Computational Engineering

Computational Engineering

Edited by **Tom Halt**

Willford Press

New York

Published by Willford Press,
118-35 Queens Blvd., Suite 400,
Forest Hills, NY 11375, USA
www.willfordpress.com

Computational Engineering
Edited by Tom Halt

International Standard Book Number: 978-1-68285-046-6 (Hardback)

Printed in the United States of America.

Contents

Preface

Every book is a source of knowledge and this one is no exception. The idea that led to the conceptualization of this book was the fact that the world is advancing rapidly; which makes it crucial to document the progress in every field. I am aware that a lot of data is already available, yet, there is a lot more to learn. Hence, I accepted the responsibility of editing this book and contributing my knowledge to the community.

Computational engineering is a promising and emerging field that deals with the development of models for providing high performance computing, to analyse designs and fix complex problems. Its framework includes data science for developing algorithms and mathematical foundations like fourier analysis and discrete fourier transforms. This book integrates physical and experimental approaches applied in the development of the discipline. It includes comprehensive techniques and applications to fabricate structures and networks. It focuses upon applied mathematics, computer modelling and other related fields. This text is an asset for anyone who is interested in the field of computational engineering.

While editing this book, I had multiple visions for it. Then I finally narrowed down to make every chapter a sole standing text explaining a particular topic, so that they can be used independently. However, the umbrella subject sinews them into a common theme. This makes the book a unique platform of knowledge.

I would like to give the major credit of this book to the experts from every corner of the world, who took the time to share their expertise with us. Also, I owe the completion of this book to the never-ending support of my family, who supported me throughout the project.

Editor

1

Optimal design and performance evaluation of a flow-mode MR damper for front-loaded washing machines

Quoc Hung Nguyen[1*], Ngoc Diep Nguyen[1] and Seung Bok Choi[2]

* Correspondence: nguyenhung2000vn@yahoo.com
[1]Department of Mechanical Engineering, Industrial University of Ho Chi Minh City, Hochiminh-12 NVBao, Vietnam
Full list of author information is available at the end of the article

Abstract

It is well known that the vibration of washing machines is a challenging issue to be considered. This research work focuses on the optimal design of a flow-mode magneto-rheological (MR) damper that can replace the conventional passive damper for a washing machine. Firstly, rigid mode vibration of the washing machine due to an unbalanced mass is analyzed and an optimal positioning of the suppression system for the washing machine is considered. An MR damper configuration for the washer is then proposed considering available space for the system. The damping force of the MR damper is derived based on the Bingham rheological behavior of the MR fluid. An optimal design problem for the proposed MR brake is then constructed. The optimization is to minimize the damping coefficient of the MR damper while the maximum value of the damping force is kept being greater than a required value. An optimization procedure based on finite element analysis integrated with an optimization tool is employed to obtain optimal geometric dimensions of the MR damper. The optimal solution of the MR damper is then presented with remarkable discussions on its performance. The results are then validated by experimental works. Finally, conclusions on the research work are given and future works for development of the research is figured out.

Keywords: Magneto-rheological; MR damper; Washing machine; Vibration control

Background

It is well known that the vibration of washing machines is a challenging issue to be considered. The vibration of the washing machine is mainly due to the unbalanced mass of clothes distributed in the washing drum. This occurs most frequently in the spin-drying stage, because the drum spins at a relatively high speed causing the clothes to be pressed against the inner wall of the spin drum, and these can become a large unbalanced mass until the end of the stage. Particularly, in a front-loaded washing machine (drum-type washing machine), the unbalanced mass of clothes easily occurs and very severe due to the effect of gravity. The vibration of the washing machine is transferred to the floor causing noises, unpleasant feeling for humans, and failure of the machine.

There are many researches on vibration control of washing machines which can be classified into two main approaches. The first approach is based on the control of the tub balance to eliminate the source of vibration [1,2]. In this approach, one type of dynamic balancer is used to self-balance the tub dynamics. A typical dynamic balancer is the hydraulic balancer containing salt water, which is attached to the upper rim of the basket. The liquid in the balancer moves to the opposite side of unbalance automatically due to the inherent nature of fluids when the rotational speed is higher than the critical speed of the spinning drum [1]. Another dynamic balancer that counteracts vibrations is to use two balancing masses. In this method, two balancing masses move along the rim of the basket. The rotation plane of the balancing masses can be easily chosen to be wherever judged suitable, always targeting at the reduction of the induced moments [2]. It is proved that the vibration of the washing machine can be significantly reduced by using a dynamic balancer. However, the complicated structure, high cost of manufacturing, and maintenance are a big obstacle for the wide application of this approach. In the second approach, the vibration of the washing machine is suppressed based on damping control of a suspension system [3]. It is noted that during the spinning process, the washing machine usually experiences the first resonance at quite low frequency, around 100 to 200 rpm. This results from the resonance of the washing drum due to the unbalanced mass. When the rotating speed exceeds 1,000 rpm, the side and rear panels of the frame may experience resonances which cause noises and vibration transferred to the floor. If a passive damper is used to reduce the vibration of the drum at low frequency, it will cause the vibration of the washing machine at high frequencies more severe. The reason is that more excitation force from the drum is transferred to the frame via the passive damper. Therefore, in order to effectively reduce the vibration of the washing machine at low frequency while the vibration of the machine at high frequencies is insignificantly affected, a semi-active suspension system such as a magneto-rheological (MR) damper should be employed.

Although there have been several researches on the design and application of MR dampers to control the vibration of washing machines [4-6], the optimal design of such MR dampers was not considered. The main objective of this study is to achieve the optimal design of the semi-active suspension system for washing machines employing MR dampers. Firstly, rigid mode vibration of the washing machine due to an unbalanced mass is analyzed and an optimal positioning of the suppression system for the washing machine is considered. An MR damper configuration for the washer is then proposed. The damping force of the MR damper is then derived based on the Bingham model of the MR fluid. An optimal design problem for the proposed MR brake is then constructed considering the damping coefficient and required damping force of the MR damper. An optimization procedure based on finite element analysis integrated with an optimization tool is employed to obtain optimal geometric dimensions of the MR damper. The optimal solution of the MR damper is then presented with remarkable discussions. The results are then validated by experimental works.

Methods

Vibration control of washing machine using MR damper

The washing machine object of this work is a prototype based on the LG F1402FDS washer manufactured by LG Electronics (Seoul, South Korea). A three-dimensional (3D) schematic diagram of the washer is shown in Figure 1. It is characterized by a suspended tub (basket) to store the water for washing linked to the cabinet by two springs

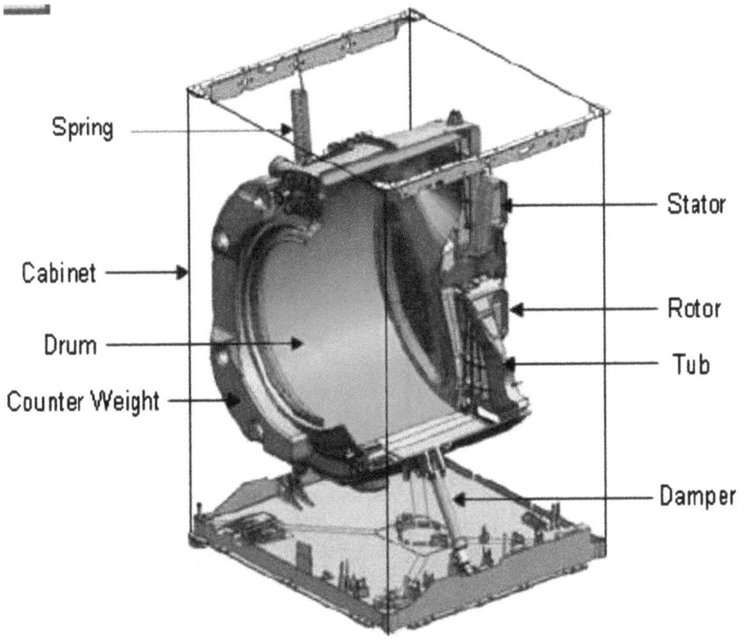

Figure 1 **3D schematic of the prototype washing machine.**

and two dampers. The rotor is directly connected with the drum which rotates against the tub while the stator is fixed on the back of the tub. When the drum is rotating, the unbalanced mass due to the eccentricity of laundry causes the vibration of the tub assembly. The vibration of the tub assembly is then transmitted to the cabinet and the bottom through the springs and the dampers. In Figure 2, a two-dimensional (2D) simplified schematic of the machine is depicted. From the figure, the following governing equation of the washing machine can be derived:

$$m\ddot{u} + c\dot{u}\left[\sin^2(\varphi + \beta_2) + \sin^2(\varphi - \beta_1)\right] + ku\left[\sin^2(\varphi + \alpha_1) + \sin^2(\varphi - \alpha_2)\right] = F_u(t) \tag{1}$$

where m is the mass of the suspended tub assembly including the drum, laundry, shaft, counter weight, rotor, and stator. For the prototype washing machine, m is roughly estimated about 40 kg. c is the damping coefficient of each damper, and k is the stiffness of each spring which is assumed to be 8 kN/m in this study. φ is the angle of an arbitrary direction (u direction) in which the vibration is considered. F_u is the excitation force due to unbalanced mass in the u direction, $F_u = F_0\cos\omega t = m_u\omega^2 R_u\cos\omega t$, in which m_u and R_u are the mass and radius from the rotation axis of the unbalanced mass. From Equation 1, the damped frequency of the suspended tub assembly is calculated by

$$\omega_d = \omega_n\sqrt{1-\xi^2} \tag{2}$$

where $\omega_n = \sqrt{\dfrac{k\left[\sin^2(\varphi+\alpha_1)+\sin^2(\varphi-\alpha_2)\right]}{m}}$ and $\xi = \dfrac{c\left[\sin^2(\varphi+\beta_2)+\sin^2(\varphi-\beta_1)\right]}{2\sqrt{mk\left[\sin^2(\varphi+\alpha_1)+\sin^2(\varphi-\alpha_2)\right]}}$.

It is seen that the damped frequency and natural frequency of the tub assembly in the u direction are a function of φ. Therefore, in general, in a different direction of vibration, the tub assembly exhibits different resonant frequency. This causes the

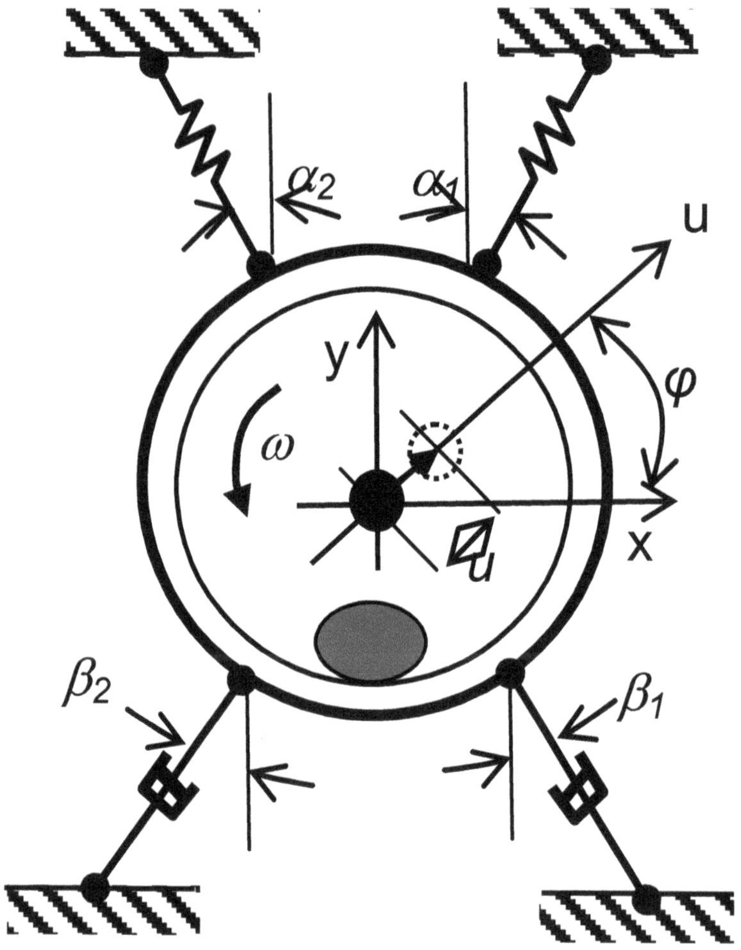

Figure 2 2D simplified schematic of the prototype washing machine.

vibration to become more severe and hard to control. In the design of the suspension system for the tub assembly, the frequency range of the resonance in all directions should be as small as possible. From the above, it is easy to show that, by choosing $\alpha_1 + \alpha_2 = 90°$ and $\beta_2 + \beta_2 = 90°$, Equation 1 can be simplified to yield

$$m\ddot{u} + c\dot{u} + ku = F_u \tag{3}$$

In this case, the damped frequency and natural frequency of the tub assembly do not depend on the direction of the vibration. We have

$$\omega_d = \omega_n\sqrt{1-\xi^2} \tag{4}$$

where $\omega_n = \sqrt{\frac{k}{m}}$ and $\xi = \frac{c}{2\sqrt{mk}}$.

An inherent drawback of the conventional damper is its high transmissibility of vibration at high excitation frequency. In order to solve this issue, semi-active suspension systems such as ER and MR dampers are potential candidates. In this study, two MR dampers are employed to control the vibration of the tub assembly.

Figure 3 shows the schematic configuration of a flow-mode MR damper proposed for the prototype washing machine. From the figure, it is observed that an MR valve structure is incorporated in the MR damper. The outer and inner pistons are combined to form the MR valve structure which divides the MR damper into two chambers: the upper and

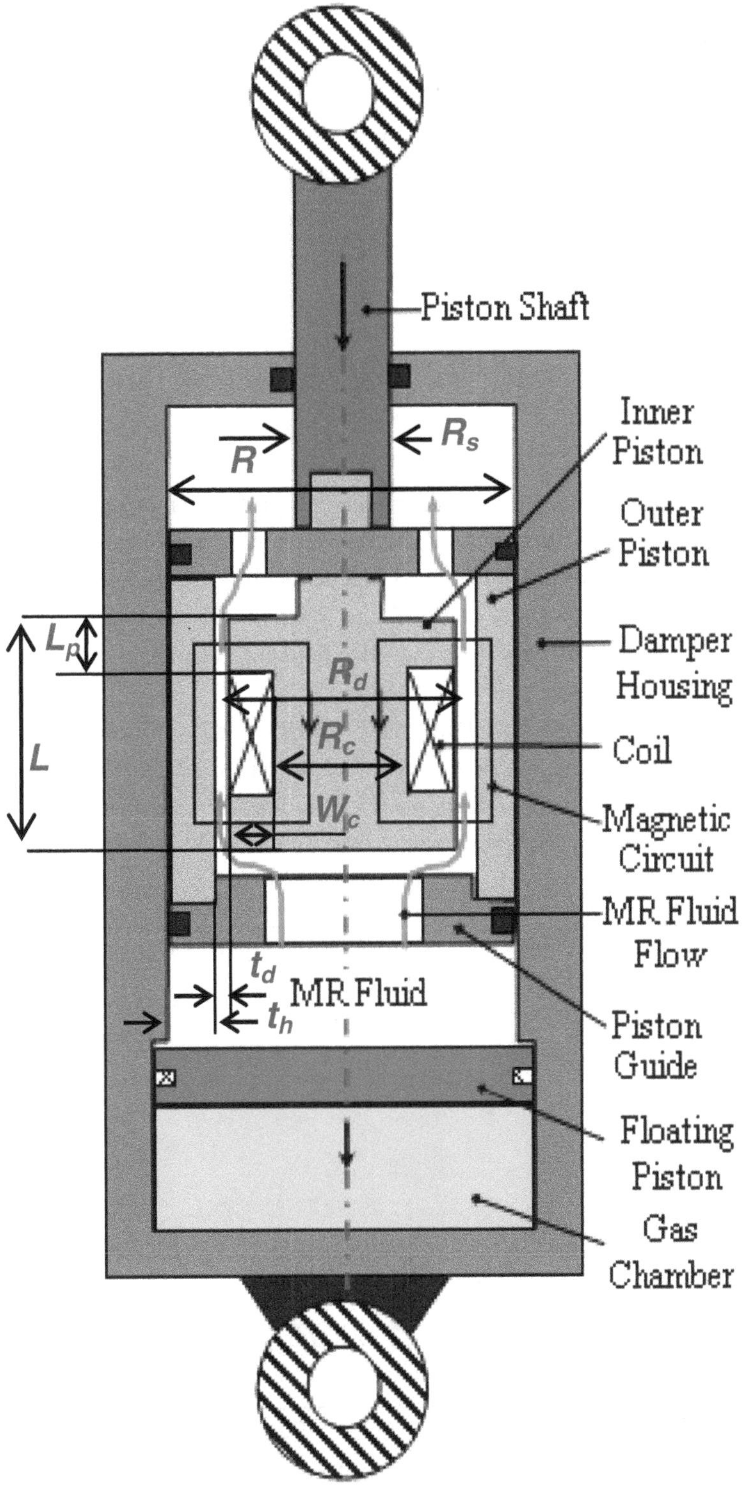

Figure 3 Schematic configuration of the MR damper.

lower chambers. These chambers are fully filled with the MR fluid. As the piston moves, the MR fluid flows from one chamber to the other through the annular duct (orifice). The floating piston incorporated with a gas chamber functions as an accumulator to accommodate the piston shaft volume as it enters and leaves the fluid chamber.

By neglecting the frictional force and assuming quasi-static behavior of the damper, the damping force can be calculated by [7]

$$F_d = P_a A_s + C_{\text{vis}} \dot{x}_p + F_{\text{MR}} \operatorname{sgn}(\dot{x}_p) \tag{5}$$

where P_a, c_{vis}, and F_{MR}, respectively, are the pressure in the gas chamber, the viscous coefficient, and the yield stress force of the MR damper which are determined as follows:

$$P_a = P_0 \left(\frac{V_0}{V_0 + A_s x_p} \right)^{\gamma} \tag{6}$$

$$C_{\text{vis}} = \frac{12\eta L}{\pi R_d t_d^3} (A_p - A_s)^2 \tag{7}$$

$$F_{\text{MR}} = 2(A_p - A_s) \frac{2.85 L_p}{t_d} \tau_y \tag{8}$$

In the above, τ_y is the induced yield stress of the MR fluid which is an unknown and can be estimated from magnetic analysis of the damper and η is the post-yield viscosity of the MR fluid which is assumed to be field independent. R_d is the average radius of the annular duct given by $R_d = R - t_h - 0.5t_d$. L and R are the overall length and outside radius of the MR valve, respectively. t_h is the valve housing thickness, t_d is the annular duct gap, and L_p is the magnetic pole length.

In this work, the commercial MR fluid (MRF132-DG) made by Lord Corporation (Cary, NC, USA) is used. The post-yield viscosity of the MR fluid is assumed to be independent on the applied magnetic field, $\eta = 0.1$ Pas. The induced yield stress of the MR fluid as a function of the applied magnetic field intensity (H) is shown in Figure 4.

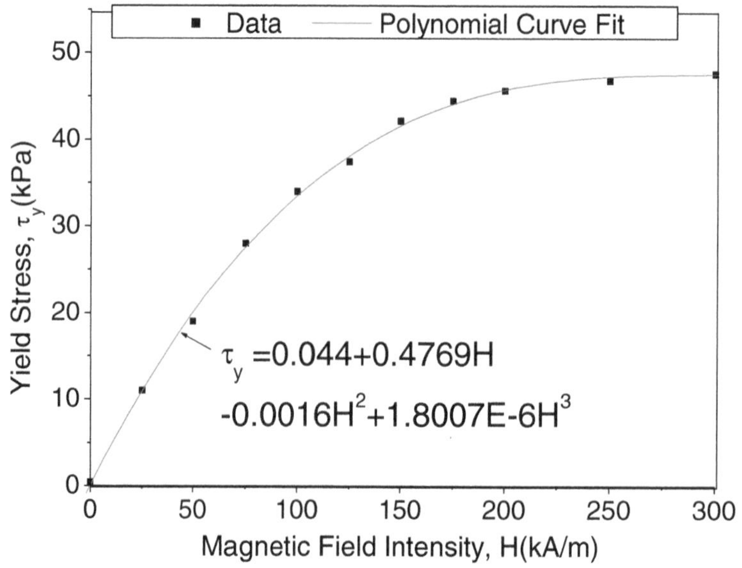

Figure 4 Yield stress of MR fluid as a function of magnetic field intensity.

By applying the least squares curve fitting method, the yield stress of the MR fluid can be approximately expressed by

$$\tau_y = C_0 + C_1 H + C_2 H^2 + C_3 H^3 \tag{9}$$

In Equation 9, the unit of the yield stress is kilopascal while that of the magnetic field intensity is kA/m. The coefficients C_0, C_1, C_2, and C_3 are respectively identified as 0.044, 0.4769, −0.0016, and 1.8007E-6. In order to estimate the induced yield stress using Equation 9, first the magnetic field intensity across the active MRF duct must be calculated. In this study, the commercial FEM software, ANSYS, is used to analyze the magnetic problem of the proposed MR damper.

Optimal design of the MR damper

In this study, the optimal design of the proposed MR damper is considered based on the quasi-static model of the MR damper and dynamic equation of the tub assembly developed in the 'Vibration control of washing machine using MR damper' section. From Figure 2 and Equation 3, the force transmissibility of the tub assembly to the cabinet can be obtained as follows:

$$\mathrm{TR} = \sqrt{\frac{1 + (2\xi r)^2}{(1 - r^2)^2 + (2\xi r)^2}} \tag{10}$$

where r is the frequency ratio, $r = \omega/\omega_n$. The dependence of the force transmissibility on excitation frequency is presented in Figure 5. As shown from the figure, at low damping, the resonant transmissibility is relatively large, while the transmissibility at higher frequencies is quite low. As the damping is increased, the resonant peaks are attenuated, but vibration isolation is lost at high frequency. This illustrates the inherent trade-off between resonance control and high-frequency isolation associated with the design of passive suspension systems. It is also observed from the figure that when the

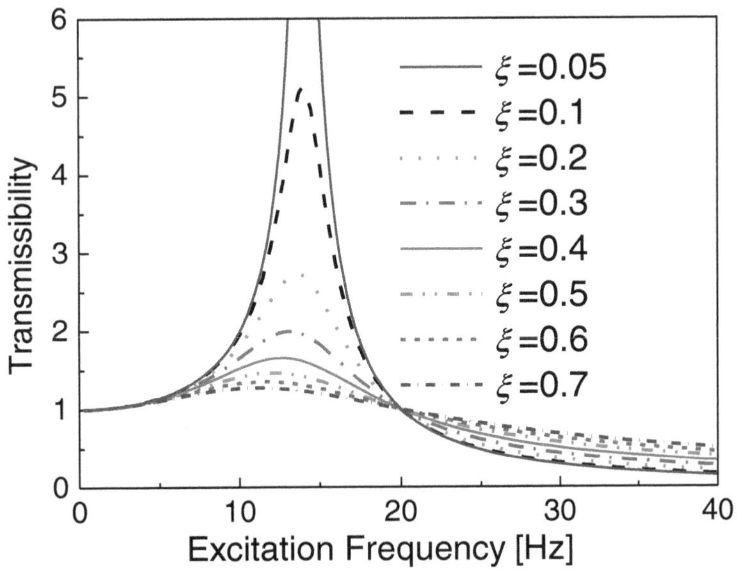

Figure 5 Transmissibility of the tub assembly.

damping ratio is 0.7 or greater, the resonant peaks are almost attenuated. Thus, the higher value of damping ratio is not necessary. It is noted that in Equation 5, the third term F_{MR} is much greater than the other and the behavior of the MR damper can is similar to that of a dry friction damper. By introducing an equivalent damping coefficient C_{eq} such that the work per cycle due to this equivalent damping coefficient equals that due to the yield stress damping force of the MR damper, the following equation holds [8]:

$$C_{eq} = \frac{4|F_{MR}|}{X\omega\pi} \tag{11}$$

or

$$|F_{MR}| = \frac{X\omega\pi C_{eq}}{4} = \frac{X\omega\pi\xi\sqrt{km}}{2} = \frac{kX\pi\xi r}{2} \tag{12}$$

In the above, X is the magnitude of the tub vibration which is determined by

$$X = \frac{F_0}{k}\sqrt{\frac{1}{(1-r^2)^2 + (2\xi r)^2}} = \frac{m_u r^2 R_u}{m}\sqrt{\frac{1}{(1-r^2)^2 + (2\xi r)^2}} \tag{13}$$

From Equations 12 and 13, the required value of F_{MR} can be determined from a required value of the damping ratio ξ as follows:

$$|F_{MR}| = \frac{k\pi\xi m_u r^3 R_u}{2m}\sqrt{\frac{1}{(1-r^2)^2 + (2\xi r)^2}} \tag{14}$$

In this study, it is assumed that the spring stiffness is $k = 10$ kN/m, the mass of the suspended tub assembly is $m = 40$ kg, and the equivalent unbalanced mass is $m_u =$ 10 kg located at the radius $R_u = 0.15$ m. With the required damping ratio $\xi = 0.7$, at the resonance $r = \sqrt{1-\xi^2}$, the required value of F_{MR} can be calculated from Equation 14 which is around 150 N in this study.

Taking all above into consideration, the optimal design of the MR brake for the washing machine can be summarized as follows: Find the optimal value of significant dimensions of the MR damper such as the pole length L_p, the housing thickness t_h, the core radius R_c, the width of the MR duct t_d, the width of the coil W_c, and the overall length of the valve structure L that

$$\text{Minimize the viscous coefficient (objective function), OBJ} = c_{vis} = \frac{12\eta L}{\pi R_d t_d^3}(A_p - A_s)^2$$

$$\text{Subjected to}: F_{MR} = 2(A_p - A_s)\frac{2.85L_p}{t_d}\tau_y \geq 150\ \text{N}$$

In order to obtain the optimal solution, a finite element analysis code integrated with an optimization tool is employed. In this study, the first-order method with the golden section algorithm of the ANSYS optimization tool is used. Figure 6 shows the flow chart to achieve optimal design parameters of the MR damper. Firstly, an analysis ANSYS file for solving the magnetic circuit of the damper and calculating the objective function is built using ANSYS parametric design language (APDL). In the analysis file, the design variables (DVs) such as the pole length L_p, the housing thickness t_h, the core radius R_c, the width of the MR duct t_d, the width of the coil W_c, and the overall length

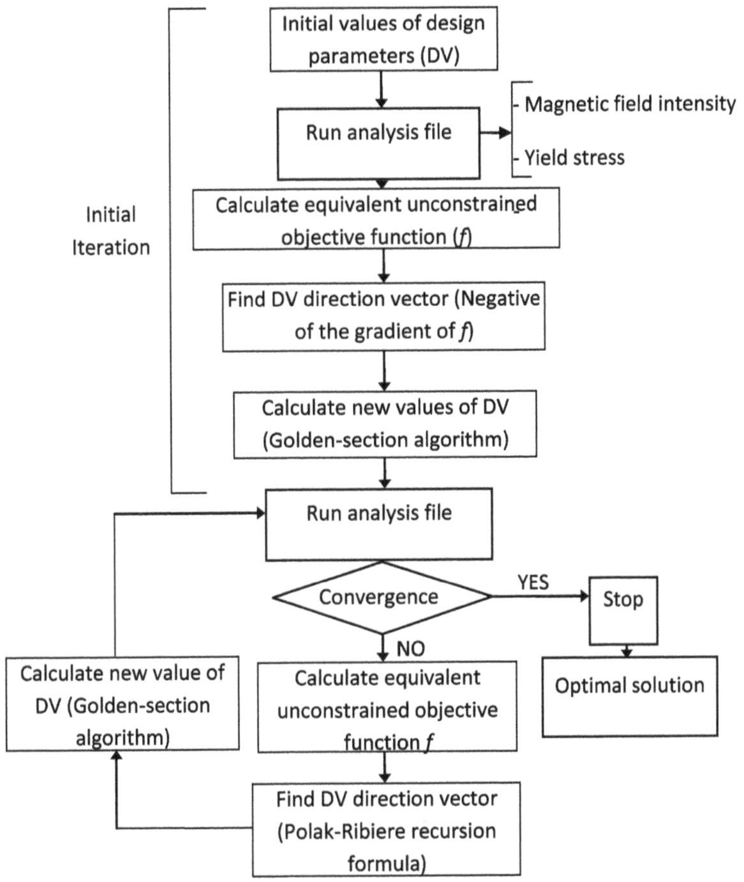

Figure 6 Flow chart to achieve optimal design parameters of the MR damper.

of the valve structure L must be coded as variables and initial values are assigned to them. The geometric dimensions of the valve structure are varied during the optimization process; the meshing size therefore should be specified by the number of elements per line rather than the element size. Because the magnetic field intensity is not constant along the pole length, it is necessary to define paths along the MR active volume where magnetic flux passes. The average magnetic field intensity across the MR ducts (H_{mr}) is calculated by integrating the field intensity along the defined path then divided by the path length. Thus, the magnetic field intensity is determined as follows:

$$H_{mr} = \frac{1}{L_p} \int_0^{L_p} H(s)ds \tag{15}$$

where $H(s)$ is the magnetic flux density and magnetic field intensity at each nodal point on the defined path.

From the figure, it is observed that the optimization is started with the initial value of DVs. By executing the analysis file, first the magnetic field intensity is derived. Then the yield stress, yield stress damping force, and objective function are respectively calculated from Equations 9, 7, and 8. The ANSYS optimization tool then transforms the optimization problem with constrained design variables to an unconstrained one via penalty functions. The dimensionless, unconstrained objective function f is formulated as follows:

$$f(x) = \frac{\text{OBJ}}{\text{OBJ}_0} + \sum_{i=1}^{n} P_{x_i}(x_i) \tag{16}$$

where OBJ_0 is the reference objective function value that is selected from the current group of design sets. P_{x_i} is the exterior penalty function for the design variable x_i. For the initial iteration ($j = 0$), the search direction of DVs is assumed to be the negative of the gradient of the unconstrained objective function. Thus, the direction vector is calculated by

$$d^{(0)} = -\nabla f\left(x^{(0)}\right) \tag{17}$$

The values of DVs in the next iteration ($j + 1$) is obtained from the following equation:

$$x^{(j+1)} = x^{(j)} + s_j d^{(j)} \tag{18}$$

where the line search parameter s_j is calculated by using a combination of the golden section algorithm and a local quadratic fitting technique. The analysis file is then executed with the new values of DVs, and the convergence of the objective function is checked. If the convergence occurs, the values of DVs at this iteration are the optimum. If not, the subsequent iterations will be performed. In the subsequent iterations, the procedures are similar to those of the initial iteration except for that the direction vectors are calculated according to the Polak-Ribiere recursion formula as follows:

$$d^{(j)} = -\nabla f\left(x^{(j)}\right) + r_{j-1} d^{(j-1)} \tag{19}$$

$$\text{where } r_{j-1} = \frac{\left[\nabla f\left(x^{(j)}\right) - \nabla f\left(x^{(j-1)}\right)\right]^T \nabla f\left(x^{(j)}\right)}{\left|\nabla f\left(x^{(j-1)}\right)\right|^2}. \tag{20}$$

Results and discussion

In this study, an optimal design of the MR damper for the washing machine is performed based on the optimization problem developed in the 'Optimal design of the MR damper' section. It is assumed that the piston part and housing of the damper are made of commercial silicon steel, and the coil wires are sized as 21 gage (diameter = 0.511 mm) whose allowable working current is 2.5A. In the optimization, the applied current is assumed to be 2A. Figure 7 shows the optimal solution of the MR damper in case the pole length L_p, the housing thickness t_h, the core radius R_c, the width of the MR duct t_d, the width of the coil W_d, and the overall length of the valve structure L are considered as design variables. From the figure, it can be found that with a convergence tolerance of 0.5%, the optimal process is converged after 14 iterations and the solution at the 14th iteration is considered as the optimal one. The optimal values of L_p, t_h, R_c, t_d, W_d, and L, respectively, are 7.4, 2.5, 5.2, 2, 1.8, and 25 mm. It is noted that the optimal values of t_d and t_h are equal to their lower limits in this case. These limits are posed considering the stability and manufacturing cost of the damper. At the optimum, the viscous coefficient is significantly reduced up to 10 Ns/m from its initial value (290 Ns/m). When no current is applied to the coil, the damping ratio at the optimum is

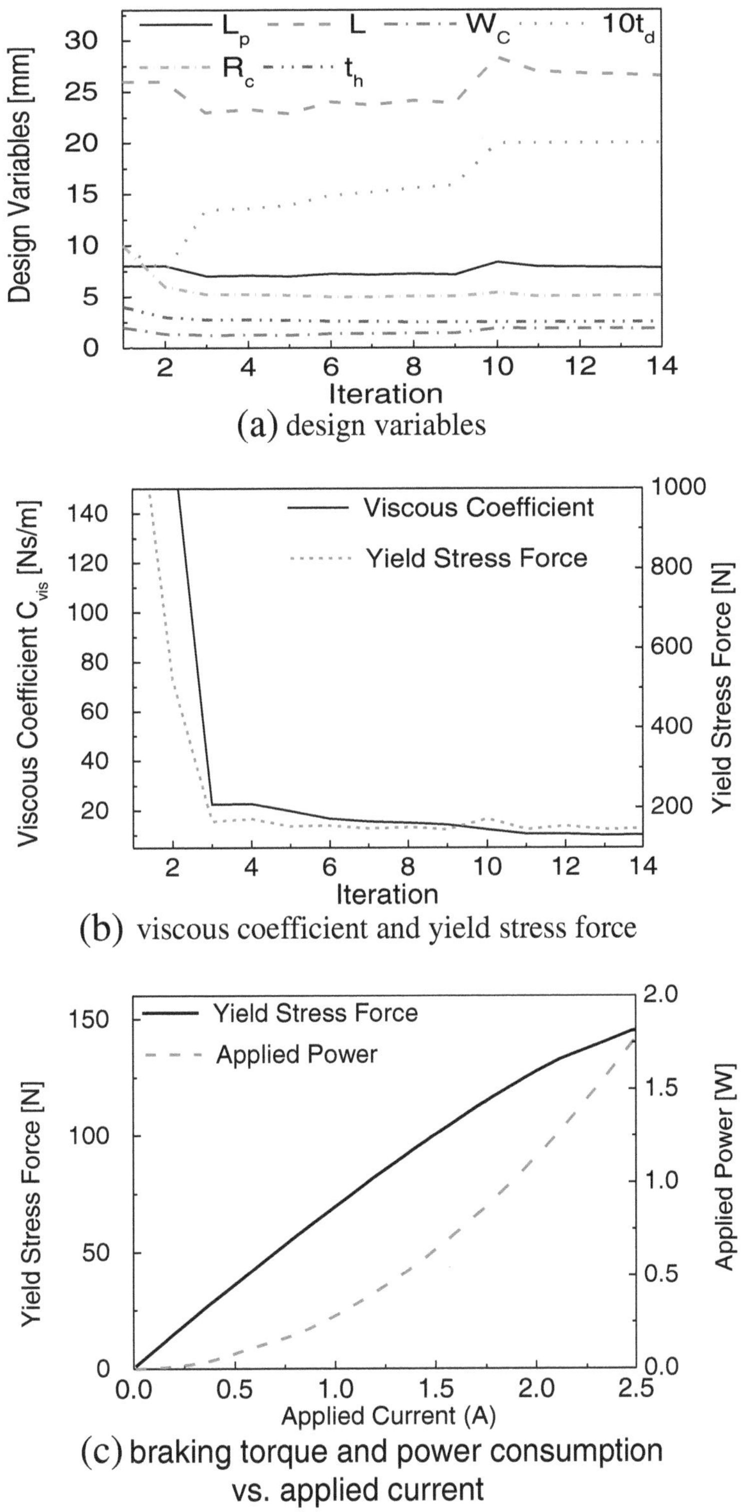

Figure 7 Optimal solution of the MR damper for the washing machine. (a) Design variables. **(b)** Viscous coefficient and yield stress force. **c)** Braking torque and power consumption vs. applied current.

around 0.01 which is very small so that a very small transmissibility of vibration from the drum to the cabinet at high excitation frequency can be achieved. It is also observed from the figure that the yield stress force of the damper at the optimum is

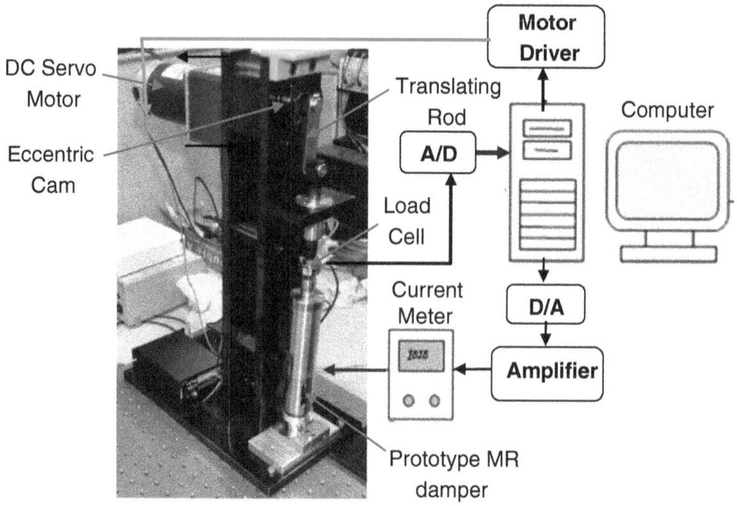

Figure 8 **Experimental setup to test the performance of the optimized MR damper.**

greater than the required value (150 N). The yield stress and power consumption as functions of the applied current of the optimized MR damper are shown in Figure 7c. From the figure, it is observed that the yield stress force almost increases proportionally to the applied current as the current varies from 0 to 2.5A.

In order to validate the above optimal results, experimental results of the optimized MR damper are obtained and presented. Figure 8 shows the experimental setup to test the performance of the optimized MR damper. In the figure, a crank-slider mechanism is employed to convert the rotary motion of the motor into the reciprocal motion of the damper shaft. The DC motor with a gearbox controlled by the computer is used to rotate the crank shaft at a constant angular speed of 0.5 rad/s. The damping force is measured by a load cell. The output signal from the load cell is then sent to the computer via the A/D converter for evaluation. Once the experiment process is stated, a step current signal from the computer is sent to the current amplifier. The output current from the amplifier, a step current of 2A, is applied to the coil of the damper.

Figure 9 shows the step response of the prototype MR damper. It is noted that in this case, the angular velocity of the motor is kept constant at 0.5π rad/s and the step response

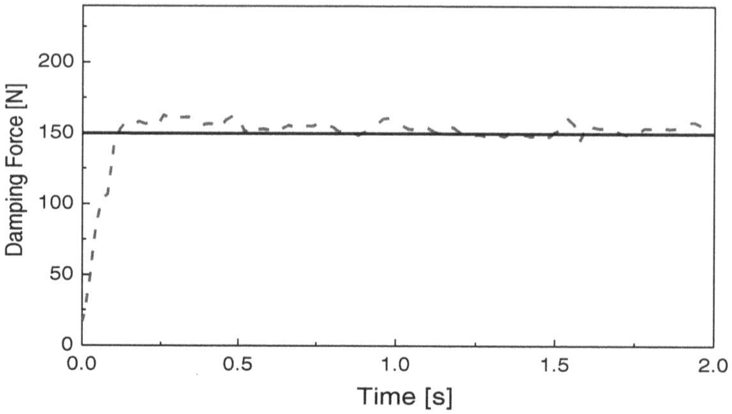

Figure 9 **Experimental step response of the optimized MR damper.**

of the MR damper is measured on the downward motion of the shaft. In the figure, the solid line presents the calculated damping force while the dash line presents the measured one. The results also show that, at the steady state, the average damping force is around 157 N which is a little greater than the calculated one (150 N). The difference may result from friction which is not taken into account in the modeling of the damper.

Conclusions

In this research, optimal design of a flow-mode MR damper to suppress the vibration of front-loaded washing machines was undertaken. After a brief introduction, the general governing equation of the washing tub assembly is derived. The position of the two springs and the two dampers to suppress the machine vibration was then optimally determined based on the governing equation. A configuration of the MR damper for the washing machine was then proposed, and the damping force was obtained based on the Bingham rheological model of the MR brake. The optimization problem for the damper was constructed such that the viscous coefficient of the damper is minimized and the yield stress force of the damper is greater than a required value that attenuates almost the resonant peak of the tub mechanism. The optimal design of the MR damper for a prototype washing machine was obtained based on the ANSYS finite element analysis of the MR damper magnetic circuit and first-order optimization method. The results show that performances of the MR damper are significantly improved with the proposed optimal design. A prototype of the optimized MR damper was manufactured, and experimental results on the performance of the prototype damper were obtained and presented. It was shown that the experimental results well agreed with the modeling one obtained from finite element analysis. As the second phase of this study, dynamics of the whole prototype washing machine equipped with the MR damper will be obtained and experimental results on the prototype washer will be conducted to evaluate the effectiveness of the optimized MR damper.

Competing interests

The authors declare that they have no competing interests.

Authors' contributions

QHN carried out the research background of the study, modeling of the system and optimal design of MR dampers. NDN carried out the experiment. SBC participated in configuration proposal of the MR damper, providing experimental data of the MR fluid and review of the manuscript. All authors read and approved the final manuscript.

Acknowledgements

This research is funded by Vietnam National Foundation for Science and Technology Development (NAFOSTED) under grant number 107.04.2011.07 and partially supported by the National Research Foundation of Korea (NRF) grant funded by the Korea government (MEST) (No. 2010-0015090).

Author details

[1]Department of Mechanical Engineering, Industrial University of Ho Chi Minh City, Hochiminh-12 NVBao, Vietnam.
[2]Department of Mechanical Engineering, Inha University, Incheon 402-751, Korea.

References

1. Bae S, Lee JM, Kang YJ, Kane JS, Yun JR (2002) Dynamic analysis of an automatic washing machine with a hydraulic balancer. Sound Vib 257(1):3–18
2. Papadopoulos E, Papadimitriou I (2001) Modeling, design and control of a portable washing machine during the spinning cycle. In: Proceedings of the 2001 IEEE/ASME international conference on advanced intelligent mechatronics systems. Como, Italy, 8-11, July 2001
3. Lim HT, Jeong WB, Kim KJ (2010) Dynamic modeling and analysis of drum-type washing machine. Int J Precis Eng Manuf 11(3):407–417

4. Michael JC, David Carson J (2001) MR fluid sponge devices and their use in vibration control of washing machines. In: Proc. SPIE 4331. Newport Beach, CA, USA, March 4, 2001
5. Cristiano S, Fibio P, Sergio MS, Giuseppe F, Nicolas G (2009) Control of magnetorheological dampers for vibration reduction in a washing machine. Mechatronics 19:410–421
6. Aydar G, Evrensel CA, Gordaninejad F, Fuchs A (2007) A low force magneto-rheological (MR) fluid damper: design, fabrication and characterization. J Intell Mater Syst Struct 18(12):1155–1160
7. Nguyen QH, Choi SB, Lee YS, Han MS (2009) An analytical method for optimal design of MR valve structures. Smart Mater Struct 18(9):385–402
8. Silva CW (2000) Vibration: fundamentals and practices. CRC, New York

2

Plastic collapse mechanisms in thin disks subject to thermo-mechanical loading

Sergei Alexandrov[1] and Chinh Pham[2*]

* Correspondence:
pdchinh@imech.ac.vn
[2]VAST, Institute of Mechanics, 264
Doi Can, Hanoi, Vietnam
Full list of author information is
available at the end of the article

Abstract

Background: A new solution for plastic collapse of a thin annular disk subject to thermo-mechanical loading is presented.

Methods: It is assumed that plastic yielding is controlled by Hill's quadratic orthotropic yield criterion. A distinguished feature of the boundary value problem considered is that there are two loading parameters. One of these parameters is temperature, and the other is pressure over the inner radius of the disk.

Results: The general qualitative structure of the solution at plastic collapse is discussed in detail.

Conclusions: It is shown that two different plastic collapse mechanisms are possible. One of these mechanisms is characterized by strain localization at the inner radius of the disk. The entire disk becomes plastic according to the other collapse mechanism. In addition, two special regimes of plastic collapse are identified. According to one of these regimes, plastic collapse occurs when the entire disk is elastic except its inner radius. According to the other regime, the entire disk becomes plastic at the same values of the loading parameters at which plastic yielding starts to develop.

Keywords: Thin disks; Plastic collapse; Plastic anisotropy; Thermo-mechanical loading; Qualitative features of solution

Background

Thin plates and disks with holes and embedded inclusions have many structural applications. A significant amount of analytical and numerical research for various material models has been carried out in the area of stress and strain analysis of such structures (see [1-20] among many others). An excellent review of previous works devoted to the problem of enlargement of a circular hole in thin plates has been given in [19]. The assumptions made regarding yield criterion, strain hardening and unloading have a significant effect on the predicted response and residual stress and strain fields [7]. Even though closed-form solutions involve more assumptions than numerical solutions, the former are necessary for studying qualitative effects and verifying numerical codes. Typical qualitative effects under plane stress conditions are the singularity of the velocity field and non-existence of the solution under certain conditions [9-12,17,20]. These features of boundary value problems can cause difficulties with their treatment by means of standard commercial numerical codes. In particular, some specific difficulties with numerical solution for plane stress problems have been mentioned in [21].

In the present paper, the effect of temperature and pressure over the inner radius of a thin hollow disk on plastic collapse is investigated. The outer radius of the disk is fixed. The state of stress is plane. The classical Duhamel-Neumann law is adopted to connect the thermal and elastic portions of the strain tensor and stress components. Plastic yielding is controlled by Hill's quadratic orthotropic yield criterion [22]. It is assumed that the principal axes of anisotropy coincide with the base vectors of a cylindrical coordinate system (r, θ, z) whose z-axis coincides with the axis of symmetry of the disk. Therefore, the boundary value problem is axisymmetric and its solution is independent of the polar angle. It is shown that the general qualitative structure of the plastic collapse solution is rather complicated. In particular, two different plastic collapse mechanisms have been found. According to one of these mechanisms, the plastic collapse occurs because the entire disk becomes plastic. The other plastic collapse mechanism is characterized by localization of plastic deformation at the inner radius of the disk.

Statement of the problem

Consider a thin disk of radius b_0 with a central hole of radius a_0, which is inserted into a rigid container of radius b_0 (Figure 1). The disk is subject to thermo-mechanical loading by a uniform pressure P over its inner radius and a uniform increase of temperature T from its initial value. By assumption, both P and T are monotonically increasing functions of a time-like parameter. Also, $P = 0$ and $T = 0$ at the initial instant. Thus, both $P \geq 0$ and $T \geq 0$. The disk has no stress at the initial instant. It is convenient to introduce a cylindrical coordinate system (r, θ, z) whose z-axis coincides with the axis of symmetry of the disk. Then, the equations for the inner and outer radii of the disk are $r = a_0$ and

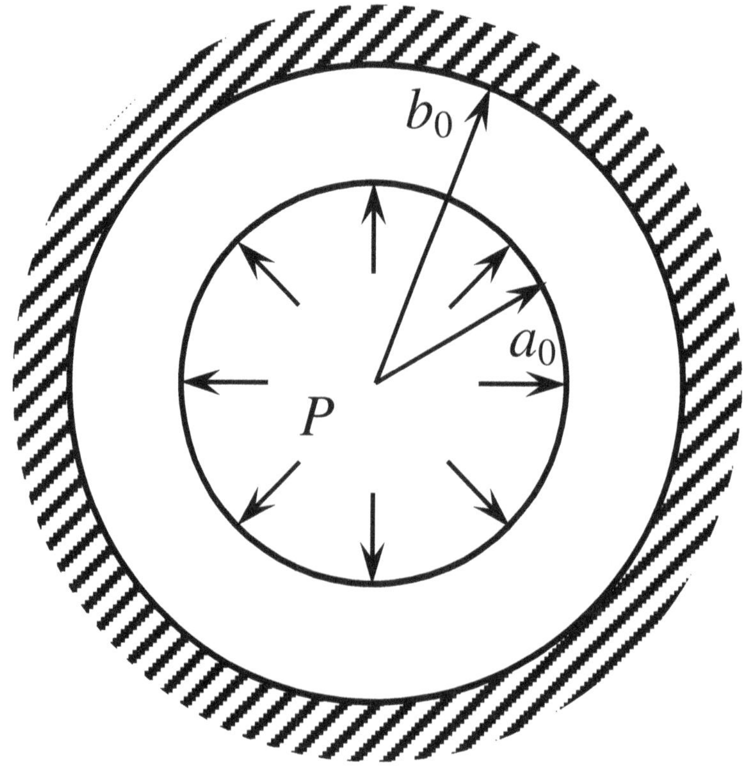

Figure 1 Illustration of the structure.

$r = b_0$, respectively. The strains are supposed to be small. Let σ_r, σ_θ and σ_z be the normal stresses in the cylindrical coordinate system. The state of stress is plane, $\sigma_z = 0$. It is evident that the problem is axisymmetric. In particular, the solution is independent of θ. Moreover, the normal stresses in the cylindrical coordinates are the principal stresses. The boundary conditions can be written as

$$\sigma_r = -P \tag{1}$$

for $r = a_0$ and

$$u_r = 0 \tag{2}$$

for $r = b_0$. Here u_r is the radial displacement.

The sum of the elastic and thermal portions of the strain tensor follows the classical Duhamel-Neumann law. In the case under consideration, this law reads

$$\varepsilon_r^e + \varepsilon_r^T = \frac{(\sigma_r - \nu\sigma_\theta)}{E} + \alpha T, \quad \varepsilon_\theta^e + \varepsilon_\theta^T = \frac{(\sigma_\theta - \nu\sigma_r)}{E} + \alpha T, \quad \varepsilon_z^e + \varepsilon_z^T = -\frac{\nu}{E}(\sigma_r + \sigma_\theta) + \alpha T \tag{3}$$

where ε_r^e, ε_θ^e and ε_z^e are the elastic portions of the strain tensor, ε_r^T, ε_θ^T and ε_z^T are the thermal portions of the strain tensor, E is Young's modulus, ν is Poisson's ratio and α is the thermal coefficient of linear expansion. The plastic portions of the strain tensor will be denoted by ε_r^p, ε_θ^p and ε_z^p. The total strain tensor is the sum of its elastic, thermal and plastic portions. In terms of the radial, circumferential and axial strains, which are also the principal strains, these relations have the form

$$\varepsilon_r = \varepsilon_r^e + \varepsilon_r^T + \varepsilon_r^p, \quad \varepsilon_\theta = \varepsilon_\theta^e + \varepsilon_\theta^T + \varepsilon_\theta^p, \quad \varepsilon_z = \varepsilon_z^e + \varepsilon_z^T + \varepsilon_z^p \tag{4}$$

It is assumed that the initiation of plastic yielding is controlled by Hill's quadratic orthotropic yield criterion [22]. By assumption, the principal axes of anisotropy coincide with the base vectors of the cylindrical coordinate system. Therefore, the aforementioned statements that the boundary value problem is axisymmetric and that the principal directions of the stress and strain tensors coincide with the base vectors of the cylindrical coordinate system are justified. Under the assumptions made, the yield criterion becomes

$$(G + H)\sigma_r^2 - 2H\sigma_r\sigma_\theta + (H + F)\sigma_\theta^2 = 1 \tag{5}$$

where G, H and F are constants which characterize the current state of anisotropy. It is convenient to rewrite (5) as [12]

$$\sigma_r^2 + p_\theta^2 - \eta\sigma_r p_\theta = \sigma_0^2 \tag{6}$$

where

$$p_\theta = \frac{\sigma_\theta}{\eta_1}, \quad \eta = \frac{2H}{\sqrt{(G + H)(H + F)}}, \quad \eta_1 = \frac{\sqrt{G + H}}{\sqrt{H + F}}, \quad \sigma_0 = \frac{1}{G + H} \tag{7}$$

No specific relation between stress and strain (or strain rate) in the plastic zone is needed for limit analysis. The only non-trivial equation of equilibrium is

$$\frac{\partial\sigma_r}{\partial r} + \frac{\sigma_r - \sigma_\theta}{r} = 0 \tag{8}$$

Since strains are small,

$$\varepsilon_r = \frac{\partial u_r}{\partial r}, \quad \varepsilon_\theta = \frac{u_r}{r} \tag{9}$$

Methods

Elastic solution

When both T and P are small enough, the entire disk is elastic. For axisymmetric deformation and the plane strain conditions, the equations of linear thermo-elasticity consisting of (3), (8) and (9) have the general solution in the form

$$\frac{\sigma_r}{\sigma_0} = \frac{A}{\rho^2} + B, \quad \frac{\sigma_\theta}{\sigma_0} = -\frac{A}{\rho^2} + B, \quad k^{-1}u = (1-\nu)B\rho - (1+\nu)\frac{A}{\rho} + \tau\rho \tag{10}$$

where $\rho = r/b_0$, $k = \sigma_0/E$, $\tau = \gamma TE/\sigma_0$, $u = u_r/b_0$, and A and B are constants of integration. When the entire disk is elastic, A and B are determined from the solution (10) using the boundary conditions (1) and (2) as

$$A = A_e = \frac{a^2[\tau - p(1-\nu)]}{a^2(1+\nu)+1-\nu}, \quad B = B_e = -\left[\frac{(1+\nu)pa^2+\tau}{a^2(1+\nu)+1-\nu}\right] \tag{11}$$

where $p = P/\sigma_0$ and $a = a_0/b_0$. As a result of an increase in τ, or p or both, a plastic zone can appear at the inner radius of the disk.

General stress solution in the plastic zone

In order to find the general stress solution in the plastic zone, it is necessary to combine the yield criterion (6) and the equilibrium equation (8). The yield criterion is satisfied automatically by the following substitution [12]:

$$\frac{\sigma_r}{\sigma_0} = \frac{2\cos\varphi}{\sqrt{4-\eta^2}}, \quad \frac{p_\theta}{\sigma_0} = \frac{\eta\cos\varphi}{\sqrt{4-\eta^2}} + \sin\varphi \tag{12}$$

where φ is a function of ρ. Substituting (12) into (8) leads to the following ordinary differential equation for φ:

$$2\sin\varphi\frac{d\varphi}{d\rho} - \left[\frac{2F\cos\varphi}{(H+F)} - \eta_1\sqrt{4-\eta^2}\sin\varphi\right]\rho^{-1} = 0 \tag{13}$$

The general solution to this equation can be found in elementary functions. However, it is more convenient to write it as

$$\rho = a\exp\left[\int_{\varphi_a}^{\varphi}\frac{d\beta}{\Omega(\beta)}\right], \quad \Omega(\beta) = \frac{F}{(H+F)}\cot\beta - \frac{\eta_1\sqrt{4-\eta^2}}{2} \tag{14}$$

where β is a dummy variable of integration and φ_a is the value of φ at $\rho = a$.

Consider the mechanism of plastic collapse according to which the plastic zone occupies the entire disk. At the instant of plastic collapse, the elastic zone reduces to the curve $\rho = 1$ in the $\rho\theta$-plane. The general solution (10) is valid in this vanishing elastic zone, though A and B are not given by (11). Since the stresses σ_r and σ_θ as well as the displacement u must be continuous across the elastic plastic boundary $\rho = 1$, it follows from the boundary condition (2) and Equations (10) and (12) that

$$(1-\nu)B-(1+\nu)A+\tau=0,\quad A+B=\frac{2\cos\varphi_m}{\sqrt{4-\eta^2}},\quad B-A=\left(\frac{\eta\cos\varphi_m}{\sqrt{4-\eta^2}}+\sin\varphi_m\right)\eta_1 \tag{15}$$

where φ_m is the value of φ at $\rho = 1$. Using Equation (14) this value is determined in implicit form as

$$1=a\exp\left[\int_{\varphi_a}^{\varphi_m}\frac{d\beta}{\Omega(\beta)}\right] \tag{16}$$

Using (1) and (12) yields

$$\frac{2\cos\varphi_a}{\sqrt{4-\eta^2}}=-p \tag{17}$$

Taking into account this equation, the solution to the system of Equations (15) and (16) gives a relation between p and τ when the entire disk becomes plastic. However, a difficulty is that this system may have no solution.

General structure of the solution at plastic collapse

It will be seen later that the set of parameters at which the plastic zone starts to develop is also of importance for understanding the general structure of the solution at plastic collapse. When plastic yielding begins, the dependence of the radial and circumferential stresses on φ is given by Equation (12) at $\rho = a$. Also, the solution (10) with A and B determined from (11) is valid in the range $a \le \rho \le 1$. The stresses and the radial displacement must be continuous across the elastic-plastic boundary $\rho = a$. Therefore,

$$\frac{A_e}{a^2}+B_e=\frac{2\cos\varphi_0}{\sqrt{4-\eta^2}},\quad -\frac{A_e}{a^2}+B_e=\eta_1\left(\frac{\eta\cos\varphi_0}{\sqrt{4-\eta^2}}+\sin\varphi_0\right) \tag{18}$$

where φ_0 is the value of φ_a at the instant of the initiation of plastic yielding. Since A_e and B_e are expressed through p and τ, the dependence of p on τ corresponding to the initiation of plastic yielding is determined from Equation (18). Using the imposed restrictions $p \ge 0$ and $\tau \ge 0$, it is possible to find the range of possible values of φ_0, say $\varphi_0^{(1)} \le \varphi_0 \le \varphi_0^{(2)}$. A typical dependence of p on τ corresponding to the initiation of plastic yielding is illustrated in Figure 2. The specific values of parameters used to find this curve are $a = 1/2$, $\nu = 0.3$ and $G = H = F$. It is seen from Figure 2 that there is a local maximum of the function $p(\tau)$ at some value of $\tau = \tau_k$ (point k in Figure 2). It is evident that $dp(\tau)/d\tau = 0$ at $\tau = \tau_k$. Replacing A_e and B_e in Equation (18) by means of Equation (11) and differentiating and excluding $d\varphi_0$ lead to

$$\frac{dp}{d\tau}=\frac{4\sin\varphi_0}{2[1-\nu-a^2(1+\nu)]\sin\varphi_0+\eta_1\left(\eta\sin\varphi_0-\sqrt{4-\eta^2}\cos\varphi_0\right)[1-\nu+a^2(1+\nu)]} \tag{19}$$

It follows from this equation that the condition $dp(\tau)/d\tau = 0$ is equivalent to

$$\varphi_0=0 \tag{20}$$

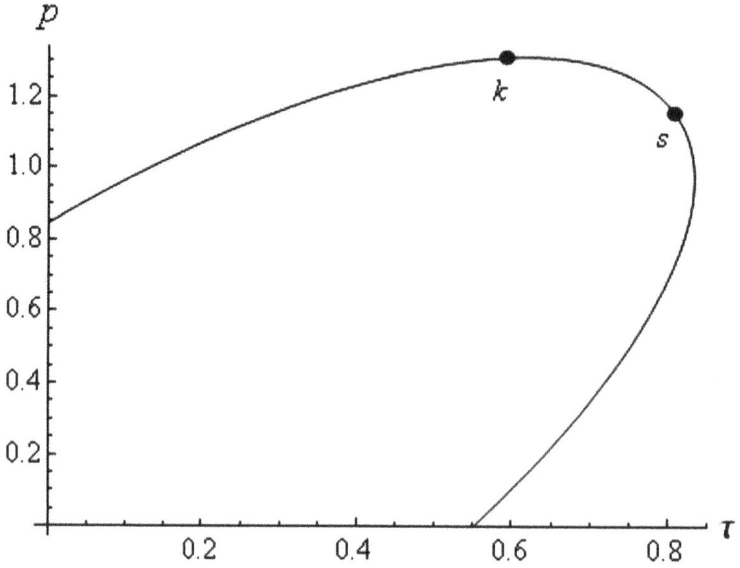

Figure 2 Curve corresponding to the initiation of plastic yielding.

Moreover, it is evident that the coefficient of the derivative in Equation (13) vanishes at $\varphi = \varphi_0$ if φ_0 is determined from (20). In the vicinity of the point $\varphi = \varphi_0 = 0$, Equation (13) transforms to

$$\varphi \frac{d\varphi}{d\rho} - \frac{F}{(H+F)a} = 0 \tag{21}$$

Integrating yields

$$\varphi^2 = \frac{2F}{(H+F)a}(\rho - a) \tag{22}$$

to leading order. It follows from this equation that the plastic zone cannot develop if $\varphi_0 = 0$. For Equation (22) is valid at any elastic/plastic boundary $\rho = \rho_c$ at which $\varphi = \varphi_c = 0$. In this case, the plastic zone occupies the domain $a \le \rho \le \rho_c$. Therefore, $\rho - \rho_c < 0$ in the plastic zone, which contradicts the left-hand side of Equation (22). Putting $\rho_c \to a$, it is possible to conclude that this statement is true at the initiation of plastic yielding as well. The physical interpretation of this mathematical feature of the solution is that plastic deformation is localized within a layer of infinitesimal thickness at $\rho = a$. This corresponds to another mechanism of plastic collapse as compared to the state in which the entire disk is plastic. A remarkable property of the set of parameters at point k (Figure 2) is that the disk losses its load-bearing capacity without any plastic deformation in the domain $a < \rho \le 1$.

Another point of great interest on the curve shown in Figure 2 is that determined by the condition $\varphi = \varphi_s$ (point s in Figure 2) where

$$\tan\varphi_s = \frac{2F}{(H+F)\eta_1\sqrt{4-\eta^2}} \tag{23}$$

It is evident that Equation (13) has a special solution $\varphi = \varphi_s$ which is not obtainable from (14). Since φ_s is constant, it follows from (12) that the stresses σ_r and σ_θ are independent of ρ. The physical meaning of this mathematical feature of Equation (13) is that the plastic zone occupies the entire disk once the plastic zone has initiated at $\rho = a$.

If the initiation of plastic yielding corresponds to any point of the curve shown in Figure 2 other than points k and s, then the elastic/plastic boundary propagates from the surface $\rho = a$ until the plastic collapse occurs. As in the special cases considered, the same two plastic collapse mechanisms are possible. In particular, once the value of φ_a has become zero, the coefficient of the derivative in (13) vanishes. Equations (21) and (22) are valid. Therefore, as before, it is possible to arrive at the conclusion that the solution cannot be extended beyond the value of $\varphi_a = 0$. The corresponding plastic collapse mechanism is localization of plastic deformation at $\rho = a$. It follows from (17) that this plastic collapse mechanism occurs at $p = p_k$ where

$$p_k = -\frac{2}{\sqrt{4-\eta^2}} \tag{24}$$

It is obvious that p_k is constant. Therefore, in the $p\tau$-space, this plastic collapse mechanism is interpreted as a straight line parallel to the τ-axis. This line is illustrated in Figure 3 for $\nu = 0.3$ and $G = H = F$. The curve corresponding to the initiation of plastic yielding (curve 1) is tangent to this line at point k.

In order to determine the curve corresponding to the other plastic collapse mechanism, it is necessary to solve Equation (16) for φ_m numerically assuming that the value of φ_a is given. Then, the value of p immediately follows from Equation (17). Excluding A and B in Equation (15) yields

$$\tau = (1+\nu)\left[\frac{\cos\varphi_m}{\sqrt{4-\eta^2}}\left(1-\frac{\eta\eta_1}{2}\right)-\frac{\eta_1}{2}\sin\varphi_m\right]-(1-\nu)\left[\frac{\cos\varphi_m}{\sqrt{4-\eta^2}}\left(1+\frac{\eta\eta_1}{2}\right)+\frac{\eta_1}{2}\sin\varphi_m\right] \tag{25}$$

Since the value of ϕ_m has been found, the corresponding value of τ can be determined from this equation with no difficulty. Thus, the dependence of p on τ is obtained in

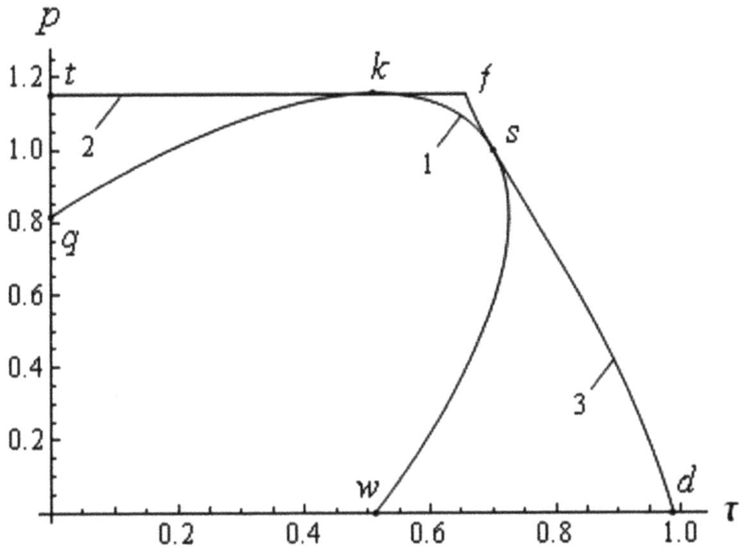

Figure 3 Illustration of the general structure of the solution. Curve 1 corresponds to the initiation of plastic yielding. Straight line 2 and curve 3 correspond to different plastic collapse mechanisms.

parametric form. This dependence is illustrated by curve 3 in Figure 3 for $a = 1/2$, $\nu = 0.3$ and $G = H = F$. Curves 1 and 3 have the same tangent line at point s.

Results and discussion

Figure 3 is a geometric illustration of the state of plastic collapse. In what follows, it is assumed that the increase in the loading parameters does not lead to unloading. It is convenient to divide curve 1 into three segments, namely qk, ks and sw. If the initiation of plastic yielding occurs at some point of the segment qk, then the only possible mechanism of plastic collapse is localization of plastic deformation at $\rho = a$. In Figure 3, this mechanism of plastic collapse corresponds to a point of the line tk. If the initiation of plastic yielding occurs at some point of the segment sw, then the only possible mechanism of plastic collapse is the fully plastic disk. In Figure 3, this mechanism of plastic collapse corresponds to a point of the curve sd. Finally, if the initiation of plastic yielding occurs at some point of the segment ks, then either mechanism of plastic collapse is possible. Moreover, both mechanisms occur simultaneously if the values of the loading parameters correspond to point f. A special feature of the solution corresponding to point k is that the plastic collapse occurs by strain localization when the entire disk is elastic (except the line $\rho = a$). A special feature of the solution corresponding to point s is that the entire disk becomes plastic at the values of the loading parameters corresponding to the initiation of plastic yielding.

Conclusions

A new semi-analytical solution for the state of plastic collapse of a thin annular plastically orthotropic disk subject to thermo-mechanical loading has been found. The numerical part of the solution reduces to solving Equation (16) for φ_m. Plastic yielding is controlled by Hill's quadratic orthotropic criterion. The study has emphasized qualitative features of the plastic collapse solution whose general structure is illustrated in Figure 3. It has been shown that there are two plastic collapse mechanisms. According to one of these mechanisms, the load-bearing capacity of the disk is lost because of strain localization at its inner radius. According to the other plastic collapse mechanism, the entire disk becomes plastic. In addition to these two general cases, there are three special cases of great interest for both numerical solutions of similar problems and the interpretation of elastic/plastic stress solutions for thin plastically anisotropic structures. These special cases are denoted by symbols k, s and f in Figure 3. If the state of stress corresponds to point k, then the disk losses its load-bearing capacity by plastic localization at its inner radius whereas the entire disk (except the inner radius) is elastic. If the state of stress corresponds to point s, then the disk becomes plastic at the same values of the loading parameters at which plastic yielding initiates. A distinguished feature of point f is that both of the aforementioned plastic collapse mechanisms occur simultaneously. It is expected that these qualitative features of the solution are rather common for a class of plastically anisotropic thin-walled structures and they can cause some difficulties with finding numerical solutions for such structures.

Competing interests
The authors declare that they have no competing interests.

Authors' contributions
SA formulated the boundary value problem and performed its qualitative analysis. CP performed numerical simulation. Both authors read and approved the final manuscript.

Acknowledgements
The research described in this paper has been supported by RFBR (Russia) and VAST (Vietnam), Project RFBR-14-01-93000.

Author details
[1]Laboratory for Strength and Fracture of Materials and Structures, A.Ishlinskii Institute for Problems in Mechanics of Russian Academy of Sciences, Moscow 119526, Russia. [2]VAST, Institute of Mechanics, 264 Doi Can, Hanoi, Vietnam.

References
1. Hsu YC, Forman RG (1975) Elastic-plastic analysis of an infinite sheet having a circular hole under pressure. Trans ASME J Appl Mech 42:347–352
2. Guven U (1992) Elastic-plastic annular disk with variable thickness subjected to external pressure. Acta Mechanica 92:29–34
3. Gamer U (1992) A concise treatment of the shrink fit with elastic-plastic hub. Int J Solids Struct 29:2463–2469
4. Lippmann H (1992) The effect of a temperature cycle on the stress distribution in a shrink fit. Int J Plast 8:567–582
5. Mack W (1993) Thermal assembly of an elastic-plastic hub and a solid shaft. Arch Appl Mech 63:42–50
6. Mack W, Bengeri M (1994) Thermal assembly of an elastic-plastic shrink fit with solid inclusion. Int J Mech Sci 36:699–705
7. Ball DL (1995) Elastic-plastic stress analysis of cold expanded fastener holes. Fatig Fract Eng Mater Struct 18:47–63
8. Poussard C, Pavier MY, Smith DJ (1995) Analytical and finite element predictions of residual stresses in cold worked fastener holes. J Strain Anal Eng Des 30:291–304
9. Alexandrov S, Alexandrova N (2001) Thermal effects on the development of plastic zones in thin axisymmetric plates. J Strain Anal Eng Des 36:169–176
10. Debski R, Zyczkowski M (2002) On decohesive carrying capacity of variable-thickness annular perfectly plastic disks. Zeitschrift für Angewandte Mathematik und Mechanik (ZAMM) 82:655–669
11. Alexandrova N, Alexandrov S (2004) Elastic-plastic stress distribution in a rotating annular disk. Mech Base Des Struct Mach 32:1–15
12. Alexandrova N, Alexandrov S (2004) Elastic-plastic stress distribution in a plastically anisotropic rotating disk. Trans ASME J Appl Mech 71:427–429
13. Gupta VK, Singh SB, Chandrawat HN, Ray S (2005) Modeling of creep behaviour of a rotating disc in the presence of both composition and thermal gradients. Trans ASME J Appl Mech 127:97–105
14. You LH, You XY, Zhang JJ, Li J (2007) On rotating circular disks with varying material properties. Zeitschrift für Angewandte Mathematik und Mechanik (ZAMM) 58:1068–1084
15. Jang JS, Kim DW (2008) Re-cold expansion process simulation to impart the residual stresses around fastener holes in 6061 A-T6 aluminium alloy. Proc IME B J Eng Manufact 222:1325–1332
16. Deepak D, Gupta VK, Dham AK (2009) Impact of stress exponent on steady state creep in a rotating composite disc. J Strain Anal Eng Des 44:127–135
17. Alexandrov SE, Lomakin EV, Jeng Y-R (2010) Effect of the pressure dependency of the yield condition on the stress distribution in a rotating disk. Doklady Physics 55:606–608
18. Chakherlou TN, Yaghoobi A (2010) Numerical simulation of residual stress relaxation around a cold-expanded fastener hole under longitudinal cyclic loading using different kinematic hardening models. Fatig Fract Eng Mater Struct 33:740–751
19. Masri R, Cohen T, Durban D (2010) Enlargement of a circular hole in a thin plastic sheet: Taylor-Bethe controversy in retrospect. Q Mech Appl Math 63:589–616
20. Alexandrov S, Jeng Y-R, Lomakin E (2011) Effect of pressure-dependency of the yield criterion on the development of plastic zones and the distribution of residual stresses in thin annular disks. Trans ASME J Appl Mech 78:031012
21. Kleiber M, Kowalczyk P (1996) Sensitivity analysis in plane stress elasto-plasticity and elasto-viscoplasticity. Comput Meth Appl Mech Eng 137:395–409
22. Hill R (1950) The mathematical theory of plasticity. Oxford University Press, Oxford

3

A numerical-analytical coupling computational method for homogenization of effective thermal conductivity of periodic composites

Quy Dong To* and Guy Bonnet

*Correspondence:
quy-dong.to@u-pem.fr
Université Paris-Est, Laboratoire Modélisation et Simulation Multi Echelle, MSME UMR 8208 CNRS, 5 Boulevard Descartes, 77454 Marne-la-Vallée, France

Abstract

Background: In the framework of periodic homogenization, the conduction problem can be formulated as an integral equation whose solution can be represented by a Neumann series. From the theory, many efficient numerical computation methods and analytical estimations have been proposed to compute the effective conductivity of composites.

Methods: We combine a Fast Fourier Transform (FFT) numerical method based on the Neumann series and analytical estimation based on the integral equation to solve the problem. Specifically, the analytical approximation is used to estimate the remainder of the series.

Results: From some numerical examples, the coupling method have shown to improve significantly the original FFT iteration scheme and results are also superior to the analytical estimation.

Conclusions: We have proposed a new efficient computation method to determine the effective conductivity of composites. This method combines the advantages of the FFT numerical methods and the analytical estimation based on integral equation.

Keywords: NIH approximation; Fourier transform; Effective conductivity; Neumann series

Background

Composite materials can exist in nature or be fabricated by purpose. Due to their technological importance, micromechanical approaches are developed to determine the overall behavior of composites from the properties of their constituents. The general procedure comprises two steps: the construction of a representative model, containing information on heterogeneities (morphologies, inclusion shape, volume fraction, local physical properties, etc.), and the analysis of the model by some mathematical methods. Analytical methods are often based on a simplification of inclusion shapes and potential theory, spherical harmonic functions, etc. Many exact and approximate closed-form solutions have been derived by such methods for materials having a linear behavior [1-7]. However, if the microstructure is known in all its complexity, numerical methods must be used. Among the numerical methods, finite element method (FEM) and boundary element method (BEM) are widely used for homogenization problems. These methods have been reported in numerous works [8-12]. A more recent method, introduced in the 1990s and described thereafter, uses extensively the Fourier transform and the introduction of a 'reference material'.

From a theoretical point of view, the introduction of a reference material allows formulation of the localization problem in the form of a Lippman-Schwinger-Dyson-type integral equation, whose solution can be represented by a Neumann series. The most convenient way to solve this integral equation is its formulation using Fourier transform of the equations governing the localization problem [13-19]. Some notable variants and improvements of this method can be found in the literature [18,20-23]. However, it is known that fast Fourier transform (FFT) iterative schemes are very sensitive to the contrast ratio between the phases and may not converge for infinite contrasts. Therefore, an important step when using FFT iterative schemes is to estimate the remainder of the Neumann series whose sum is computed up to a finite number of terms. This paper is devoted to this fundamental question.

In this paper, the remainder of the Neumann series is estimated by a combination between FFT schemes and the Nemat-Nasser-Iwakuma-Hejazi (NIH) [24,25] estimation of the effective properties. For two-phase systems with spherical inclusions, the NIH estimation in thermal problems leads to closed-form solutions which agree with numerical results for a large range of volume fractions. However, the NIH estimation departs from the sum of the Neumann series at high concentrations of inclusions. Since both NIH approximation and FFT schemes are based on integral equations, we use the former to estimate analytically the remainder of the Neumann series and derive the improved effective properties.

The present paper contains four parts. After a brief introduction of the paper's context, the 'Methods' Section is dedicated to the computational methods. The problem statement, FFT methods, and the FFT-NIH coupling are also presented in this section. Implementations of the coupling are discussed in the 'Results and discussion' Section. Finally, concluding remarks are given in the 'Conclusions' Section.

Methods

Problem statement and integral equation formulation

A periodic composite material is constructed by repeating infinitely a unit rectangular cell V of dimensions a_1, a_2, a_3 along three directions x_1, x_2, x_3. The homogenization of its thermal conductivity is reduced to solving the periodic heat transfer problem defined by the system of equations:

$$\begin{aligned}
&\mathbf{q}(\mathbf{x}) = \mathbf{K}(\mathbf{x})\mathbf{e}(\mathbf{x}) \quad \forall \mathbf{x} \in V \\
&\mathbf{e}(\mathbf{x}) = -\nabla T(\mathbf{x}), \quad \forall \mathbf{x} \in V \\
&\nabla \cdot \mathbf{q} = 0, \quad \forall \mathbf{x} \in V \\
&T - \mathbf{E} \cdot \mathbf{x} \quad \text{periodic}, \\
&\mathbf{q} \cdot \mathbf{n} \quad \text{antiperiodic.}
\end{aligned} \tag{1}$$

In (1), $\mathbf{q}(\mathbf{x})$ is the flux vector, $T(\mathbf{x})$ the temperature, $\mathbf{e}(\mathbf{x})$ the (minus) temperature gradient, $\mathbf{K}(\mathbf{x})$ the local second-order conductivity, and $\mathbf{n}$ the outward normal vector on the surface of the unit cell. Solution of (1) allows computation of the volume averages of $\mathbf{e}$ and

$\mathbf{q}$, denoted, respectively, by $\mathbf{E}$ and $\mathbf{Q}$ and finally the overall conductivity $\mathbf{K}^{\text{eff}}$. In summary, we can write

$$\mathbf{Q} = \mathbf{K}^{\text{eff}}\mathbf{E}, \quad \mathbf{E} = \langle \mathbf{e} \rangle_V, \quad \mathbf{Q} = \langle \mathbf{q} \rangle_V. \tag{2}$$

Here and from now on, we use the angular brackets $\langle . \rangle_V$ to denote the volume average over V, for example,

$$\langle \phi \rangle_V = \frac{1}{V} \int_V \phi d\mathbf{x}. \tag{3}$$

Instead of solving the system of (1), the integral equation approach reformulates the boundary value problem using a reference material with arbitrary conductivity $\mathbf{K}^0$. This allows the introduction of the *free gradient* $\mathbf{e}^*$ through the following formula:

$$\mathbf{q}(\mathbf{x}) = \mathbf{K}^0(\mathbf{e}(\mathbf{x}) - \mathbf{e}^*(\mathbf{x})) \text{ or } \mathbf{K}^0\mathbf{e}^*(\mathbf{x}) = \delta\mathbf{K}\mathbf{e}(\mathbf{x}) \tag{4}$$

with

$$\delta\mathbf{K} = \mathbf{K}^0 - \mathbf{K}(\mathbf{x}). \tag{5}$$

Since any V-periodic function ϕ can be represented by a Fourier series,

$$\phi(\mathbf{x}) = \sum_{\boldsymbol{\xi}} \widehat{\phi}(\boldsymbol{\xi}) e^{i\boldsymbol{\xi}\cdot\mathbf{x}}, \quad \widehat{\phi}(\boldsymbol{\xi}) = \left\langle \phi(\mathbf{x}) e^{-i\boldsymbol{\xi}\cdot\mathbf{x}} \right\rangle_V, \tag{6}$$

applying Fourier analysis to (1) and (4) yields an integral equation for $\mathbf{e}^*(\mathbf{x})$:

$$\delta\mathbf{K}\left[\mathbf{E} + \sum_{\boldsymbol{\xi}\neq 0} e^{i\boldsymbol{\xi}\cdot\mathbf{x}} \widehat{\boldsymbol{\Gamma}}^0(\boldsymbol{\xi}) \mathbf{K}^0 \widehat{\mathbf{e}}^*(\boldsymbol{\xi})\right] = \mathbf{K}^0\mathbf{e}^*(\mathbf{x}),$$
$$\text{or} \quad \delta\mathbf{K}\left[\mathbf{E} + \boldsymbol{\Gamma}^0 * \mathbf{K}^0\mathbf{e}^*(\mathbf{x})\right] = \mathbf{K}^0\mathbf{e}^*(\mathbf{x}). \tag{7}$$

The Green tensor $\widehat{\boldsymbol{\Gamma}}^0(\boldsymbol{\xi})$ in (7), the Fourier representation of the periodic Green operator $\boldsymbol{\Gamma}^0$, is defined by the following formula:

$$\widehat{\boldsymbol{\Gamma}}^0(\boldsymbol{\xi}) = \frac{\boldsymbol{\xi} \otimes \boldsymbol{\xi}}{\boldsymbol{\xi} \cdot \mathbf{K}^0 \boldsymbol{\xi}}. \tag{8}$$

The infinite sums in (6) and (7) involve all vectors $\boldsymbol{\xi}$ with components ξ_i satisfying the conditions

$$\xi_i = \frac{\pi n_i}{a_i}, \quad n_i = 0, \pm 1, \ldots, \pm\infty, \quad i = 1, 2, 3. \tag{9}$$

Method of resolution

Full field solution of (1) and the effective properties can be determined by FFT-based methods at any accuracy. By recasting (7), a more convenient form is obtained [18,26,27]:

$$\mathbf{e}(\mathbf{x}) = \mathbf{E} + \boldsymbol{\Gamma}^0 * \delta\mathbf{K}\mathbf{e}(\mathbf{x}). \tag{10}$$

A classical way of solving the integral equation is to sum the Neumann series

$$\mathbf{e}(\mathbf{x}) = \sum_{j=0}^{\infty} (\boldsymbol{\Gamma}^0 * \delta\mathbf{K})^j \mathbf{E}, \tag{11}$$

under the condition that the Neumann series is convergent, which is achieved for a specific range of admissible values of $\mathbf{K}^0$. To solve (10), iterative schemes are usually employed. For example, starting from the initial value $\mathbf{e}^0(\mathbf{x}) = \mathbf{E}$, one can repeatedly compute $\mathbf{e}^1, \mathbf{e}^2, \ldots, \mathbf{e}^N$ via the recurrence relation

$$\mathbf{e}^{N+1} = \mathbf{E} + \boldsymbol{\Gamma}^0 * \delta\mathbf{K}\mathbf{e}^N. \tag{12}$$

Stopping the recurrence at N_0 iterations produces the sum of the N_0 first terms in the Neumann series (11). It is worthwhile mentioning that relation

$$\mathbf{e} = \mathbf{E} + \boldsymbol{\Gamma}^0 * \mathbf{K}^0\mathbf{e} \tag{13}$$

holds for all rotational free vector $\mathbf{e}$ and leads to another equivalent form of (12):

$$\mathbf{e}^{N+1} = \mathbf{e}^N - \boldsymbol{\Gamma}^0 * \mathbf{q}^N, \quad \mathbf{q}^N = \mathbf{K}\mathbf{e}^N. \tag{14}$$

Although the FFT-based methods produce $\mathbf{e}(\mathbf{x})$ at convergence, the main concern is the convergence rate at high contrast ratio. The basic iterative scheme described in (12) and (14) is called the primal iterative scheme (PIS). In the literature, there have been numerous works to improve the convergence of the basic method such as dual iterative scheme (DIS) [20,28], polarization-based iterative scheme (PBIS) [21,22], accelerated scheme (AS) [18], augmented Lagrangian scheme (ALS) [16], etc.

Instead of finding the full field solution of (1), the mean value of $\mathbf{e}^*$ and the effective thermal conductivity $\mathbf{K}^{\text{eff}}$ can be estimated from (7) with NIH approximation [24,25]. Such an approximation has been shown to predict very well the overall elastic and thermal properties of two-phase composites for a large range of volume fractions of inclusions [25,29]. However, it fails at higher concentrations. Generally, the estimation of $\mathbf{K}^{\text{eff}}$ requires only the computation of a lattice sum which admits closed-form expressions in many cases, as seen thereafter.

Residual integral equation and estimation of the remainder of the Neumann series

The main scope of this paper is to combine the advantages of the analytical approximation and FFT numerical methods to improve the prediction of the effective properties. The material under consideration is a two-phase matrix-inclusion composite with conductivity of both phases being $\mathbf{K}^M$ (matrix) and $\mathbf{K}^I$ (inclusion). The volume fraction of the inclusions is f, and the distribution of the inclusions in the unit cell is taken to be general at this stage.

Starting with any conventional FFT method (e.g., PIS, PBIS), we assume that after N iterations, we have obtained $\mathbf{e}^N$ which is an estimation of the exact solution $\widetilde{\mathbf{e}}$. In the coupled method, we consider the residual $\mathbf{r}^N$ at step N defined by

$$\mathbf{r}^N = \left[\mathbf{K}(\mathbf{x}) - \mathbf{K}^M\right](\widetilde{\mathbf{e}} - \mathbf{e}^N). \tag{15}$$

Knowing the average of $\mathbf{r}^N$ allows computation of the macroscopic flux $\widetilde{\mathbf{Q}}$ associated to $\widetilde{\mathbf{e}}$. Indeed, by averaging (15) over V and accounting for the following properties:

$$\langle\widetilde{\mathbf{e}}\rangle_V = \mathbf{E}, \quad \mathbf{r}^N = \mathbf{0} \text{ outside } \Omega, \tag{16}$$

we can deduce that

$$\begin{aligned} f\langle\mathbf{r}^N\rangle_\Omega &= \widetilde{\mathbf{Q}} - \mathbf{Q}^N - \mathbf{Q}^*, \quad \mathbf{Q}^N = \langle\mathbf{K}\mathbf{e}^N\rangle_V, \\ \widetilde{\mathbf{Q}} &= \langle\mathbf{K}\widetilde{\mathbf{e}}\rangle_V, \quad \mathbf{Q}^* = \mathbf{K}^M[\mathbf{E} - \langle\mathbf{e}^N\rangle_V]. \end{aligned} \tag{17}$$

When $\mathbf{e}^N$ is computed from the primal iterative scheme, $\langle\mathbf{e}^N\rangle_V = \mathbf{E}$ is always true and $\mathbf{Q}^*$ always vanishes (for other schemes, this quantity is known). The other terms $\mathbf{Q}^N$

and $\widetilde{\mathbf{Q}}$ in (17), respectively, are the macroscopic flux calculated by the conventional FFT method and the real flux. They are different by a correcting term $f\langle \mathbf{r}^N \rangle_\Omega$ which will be estimated through the NIH approach. Substituting (15) into (10) with the matrix as the reference material and accounting for (12), we obtain the following integral equation for $\mathbf{r}^N$:

$$\mathbf{r}^N = \mathbf{w}^N - [\mathbf{K}(\mathbf{x}) - \mathbf{K}^M]\, \mathbf{\Gamma}^M * \mathbf{r}^N, \tag{18}$$

in which $\mathbf{w}^N$ is known from the expressions

$$\mathbf{w}^N = \left[\mathbf{K}(\mathbf{x}) - \mathbf{K}^M\right][\boldsymbol{\epsilon} - \mathbf{e}^N], \quad \boldsymbol{\epsilon} = \mathbf{E} - \mathbf{\Gamma}^M * \left[\mathbf{K}(\mathbf{x}) - \mathbf{K}^M\right]\mathbf{e}^N. \tag{19}$$

Since the convolution $\mathbf{\Gamma}^M * \mathbf{r}^N$ admits the Fourier representation

$$\mathbf{\Gamma}^M * \mathbf{r}^N = \sum_{\boldsymbol{\xi} \neq 0} e^{i\boldsymbol{\xi}\cdot\mathbf{x}} \widehat{\mathbf{\Gamma}}^M(\boldsymbol{\xi}) \widehat{\mathbf{r}}^N(\boldsymbol{\xi}), \tag{20}$$

averaging both sides of (18) over the inclusion Ω yields

$$\langle \mathbf{r}^N \rangle_\Omega = \langle \mathbf{w}^N \rangle_\Omega - \left[\mathbf{K}^I - \mathbf{K}^M\right] \sum_{\boldsymbol{\xi} \neq 0} \langle e^{i\boldsymbol{\xi}\cdot\mathbf{x}} \rangle_\Omega \widehat{\mathbf{\Gamma}}^M(\boldsymbol{\xi}) \widehat{\mathbf{r}}^N(\boldsymbol{\xi}). \tag{21}$$

Next, the NIH approximation is applied to $\widehat{\mathbf{r}}^N(\boldsymbol{\xi})$ as follows:

$$\widehat{\mathbf{r}}^N(\boldsymbol{\xi}) = \frac{1}{V} \int_V \mathbf{r}^N e^{-i\boldsymbol{\xi}\cdot\mathbf{x}} d\mathbf{x} \simeq f \langle e^{-i\boldsymbol{\xi}\cdot\mathbf{x}} \rangle_\Omega \langle \mathbf{r}^N \rangle_\Omega. \tag{22}$$

By denoting $I(\boldsymbol{\xi}), P(\boldsymbol{\xi})$ the following shape functions:

$$I(\boldsymbol{\xi}) = \langle e^{i\boldsymbol{\xi}\cdot\mathbf{x}} \rangle_\Omega, \quad P(\boldsymbol{\xi}) = fI(\boldsymbol{\xi})I(-\boldsymbol{\xi}), \tag{23}$$

we can now obtain the average of the residual term $\langle \mathbf{r}^N \rangle_\Omega$ through the new relation

$$\langle \mathbf{r}^N \rangle_\Omega = \left[\mathbf{I} + [\mathbf{K}^I - \mathbf{K}^M] \sum_{\boldsymbol{\xi} \neq 0} P(\boldsymbol{\xi}) \widehat{\mathbf{\Gamma}}^M(\boldsymbol{\xi})\right]^{-1} [\mathbf{K}^I - \mathbf{K}^M] \langle \boldsymbol{\epsilon} - \mathbf{e}^N \rangle_\Omega. \tag{24}$$

Substituting (24) back into (17), we obtain $\mathbf{Q}^N_{\text{cor}}$, an improved estimation of the macroscopic flux $\widetilde{\mathbf{Q}}$. It is noteworthy that if we apply the property at convergence (13) to $\mathbf{e}^N$ in (19), the term $\boldsymbol{\epsilon} - \mathbf{e}^N$ can be computed from the expression

$$\boldsymbol{\epsilon} - \mathbf{e}^N = -\mathbf{\Gamma}^M * \mathbf{q}^N, \quad \mathbf{q}^N = \mathbf{K}\mathbf{e}^N. \tag{25}$$

The method presented in this paper can be used in coupling with any FFT-based iterative scheme. An algorithm presenting the implementation with the basic scheme (PIS) is presented in Algorithm 1 and used later in this work. In the following, this scheme will be stopped before convergence, in view to evaluate the performance of the estimation of the remainder of the series.

Algorithm 1 Algorithm of the iterative scheme PIS coupled with NIH approximation

$\mathbf{e}^0(\mathbf{x}) = \mathbf{E}$

$\mathbf{q}^N(\mathbf{x}) = \mathbf{K}(\mathbf{x}).\mathbf{e}^N(\mathbf{x})$

$\widehat{\mathbf{q}}^N(\boldsymbol{\xi}) = \mathcal{F}(\mathbf{q}^N(\mathbf{x}))$

compute $\langle \mathbf{w}^N \rangle_\Omega$, $\langle \mathbf{r}^N \rangle_\Omega$, $\mathbf{Q}^N_{\text{cor}}$

convergence test

$\widehat{\mathbf{e}}^{N+1}(\boldsymbol{\xi}) = \widehat{\mathbf{e}}^N(\boldsymbol{\xi}) - \widehat{\mathbf{\Gamma}}^0(\boldsymbol{\xi}).\widehat{\mathbf{q}}^N(\boldsymbol{\xi})$

$\mathbf{e}^{N+1}(\mathbf{x}) = \mathcal{F}^{-1}(\widehat{\mathbf{e}}^{N+1}(\boldsymbol{\xi}))$

Although the original NIH estimation is obtained by making approximation to (7) instead of (10), the NIH estimation can also be recovered as a special case of (24). Indeed, by replacing $\mathbf{e}^N$ with a zero field $\mathbf{0}$ and repeating the same steps to derive $\mathbf{Q}^N_{\mathrm{cor}}$, the final result is the flux $\mathbf{Q}^{\mathrm{NIH}}$ defined by

$$\mathbf{Q}^{NIH} = \mathbf{K}^M\mathbf{E} + f\left[\mathbf{I} + [\mathbf{K}^I - \mathbf{K}^M]\sum_{\xi\neq\mathbf{0}} P(\xi)\widehat{\boldsymbol{\Gamma}}^M(\xi)\right]^{-1} [\mathbf{K}^I - \mathbf{K}^M]\,\mathbf{E}, \tag{26}$$

It is clear that, from (26), the effective conductivity is obtained in the same form as in the previous work [25].

Coupled method in special cases

The coupled algorithm is significantly accelerated if the shape functions $I(\xi)$ or $P(\xi)$ are determined from closed-form expressions, for example, in the case of ellipsoidal inclusions. Firstly, it is no longer necessary to compute numerically the Fourier transform of the characteristic function [28]. Secondly, the lattice sum $\sum_{\xi\neq\mathbf{0}} P(\xi)\widehat{\boldsymbol{\Gamma}}^M(\xi)$ can also be estimated by a closed-form expression.

To illustrate these ideas, we consider the special cases where the spherical inclusions of radius R are located at the lattice points of cubic lattice systems (see Figure 1). The matrix and inclusions are assumed to be isotropic with conductivities k_M and k_I :

$$\mathbf{K}^M = k_M\mathbf{I}, \quad \mathbf{K}^I = k_I\mathbf{I}, \tag{27}$$

with $\mathbf{I}$ being the identity tensor. The Green tensor associated to the matrix admits a simple form:

$$\widehat{\boldsymbol{\Gamma}}^M(\xi) = \bar{\xi}\otimes\bar{\xi}/k_M, \quad \bar{\xi} = \xi/|\xi|. \tag{28}$$

By considering the symmetry with respect to $\xi_i = 0$ planes and the permutation invariance, the lattice sum $\sum_{\xi\neq\mathbf{0}} P(\xi)\widehat{\boldsymbol{\Gamma}}^M(\xi)$ can be simplified into

$$\sum_{\xi\neq\mathbf{0}} P(\xi)\widehat{\boldsymbol{\Gamma}}^M(\xi) = \frac{\mathbf{I}}{3k_M}\sum_{\xi\neq\mathbf{0}} P(\xi). \tag{29}$$

Finally, the improved estimation $\mathbf{Q}^N_{cor}$ is reduced to

$$\mathbf{Q}^N_{cor} = \mathbf{Q}^N - \frac{f k_M \langle \boldsymbol{\Gamma}^M * \mathbf{q}^N\rangle_\Omega}{\frac{k_M}{k_M - k_I} - \frac{1}{3}\sum_{\xi\neq\mathbf{0}} P(\xi)}. \tag{30}$$

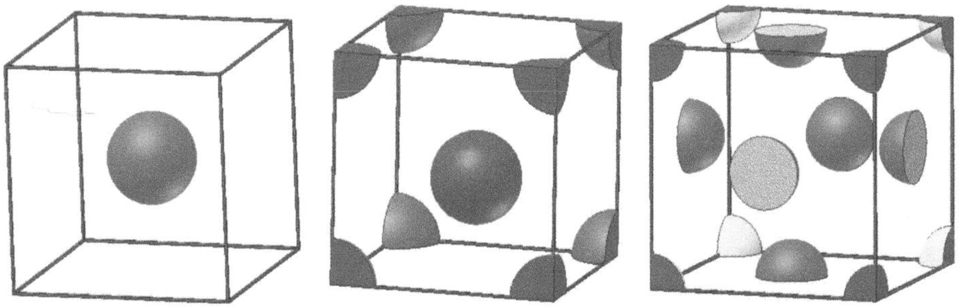

Figure 1 Unit cell of cubic lattice structures (from left to right: simple cubic, body-centered cubic, face-centered cubic).

The macroscopic flux from NIH approximation (26) has also a simple form:

$$\mathbf{Q}^{NIH} = \left(k_M - \frac{f k_M}{\frac{k_M}{k_M - k_I} - \frac{1}{3}\sum_{\boldsymbol{\xi}\neq 0} P(\boldsymbol{\xi})} \right) \mathbf{E}, \tag{31}$$

where the term inside the parenthesis is the effective conductivity k_{eff} predicted by the approach. Since $P(\boldsymbol{\xi})$ decays rapidly with $|\boldsymbol{\xi}|$, the infinite sum $\sum_{\boldsymbol{\xi}\neq 0} P(\boldsymbol{\xi})$ can be estimated by keeping several initial terms and approximating the remainder with an improper integral:

$$\sum_{\boldsymbol{\xi}\neq 0} P(\xi) \simeq \sum_{0<|\boldsymbol{\xi}|<\xi_c} P(\xi) + \frac{a^3}{2\pi^2} \int_{\xi_c}^{\infty} P(\xi)\xi^2 d\xi. \tag{32}$$

The parameter ξ_c defines the number of initial terms of the sum that we keep in the approximation formula. The final analytical expression is given in the following:

- Simple cubic system

$$P(\boldsymbol{\xi}) = P(\xi) = \frac{9f(\eta\cos\eta - \sin\eta)^2}{\eta^6},$$

$$\sum_{\boldsymbol{\xi}\neq 0} P(\xi) \simeq \sum_{0<|\boldsymbol{\xi}|<\xi_c} P(\xi) + \frac{3-\cos 2\eta_c}{\pi\eta_c} + \frac{2\sin^2\eta_c}{\pi\eta_c^3} - \frac{2\sin 2\eta_c}{\pi\eta_c^2} - \frac{2}{\pi}\text{Si}(2\eta_c) + 1, \quad \eta = \xi R, \quad \eta_c = \xi_c R, \tag{33}$$

with $\text{Si}(\eta)$ being the sine integral

$$\text{Si}(\eta) = \int_0^{\eta} \frac{\sin\eta'}{\eta'} d\eta'. \tag{34}$$

- Body-centered cubic system

$$P(\boldsymbol{\xi}) = \frac{9f}{4} \frac{[\eta\cos\eta - \sin\eta]^2}{\eta^6} [1 + \cos\pi(n_1+n_2+n_3)]^2,$$

$$\sum_{\boldsymbol{\xi}\neq 0} P(\xi) \simeq \sum_{0<|\boldsymbol{\xi}|<\xi_c} P(\xi) + \frac{3-\cos 2\eta_c}{\pi\eta_c} + \frac{2\sin^2\eta_c}{\pi\eta_c^3} - \frac{2\sin 2\eta_c}{\pi\eta_c^2} - \frac{2}{\pi}\text{Si}(2\eta_c) + 1. \tag{35}$$

- Face-centered cubic system

$$P(\boldsymbol{\xi}) = \frac{9f}{16} \frac{[\eta\cos\eta - \sin\eta]^2}{\eta^6} [\cos\pi n_1 + \cos\pi n_2 + \cos\pi n_3 + \cos\pi(n_1+n_2+n_3)]^2,$$

$$\sum_{\boldsymbol{\xi}\neq 0} P(\xi) \simeq \sum_{0<|\boldsymbol{\xi}|<\xi_c} P(\xi) + \frac{1}{4}\left[\frac{3-\cos 2\eta_c}{\pi\eta_c} + \frac{2\sin^2\eta_c}{\pi\eta_c^3} - \frac{2\sin 2\eta_c}{\pi\eta_c^2} - \frac{2}{\pi}\text{Si}(2\eta_c) + 1\right]. \tag{36}$$

Results and discussion

In this section, we study the results coming from the implementation of the coupled method for the case of a simple cubic system. The representative cell is a cube with the spherical inclusion located at its center (the first figure from the left in Figure 1). The

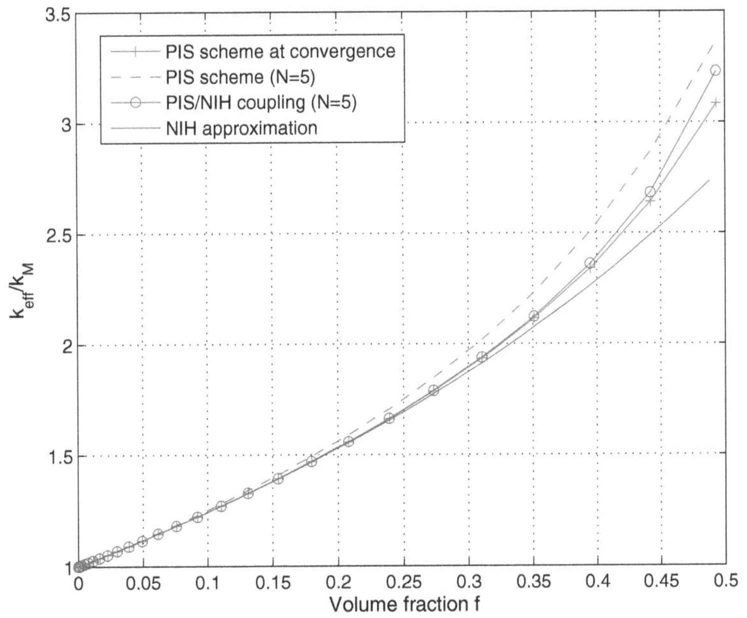

Figure 2 Estimation of the effective conductivity after 5 iterations (N=5). PIS, PIS/NIH coupling at $N = 5$ and NIH approximation for $k_I/k_M = 10$.

periodic problem with prescribed temperature gradient **E** is solved by three approaches: the NIH approximation (31), the conventional PIS, and the coupled method. The last two methods are based on the same iterative scheme, and in the coupled method, the reevaluation of the effective conductivity after each iteration is done using (30). All results are compared with the results coming from the conventional PIS method at convergence. The analytical expression of $\sum_{\xi \neq 0} P(\xi)$ described in (33) is used to accelerate the computation and to improve the accuracy. Regarding the iterative scheme, the number of harmonic

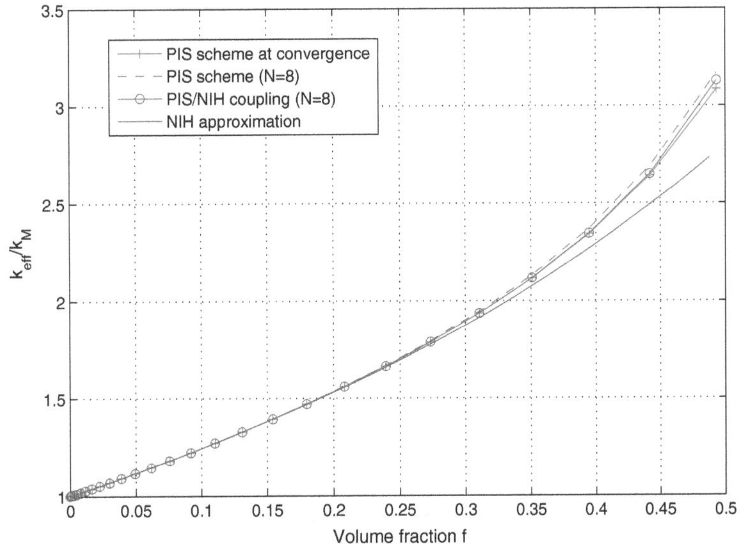

Figure 3 Estimation of the effective conductivity after 8 iterations (N=8). PIS, PIS/NIH coupling at $N = 8$ and NIH approximation for $k_I/k_M = 10$.

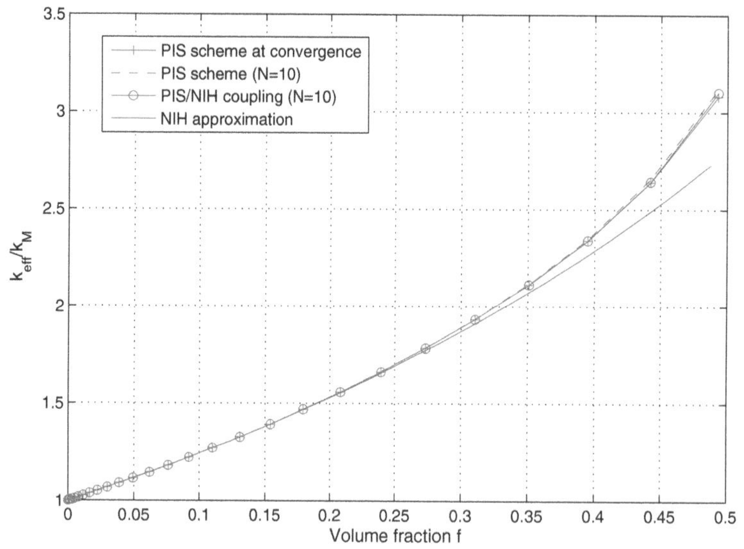

Figure 4 Estimation of the effective conductivity after 10 iterations (N=10). PIS, PIS/NIH coupling at $N = 10$ and NIH approximation for $k_I/k_M = 10$.

terms retained in the Fourier series is limited to 128*128*128, i.e., $|n_i| < 128$, $i = 1, 2, 3$, and the precision of the computation $\varepsilon = 0.001$ is adopted. Different contrast ratios k_I/k_M ranging from 0.1 to 50 are considered in this work, and the results of the three approaches are discussed and compared.

From Figures 2,3,4, all curves, associated to the first case $k_I/k_M = 10$, are quite close at small volume fraction f but separate at high f. The significant improvement of the coupled

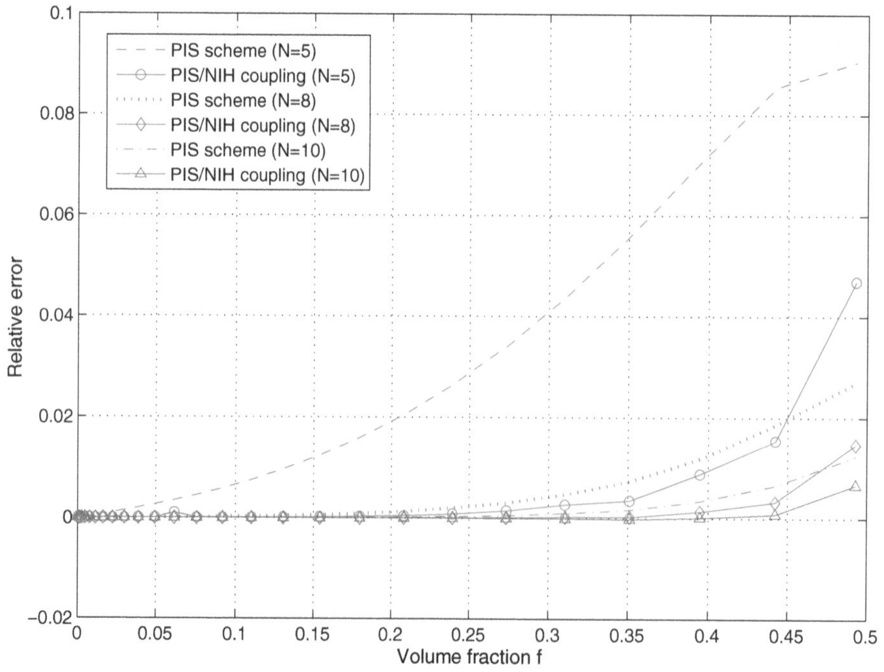

Figure 5 Relative error induced by different approaches at kI/kM=10. PIS, PIS/NIH coupling at $N = 5, 8, 10$, $k_I/k_M = 10$. Case study: simple cubic system.

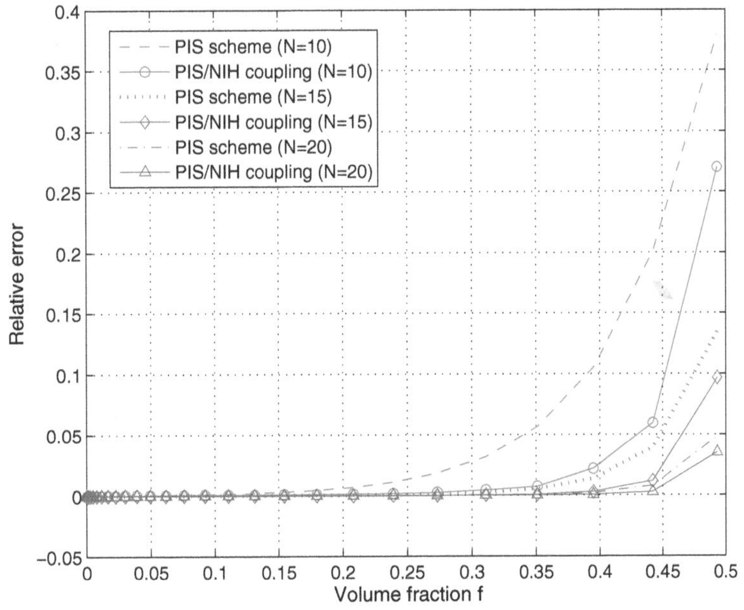

Figure 6 Relative error induced by different approaches at kI/kM=50. PIS, PIS/NIH coupling at $N = 10, 15, 20$, $k_I/k_M = 50$. Case study: simple cubic system.

method can be found at a small number of iterations, e.g., $N = 5$. In all cases under consideration, the coupling reduces significantly the difference between the conventional FFT method and the exact solution (see Figures 5,6,7). The coupled method results are also much more accurate than those issued from the pure NIH approximation which fails at high f.

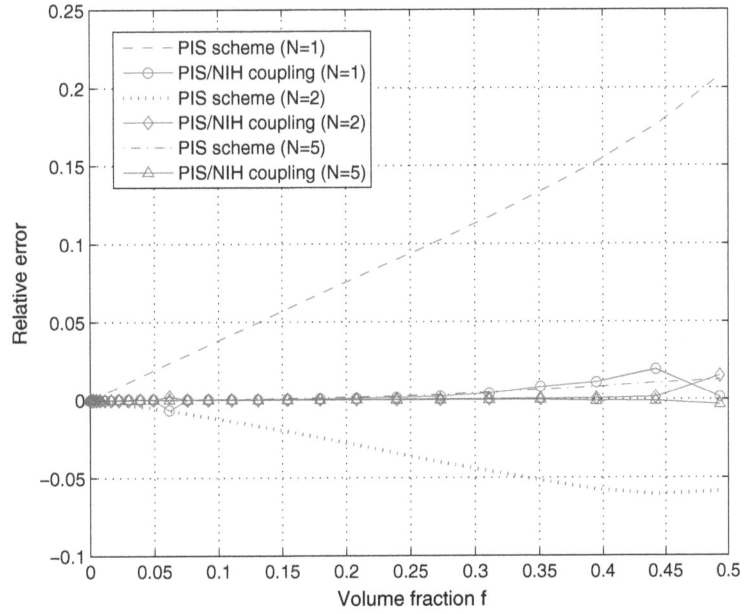

Figure 7 Relative error induced by different approaches at kI/kM=0.1. PIS, PIS/NIH coupling at $N = 1, 2, 5$, $k_I/k_M = 0.1$. Case study: simple cubic system.

Numerical examples at different contrast ra tios k_I/k_M also demonstrate a considerable improvement of the coupling in comparison with the basic FFT method. More particularly, for small $k_I/k_M = 0.1$, it generates a very good approximation of k_{eff} even at $N = 1, 2$, where the error of the FFT method is of order 20%. At high $k_I/k_M = 50$, the coupling performs less well but still reduces the relative error, the effect being important for lower number of iterations.

Conclusions

A coupled method is developed for computing the effective conductivity of periodic composites. The method uses a FFT iterative scheme to solve the localization problem and the NIH approximation to estimate analytically the remainder at any iteration N of the Neumann series. As a result, a new expression for the effective conductivity is derived on the basis of the current flux and temperature gradient field. Numerical tests on various cases have shown that the expression coming from the coupled method improves considerably the results issued from the uncoupled methods for small numbers of iterations. The contribution of the coupling improves the results at any contrast ratio and any volume fraction.

The application domain of the coupled method is large. Although the numerical examples given in this work concern the PIS scheme and spherical inclusions, the method can be applied to any existing FFT-based methods and arbitrary inclusion shapes to improve the accuracy of the predicted properties. The method can be extended to deal with other physical problems such as elasticity, piezoelectricity, etc.

Competing interests

The authors declare that they have no competing interests.

Authors' contributions

To Q.D. carried out the numerical and analytical computation. Bonnet G. provided his original numerical FFT code and proposed the present estimation scheme.

References

1. Kellogg O (1929) Foundations of potential theory. Frederick Ungar, New York
2. Rayleigh L (1892) On the influence of obstacles arranged in rectangular order upon the properties of a medium. Phil Mag 34: 481–502
3. McPhedran RC, McKenzie DR (1978) The conductivity of lattices of spheres. I. The simple cubic lattice. Proc R Soc Lond A 359: 45–63
4. McKenzie DR, McPhedran RC, Derrick G (1978) The conductivity of lattices of spheres. II. The body centred and face centred cubic lattices. Proc R Soc Lond A 362: 211–232
5. Cheng H, Torquato S (1997) Effective conductivity of periodic arrays of spheres with interfacial resistance. Proc R Soc Lond A 453: 145–161
6. Sangani AS, Acrivos A (1983) The effective conductivity of a periodic array of spheres. Proc R Soc Lond A 386: 263–275
7. Eshelby JD (1957) The determination of the elastic field of an ellipsoidal inclusion, and related problems. Proc R Soc Lond A 241: 376–396
8. McPhedran RC, Movchan AB (1994) The Rayleigh multipole method for linear elasticity. J Mech Phys Solids 42: 711–727
9. Helsing J (1995) An integral equation method for elastostatics of periodic composites. J Mech Phys Solids 43: 815–828
10. Eischen JW, Torquato S (1993) Determining elastic behavior of composites by boundary element method. J Appl Phys 74: 159–170
11. Kaminski M (1999) Boundary element method homogenization of the periodic linear elastic fiber composites. Eng Anal Bound Elem 23: 815–823
12. Liu YJ, Nishimura N, Otani Y, Takahashi T, Chen XL, Munakata H (2005) A fast boundary element method for the analysis of fiber-reinforced composites based on a rigid-inclusion model. J Appl Mech ASME 72: 115–128
13. Sheng P, Tao R (1985) First-principles approach for effective elastic-moduli calculation: application to continuous fractal structure. Phys Rev B 31: 6131–6133
14. Tao R, Chen Z, Sheng P (1990) First-principles Fourier approach for the calculation of the effective dielectric constant of periodic composites. Phys Rev B 41: 2417–2420

15. Michel JC, Moulinec H, Suquet P (1999) Effective properties of composite materials with periodic microstructure: a computational approach. Comput Method Appl Mech 172: 109–143
16. Michel JC, Moulinec H, Suquet P (2000) A computational method based on augmented Lagrangians and fast Fourier transforms for composites with high contrast. Comput Model Eng Sci 1: 79–88
17. Michel JC, Moulinec H, Suquet P (2001) A computational scheme for linear and non-linear composites with arbitrary phase contrast. Int J Numer Meth Engng 52: 139–160
18. Eyre DJ, Milton GW (1999) A fast numerical scheme for computing the response of composites using grid refinement. Eur Phys J Appl Phys: 41–47
19. Milton G (2002) The theory of composites. Cambridge University Press, New York
20. Bhattacharya K, Suquet P (2005) A model problem concerning recoverable strains of shape-memory polycrystals. Proc R Soc A 461: 2797–2816
21. Monchiet V, Bonnet G (2013) A polarization-based fast numerical method for computing the effective conductivity of composites. Int J Numer Meth Heat Fluid Flow 23(7): 1256–1271
22. Monchiet V, Bonnet G (2012) A polarization-based FFT iterative scheme for computing the effective properties of elastic composites with arbitrary contrast. Int J Numer Meth Eng 89: 1419–1436
23. Chen Y, Schuh CA (2009) Analytical homogenization method for periodic composite materials. Phys Rev B 79: 094104–094114
24. Nemat-Nasser S, Iwakuma T, Hejazi M (1982) On composites with periodic structure. Mech Mater 1: 239–267
25. To QD, Bonnet G, To VT (2013) Closed-form solutions for the effective conductivity of two-phase periodic composites with spherical inclusions. Proc R Soc A 469: 1471–2946
26. Strelniker YM, Bergman DJ (1994) Theory of magnetotransport in a composite medium with periodic microstructure for arbitrary magnetic fields. Phys Rev B 50: 14001–14015
27. Bergman DJ, Strelniker YM (1994) Calculation of strong-field magnetoresistance in some periodic composites. Phys Rev B 49: 16256–16268
28. Bonnet G (2007) Effective properties of elastic periodic composite media with fibers. J Mech Phys Solids 55: 881–899
29. Hoang DH (2011) Contribution à l'homogénéisation de matériaux hétérogènes viscoélastiques. Milieux aléatoires et périodiques et prise en compte des interfaces. PhD thesis, Université Paris Est Marne la Vallée

4

Modelling of shear localization in solids by means of energy relaxation

Tuyet B Trinh* and Klaus Hackl

*Correspondence:
Tuyet.Trinh@rub.de
Lehrstuhl für Mechanik-Materialtheorie, Ruhr-Universität Bochum, Universitätsstr. 150, D-44801 Bochum, Germany

Abstract

An approach to the problem of shear localization is proposed. It is based on energy minimization principles associated with micro-structure developments. Shear bands are treated as laminates of first order. The micro-shear band is assumed to have a zero thickness, leading to an unbounded strain field and the special form of the energy within this micro-band. The energy is approximated by the mixture of potential of two low-strain and high-strain domains and it is non-convex. The problem of the non-convex energy arising due to the formation of shear bands is solved by energy relaxation in order to ensure that the corresponding problem is well-posed. An application of the proposed formulation to isotropic material is presented. The capability of the proposed concept is demonstrated through numerical simulation of a tension test.

Keywords: Energy relaxation; Shear band; Strain localization

Background

Strain localization phenomena are observed in various materials as narrow zones of intense shearing, known as shear bands. In many cases, the formation of shear bands is accompanied by a softening response, characterized by a decrease in strength of the material with accumulated inelastic strain, often leading to complete failure [1,2]. Therefore, research on formation of shear bands has received much attention.

In simulation of strain localization, mesh dependence is the direct consequence of the ill-posedness of the corresponding boundary value problem [3]. Some enhanced continuum approaches can be found in literatures such as *Cosserat theory* [4-6], *nonlocal approaches* [7,8], and *gradient-enhanced approach* [9,10]. In these, an internal length scale is introduced to reflect certain small-scale effects assumed to be present in shear bands. The disadvantage of the corresponding numerical models is, however, that the element size is required be at least an order of magnitude smaller than the width of shear zones in order to obtain results independent of the mesh size [11].

The *strong discontinuity approach*, known as an alternative way to simulate strain localization without the introduction of characteristic lengths, rests upon the assumption that the displacement field is discontinuous [12-14]. This approach can be categorized into unregularized and regularized strong discontinuities. For *unregularized strong discontinuities*, the discontinuous displacement field induces an unbounded strain field having the character of a Dirac-delta distribution [14]. For *regularized strong discontinuity*

[11,15], one considers a transition from continuous to discontinuous response by using an approximation of the Dirac-delta distribution. In both variants, however, it is necessary to determine the position of a shear band by tracking strong discontinuities.

Furthermore, another possibility to tackle the localization problem is the use of phenomenological plasticity frameworks, in which the shear band and its constitutive response are embedded in the macroscopic constitutive behavior. Pietruszczak and Xu [16,17] suggested a theoretical framework for the analysis of brittle materials. Constituent materials including the intact and localized zone are used to determine the average mechanical properties through homogenization technique. The constitutive equation in the region confined by the shear band involves the resultant force rate acting at the interface and the displacement discontinuity. Amero [18] suggested a procedure for incorporating localized small-scale effects of the material response in the large-scale problem, which is characterized by the standard local continuum. The large-scale regularization of rate-dependent models is accomplished with the formalism of strong discontinuities to model effectively the localized dissipation observed in localized failures of solids and structures. Nguyen et al. [19,20] presented an approach with enhanced kinematics to capture localized mode of deformation for quasi-brittle materials. The volume element intersected by a localization band is considered as a two-phase material. The continuity condition of the traction across the boundary of the localization boundary is enforced to couple two stresses corresponding to the behavior in the localization zone and the bulk elastic one.

In recent years a new methodology based on *energy relaxation* has been developed to simulate not only the development of material microstructures [21-28] but also localization phenomena in plasticity and damage [29-33]. For problems involving microstructure evolution and localization which is related to various local instability effects such as buckling, crashing, and cracking, integration of the stress-strain relation leads to a nonconvexity of the potential energy. This behaviour can be seen in many kinds of materials such as geomaterials, concrete, steel, composite. For detailed expositions of the different monotone stress-strain curves and the corresponding nonconvex energies consult [34]. Dacorogna [23] showed that minimizers cannot be obtained in nonconvex variational problems. Instead, the quasiconvex envelope of the nonconvex energy, called the relaxed energy, should be studied to ensure the existence of minimizers. For the problem of strain localization, shear bands are treated as laminates of first order in microscopic level. The advantage of this theory, when applied to the problem at hand, is the natural formation of shear bands based on the energy minimization principles associated with micro-structure developments. In the works of Miehe and his coworkers [29-31], the laminate orientation corresponding to a mode-II simple shear is approximated to the critical direction of nonconvex energy based on the minimization of the determinant of the acoustic tensor. The width of a micro-shear band is finite. An incrementally variational formulation is based on an energy storage function and a dissipation function. Relaxation methods have been applied to crystal plasticity, see [25,35], and the references therein. However, the model in this paper is different in the sense as the direction of the shear band is variable, while in crystal plasticity, it is fixed.

Our model is based on the energy relaxation approach and aims to be applicable to any material which softens towards a critical state, for example geomaterials such as dense sands and over-consolidated clay. We treat shear bands as special laminates mixing two co-existing phases. When a shear band develops, the material at a point located inside the shear band is viewed as being decomposed into a high-strain and a low-strain domain. We will introduce specific potentials for the low strain and the high strain material behavior as depicted in Figure 1b.

This approach has some similarities with that one of Miehe and coworkers [29-31]. There, a non-convex potential obtained as condensed energy of an incremental variational approach is used. This leads to microstructures given as laminates of finite width. In our approach, we start from an energy given as the minimum of a low strain and a high strain potential where the latter one has linear growth only, while Miehe's energy has superlinear growth. This leads to degenerated laminates which can be interpreted as true shear bands.

This work is based on the formulation introduced in [36]. An application of the relaxation theory to linear elastic isotropic material and numerical simulations of a tension test under displacement control are shown. For inelastic materials, we assume that the elastic deformation is small compared to the inelastic deformation and can be neglected. A numerical example involving loading and unloading is studied in order to evaluate the performance of the proposed concept.

Existence of solutions of non-linear boundary value problems and relaxation

The existence of equilibrium solutions of non-linear boundary value problems can be proved by employing the direct methods of calculus of variations. The basic idea of this method is the minimization of an energy functional. Let us consider the following total potential energy:

$$\Pi(\boldsymbol{u}) = \int_{\Omega} W(\boldsymbol{\varepsilon})\, d\Omega - \int_{\Omega} \boldsymbol{u} \cdot \boldsymbol{f}\, d\Omega - \int_{\partial\Omega_{\sigma}} \boldsymbol{u} \cdot \bar{\boldsymbol{t}}\, dA \tag{1}$$

where $\boldsymbol{u}$ is the displacement, $\boldsymbol{f}$ is the body force per unit volume, $\bar{\boldsymbol{t}}$ is the traction acting on the part $\partial\Omega_{\sigma}$ of the surface, and W is the nonlinear elastic strain energy. The strain field $\boldsymbol{\varepsilon}$ is given as the symmetric part of the displacement-gradient.

$$\boldsymbol{\varepsilon} = \nabla^{s}\boldsymbol{u}. \tag{2}$$

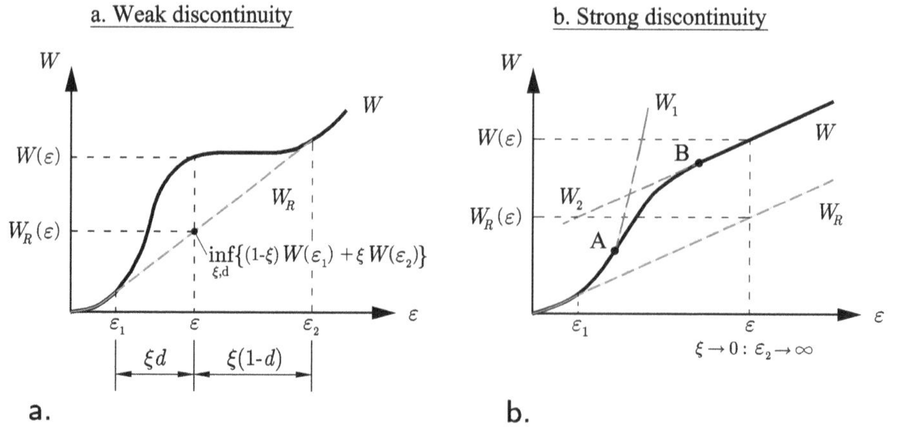

Figure 1 Two micro-strains ε_1, ε_2 and the relaxed energy W_R. (a) A finite thickness of a micro-shear band. **(b)** A zero thickness of a micro-shear band.

Now we look at solutions of minimization problems of the form

$$(\mathcal{P}) \quad \inf_{\boldsymbol{u}} \{ \Pi(\boldsymbol{u}) | \, \boldsymbol{u} = \bar{\boldsymbol{u}} \text{ on } \partial\Omega_u \} . \tag{3}$$

For elastic materials, this corresponds to the well-known principle of minimum of the potential energy. But inelastic materials can be incorporated as well *via* a time-incremental formulation. In this case, W denotes the so-called condensed energy [27,28,37].

However, for the case of negligible elastic deformations, inelastic materials can be treated in a completely analogous manner employing the theory established in [27,28]. Fur this purpose, let us decompose the displacement gradient into rotation $\boldsymbol{\omega}$ and total strain $\boldsymbol{\varepsilon}$ and the latter into its elastic and inelastic parts

$$\nabla \boldsymbol{u} = \omega + \boldsymbol{\varepsilon}_{\mathrm{E}} + \boldsymbol{\varepsilon}_{\mathrm{I}}. \tag{4}$$

If $\boldsymbol{\varepsilon}_{\mathrm{E}}$ is negligible, it follows

$$\boldsymbol{\varepsilon}_{\mathrm{I}} = \nabla^{\mathrm{s}} \boldsymbol{u}. \tag{5}$$

Let a local dissipation functional for inelastic deformation be given by $\Delta(\dot{\boldsymbol{\varepsilon}}_{\mathrm{I}})$, see [27,28]. Then the total dissipation functional reads

$$D(\dot{\boldsymbol{u}}) = \int_{\Omega} \Delta(\dot{\boldsymbol{\varepsilon}}_{\mathrm{I}}) \, d\Omega \tag{6}$$

while the total Gibbs energy is given by

$$G(\boldsymbol{u}) = - \int_{\Omega} \boldsymbol{u} \cdot \boldsymbol{f} \, d\Omega - \int_{\partial\Omega_\sigma} \boldsymbol{u} \cdot \bar{\boldsymbol{t}} \, dA. \tag{7}$$

The principle of minimum of the dissipation functional, [28], can now be formulated as

$$\inf_{\dot{\boldsymbol{u}}} \left\{ \dot{G} + D \middle| \, \dot{\boldsymbol{u}} = \dot{\bar{\boldsymbol{u}}} \text{ on } \partial\Omega_u \right\} . \tag{8}$$

Because the terms $\left(- \int_{\Omega} \boldsymbol{u} \cdot \dot{\boldsymbol{f}} \, d\Omega - \int_{\partial\Omega_\sigma} \boldsymbol{u} \cdot \dot{\bar{\boldsymbol{t}}} \, dA \right)$ occurring in $\dot{G}$ are not dependent on $\dot{\boldsymbol{u}}$ and thus do not enter the variation in (8), the functional in (8) can be equivalently replaced by

$$\Pi_{\mathrm{I}}(\dot{\boldsymbol{u}}) = \int_{\Omega} \Delta(\dot{\boldsymbol{\varepsilon}}_{\mathrm{I}}) \, d\Omega - \int_{\Omega} \dot{\boldsymbol{u}} \cdot \boldsymbol{f} \, d\Omega - \int_{\partial\Omega_\sigma} \dot{\boldsymbol{u}} \cdot \bar{\boldsymbol{t}} \, dA. \tag{9}$$

The principle of minimum of the dissipation potential can now be reformulated as

$$(\mathcal{P}_{\mathrm{I}}) \quad \inf_{\dot{\boldsymbol{u}}} \left\{ \Pi_{\mathrm{I}}(\dot{\boldsymbol{u}}) | \, \dot{\boldsymbol{u}} = \dot{\bar{\boldsymbol{u}}} \text{ on } \partial\Omega_u \right\} . \tag{10}$$

Obviously the structure defined in (5), (9), (10) is completely analogous to that one given by (2), (1), (3) with $\boldsymbol{u}$ replaced by $\dot{\boldsymbol{u}}$ and $W(\boldsymbol{\varepsilon})$ by $\Delta(\dot{\boldsymbol{\varepsilon}}_{\mathrm{I}})$.

From now on, we will focus our exposition on the elastic case keeping in mind that everything can be readily transferred to the inelastic case using the scheme explained above.

If the potential energy W is not quasiconvex in some region of the material body Ω, the functional

$$I(\boldsymbol{u}) = \int_{\Omega} W(\boldsymbol{\varepsilon}) \, d\Omega \tag{11}$$

is not sequentially weakly lower semicontinuous, thus the minimizer in problem $(\mathcal{P})$ may be unattained [23]. This is precisely the case for softening materials. As a result, numerical solutions suffer from discretization sensitivity [38]. Following [23], the functional $I(\boldsymbol{u})$ may be replaced by a *relaxed* functional $I_Q(\boldsymbol{u})$

$$I_Q(\boldsymbol{u}) = \int_{\Omega} QW(\boldsymbol{\varepsilon})\, d\Omega\,, \tag{12}$$

where the *quasiconvexified* functional $QW(\boldsymbol{\varepsilon})$, also called *quasiconvex envelope* of W or *quasiconvex hull* of W, is defined by the minimization problem

$$QW(\boldsymbol{\varepsilon}) = \inf_{\boldsymbol{\varphi}} \frac{1}{\omega} \int_{\omega} W\left(\boldsymbol{\varepsilon} + \nabla^{s}\boldsymbol{\varphi}\right) d\Omega \tag{13}$$

for a fixed but arbitrary bounded domain ω and every $\boldsymbol{\varphi}$ with $\boldsymbol{\varphi} = \boldsymbol{0}$ on $\partial\omega$, herein $\boldsymbol{\varphi}$ is denoted as fluctuation field. Using QW instead of W in $(\mathcal{P})$ ensures the existence of minimizers [23]. Let us now approximate QW by introducing specific fluctuation fields, so-called laminates, in Equation 13. We define a scalar function by

$$\psi(x) = \begin{cases} \dfrac{x}{\xi}, & 0 \le x \le \xi, \\ \dfrac{1-x}{1-\xi} & \xi \le x \le 1, \text{ periodically repeated,} \end{cases} \tag{14}$$

which is depicted in Figure 2a. The fluctuation field is defined by

$$\boldsymbol{\varphi}(\boldsymbol{x}) = \boldsymbol{a}\psi\left(\boldsymbol{n}\cdot\boldsymbol{x}\right), \quad \|\boldsymbol{n}\| = 1 \tag{15}$$

corresponding to the laminate depicted in Figure 2b, where $\boldsymbol{n}$ is the unit normal vector to laminates and $\boldsymbol{a}$ is an arbitrary vector. Then the gradient of the fluctuation field $\boldsymbol{\varphi}$ has the following values:

$$\nabla\boldsymbol{\varphi}(\boldsymbol{x}) = \begin{cases} \dfrac{1}{\xi}\boldsymbol{a}\otimes\boldsymbol{n}, & \text{if } \boldsymbol{x} \text{ belongs to region 1,} \\ -\dfrac{1}{1-\xi}\boldsymbol{a}\otimes\boldsymbol{n}, & \text{if } \boldsymbol{x} \text{ belongs to region 2.} \end{cases} \tag{16}$$

Without restriction we consider a representative volume element as shown in Figure 2b. Then the definition of quasiconvexified energy (13) reduces to

$$W_R(\boldsymbol{\varepsilon}) = \inf\left\{\xi W\left(\boldsymbol{\varepsilon} + \frac{1}{\xi}(\boldsymbol{a}\otimes\boldsymbol{n})^{s}\right) + (1-\xi)W\left(\boldsymbol{\varepsilon} - \frac{1}{1-\xi}(\boldsymbol{a}\otimes\boldsymbol{n})^{s}\right) \mid \xi\,,\, \boldsymbol{a}\,,\, \boldsymbol{n}\,; \right.$$
$$\left. 0 \le \xi \le 1\,,\, \|\boldsymbol{n}\| = 1\right\}, \tag{17}$$

which can be written in the alternative form

$$\begin{aligned} W_R(\boldsymbol{\varepsilon}) = \inf\{&\xi_1 W(\boldsymbol{\varepsilon}_1) + \xi_2 W(\boldsymbol{\varepsilon}_2) \mid \xi_1\,,\, \xi_2,\, \boldsymbol{\varepsilon}_1\,,\, \boldsymbol{\varepsilon}_2\,;\, 0 \le \xi_i \le 1\,, \\ &\xi_1 + \xi_2 = 1\,,\, \boldsymbol{\varepsilon} = \xi_1\boldsymbol{\varepsilon}_1 + \xi_2\boldsymbol{\varepsilon}_2\,,\, \operatorname{rank}(\boldsymbol{\varepsilon}_1 - \boldsymbol{\varepsilon}_2) \le 1\}\,, \end{aligned} \tag{18}$$

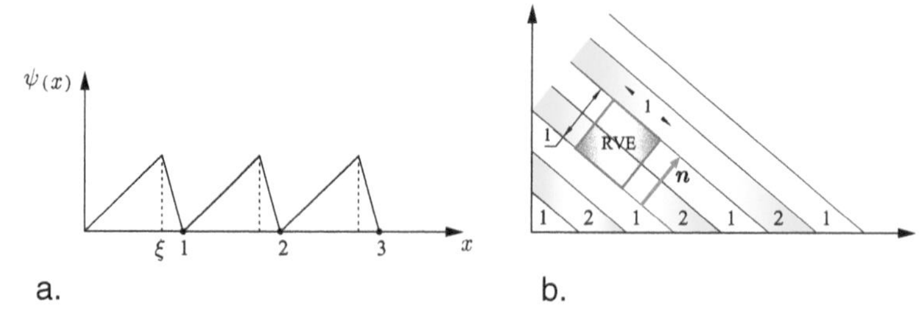

Figure 2 Laminates as special fluctuation fields $\boldsymbol{\varphi}$. (a) Scalar function $\Psi(x)$. **(b)** Laminate of first order and representative volume element (RVE).

where ξ_1 and ξ_2, respectively, are two volume fractions of the regions 1 and 2; $\boldsymbol{\varepsilon}_1$ and $\boldsymbol{\varepsilon}_2$, respectively, are the strain fields within regions 1 and 2.

In Equation 17, or equivalently 18, we find the definition of the so-called first order lamination hull [23,39]. This is nothing more than quasiconvexification restricted to first-order laminates as possible fluctuation fields. The formulation proposed in this paper is developed based on that very notion.

Shear bands as special laminates

In this paper, localization phenomena are regarded as microstructure developments associated with nonconvex potentials. We assume that the micro-structures consist of two domains: a low-strain domain and a high-strain one. Let us consider a representative volume element (RVE) obtained by zooming in on the region around point A as shown in Figure 3. The RVE is split into two volume fractions: the volume fraction ξ of the high-strain domain and the volume fraction $(1-\xi)$ of the low-strain domain.

When strain localization occurs, the potential (energy) inside the shear band W_2 is assumed to satisfy

$$W_2(\xi\boldsymbol{\varepsilon}) = |\xi|\, W_2(\boldsymbol{\varepsilon}). \tag{19}$$

For example, $W_2(\boldsymbol{\varepsilon})$ may be taken in the following form

$$W_2(\boldsymbol{\varepsilon}) = (\boldsymbol{\varepsilon} : \boldsymbol{\mathcal{D}} : \boldsymbol{\varepsilon})^{\frac{1}{\alpha}}, \tag{20}$$

$\alpha = 2$, where $\boldsymbol{\mathcal{D}}$ is symmetric fourth-order, positive definite tensor. For $\alpha = 1$, this energy corresponds to a linear-elastic material with elastic stiffness tensor given by $\boldsymbol{\mathcal{D}}$. For varying α, it behaves more or less stiff in a nonlinear way.

According to the assumption above, the potential inside a shear band is positive homogeneous of first-order in the strain field (19). We will see later on, that only for this very form of the potential as given in Equation 20 corresponding to $\alpha = 2$, it has the desired property leading to strong discontinuities. If α is smaller than 2, the material will exhibit

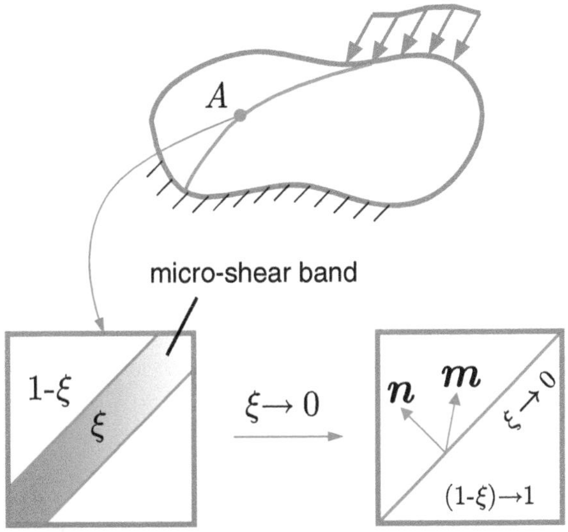

Figure 3 Shear bands are treated as laminates of first order.

only weak discontinuities. If α is larger than 2, a relaxed energy does not exist because of lack of coercivity.

Based upon these considerations, let us start with the consideration of a very simple one-dimensional model to discuss the physical implications of the proposed approach. Then it will be generalized to two dimensions.

One-dimensional problem

Micro-strain

Shear bands are treated as special laminates mixing two co-existed phases (Figure 3). The volume fraction ξ characterizing the width of the micro-band may be defined by the ratio between the length scale and a characteristic geometric parameter [30,31]. If the volume fraction ξ is finite ($0 < \xi < 1$), shear bands are represented as *weak discontinuity*. In this case, let us denote by ε_1 the strain present outside and by ε_2 the strain present within a micro-shear band (see Figure 1a). A visualization given in Figure 1a depicts the shape of a non-convex potential W and its convexification.

The volume fraction ξ of the micro-band varies between 0 and 1. Let us assume that the volume fraction ξ is rather small in comparison to the volume fraction of the RVE, then, the latter case does not happen. If ξ tends to zero, the micro-strain ε_2 of the high-strain domain is unbounded. Then, a potential W responsible for a *strong discontinuity* ($\xi \to 0$) is depicted in Figure1b.

To clarify why ε_2 is unbounded, let us start with the relation between the macro-strain ε and the two micro-strains ε_1, ε_2

$$\varepsilon = (1 - \xi)\varepsilon_1 + \xi\, \varepsilon_2. \tag{21}$$

Following Lambrecht and Miehe [29], we assume that

$$\varepsilon_1 = \varepsilon - \xi\, d, \tag{22}$$

$$\varepsilon_2 = \varepsilon + (1 - \xi)\, d = \varepsilon - \xi\, d + d, \tag{23}$$

where $0 \leq \xi \leq 1$. Let us consider here the case $d \geq 0$ and $\varepsilon \geq 0$. In the case $d \leq 0$ and $\varepsilon \leq 0$, the procedure is completely similar. The case $\varepsilon\, d < 0$ leading to $|\varepsilon_2| < |\varepsilon|$ does not exist. In order to analyze the limit $\xi \to 0$, we have to introduce an appropriately rescaled variable. Let us define s by

$$s = \xi d. \tag{24}$$

Substituting (24) into Equations 22 and 23 yields

$$\varepsilon_1 = \varepsilon - s, \tag{25}$$

$$\varepsilon_2 = \varepsilon - s + \frac{s}{\xi}. \tag{26}$$

Let ξ tend to zero for fixed s. Then $\frac{s}{\xi}$ will grow out of bounds in comparison with $(\varepsilon - s)$. Thus, Equation 26 can be simplified as

$$\varepsilon_2 \approx \frac{s}{\xi} \to \infty \quad \text{as}\ \xi \to 0\,. \tag{27}$$

The assumption of a zero-width micro-shear band immediately leads to an unbounded strain (27) within the high-strain domain of the micro-shear band.

Relaxed energy

Based on the values of the two micro-strains ε_1 and ε_2 the potential W can be divided into three domains (see Figure 1b). The quadratic part, denoted as W_1, is the potential representing the behaviour at small strains. The linear part W_2 is the potential representing the behaviour at very large strains. The energy W in the domain in strain space where $W(\boldsymbol{\varepsilon}) \neq W_1(\boldsymbol{\varepsilon})$ and $W(\boldsymbol{\varepsilon}) \neq W_2(\boldsymbol{\varepsilon})$ is of no importance since it does not influence the relaxed energy. Hence, using (25) and (27), we can formulate a mixture potential of the two energies as

$$W^{\text{mix}}(\varepsilon) = (1-\xi)W_1(\varepsilon_1) + \xi W_2(\varepsilon_2) = (1-\xi)W_1(\varepsilon - s) + \xi W_2\left(\frac{s}{\xi}\right). \tag{28}$$

Based on the assumption (20) with the special case $\mathcal{D} = A^2\mathcal{I}$, it can be simplified as

$$W^{\text{mix}}(\varepsilon) \;=\; W_1(\varepsilon - s) + A\,|s|\,. \tag{29}$$

It should be noted that the classical Hencky model of deformation [40-42] bears a strong relation to our theory. To this end, the energy (29) can be viewed a composed of the elastic energy $W_1(\varepsilon - s)$ and the dissipated energy $A\,|s|$. The displacement u and the plastic strain s can then be determined by the following minimization problem

$$\inf\left\{\int_\Omega W^{\text{mix}}(\varepsilon(u) - s)\,d\Omega - \int_\Omega u\cdot f\,d\Omega - \int_{\partial\Omega_\sigma} u\cdot\bar{t}\,dA \;\mid u, s\right\}, \tag{30}$$

where W^{mix} is refered to in the literature as the elasto-plastic superpotential [43]. In the plastic regime, the stress state lies on the yield surface, indicating that $\sigma = A$ is in agreement with Equation 34.

The non-convex mixture potential (29) gives rise to an ill-posed boundary value problem making the calculation of shear bands dependent on the particularities of the numerical discretization used. By introducing the concept of relaxation the problem can be resolved and becomes well-posed. The relaxed potential is obtained by the minimization procedure

$$W_R(\varepsilon) = \inf\left\{W^{\text{mix}}(\varepsilon) \mid s\right\}. \tag{31}$$

As mentioned in section 'Micro-strain' we consider here the case $d \geq 0$ and $\varepsilon \geq 0$. Then the relaxed potential (31) can be rewritten as follows:

$$W_R(\varepsilon) = \inf\left\{W^{\text{mix}}(\varepsilon) \mid s,\, s \geq 0\right\}. \tag{32}$$

The corresponding stress is obtained by taking the derivative of the mixture potential (28) with respect to ε

$$\sigma(\varepsilon) = (1-\xi)\sigma(\varepsilon_1) + \xi\sigma(\varepsilon_2). \tag{33}$$

The unique stationary point of Equation 32 can be obtained from

$$\sigma(\varepsilon) = \sigma(\varepsilon_1) = \sigma(\varepsilon_2) = A. \tag{34}$$

The slope of the relaxed potential represented by (34), i.e. at values of ε where it differs from W_1, is constant, consequently, the relaxed tangent modulus is equal to zero. Here, the material parameter A can be interpreted as stress level inside the shear band. The relaxed potential W_R is depicted in Figure 1b. The relaxed stress corresponding to a weak and strong discontinuity is shown in Figure 4a,b, respectively. For the weak discontinuity, the slope of the relaxed potential is constant for $\varepsilon_1 \leq \varepsilon \leq \varepsilon_2$, thus, the relaxed stress

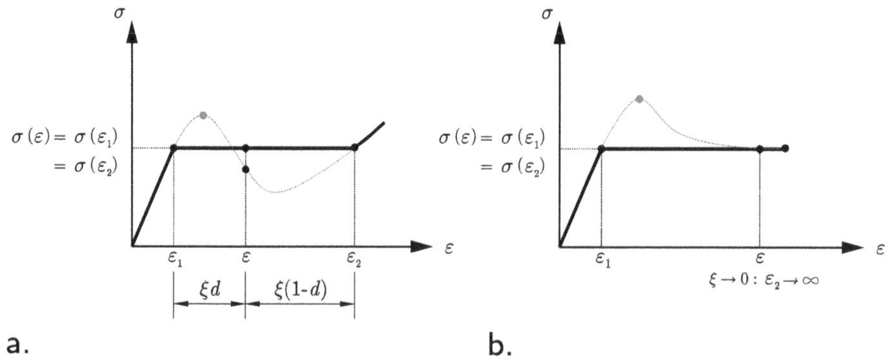

Figure 4 Two micro-strains ε_1, ε_2 and the relaxed stress σ. (a) A finite thickness of a micro-shear band. **(b)** A zero thickness of a micro-shear band.

is constant in this strain interval [29]. For the strong discontinuity, the relaxed stress is constant in the range $\varepsilon_1 \leq \varepsilon$ where $\varepsilon_2 \to \infty$ as $\xi \to 0$. When the material softens towards the critical state, it is shown in Figure 4b that the relaxed stress can be approximated as being constant. This kind of stress-strain curve can be observed, for example, in dense sands and over-consolidated clays [44]. Using Equations 29 and 31, we can approximate the response as perfectly plastic as soon as strain localization occurs, and A in this case is interpreted as the stress at the critical state.

Example 1

The proposed formulation in the previous section is applied to a linear isotropic material. The mixture potential of the low-strain and high-strain domains obtained in Equation 28 simplifies to

$$W^{\text{mix}}(\varepsilon) = \frac{1}{2}E\,(\varepsilon - s)^2 + A\,|s|\,. \tag{35}$$

where E is the Young's modulus and A is a material parameter. The local minimizer of problem (32) is

$$s = \begin{cases} 0 & \text{for } \varepsilon < \dfrac{A}{E}\,. \\ \varepsilon - \dfrac{A}{E} & \text{for } \varepsilon \geq \dfrac{A}{E}. \end{cases} \tag{36}$$

Now strains and stresses can be calculated as follows:

For $\varepsilon < \dfrac{A}{E}$, we have $s = 0$. The relaxed potential is equal to the elastic strain energy

$$W_R(\varepsilon) = W^{\text{mix}}(\varepsilon) = \frac{1}{2}E\varepsilon^2. \tag{37}$$

The macroscopic strain ε is equal to ε_1 and ε_2 due to $\xi = 0$

$$\varepsilon = \varepsilon_1 = \varepsilon_2. \tag{38}$$

The material obeys Hooke's law

$$\sigma = \frac{\partial W^{\text{mix}}}{\partial \varepsilon} = E\varepsilon. \tag{39}$$

For $\varepsilon \geq \frac{A}{E}$, we obtain the micro-strains

$$\varepsilon_1 = \varepsilon - s = \frac{A}{E} \quad ; \quad \varepsilon_2 \to \infty. \tag{40}$$

The relaxed potential is the sum of the contributions of the low-strain domain here denoted by $[\,(1-\xi)W_1]_R$ and the high-strain domain denoted by $[\,\xi W_2]_R$:

$$W_R(\varepsilon) = \underbrace{\frac{A^2}{2E}}_{[(1-\xi)W_1]_R} + \underbrace{A\,|s|}_{[\xi W_2]_R}\,, \tag{41}$$

The stress is given by

$$\sigma = \sigma_1 = \sigma_2 = \frac{\partial W_R}{\partial \varepsilon} = A. \tag{42}$$

The relaxed potential as well as the stress is depicted in Figure 5.

Two-dimensional problem

Micro-strain

In the two-dimensional problem, the micro-strains $\boldsymbol{\varepsilon}_1$ and $\boldsymbol{\varepsilon}_2$ can be written as

$$\boldsymbol{\varepsilon}_1 = \boldsymbol{\varepsilon} - \xi(\boldsymbol{a}\otimes\boldsymbol{n})^{\mathrm{s}}, \tag{43}$$

$$\boldsymbol{\varepsilon}_2 = \boldsymbol{\varepsilon} + (1-\xi)(\boldsymbol{a}\otimes\boldsymbol{n})^{\mathrm{s}} = \boldsymbol{\varepsilon} - \xi(\boldsymbol{a}\otimes\boldsymbol{n})^{\mathrm{s}} + (\boldsymbol{a}\otimes\boldsymbol{n})^{\mathrm{s}}, \tag{44}$$

where $\boldsymbol{\varepsilon}_1 - \boldsymbol{\varepsilon}_2 = (\boldsymbol{a}\otimes\boldsymbol{n})^{\mathrm{s}} = \frac{1}{2}(\boldsymbol{a}\otimes\boldsymbol{n}+\boldsymbol{n}\otimes\boldsymbol{a})$ satisfies rank $(\boldsymbol{\varepsilon}_1 - \boldsymbol{\varepsilon}_2) \leq 1$ in Equation 18.

Let us define s by

$$\xi\boldsymbol{a} = s\boldsymbol{m}, \tag{45}$$

where $\|\boldsymbol{m}\| = 1$. Herein $\boldsymbol{m}$ and $\boldsymbol{n}$ are two unit vectors giving the direction of shear band evolution; s is an appropriately rescaled variable.

On inserting Equation 45 into Equations 43 and 44, we have

$$\boldsymbol{\varepsilon}_1 = \boldsymbol{\varepsilon} - s(\boldsymbol{m}\otimes\boldsymbol{n})^{\mathrm{s}}, \tag{46}$$

$$\boldsymbol{\varepsilon}_2 = \boldsymbol{\varepsilon} - s(\boldsymbol{m}\otimes\boldsymbol{n})^{\mathrm{s}} + \frac{s}{\xi}(\boldsymbol{m}\otimes\boldsymbol{n})^{\mathrm{s}}. \tag{47}$$

As ξ tends to zero, $\frac{s}{\xi}$ will grow out of bounds. Thus, Equation 47 can be simplified as

$$\boldsymbol{\varepsilon}_2 \approx \frac{s}{\xi}(\boldsymbol{m}\otimes\boldsymbol{n})^{\mathrm{s}}. \tag{48}$$

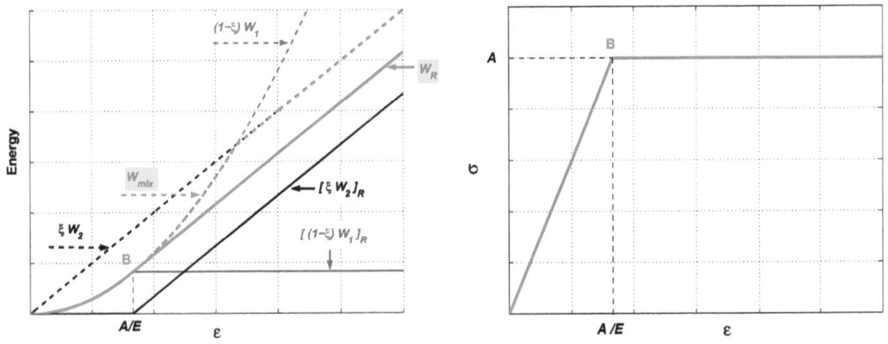

Figure 5 Relaxed potential and stress in the one-dimensional problem.

Relaxed potential

The mixture potential of the two domains can be written in the following form

$$W^{\text{mix}}(\boldsymbol{\varepsilon}) = W_1(\boldsymbol{\varepsilon} - s(\boldsymbol{m} \otimes \boldsymbol{n})^{\text{s}}) + |s|\, W_2((\boldsymbol{m} \otimes \boldsymbol{n})^{\text{s}}). \tag{49}$$

As explained in section 'Relaxed energy', the relaxed potential is computed in order to ensure the well-posedness of the boundary-value problem, governing the emergence of a shear band. The relaxed potential is obtained by the minimization procedure

$$W_R(\boldsymbol{\varepsilon}) = \inf\left\{ W^{\text{mix}}(\boldsymbol{\varepsilon}) \;\middle|\; s\,,\, \boldsymbol{m}\,, \boldsymbol{n}\,;\ \|\boldsymbol{m}\| = \|\boldsymbol{n}\| = 1 \right\}. \tag{50}$$

Let us consider two specific potentials representing the behaviour at low and high strains, respectively

$$W_1(\boldsymbol{\varepsilon}) = \frac{1}{2}\,\boldsymbol{\varepsilon} : \boldsymbol{\mathcal{C}} : \boldsymbol{\varepsilon}, \tag{51}$$

$$W_2(\boldsymbol{\gamma}) = h\,(\boldsymbol{\gamma} : \boldsymbol{\mathcal{D}} : \boldsymbol{\gamma})^{\frac{1}{2}}\,, \tag{52}$$

where $\boldsymbol{\mathcal{C}}$ and $\boldsymbol{\mathcal{D}}$ are symmetric fourth-order, positive definite tensors. Here, $\boldsymbol{\varepsilon}$ and $\boldsymbol{\gamma}$ are the strains in the low-strain and high-strain domains, respectively, whose domains are depicted in Figure 3. The energy $W_2(\boldsymbol{\gamma})$ is expected to be homogeneous of first order in $\boldsymbol{\gamma}$, as shown in Figure 1b for the one-dimensional problem. Therefore, $W_2(\boldsymbol{\gamma})$ raised by the exponent of $\frac{1}{2}$ has the desired property leading to strong discontinuities. For convenience, $h = 1\sqrt{N}/mm$ is introduced as a parameter to guarantee that $W_2(\boldsymbol{\gamma})$ has the dimension of energy density.

Substituting (51) and (52) into (49), one gets

$$\begin{aligned} W^{\text{mix}}(\boldsymbol{\varepsilon}) &= \frac{1}{2}\,(\boldsymbol{\varepsilon} - s\boldsymbol{\gamma}) : \boldsymbol{\mathcal{C}} : (\boldsymbol{\varepsilon} - s\boldsymbol{\gamma}) + |s|\, h\,(\boldsymbol{\gamma} : \boldsymbol{\mathcal{D}} : \boldsymbol{\gamma})^{\frac{1}{2}} \\ &= \frac{1}{2}\boldsymbol{\varepsilon} : \boldsymbol{\mathcal{C}} : \boldsymbol{\varepsilon} + \frac{1}{2}s^2\boldsymbol{\gamma} : \boldsymbol{\mathcal{C}} : \boldsymbol{\gamma} - s\,\boldsymbol{\varepsilon} : \boldsymbol{\mathcal{C}} : \boldsymbol{\gamma} + |s|\, h\,(\boldsymbol{\gamma} : \boldsymbol{\mathcal{D}} : \boldsymbol{\gamma})^{\frac{1}{2}} \end{aligned} \tag{53}$$

where $\boldsymbol{\gamma} = (\boldsymbol{m} \otimes \boldsymbol{n})^{\text{s}}$. Let us denote by W_1^{mix} and W_2^{mix}

$$W_1^{\text{mix}} = \frac{1}{2}\boldsymbol{\varepsilon} : \boldsymbol{\mathcal{C}} : \boldsymbol{\varepsilon} + \frac{1}{2}s^2\boldsymbol{\gamma} : \boldsymbol{\mathcal{C}} : \boldsymbol{\gamma} - s\,\boldsymbol{\varepsilon} : \boldsymbol{\mathcal{C}} : \boldsymbol{\gamma}, \tag{54}$$

$$W_2^{\text{mix}} = |s|\, h\,(\boldsymbol{\gamma} : \boldsymbol{\mathcal{D}} : \boldsymbol{\gamma})^{\frac{1}{2}}\,, \tag{55}$$

then, the mixture energy W^{mix} is the sum of W_1^{mix} and W_2^{mix}.

Using the results in Table 1, minimization of (53) with respect to s yields

$$s = \frac{\text{sign}(\boldsymbol{\varepsilon} : \boldsymbol{\mathcal{C}} : \boldsymbol{\gamma})}{(\boldsymbol{\gamma} : \boldsymbol{\mathcal{C}} : \boldsymbol{\gamma})^{\frac{1}{2}}} \left[\frac{|\boldsymbol{\varepsilon} : \boldsymbol{\mathcal{C}} : \boldsymbol{\gamma}|}{(\boldsymbol{\gamma} : \boldsymbol{\mathcal{C}} : \boldsymbol{\gamma})^{\frac{1}{2}}} - h \left(\frac{\boldsymbol{\gamma} : \boldsymbol{\mathcal{D}} : \boldsymbol{\gamma}}{\boldsymbol{\gamma} : \boldsymbol{\mathcal{C}} : \boldsymbol{\gamma}} \right)^{\frac{1}{2}} \right]_+ \,, \tag{56}$$

and the potential (49) with s given by (56) takes the form

$$\inf_s W^{\text{mix}}(\boldsymbol{\varepsilon}) = \frac{1}{2}\boldsymbol{\varepsilon} : \boldsymbol{\mathcal{C}} : \boldsymbol{\varepsilon} - \frac{1}{2} \left[\frac{|\boldsymbol{\varepsilon} : \boldsymbol{\mathcal{C}} : \boldsymbol{\gamma}|}{(\boldsymbol{\gamma} : \boldsymbol{\mathcal{C}} : \boldsymbol{\gamma})^{\frac{1}{2}}} - h \left(\frac{\boldsymbol{\gamma} : \boldsymbol{\mathcal{D}} : \boldsymbol{\gamma}}{\boldsymbol{\gamma} : \boldsymbol{\mathcal{C}} : \boldsymbol{\gamma}} \right)^{\frac{1}{2}} \right]_+^2 . \tag{57}$$

Herein $a = \frac{1}{2}\boldsymbol{\gamma} : \boldsymbol{\mathcal{C}} : \boldsymbol{\gamma}$, $b = -\,\boldsymbol{\varepsilon} : \boldsymbol{\mathcal{C}} : \boldsymbol{\gamma}$, $c = h\,(\boldsymbol{\gamma} : \boldsymbol{\mathcal{D}} : \boldsymbol{\gamma})^{\frac{1}{2}}$. Easily one can recognise that a is positive due to the positive definiteness of the fourth-order tensor $\boldsymbol{\mathcal{C}}$.

Table 1 Minimization problem: $\inf_s W(s)$

	Expression
Scalar minimization problem	$\inf_s W(s)$
Potential	$W(s) = as^2 + bs + c\,\lvert s\rvert \ (c > 0,\, a > 0)$
Solution	$\inf_s W(s) = -\frac{1}{4a}(\lvert b\rvert - c)_+^2$
Minimizer	$s = -\frac{1}{2a}(\lvert b\rvert - c)_+ \operatorname{sign}(b)$
Abbreviations	$(\lvert b\rvert - c)_+ = \begin{cases} 0 & \text{for } \lvert b\rvert \leq c \\ \lvert b\rvert - c & \text{for } \lvert b\rvert > c \end{cases}$
	$\operatorname{sign}(b) = \frac{\lvert b\rvert}{b} \quad \text{for } b \neq 0$

Computation of stress and the tangent operator

The stress and the tangent operator are derived from the direct derivative of the relaxed potential (50). The derivative of (50) reads

$$\frac{\partial W_R}{\partial \boldsymbol{\varepsilon}} = \frac{\partial W^{\text{mix}}}{\partial \boldsymbol{\varepsilon}} + \frac{\partial W^{\text{mix}}}{\partial s}\frac{\partial s}{\partial \boldsymbol{\varepsilon}} + \frac{\partial W^{\text{mix}}}{\partial \boldsymbol{m}}\frac{\partial \boldsymbol{m}}{\partial \boldsymbol{\varepsilon}} + \frac{\partial W^{\text{mix}}}{\partial \boldsymbol{n}}\frac{\partial \boldsymbol{n}}{\partial \boldsymbol{\varepsilon}}. \tag{58}$$

It is observed that the three last terms in Equation 58 vanish due to the stationarity condition of the minimization problem (50). Thus, the relaxed stress which is an appropriate average of the two micro-stresses has the form

$$\boldsymbol{\sigma} = \frac{\partial W^{\text{mix}}}{\partial \boldsymbol{\varepsilon}}. \tag{59}$$

Considering the form of the potential (57), we obtain

$$\boldsymbol{\sigma} = \boldsymbol{\mathcal{C}} : \boldsymbol{\varepsilon} - s\boldsymbol{\mathcal{C}} : \boldsymbol{\gamma}. \tag{60}$$

The tangent operator is given by

$$\boldsymbol{\mathcal{A}} = \frac{\partial^2 W_R}{\partial \boldsymbol{\varepsilon}^2} = \frac{\partial \boldsymbol{\sigma}}{\partial \boldsymbol{\varepsilon}} = \boldsymbol{\mathcal{C}} - (\boldsymbol{\mathcal{C}} : \boldsymbol{\gamma}) \otimes \frac{\partial s}{\partial \boldsymbol{\varepsilon}} - s\frac{\partial\,(\boldsymbol{\mathcal{C}} : \boldsymbol{\gamma})}{\partial \boldsymbol{\varepsilon}}. \tag{61}$$

Localization criterion

In the derivations above, a central role is played by the quantity

$$L = \left[\frac{\lvert \boldsymbol{\varepsilon} : \boldsymbol{\mathcal{C}} : \boldsymbol{\gamma}\rvert}{(\boldsymbol{\gamma} : \boldsymbol{\mathcal{C}} : \boldsymbol{\gamma})^{\frac{1}{2}}} - h\left(\frac{\boldsymbol{\gamma} : \boldsymbol{\mathcal{D}} : \boldsymbol{\gamma}}{\boldsymbol{\gamma} : \boldsymbol{\mathcal{C}} : \boldsymbol{\gamma}}\right)^{\frac{1}{2}}\right]. \tag{62}$$

As the process of deformation progresses, L may be negative, zero or positive. A positive value in turn signals the onset of localization, a criterion that can be shown to be equivalent to the well-known notion of loss of ellipticity:

i. $L \leq 0$: we have $s = 0$. The relaxed potential $W_R(\boldsymbol{\varepsilon})$ reduces to the elastic strain energy $W_1(\boldsymbol{\varepsilon})$.
ii. $L > 0$: we have $s \neq 0$. A shear band starts to develop. The homogeneous deformation $\boldsymbol{\varepsilon}$ decomposes into the two micro-strains $\boldsymbol{\varepsilon}_1$ and $\boldsymbol{\varepsilon}_2$. The nonconvex potential energy W^{mix} is replaced with the approximated rank-one convexification $W_R(\boldsymbol{\varepsilon})$ to ensure well-posedness of the problem.

Application of relaxation theory to linear isotropic material

Relaxed potential

Let us consider the potential W_2 of the high-strain domain in Equation 52

$$W_2(\boldsymbol{\gamma}) = h(\boldsymbol{\gamma} : \boldsymbol{\mathcal{D}} : \boldsymbol{\gamma})^{\frac{1}{2}}. \tag{63}$$

In what follows, the case $\boldsymbol{\mathcal{D}}$ being equal to $\boldsymbol{\mathcal{C}}$ is investigated.

On inserting $\boldsymbol{\mathcal{D}} = \boldsymbol{\mathcal{C}}$ into (63) and (53), we obtain the mixture potential

$$\begin{aligned} W^{\text{mix}}(\boldsymbol{\varepsilon}) &= \frac{1}{2}\boldsymbol{\varepsilon} : \boldsymbol{\mathcal{C}} : \boldsymbol{\varepsilon} + \frac{1}{2}s^2\boldsymbol{\gamma} : \boldsymbol{\mathcal{C}} : \boldsymbol{\gamma} - s\,\boldsymbol{\varepsilon} : \boldsymbol{\mathcal{C}} : \boldsymbol{\gamma} + |s|\,h\,(\boldsymbol{\gamma} : \boldsymbol{\mathcal{C}} : \boldsymbol{\gamma})^{\frac{1}{2}} \\ &= \frac{\lambda}{2}(\text{tr}\boldsymbol{\varepsilon})^2 + \mu\,\|\boldsymbol{\varepsilon}\|^2 + \frac{1}{2}s^2\boldsymbol{\gamma} : \boldsymbol{\mathcal{C}} : \boldsymbol{\gamma} - s\,\boldsymbol{\varepsilon} : \boldsymbol{\mathcal{C}} : \boldsymbol{\gamma} \\ &\quad + |s|\,h\,(\boldsymbol{\gamma} : \boldsymbol{\mathcal{C}} : \boldsymbol{\gamma})^{\frac{1}{2}}, \end{aligned} \tag{64}$$

where $\boldsymbol{\gamma} = (\boldsymbol{m} \otimes \boldsymbol{n})^s$. Herein, $\boldsymbol{\mathcal{C}}$ is the fourth-order isotropic elastic tensor

$$\mathcal{C}_{ijkl} = \lambda\delta_{ij}\delta_{kl} + \mu\left(\delta_{ik}\delta_{jl} + \delta_{il}\delta_{jk}\right), \tag{65}$$

or in the tensor notation

$$\boldsymbol{\mathcal{C}} = \lambda\boldsymbol{I} \otimes \boldsymbol{I} + \mu\,(\boldsymbol{\mathcal{I}} + \bar{\boldsymbol{\mathcal{I}}}), \tag{66}$$

where λ and μ are Lamé constants. The relaxed potential can be defined in the form

$$W_R(\boldsymbol{\varepsilon}) = \inf\left\{W^{\text{mix}}(\boldsymbol{\varepsilon}) \mid s,\, \boldsymbol{m}, \boldsymbol{n};\; \|\boldsymbol{m}\| = \|\boldsymbol{n}\| = 1\right\}. \tag{67}$$

Using the result of Equation 57 we obtain

$$\inf_s W^{\text{mix}}(\boldsymbol{\varepsilon}) = \frac{\lambda}{2}(\text{tr}\boldsymbol{\varepsilon})^2 + \mu\,\|\boldsymbol{\varepsilon}\|^2 - \frac{1}{2}\,[L]_+^2\,, \tag{68}$$

where the quantity L in (62) reduces to

$$L = \left[\frac{|\boldsymbol{\varepsilon} : \boldsymbol{\mathcal{C}} : \boldsymbol{\gamma}|}{(\boldsymbol{\gamma} : \boldsymbol{\mathcal{C}} : \boldsymbol{\gamma})^{\frac{1}{2}}} - h\right]. \tag{69}$$

Let φ be the angle between two vectors $\boldsymbol{m}$ and $\boldsymbol{n}$ as depicted in Figure 6, where the unit vector $\boldsymbol{t}$ is perpendicular to the vector $\boldsymbol{m}$. Then, we may write

$$\boldsymbol{n} = \boldsymbol{m}\cos\varphi + \boldsymbol{t}\sin\varphi, \tag{70}$$

$$\boldsymbol{m}.\boldsymbol{\varepsilon}\,\boldsymbol{n} = (\boldsymbol{m}.\boldsymbol{\varepsilon}\,\boldsymbol{m})\cos\varphi + (\boldsymbol{m}.\boldsymbol{\varepsilon}\,\boldsymbol{t})\sin\varphi. \tag{71}$$

Now we consider a plane which has $(\boldsymbol{m}, \boldsymbol{t})$ as the unit tangent and normal vectors. It is recognized that $(\boldsymbol{m}.\boldsymbol{\varepsilon}\,\boldsymbol{m})$ is the normal strain whose direction is perpendicular to the plane and $(\boldsymbol{m}.\boldsymbol{\varepsilon}\,\boldsymbol{t})$ is the shear strain in this plane. Using Mohr's circle we can transform (71) into principal strains

$$\begin{aligned} \boldsymbol{m}.\boldsymbol{\varepsilon}\,\boldsymbol{n} &= (\varepsilon_m + R\cos 2\psi)\cos\varphi + R\sin 2\psi\,\sin\varphi \\ &= \varepsilon_m\cos\varphi + R\cos(\varphi - 2\psi), \end{aligned} \tag{72}$$

where R and ε_m, respectively, are the maximum shear strain and the average strain

$$R = \frac{1}{2}(E_1 - E_2) \quad ; \quad \varepsilon_m = \frac{1}{2}(E_1 + E_2). \tag{73}$$

Herein, ψ is an angle between the vector $\boldsymbol{m}$ and the eigenvector $\boldsymbol{e}_1$ corresponding to the major principal strain E_1 as denoted in Figure 7.

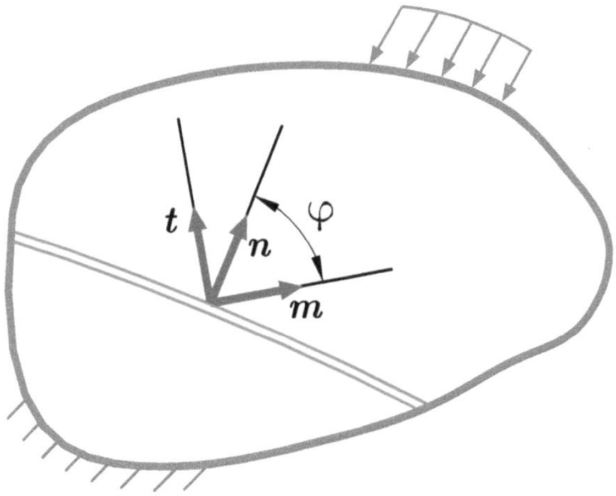

Figure 6 Orientation of the shear band.

Instead of minimizing (67) with respect to s, $\boldsymbol{m}$ and $\boldsymbol{n}$, now we minimize (74) with respect to s, ψ and φ based on Equations 70 to 73

$$W_R(\boldsymbol{\varepsilon}) = \inf\left\{W^{\text{mix}}(\boldsymbol{\varepsilon}) \mid s\,,\,\psi\,,\varphi\,;\,0 \le \psi\,,\,\varphi \le \pi\,\right\}. \tag{74}$$

The minimization of (74) with respect to s, ψ and φ yields

- $R = 0$:

$$\psi = \varphi = 0, \tag{75}$$

$$s = \frac{\text{sign}\left[\lambda \text{tr}\boldsymbol{\varepsilon} + 2\mu\varepsilon_m\right]}{\left[2\mu + \lambda\right]^{\frac{1}{2}}}\,[L]_+\,, \tag{76}$$

$$\text{where } L = \frac{\left|\lambda \text{tr}\boldsymbol{\varepsilon} + 2\mu\epsilon_m\right|}{\left[2\mu + \lambda\right]^{\frac{1}{2}}} - h, \tag{77}$$

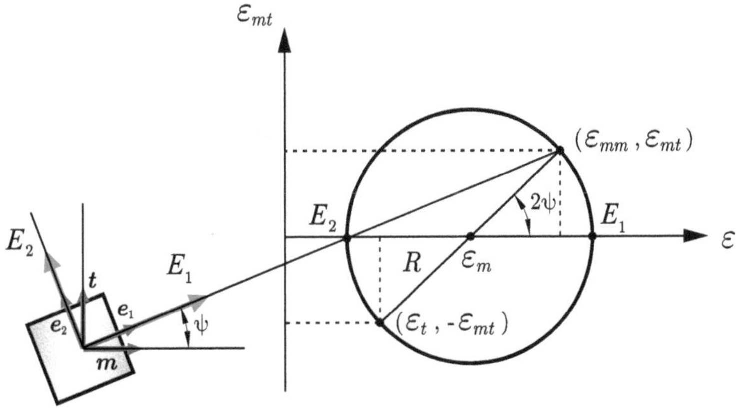

Figure 7 Mohr strain circle.

- $R \neq 0$:

$$\cos\varphi = \frac{2\varepsilon_m\mu + \lambda tr\boldsymbol{\varepsilon}}{2R\left(\lambda + \mu\right)}, \tag{78}$$

$$\psi = \frac{\varphi}{2}, \tag{79}$$

$$s = \frac{\text{sign}\left[\left(\lambda \text{tr}\boldsymbol{\varepsilon} + 2\mu\varepsilon_m\right)\cos\varphi + 2\mu R\right]}{\left[\mu + (\lambda+\mu)\cos^2\varphi\right]^{\frac{1}{2}}}\,[L]_+, \tag{80}$$

$$\text{where } L = \sqrt{\frac{4\mu R^2(\lambda+\mu) + (2\mu\varepsilon_m + \lambda\text{tr}\boldsymbol{\varepsilon})^2}{\lambda+\mu}} - h. \tag{81}$$

The capability of the proposed model is demonstrated through numerical simulation of a tension test in the next section.

Example 2

In this section, the model presented in section 'Relaxed potential' are implemented into the finite element code FEAP [45]. In what follows, we investigate a tension test under plane strain conditions. The main goal of the study is the analysis of the developing shear bands and the demonstration of mesh independent results due to the proposed relaxation technique. Two kinds of elements are used in this example as summarized in Figure 8.

A sample is subjected to a prescribed vertical displacement under plane strain conditions. The geometry of the specimen, the boundary conditions and the material parameters are given in Figure 9. $h = 1\sqrt{N}/mm$. In order to trigger the shear band formation, a geometrical imperfection along the height of specimen is introduced.

Four discretizations of the domain are considered: 3×8, 7×18, 14×36, 21×54 elements. The response obtained using the four different meshes is the same with respect to load-displacement curves as shown in Figure 10a, thus verifying the lack of pathological mesh-dependence of the proposed concept. As soon as the onset of localization is met at $v \approx 0.2427\,mm$ which signals the loss of convexity, the performance of the diverse element formulations employed starts to differ.

The displacement method is unable to capture the localization and shows a hardening behaviour as depicted in Figure 10a,b.

However, Figure 11 demonstrates that the mixture element formulation can resolve the effect of strain localization. While in Figure 11a,b, the mesh is still too coarse to exhibit shear bands, these are clearly represented in a mesh-independent way in Figure 11c,d. There exist two symmetric shear bands in this example and their orientations are about 60° and 120° with respect to the horizontal axis.

The behaviour of the relaxed potential as well as the relaxed vertical stress σ_y of the element 465 (Figure 11e) is shown in Figure 12 at the first Gauss point inside the shear band. After the bifurcation point, the relaxed potential of the low-strain domain approaches asymptotically a constant value, whereas the relaxed potential of the high-strain domain

Element type	Method	Number of Gauss points	Notation
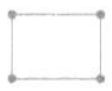	MES[1]	2×2	MES
	Disp[2]	2×2	Q4

Figure 8 Notation of element type. MES[1], the mixed enhanced strain method [46]; Disp[2], the displacement method [47].

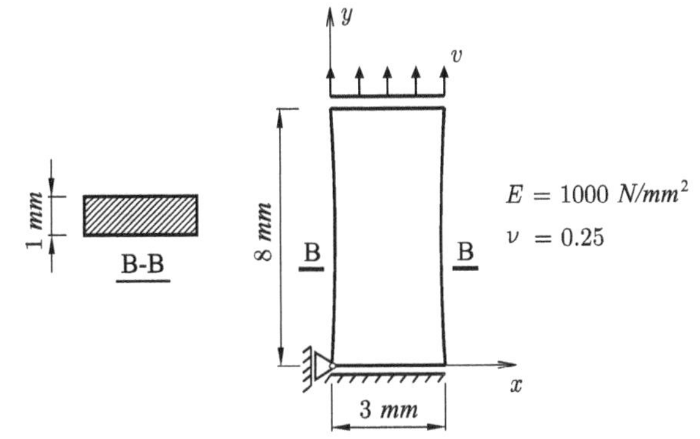

Figure 9 Example 2: geometry and boundary conditions.

is active inside the shear band only and increases continuously with the prescribed displacement v. As a result, the relaxed stress approaches a constant value.

Application of relaxation theory to inelastic materials

Relaxed potential

For simplicity we consider the special case $\mathcal{D} = A^2\mathcal{I}$ [36] in this section with assuming orthogonality, i.e. $\boldsymbol{m}.\boldsymbol{n} = 0$ of the two unit vectors giving the direction of shear band evolution. Herein, A is a material parameter and $\mathcal{I}$ is the fourth-order unity tensor. Furthermore, we assume that evolution of these two vectors over time is not remarkable.

We assume that the elastic deformation is small compared to the inelastic deformation and can be neglected, yielding Equation 5:

$$\boldsymbol{\varepsilon}_{\mathrm{I}} = \nabla^{\mathrm{s}}\boldsymbol{u}. \tag{82}$$

Together with the above assumptions, the mixture dissipation potential can be obtained with s replaced by $\dot{s}$ and $W^{\mathrm{mix}}(\boldsymbol{\varepsilon})$ by $\Delta^{\mathrm{mix}}(\dot{\boldsymbol{\varepsilon}}_{\mathrm{I}})$ in Equation 53

$$\Delta^{\mathrm{mix}}(\dot{\boldsymbol{\varepsilon}}_{\mathrm{I}}) = \frac{1}{2}\left(\dot{\boldsymbol{\varepsilon}}_{\mathrm{I}} - \dot{s}\boldsymbol{\gamma}\right) : \boldsymbol{C} : \left(\boldsymbol{\varepsilon}_{\mathrm{I}} - \dot{s}\boldsymbol{\gamma}\right) + \frac{A}{\sqrt{2}}\,|\dot{s}| \tag{83}$$

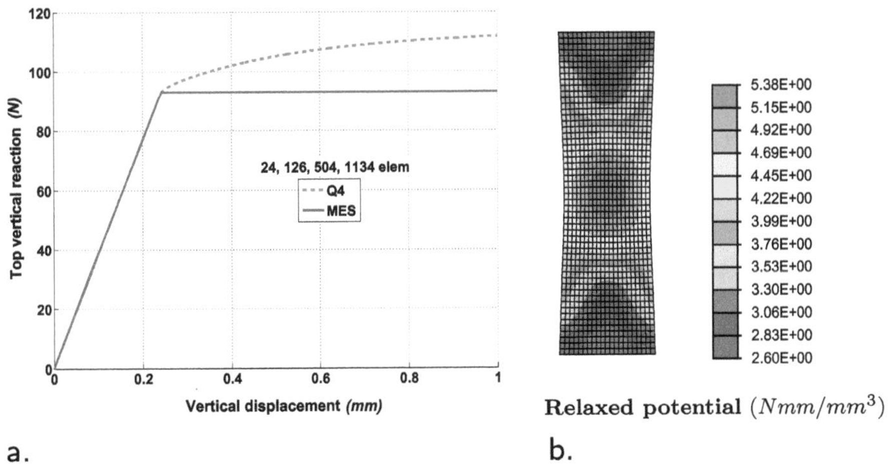

Figure 10 Localization in tension using MES elements (mixed enhanced strain method) and Q4 elements (displacement method). (a) Load-displacement response. **(b)** Distribution of relaxed potential.

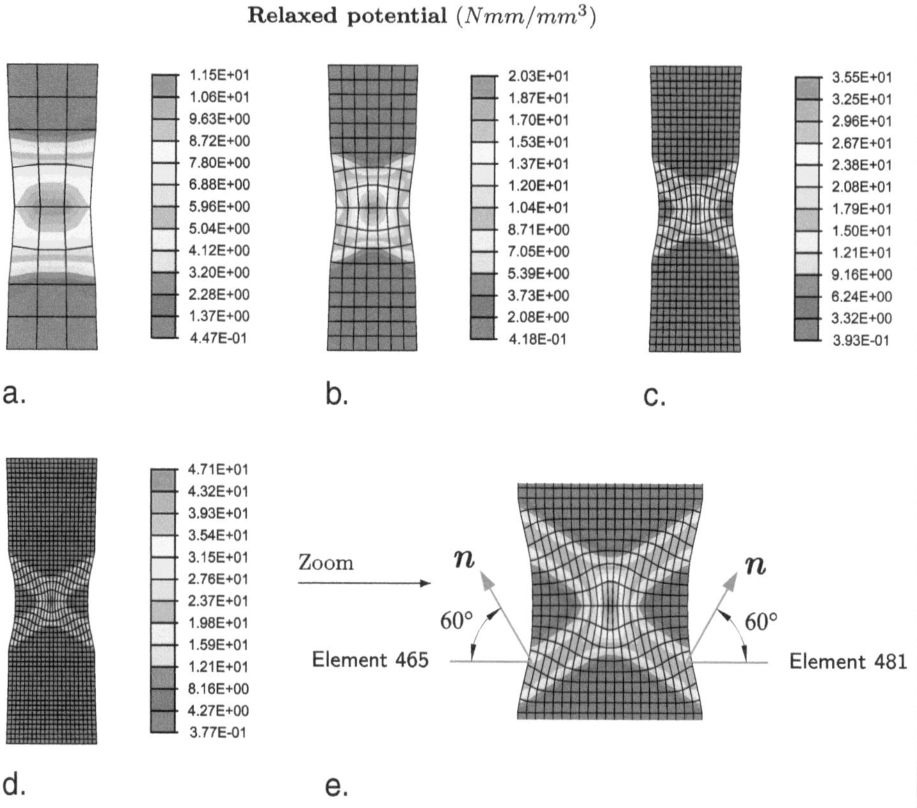

Figure 11 Example 2: comparison of different finite element meshes. Distribution of relaxed potential at $v = 1.0$ mm. **(a)** 24 MES elements. **(b)** 126 MES elements. **(c)** 504 MES elements. **(d)** 1,134 MES elements. **(e)** Orientation of shear bands at element 465 and element 481.

where $\boldsymbol{\gamma} = (\boldsymbol{m} \otimes \boldsymbol{n})^s$. Let us denote by Δ_1^{mix} and Δ_2^{mix}

$$\Delta_1^{\text{mix}} = \frac{1}{2} (\dot{\boldsymbol{\varepsilon}}_{\text{I}} - \dot{s}\boldsymbol{\gamma}) : \boldsymbol{C} : (\boldsymbol{\varepsilon}_{\text{I}} - \dot{s}\boldsymbol{\gamma}), \tag{84}$$

$$\Delta_2^{\text{mix}} = \frac{A}{\sqrt{2}} |\dot{s}|, \tag{85}$$

then, the mixture dissipation potential Δ^{mix} is the sum of Δ_1^{mix} and Δ_2^{mix}.

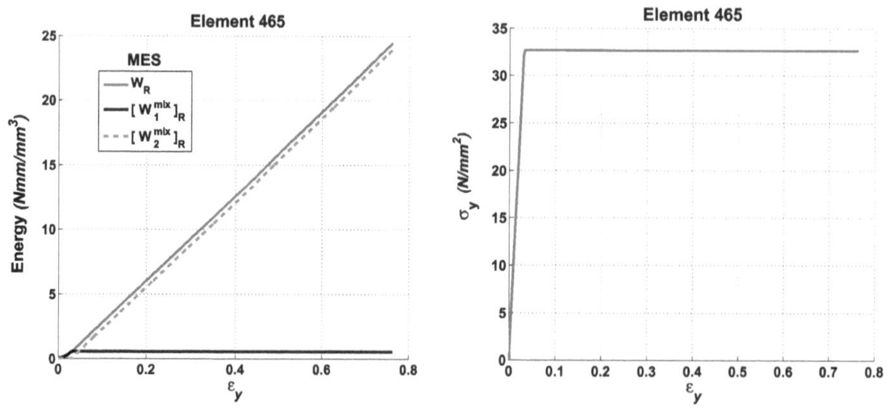

Figure 12 Example 2: relaxed potential and relaxed normal stress σ_y at the first Gauss point of the element 465.

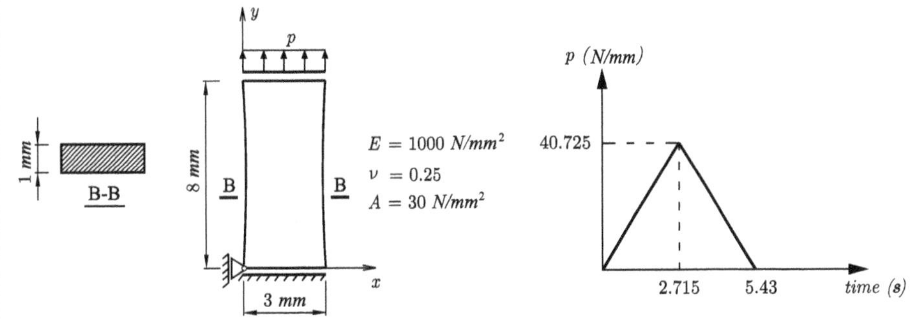

Figure 13 Example 3: geometry and boundary conditions.

By substituting (66) into (83), the relaxed potential reads

$$W_R = \inf_{\dot{s},\boldsymbol{m},\boldsymbol{n}} \Delta^{\text{mix}} = \frac{\lambda}{2} \text{tr}\,(\dot{\boldsymbol{\varepsilon}}_{\text{I}})^2 + \mu\,\|\dot{\boldsymbol{\varepsilon}}_{\text{I}}\|^2 - 2\mu\left[|\dot{\varepsilon}_{mn}| - \frac{\alpha}{2}\right]_+^2, \tag{86}$$

where $\alpha = \dfrac{A}{\sqrt{2\mu}}$, $|\dot{\varepsilon}_{mn}|$ is the maximum shear strain rate.

Solution $\dot{s}$ yields

$$\dot{s} = (2\,|\dot{\varepsilon}_{mn}| - \alpha)_+ \text{sign}(\dot{\varepsilon}_{mn}) = \begin{cases} 0 & \text{if } |\dot{\varepsilon}_{mn}| < \alpha/2 \\ (2\,|\dot{\varepsilon}_{mn}| - \alpha)\,\text{sign}(\dot{\varepsilon}_{mn}) & \text{if } |\dot{\varepsilon}_{mn}| \geq \alpha/2 \end{cases} \tag{87}$$

Unlike elastic materials, inelastic materials can be incorporated as well *via* a time-incremental formulation

$$W_{R,n+1} = W_{R,n} + \Delta W_R \tag{88}$$

where $W_{R,n+1}$ and $W_{R,n}$, respectively, are the potential energies at times t_{n+1} and t_n, ΔW is the incremental potential at time interval Δt

$$\Delta W_R = \int_{t_n}^{t_{n+1}} W_R\,dt. \tag{89}$$

The proposed formulation is implemented in the general code FEAP [45]. Based on the mixed enhanced strain method [46], the four-node quadrilateral element (MES element) will be considered in the next section.

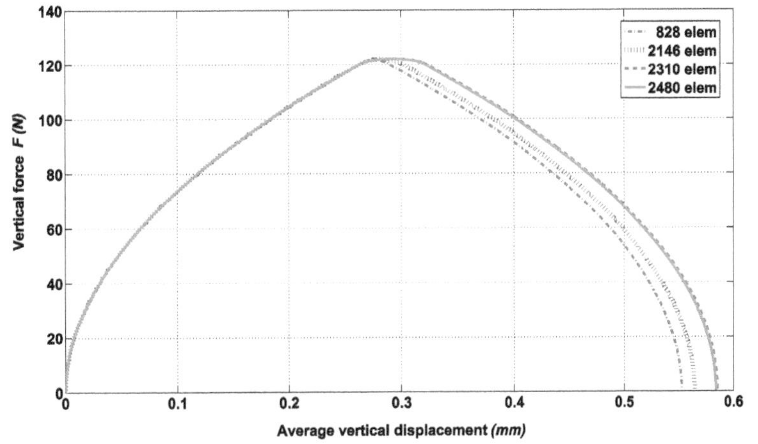

Figure 14 Example 3: load-displacement response.

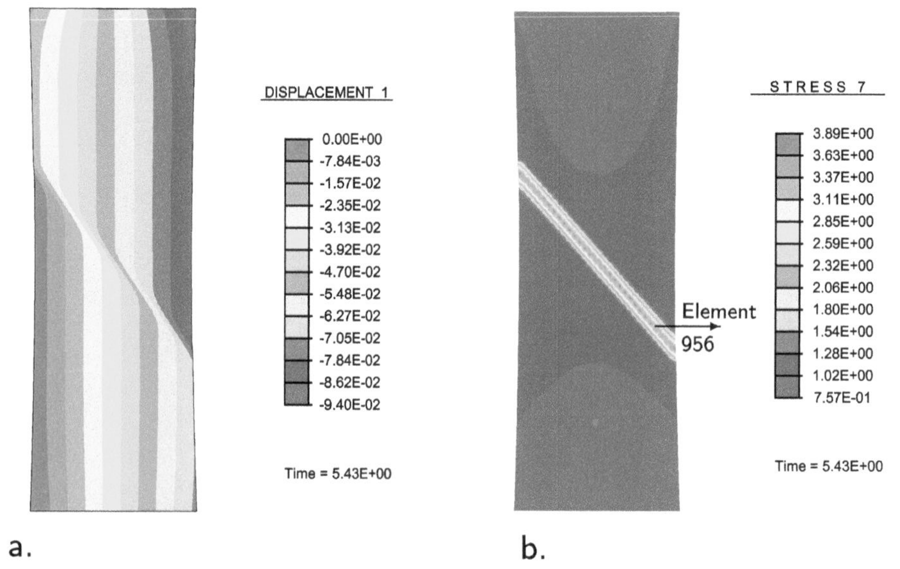

Figure 15 Example 3: distributions of horizontal displacement and of relaxed energy at $t = 5.43$ s (2,480 MES elements). (a) Horizontal displacement (mm). **(b)** Relaxed potential (Nmm/mm^3).

Example 3

A sample is subjected to vertical loading and unloading under plane strain conditions as shown in Figure 13. A geometrical imperfection along the height of specimen is introduced to trigger the shear band formation.

Four discretizations of the domain are considered: 828, 2,146, 2,310 and 2,480 elements. As depicted in Figure 14, mesh-independence response obtained by use of MES element becomes evident by considering load-displacement diagram at the top of the specimen. The distributions of the horizontal displacement and of the relaxed energy shown in Figure 15 point out the localized region. The relaxed energy and the relaxed vertical stress of the element 956 at the first Gauss point are shown in Figure 16. The relaxed potential of the large-strain domain $(\Delta_2^{\text{mix}})_R$ develops linearly between $\varepsilon_y = 0.035$ and $\varepsilon_y = 0.095$ ($2.7\,\text{s} \leq t \leq 2.73\,\text{s}$), then remains constant when $\varepsilon_y \geq 0.095$ corresponding

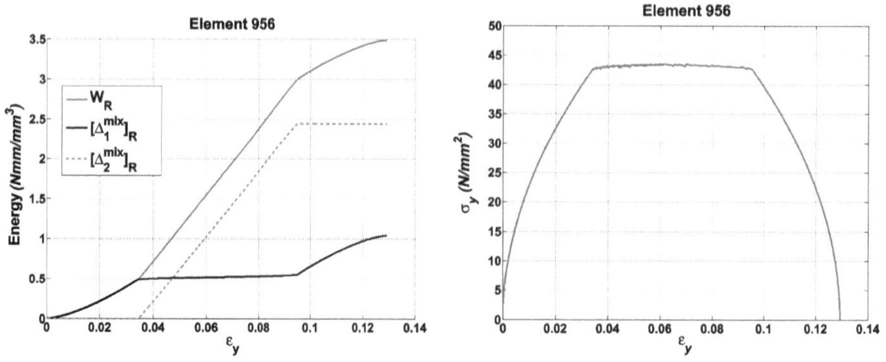

Figure 16 Example 3: relaxed potential and relaxed normal stress σ_y at first Gauss point of element 956.

to the unloading path. The relaxed stress is also constant for $0.035 \leq \varepsilon_y \leq 0.095$, and it diminishes after $\varepsilon_y \geq 0.095$ due to the prescribed unloading.

Conclusions

The paper focuses on a theoretical framework for the treatment of shear localization in solid materials. The theory is based on minimization principles associated with micro-structure developments under the assumptions of a micro-shear band of a zero thickness and the presence of a mixture potential inside the shear band.

Localization phenomena are regarded as micro-structure developments associated with nonconvex potentials. The nonconvexity of the mixture potential occurring due to the formation of strain localization is resolved by relaxation in order to ensure the well-posedness of the associated boundary value problem. The relaxed potential, which is approximated by a first-order rank-one convexification, is obtained *via* local minimization problem of the mixture potential. The onset of localization is detected through the proposed optimization process. The model can be applied to any material which softens towards the critical state. The relaxed stress can be computed directly and approaches the critical stress as soon as strain localization occurs. Material points located inside the shear bands can be considered as decomposed into a low strain and a high strain phase at the microscopic level. The theoretical solutions satisfy possessing a zero micro-band width at the microscopic level. At the macroscopic scale, the width of a shear band is still finite. Numerical results clearly show a mesh-independent behaviour in the sense that shear bands are as narrow as the mesh resolution allows, while all other features of the solution are independent of the chosen discretization.

Competing interests

The authors declare that they have no competing interests.

Authors' contributions

TT and KH contributed in equal measure. Both authors read and approved the final manuscript.

Acknowledgements

The research was supported through grants by the Vietnamese Government and Ministry of Education and Training as well as the Research School at Ruhr University Bochum, Germany.

References

1. Borja R (2000) A finite element model for strain localization analysis of strongly discontinuous fields based on standard Galerkin approximation. Comput Methods Appl Mech Engrg 190:1529–1549
2. Lott-Crumpler DA (1997) The formation and properties of shear bands in viscoplastic materials. Model Simul Mater Sc 5:317–336
3. Engelen RAB, Geers MGD, Baaijens FPT (2003) Nonlocal implicit gradient-enhanced elasto-plasticity for the modelling of softening behaviour. Int J Plasticity 19:403–433
4. Mühlhaus HB, Vardoulakis I (1987) The thickness of shear bands in granular materials. Géotechnique 37:271–283
5. de Borst R, Sluys LJ (1991) Localization in a Cosserat continuum under static and dynamics loading conditions. Comput Methods Appl Mech Engrg 90:805–827
6. Huang W, Bauer E (2003) Numerical investigations of shear localization in a micro-polar hypoplastic material. Int J Numer Anal Methods Geomech 27:325–352
7. Strömberg L, Ristinmaa M (1996) FE-formulation of a non-local plasticity theory. Comput Methods Appl Mech Engrg 136:127–144
8. Bažant ZP, Belytschko TB, Chang TP (1984) Continuum model for strain softening. J Eng Mech (ASCE) 110:1666–1692
9. de Borst R, Mühlhaus HB (1992) Gradient-dependent plasticity: formulation and algorithmic aspects. Int J Numer Meth Eng 35:521–539
10. Pamin J (1994) Gradient-dependent plasticity in numerical simulation of localization phenomena. Dissertation. Delft University of Technology, The Netherlands
11. Larsson R, Steinmann P, Runesson K (1998) Finite element embedded localization band for finite strain plasticity based on a regularized strong discontinuity. Mech Cohes-Frict Mat 4:171–194

12. Simo JC, Oliver J, Armero F (1993) An analysis of strong discontinuities induced by strain-softening in rate-independent inelastic solids. Comput Mech 12:277–296
13. Oliver J (1995) Modelling strong discontinuities in solid mechanics via strain softening constitutive equations: fundamental and numerical simulation. Monograph CIMNE No. 28. Internacional Center for Numerical Methods in Engineering, Barcelona
14. Armero F, Garikipati K (1996) An analysis of strong discontinuities in multiplicative finite strain plasticity and their relation with the numerical simulation of strain localization in solids. Int J Solids Struct 33:2863–2885
15. Steinmann P, Larsson R, Runesson K (1997) On the localization properties of multiplicative hyperelasto-plastic continua with strong discontinuities. Int J Solids Struct 34:969–990
16. Pietruszczak S, Xu G (1995) Brittle response of concrete as a localization problem. Int J Solids Struct 32:1517–1533
17. Xu G, Pietruszczak S (1997) Numerical analysis of concrete fracture based on a homogenization technique. Comput Struc 63:497–509
18. Armero F (1999) Large-scale modeling of localized dissipative mechanisms in a local continuum: applications to the numerical simulation of strain localization in rate-dependent inelastic solids. Mech Cohes-Frict Mater 4:101–131
19. Nguyen GD, Einav I, Korsunsky AM (2012) How to connect two scales of behaviour in constitutive modelling of geomaterials. Geotech Lett 2:129–134
20. Nguyen GD, Einav I, Korsunsky AM (2012) A constitutive modelling framework featuring two scales of behaviour: Fundamentals and applications to quasi-brittle failure. Eng Fract Mech 115:221–240
21. Hackl K, Hoppe U (2001) On the calculation of microstructures for inelastic materials using relaxed enegies. In: Miehe C (ed) Proceedings of the IUTAM Symposium on Computational Mechanics of Solid Materials at Large Strains, Boston, pp 77–86
22. Ball JM, James RD (1987) Fine phase mixtures as minimizer of energy. Arch Ration Mech Ana 100:13–52
23. Dacorogna B (1989) Direct methods in the calculus of variations. Springer-Verlag, Berlin
24. Kohn R (1991) The relaxation of a double-well energy. Continuum Mech Therm 3:193–236
25. Bartel S, Carstensen C, Hackl K, Hoppe U (2004) Effective relaxation for microstructure simulations: algorithms and applications. Comput Methods Appl Mech Engrg 193:5143–5175
26. Hackl K, Heinen R (2008) A micromechanical model for pretextured polycrystalline shape-memory alloys including elastic anisotropy. Continuum Mech Therm 19:499–510
27. Carstensen C, Hackl K, Mielke A (2002) Non-convex potentials and microstructures in finite-strain plasticity. Proc R Soc Lond A 458:299–317
28. Hackl K, Fischer FD (2008) On the relation between the principle of maximum dissipation and inelastic evolution given by dissipation potentials. Proc R Soc Lond A 464:117–132
29. Lambrecht M, Miehe C, Dettmar J (2003) Energy relaxation of non-convex incremental stress potentials in a strain-softening elastic-plastic bar. Int J Solids Struct 40:1369–1391
30. Miehe C, Lambrecht M (2003) A two-scale finite element relaxation analysis of shear bands in non-convex inelastic solids: small-strain theory for standard dissipative materials. Comput Methods Appl Mech Engrg 192:473–508
31. Miehe, C, Lambrecht, M (2003) Analysis of microstructure development in shearbands by energy relaxation of incremental stress potentials: large-strain theory for standard dissipative solids. Int J Numer Meth Eng 58:1–41
32. Miehe C, Lambrecht M, Guerses E (2004) Analysis of microstructure development in shearbands by energy relaxation of incremental stress potentials: large-strain theory for standard dissipative solids. J Mech Phys Solids 52:2725–2769
33. Guerses E, Miehe C (2011) On evolving deformation microstructures in non-convex partially damaged solids. J Mech Phys Solids 59:1268–1290
34. Mistakidis ES (1997) On the solution of structures involving elements with nonconvex energy potentials. Struct Optimization 13:182–190
35. Kochmann DM, Hackl K (2011) The evolution of laminates in finite plasticity: a variational approach. Continuum Mech Thermodyn 23:63–85
36. Trinh BT, Hackl K (2011) Finite element simulation of strain localization in inelastic solids by energy relaxation. Vietnam J Mech 33:203–213
37. Mielke A (2004) Deriving new evolution equations for microstructures via relaxation of variational incremental problems. Comput Methods Appl Mech Engrg 193:5095–5127
38. de Borst R (2004) Damage, material instabilities, and failure, Chapter 10. In: Stein E, de Borst R, Hughes TJR (eds) Encyclopedia of Computational Mechanics, vol. 2. Wiley, Chichester, pp 335–373
39. Kohn RV, Strang G (1986) Optimal design and relaxation of variational problems I, II, III. Comm Pure Appl Math 39:113–137
40. Hencky H (1924) Zur Theorie plastischer Deformation und der hierdurch im Material hervorgerufenen Nachspannungen. Z Angew Nath Mech 4:323–333
41. Ilyushin AA (1943) Some problems of plastic deformations. PMM 7:245–272
42. Ilyushin AA (1947) Theory of plasticity at simple loading of the bodies exhbiting plastic hardening. PMM 11:291–296
43. Gao Y, Huang K (1988) Complementary energy principles for elasto-perfectly plasticity. Scientia Sinica 31:1469–1476
44. Budhu M (2000) Soil mechanics and foundations. United States of America, Wiley
45. Taylor RL (2004) A finite element analysis program: User manual, University of California at Berkeley
46. Kasper EP, Taylor RL (1997) A mixed-enhanced strain method: linear problems. Report No. UCB/SEMM-97/02, University of California at Berkeley
47. Zienkiewicz OC, Taylor RL (2000) The finite element method. Volume 1: The Basis (5nd edn). Butterworth-Heinmann, London

5

FEM-based shakedown analysis of hardening structures

Phú Tình Phạm[1*] and Manfred Staat[2]

* Correspondence: phamphutinh@yahoo.com
[1]Faculty of Civil Engineering, Hanoi Architectural University, Nguyen Trai Street, Thanh Xuân District, Hanoi, Vietnam
Full list of author information is available at the end of the article

Abstract

This paper develops a new finite element method (FEM)-based upper bound algorithm for limit and shakedown analysis of hardening structures by a direct plasticity method. The hardening model is a simple two-surface model of plasticity with a fixed bounding surface. The initial yield surface can translate inside the bounding surface, and it is bounded by one of the two equivalent conditions: (1) it always stays inside the bounding surface or (2) its centre cannot move outside the back-stress surface. The algorithm gives an effective tool to analyze the problems with a very high number of degree of freedom. Our numerical results are very close to the analytical solutions and numerical solutions in literature.

Keywords: Ratchetting; Kinematic hardening; Two-surface plasticity; Shakedown; FEM

Background

Shakedown analysis for hardening structures has been investigated by many researchers. Among hardening models, the isotropic hardening law is generally not reasonable in situations where structures are subjected to cyclic loading because it does not account for the Bauschinger effect and rejects the possibility of incremental plasticity. The unbounded kinematic hardening model has already been introduced theoretically by Melan [1] and later by Prager [2]. Applications of this model have been investigated by Maier [3] and Ponter [4]. The unbounded kinematic hardening model cannot estimate the plastic collapse and also incremental plasticity but only low-cycle fatigue, while low-cycle fatigue limit with the kinematical hardening model seems not to be essentially different from the perfectly plastic model, cf. Gokhfeld and Cherniavsky [5] and Stein and Huang [6].

Introducing a bounding surface in Melan-Prager's model, a two-surface model of plasticity with a fixed bounding surface is achieved which appears to be most basic, suitable and simple for shakedown analysis. Application of bounded kinematic hardening model was introduced theoretically and numerically by Weichert and Groß-Weege [7] who used the generalized standard material model (GSM). They used Airy's stress function to satisfy the equilibrium conditions in the interior of the structures fulfilled. Shakedown theorems for bounded linear and nonlinear kinematic hardening have been proposed by Bodovillé and de Saxcé [8], Pham [9,10] and Nguyen [11].

Numerical investigations for bounded kinematic hardening using basic reduction technique have been introduced by Staat and Heitzer [12,13] and Stein and Zhang [14]. By the lower bound approach, it permits to avoid the nondifferentiability of the objective function, which must be regularized via internal dissipation energy and there is no incompressibility constraint in nonlinear programming problem, but this approach suffers from nonlinear inequality constraints.

A company of lower bound algorithm is the upper bound algorithm, which is based on Koiter theorem. For perfectly plastic structures, the upper bound algorithm has been established by Yan and Nguyen Dang [15,16] and Yan et al. [17]. The major numerical obstacle in this approach is the singular property of plastic dissipation function. Dealing with this difficulty, the researchers replaced the original dissipation function $D^p\left(\dot{\varepsilon}_{ij}^p\right)$ by $D^p\left(\dot{\varepsilon}_{ij}^p + \varepsilon_0^2\right)$, where ε_0 is a very small number. This technique is also used in our algorithm.

By using the static approach and the criterion of the mean, Nguyen Dang and König [18] showed that the shakedown solution can be obtained by a maximization or a minimization problem. The yield criterion of the mean was further applied in practical computations by displacement method and equilibrium finite element by Nguyen Dang and Palgen [19].

A very efficient primal-dual algorithm, which can derive lower and upper bound simultaneously of shakedown limit load factor for complicated structures, has been introduced by Vu, Yan and Nguyen Dang [20-22] and Vu [23]. In these works, dual relationship between upper bound and lower bound for shakedown analysis of perfectly plastic structures has been proven. Theoretically speaking, primal-dual algorithm helps to find a very accurate solution of shakedown analysis problem.

While using the finite element method (FEM) for limit and shakedown analysis, the stress method can be used, but this method is restricted since for certain structures, it is very difficult to find appropriate stress function, so the displacement method is preferred to make the numerical approach as general as possible.

For the structures with hardening material, it is difficult to prove the relationship between upper bound and lower bound because of the complication of the objective function. Furthermore, in the static approach, it is difficult to present alternating limit and ratcheting limit separately. In this paper, we have presented a FEM-based upper bound algorithm for shakedown analysis of bounded kinematic hardening structures with von Mises yield criterion. By the direct plasticity methods, shakedown analysis is a nonlinear programming problem. The present algorithm can deal with complicated realistic structures which are modelled by 3D, 20-node elements with huge number of degree of freedom. Two numerical examples are included to validate the algorithm and to study the influence of hardening effect.

Methods

Bounded kinematic hardening model

For kinematic hardening model, the initial yield surface can translate in the multi-axial stress space, without changing its shape and size. If the translation is unlimited, or in other words, the ultimate strength of material σ_u is infinite, we have unbounded model (Figure 1). This model is inadequate to predict the plastic collapse (both incremental and instantaneous) of structure. It can only describe the alternating plasticity mode.

The initial yield surface for von Mises material is defined as below

$$F[\boldsymbol{\sigma}] - \sigma_y^2 = 0. \tag{1}$$

The subsequent surface is defined as

$$F[\boldsymbol{\sigma} - \boldsymbol{\pi}] - \sigma_y^2 = 0 \tag{2}$$

where $\boldsymbol{\pi}$ is the back stress. If hardening is unbounded, $\boldsymbol{\pi}$ is infinite.

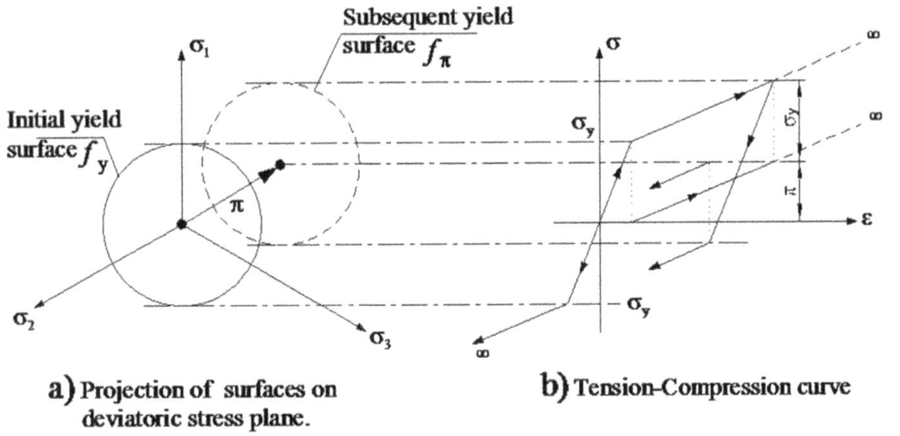

Figure 1 Unbounded kinematic hardening model.

For more realistic material, yield stress σ_y must be bounded by ultimate strength σ_u. A simple two-surface model is used to model the bounded hardening. The subsequent yield surface may or may not touch the fixed bounding surface; see Figure 2. This is satisfied by one of the two following conditions:

1. Centre of subsequent yield surface cannot move outside the back-stress surface. This is expressed by

$$F[\pi] \leq (\sigma_u - \sigma_y)^2. \tag{3}$$

2. Subsequent yield surface always stays inside bounding surface. This is expressed by

$$F[\sigma] \leq \sigma_u^2. \tag{4}$$

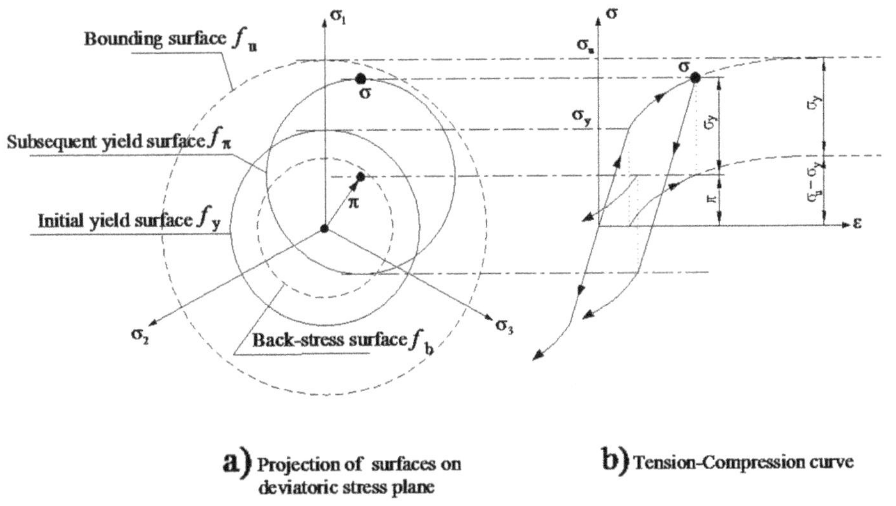

Figure 2 A simple two-surface plasticity with fixed bounding surface.

In the preceding conditions, Equations 3 and 4, equalities occur when the subsequent surface touches bounding surface. We have proven that bounding conditions (3) and (4) are exactly equivalent. See detail in the study of Pham and Staat [24].

Shakedown formulation based on Koiter's theorem

Problem establishment

Upper bound solution of shakedown load multiplier is the solution of a constrained nonlinear programming problem

$$\alpha_{\mathrm{sd}} = \min_{\dot{\boldsymbol{\varepsilon}}^p} \int_0^T \int_V D^p(\dot{\boldsymbol{\varepsilon}}^p) dV dt \qquad \text{(a)}$$
$$\text{s.t.}: \begin{cases} \Delta\boldsymbol{\varepsilon}^p = \int_0^T \dot{\boldsymbol{\varepsilon}}^p dt & \text{(b)} \\ \mathrm{tr}(\dot{\boldsymbol{\varepsilon}}^p) = 0 & \text{(c)} \\ \Delta\boldsymbol{\varepsilon}^p = \frac{1}{2}\left(\nabla(\Delta\mathbf{u}) + \nabla(\Delta\mathbf{u})^T\right) \quad \text{in } V & \text{(d)} \\ \Delta\mathbf{u} = \mathbf{0} \quad \text{on } \partial V_u & \text{(e)} \\ \int_0^T \int_V \boldsymbol{\sigma}^E(\mathbf{x}, t) : \dot{\boldsymbol{\varepsilon}}^p dV dt = 1 & \text{(g)} \end{cases} \tag{5}$$

where total plastic energy dissipation $D^p(\dot{\boldsymbol{\varepsilon}}^p)$ in the structure is as follows:

$$\int_0^T \int_V D^p(\dot{\boldsymbol{\varepsilon}}^p) dV dt = \int_0^T \int_V \sqrt{\frac{2}{3}} \sigma_y \|\dot{\boldsymbol{\varepsilon}}^p\| dV dt + \int_V \sqrt{\frac{2}{3}} (\sigma_u - \sigma_y) \|\Delta\boldsymbol{\varepsilon}^p\| dV \tag{6}$$

The first term in the right hand side of Equation 6 is plastic energy dissipation of perfect plasticity material, and the second term is hardening effect. Evidently, if $\sigma_u = \sigma_y$, we have ideal plastic material.

Constraint (5b) is the definition of plastic strain accumulation. The plastic strain rate $\dot{\boldsymbol{\varepsilon}}^p$ may not necessarily be compatible, but $\Delta\boldsymbol{\varepsilon}^p$ must be compatible. This is expressed by constraints (5d) and (5e). Constraint (5c) is the incompressibility condition, and (5g) is the normalized condition.

Problem discretization

Based on FEM, whole structure V is discretized into n_e finite elements with NG = $n_e \times n_g$ Gaussian points, where n_g is number of Gaussian points in each element. If the load domain $\mathcal{L}$ is convex, it is sufficient to check if shakedown will happen at all vertices of $\mathcal{L}$. So the load domain can be discretized into finite number of load combinations $\hat{\mathbf{P}}_k$, $k = 1, \ldots, m$, and m is total number of vertices of $\mathcal{L}$. By these discretizations, the shakedown analysis is reduced to checking shakedown conditions at all Gaussian points and all load vertices m, instead of checking for whole structure V and entire load domain $\mathcal{L}$. Then, numerical form of Equation 5 is as follows:

$$\begin{aligned}
&\alpha_{\text{sd}}^{\text{blkh}} = \min_{\dot{\varepsilon}^p}\left\{\sqrt{\tfrac{2}{3}}\sigma_y\sum_{k=1}^{m}\sum_{i=1}^{\text{NG}}\sqrt{w_i^2\boldsymbol{\varepsilon}_{ik}^T\mathbf{D}\boldsymbol{\varepsilon}_{ik}+w_i^2\varepsilon_0^2}+\sqrt{\tfrac{2}{3}}(\sigma_u-\sigma_y)\sum_{i=1}^{\text{NG}}\sqrt{w_i^2\sum_{k=1}^{m}\boldsymbol{\varepsilon}_{ik}^T\mathbf{D}\sum_{k=1}^{m}\boldsymbol{\varepsilon}_{ik}+w_i^2\varepsilon_0^2}\right\} && \text{(a)}\\
&\text{s.t.}:\\
&\begin{cases}
\sum_{k=1}^{m}\boldsymbol{\varepsilon}_{ik}=\mathbf{B}_i\mathbf{u} & \forall i=\overline{1,\text{NG}} \qquad\qquad \text{(b)}\\
\mathbf{D}_M\boldsymbol{\varepsilon}_{ik}=\mathbf{0} & \forall i=\overline{1,\text{NG}}\quad \forall k=\overline{1,m} \qquad \text{(c)}\\
\sum_{k=1}^{m}\sum_{i=1}^{\text{NG}}w_i\boldsymbol{\varepsilon}_{ik}^T\boldsymbol{\sigma}_{ik}^E=1 & \qquad\qquad \text{(d)}
\end{cases}
\end{aligned} \tag{7}$$

where $\alpha_{\text{sd}}^{\text{blkh}}$ denotes the shakedown multiplier in bounded linearly kinematic hardening. $\boldsymbol{\varepsilon}_{ik}$ is the strain vector corresponding to load vertex k at Gaussian point i

$$\begin{aligned}
\boldsymbol{\varepsilon}_{ik} &= \begin{bmatrix}\varepsilon_{11}^{ik} & \varepsilon_{22}^{ik} & \varepsilon_{33}^{ik} & 2\varepsilon_{12}^{ik} & 2\varepsilon_{23}^{ik} & 2\varepsilon_{13}^{ik}\end{bmatrix}^T\\
&= \begin{bmatrix}\varepsilon_{11}^{ik} & \varepsilon_{22}^{ik} & \varepsilon_{33}^{ik} & \gamma_{12}^{ik} & \gamma_{23}^{ik} & \gamma_{13}^{ik}\end{bmatrix}^T.
\end{aligned} \tag{8}$$

$\boldsymbol{\sigma}_{ik}^E$ is the fictitious elastic stress vector corresponding to load vertex k at Gaussian point i, $\mathbf{u}$ is the nodal displacement vector, $\mathbf{B}_i$ is the deformation matrix and ε_0 is the small number to avoid singularity. $\mathbf{D}$ and $\mathbf{D}_M$ are square matrices, expressed in Equation 9:

$$\mathbf{D} = \text{Diag}\begin{bmatrix}1 & 1 & 1 & \frac{1}{2} & \frac{1}{2} & \frac{1}{2}\end{bmatrix}, \quad \mathbf{D}_M = \begin{bmatrix}1&1&1&0&0&0\\1&1&1&0&0&0\\1&1&1&0&0&0\\0&0&0&0&0&0\\0&0&0&0&0&0\\0&0&0&0&0&0\end{bmatrix}. \tag{9}$$

For the sake of simplicity, we define some new plastic strain $\mathbf{e}_{ik}$, fictitious elastic stress $\mathbf{t}_{ik}$, deformation matrix $\hat{\mathbf{B}}_i$, respectively as

$$\mathbf{e}_{ik} = w_i\mathbf{D}^{1/2}\boldsymbol{\varepsilon}_{ik};\ \ \mathbf{t}_{ik} = \mathbf{D}^{-1/2}\boldsymbol{\sigma}_{ik}^E;\, \hat{\mathbf{B}}_i = w_i\mathbf{D}^{1/2}\mathbf{B}_i. \tag{10}$$

Then Equation (7) becomes

$$\begin{aligned}
&\alpha_{sd}^{blkh} = \sqrt{\tfrac{2}{3}}\sigma_y\,\min_{\dot{\mathbf{e}}_{ik}}\left\{\sum_{k=1}^{m}\sum_{i=1}^{NG}\sqrt{\mathbf{e}_{ik}^T\mathbf{e}_{ik}+\varepsilon^2}+a\sum_{i=1}^{NG}\sqrt{\sum_{k=1}^{m}\mathbf{e}_{ik}^T\sum_{k=1}^{m}\mathbf{e}_{ik}+\varepsilon^2}\right\} && \text{(a)}\\
&\text{s.t.}:\begin{cases}
\sum_{k=1}^{m}\mathbf{e}_{ik}=\hat{\mathbf{B}}_i\mathbf{u} & \forall i=\overline{1,NG} \qquad\qquad \text{(b)}\\
\frac{1}{3}\mathbf{D}_M\mathbf{e}_{ik}=\mathbf{0} & \forall i=\overline{1,NG}\quad \forall k=\overline{1,m} \qquad \text{(c)}\\
\sum_{k=1}^{m}\sum_{i=1}^{NG}\mathbf{e}_{ik}^T\mathbf{t}_{ik}=1 & \qquad\qquad \text{(d)}
\end{cases}
\end{aligned} \tag{11}$$

where

$$a = (\sigma_u-\sigma_y)/\sigma_y. \tag{12}$$

to solve problem (11), using penalty function method for constraints (11b) and (11c), combined with Lagrange multiplier method for constraint (11d). Penalty function F_{P} and Lagrange function F_{PL} are expressed in Equations 13 and 14, respectively.

$$F_{\mathrm{P}} = \sum_{i=1}^{\mathrm{NG}} \left\{ \sum_{k=1}^{m} \sqrt{\mathbf{e}_{ik}^{T}\mathbf{e}_{ik} + \varepsilon^{2}} + a\sqrt{\sum_{k=1}^{m}\mathbf{e}_{ik}^{T}\sum_{k=1}^{m}\mathbf{e}_{ik} + \varepsilon^{2}} \right.$$
$$\left. + \frac{c}{2}\sum_{k=1}^{m}\mathbf{e}_{ik}^{T}\mathbf{D}_{M}\mathbf{e}_{ik} + \frac{c}{2}\left(\sum_{k=1}^{m}\mathbf{e}_{ik} - \hat{\mathbf{B}}_{i}\mathbf{u}\right)^{T}\left(\sum_{k=1}^{m}\dot{\mathbf{e}}_{ik} - \hat{\mathbf{B}}_{i}\mathbf{u}\right)\right\}$$

s.t. :

$$\sum_{k=1}^{m}\sum_{i=1}^{\mathrm{NG}}\mathbf{e}_{ik}^{T}\mathbf{t}_{ik} = 1 \tag{13}$$

$$F_{\mathrm{PL}} = \sum_{i=1}^{\mathrm{NG}} \left\{ a\sqrt{\sum_{k=1}^{m}\mathbf{e}_{ik}^{T}\sum_{k=1}^{m}\mathbf{e}_{ik} + \varepsilon^{2}} + \sum_{k=1}^{m}\sqrt{\mathbf{e}_{ik}^{T}\mathbf{e}_{ik} + \varepsilon^{2}} \right.$$
$$\left. + \frac{c}{2}\sum_{k=1}^{m}\mathbf{e}_{ik}^{T}\mathbf{D}_{M}\mathbf{e}_{ik} + \frac{c}{2}\left(\sum_{k=1}^{m}\mathbf{e}_{ik} - \hat{\mathbf{B}}_{i}\mathbf{u}\right)^{T}\left(\sum_{k=1}^{m}\mathbf{e}_{ik} - \hat{\mathbf{B}}_{i}\mathbf{u}\right)\right\} + \alpha\left(\sum_{k=1}^{m}\sum_{i=1}^{\mathrm{NG}}\mathbf{e}_{ik}^{T}\mathbf{t}_{ik} - 1\right) \tag{14}$$

Algorithm

Step 1: Choose starting point: displacement and strain vectors $\mathbf{u}^{0}$ and $\mathbf{e}^{0}$ such that the normalized condition (11d) is satisfied:

$$\sum_{i=1}^{\mathrm{NG}}\sum_{k=1}^{m}\mathbf{t}_{ik}^{T}\mathbf{e}_{ik}^{0} = 1 \tag{15}$$

Step 2: Calculate $d\mathbf{u}$, $d\mathbf{e}_{ik}$, $(\alpha + d\alpha)$ from current values of $\mathbf{u}$, $\mathbf{e}$

$$\begin{cases} d\mathbf{u} = \left(-\mathbf{u} + \tilde{\mathbf{S}}^{-1}\tilde{\mathbf{f}}_{1}\right) + (\alpha + d\alpha)\tilde{\mathbf{S}}^{-1}\tilde{\mathbf{f}}_{2} \\ d\mathbf{e}_{ik} = \left(\tilde{\mathbf{M}}_{ik}^{-1}\mathbf{N}_{ik}\mathbf{Q}_{i}^{-1}\sum_{k=1}^{m}\tilde{\mathbf{M}}_{ik}^{-1} - \tilde{\mathbf{M}}_{ik}^{-1}\right)\boldsymbol{\beta}_{1} + (\alpha + d\alpha)\left(\tilde{\mathbf{M}}_{ik}^{-1}\mathbf{N}_{ik}\mathbf{Q}_{i}^{-1}\sum_{k=1}^{m}\tilde{\mathbf{M}}_{ik}^{-1} - \tilde{\mathbf{M}}_{ik}^{-1}\right)\boldsymbol{\beta}_{2} \end{cases} \tag{16}$$

where

$$\tilde{\mathbf{S}} = \sum_{i=1}^{\mathrm{NG}}\hat{\mathbf{B}}_{i}^{T}\tilde{\mathbf{E}}_{i}\hat{\mathbf{B}}_{i} \tag{17}$$

$$\tilde{\mathbf{f}}_{1} = \sum_{i=1}^{\mathrm{NG}}\hat{\mathbf{B}}_{i}^{T}\tilde{\mathbf{E}}_{i}\sum_{k=1}^{m}\mathbf{e}_{ik} - \sum_{i=1}^{\mathrm{NG}}\hat{\mathbf{B}}_{i}^{T}\mathbf{Q}_{i}^{-1}\sum_{k=1}^{m}\tilde{\mathbf{M}}_{ik}^{-1}\left(a\sum_{k=1}^{m}\mathbf{e}_{ik}\sqrt{\dot{\mathbf{e}}_{ik}^{T}\mathbf{e}_{ik} + \varepsilon^{2}} + \mathbf{e}_{ik}\sqrt{\sum_{k=1}^{m}\mathbf{e}_{ik}^{T}\sum_{k=1}^{m}\mathbf{e}_{ik} + \varepsilon^{2}}\right)$$
$$-\sum_{i=1}^{\mathrm{NG}}\hat{\mathbf{B}}_{i}^{T}\mathbf{Q}_{i}^{-1}\sum_{k=1}^{m}\tilde{\mathbf{M}}_{ik}^{-1}cb_{ik}\mathbf{D}_{M}\mathbf{e}_{ik} \tag{18}$$

$$\tilde{\mathbf{f}}_{2} = -\sum_{i=1}^{\mathrm{NG}}\hat{\mathbf{B}}_{i}^{T}\mathbf{Q}_{i}^{-1}\sum_{k=1}^{m}\tilde{\mathbf{M}}_{ik}^{-1}\mathbf{t}_{ik}b_{ik} \tag{19}$$

$$\tilde{\mathbf{E}}_{i} = \left(\mathbf{I}_{i} - c\mathbf{Q}_{i}^{-1}\sum_{k=1}^{m}b_{ik}\tilde{\mathbf{M}}_{ik}^{-1}\right) \tag{20}$$

$$\mathbf{Q}_i = \mathbf{I}_i + \sum_{k=1}^{m} \tilde{\mathbf{M}}_{ik}^{-1} \mathbf{N}_{ik} \tag{21}$$

$$\tilde{\mathbf{M}}_{ik} \approx \left(\sqrt{\sum_{k=1}^{m} \mathbf{e}_{ik}^T \sum_{k=1}^{m} \mathbf{e}_{ik} + \varepsilon^2} \mathbf{I}_{ik} + c b_{ik} \mathbf{D}_M \right) \tag{22}$$

$$\mathbf{N}_{ik} \approx \left(a \sqrt{\mathbf{e}_{ik}^T \mathbf{e}_{ik} + \varepsilon^2} + c b_{ik} \right) \mathbf{I}_{ik} \tag{23}$$

$$b_{ik} = \sqrt{\sum_{k=1}^{m} \mathbf{e}_{ik}^T \sum_{k=1}^{m} \mathbf{e}_{ik} + \varepsilon^2} \sqrt{\mathbf{e}_{ik}^T \mathbf{e}_{ik} + \varepsilon^2} \tag{24}$$

$$\begin{aligned} \boldsymbol{\beta}_1 = {} & a \sum_{k=1}^{m} \mathbf{e}_{ik} \sqrt{\mathbf{e}_{ik}^T \mathbf{e}_{ik} + \varepsilon^2} + \mathbf{e}_{ik} \sqrt{\sum_{k=1}^{m} \mathbf{e}_{ik}^T \sum_{k=1}^{m} \mathbf{e}_{ik} + \varepsilon^2} + c\mathbf{D}_M \mathbf{e}_{ik} b_{ik} \\ & + c \left(\sum_{k=1}^{m} \mathbf{e}_{ik} - \hat{\mathbf{B}}_i \mathbf{u} \right) b_{ik} - c b_{ik} \hat{\mathbf{B}}_i d\mathbf{u}_1 \end{aligned} \tag{25}$$

$$\boldsymbol{\beta}_2 = \left(\mathbf{t}_{ik} - c \hat{\mathbf{B}}_i d\mathbf{u}_2 \right) \tag{26}$$

$$(\alpha + d\alpha) = \frac{1 - \sum_{i=1}^{NG} \sum_{k=1}^{m} \mathbf{t}_{ik}^T \left(\mathbf{e}_{ik} + (d\mathbf{e}_{ik})_1 \right)}{\sum_{i=1}^{NG} \sum_{k=1}^{m} \mathbf{t}_{ik}^T (d\mathbf{e}_{ik})_2} = - \frac{\sum_{i=1}^{NG} \sum_{k=1}^{m} \mathbf{t}_{ik}^T (d\mathbf{e}_{ik})_1}{\sum_{i=1}^{NG} \sum_{k=1}^{m} \mathbf{t}_{ik}^T (d\mathbf{e}_{ik})_2} \tag{27}$$

Step 3: Perform a line search to find λ_u such that

$$\lambda_u = F_P(\mathbf{u} + \lambda d\mathbf{u}, \mathbf{e} + \lambda d\mathbf{e}) \rightarrow \min \tag{28}$$

Update displacement $\mathbf{u}$, plastic strain $\mathbf{e}_{ik}$

$$\begin{aligned} \mathbf{u} &= \mathbf{u} + \lambda_u d\mathbf{u} && \text{(a)} \\ \mathbf{e}_{ik} &= \mathbf{e}_{ik} + \lambda_u d\mathbf{e}_{ik} && \text{(b)} \end{aligned} \tag{29}$$

Step 4: Check convergence criteria: if they are all satisfied, then stop; otherwise go to step 2.

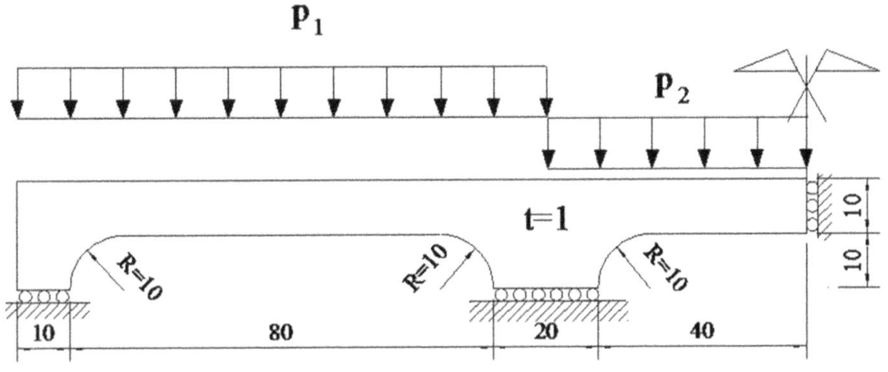

Figure 3 Continuous beam.

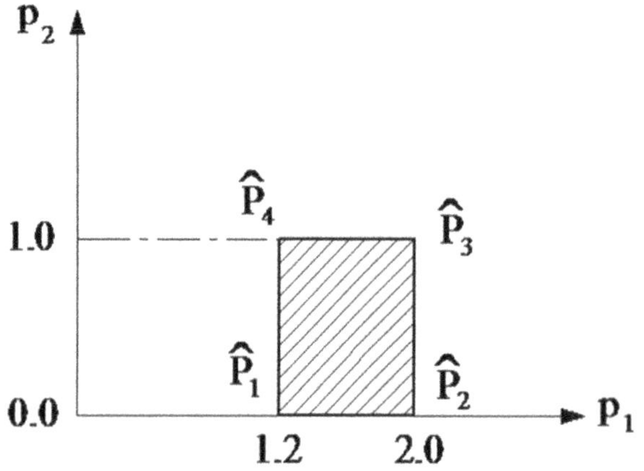

Figure 4 Load domain for example 4.1.

Results and discussions

Two examples are reported. To compare the results on shakedown limit for perfectly plastic materials with other researches, we choose $\sigma_u = \sigma_y$. To investigate the effect of bounded hardening, we choose $\sigma_y < \sigma_u < 2\sigma_y$. When $\sigma_u \geq 2\sigma_y$, we have unbounded kinematic hardening model.

Continuous beam

The continuous steel beam is described in Figure 3 subjected to uniform distributed loads: p_1 and P_2 vary independently in the domain: $p_1 \in [1.2, 2]$, $p_2 \in [0, 1]$. The load domain is described in Figure 4.

The material mechanical properties are Young's modulus, $E = 1.8 \cdot 10^5$ N/mm^2; yield stress, $\sigma_y = 100$ N/mm^2; ultimate strength, $\sigma_u = 1.35\sigma_y$ and Poisson's ratio, $\nu = 0.3$. By the symmetry of the problem, only half of the structure is discretized into 589 elements, 8-node quadrangle, Figure 5. The structure is considered as a plane stress problem. Numerical limit and shakedown analysis for this structure made of perfectly plastic material were presented in Garcea et al. [25] and Tran et al. [26].

Table 1 shows the results of limit and shakedown analysis. Present results are close to others in literature.

Interaction diagram of shakedown load multiplier is plotted in Figure 6. In this structure, when p_2 is not very large, the structure fails in ratcheting mode, and benefit of hardening is quite clear.

Cylindrical pipe under complex loading

This closed-end pipe is investigated for perfectly plastic material in Vu [23] using primal-dual shakedown algorithm. The structure is subjected to bending M_b and

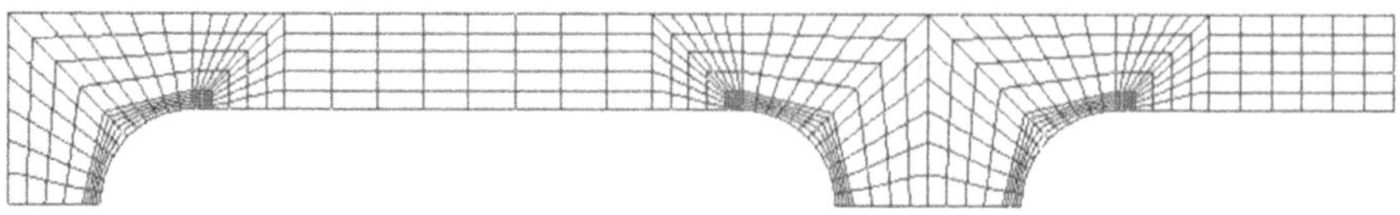
Figure 5 FEM mesh.

Table 1 Comparison of plastic limit collapse and shakedown results

Author	Limit				Shakedown
	$[p_1, p_2] = [2.0, 0.0]$	$[p_1, p_2] = [0.0, 1.0]$	$[p_1, p_2] = [1.2, 1.0]$	$[p_1, p_2] = [2.0, 1.0]$	$p_1 \in [1.2, 2]$ $p_2 \in [0, 1]$
Garcea et al. [25]	3.280	8.718	5.467	3.280	3.244
Tran et al. [26]	3.402	9.192	5.720	3.388	3.377
Present (perfectly plastic)	3.300	8.744	5.500	3.300	3.264
Present (kin. hardening)	4.455	11.804	7.425	4.455	4.406

torsion M_t moments, internal pressure p and axial tension T. Material properties are Young's modulus, $E = 2.1 \cdot 10^5$ N/mm^2; yield stress, $\sigma_y = 160$ N/mm^2; ultimate strength, $\sigma_u = 1.25\sigma_y$ and Poisson's ratio, $\nu = 0.3$. Using 20-node 3D elements to model whole structure with the dimensions: length $L = 2,700$ mm, mean radius $r = 300$ mm and thickness $h = 60$ mm, see Figure 7.

The analytical solutions of plastic collapse limit for cylindrical pipe under complex loading can be cited from Vu [23].

Pure bending capacity:

$$M_{b\lim} = 4\sigma_y h\left(r^2 + \frac{h^2}{12}\right) = 3647.52{\cdot}10^6 \text{ Nmm.} \tag{30}$$

Pure torsion capacity:

$$M_{t\lim} = \frac{2}{\sqrt{3}}\pi r^2 h\sigma_y = 3134.24{\cdot}10^6 \text{ Nmm.} \tag{31}$$

Pure tension capacity:

$$T_{\lim} = 2\pi r h\sigma_y = 18095573.6 \text{ N.} \tag{32}$$

Pure internal pressure capacity:

$$p_{\lim} = \sigma_y\frac{h}{r} = 32 \text{ N/mm}^2 \tag{33}$$

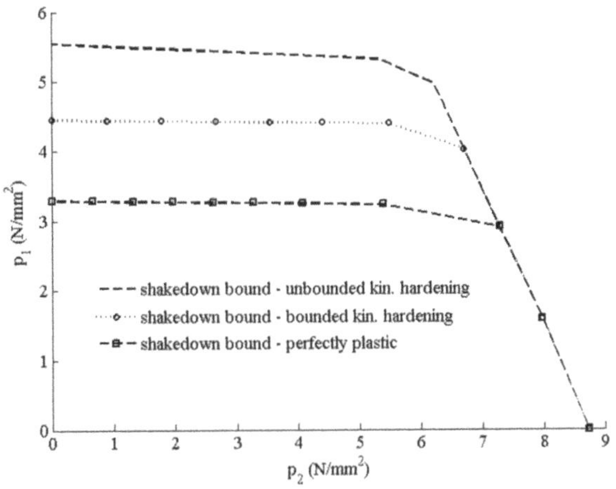

Figure 6 Interaction diagram for shakedown bounds of continuous beam. The results are not normalized.

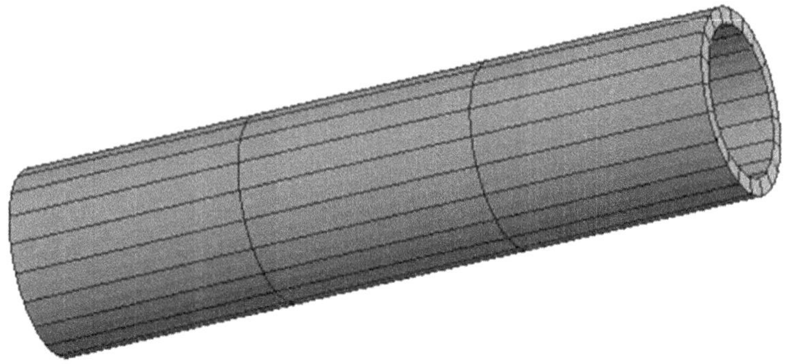

Figure 7 FEM mesh of cylindrical pipe.

and the normalized load multiplier when bending, internal pressure and tension are combined is as follows:

$$m = \frac{\sqrt{4-3n_\varphi^2}}{2} \cos\left[\frac{n_\varphi-2n_x}{\sqrt{4-3n_\varphi^2}}\frac{\pi}{2}\right], \tag{34}$$

where

$$\begin{cases} m = M/M_{b\,\lim} \\ n_\phi = p/p_{\lim} \\ n_x = T/T_{\lim} \end{cases}. \tag{35}$$

If the axial tension force comes from only internal pressure on closed ends, then $n_x = n_\phi/2$, and formula (35) can be rewritten as

$$m = \frac{\sqrt{4-3n_\varphi^2}}{2} \tag{36}$$

FE analysis is fulfilled for structure subjected to combined internal pressure p and bending M_b. Results are presented in Table 2, normalized by pure bending capacity in

Table 2 Limit and shakedown load multipliers of cylindrical pipe subjected to internal pressure and bending

Load combination	Elastic factor	Limit factor (perfectly plastic)	Shakedown factor (perfectly plastic)	Shakedown factor (bounded hardening)	Shakedown factor (unbounded hardening)
0.0p_1.0 M	0.7338	1.0012	0.7338	0.7338	0.7338
0.2p_1.0 M	0.7228	0.9870	0.7297	0.7310	0.7304
0.4p_1.0 M	0.7011	0.9478	0.7228	0.7236	0.7231
0.6p_1.0 M	0.6570	0.8914	0.7131	0.7132	0.7134
0.8p_1.0 M	0.6023	0.8267	0.7011	0.7013	0.7014
1.0p_1.0 M	0.5509	0.7608	0.6667	0.6855	0.6853
1.0p_0.8 M	0.6168	0.8540	0.7696	0.8128	0.8127
1.0p_0.6 M	0.6921	0.9556	0.8906	0.9894	0.9894
1.0p_0.4 M	0.7727	1.0546	1.0179	1.2318	1.2346
1.0p_0.2 M	0.8486	1.1306	1.1204	1.3874	1.5506
1.0p_0.0 M	0.9019	1.1589	1.1586	1.4482	1.8091

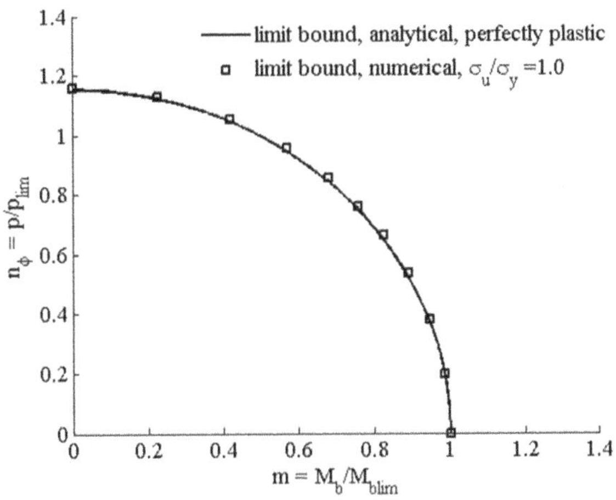

Figure 8 Interaction diagram for limit bounds. Comparison between analytical and numerical solutions.

formula (28) and pure internal pressure in formula (33). Limit analysis is implemented for $\sigma_u/\sigma_y = 1.0$ to be compared to formula (36), and interaction diagram is plotted in Figure 8. Shakedown analysis with and without hardening effect is implemented for the load domain: $p \in [0, 1]; M_b \in [-1, 1]$. Interaction diagram is plotted in Figure 9.

Figure 8 shows that the present results of limit analysis for $\sigma_u/\sigma_y = 1$ are close to analytical solutions. Figure 9 shows that the hardening effect is clear if the applied moment is less than $0.5M_{b\,\mathrm{lim}}$. If $\sigma_u \geq 2\sigma_y$, bounded hardening model becomes unbounded, and shakedown limit of structure cannot exceed two times of elastic limit.

Conclusions

The paper developed a new upper bound algorithm for shakedown analysis of elastic plastic-bounded linearly kinematic hardening structures. This is an efficient tool for practical computation, especially for complicated structures subject to mechanical loads.

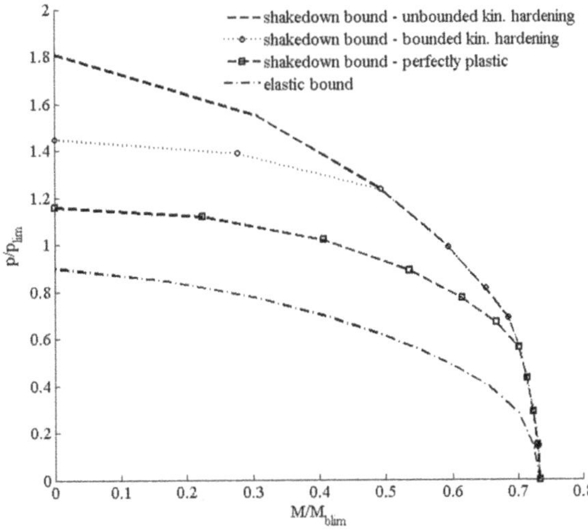

Figure 9 Interaction diagram for elastic and shakedown bounds, normalized by pure plastic collapse limits, $M_{b\,\mathrm{lim}}$ and p_{lim}.

The proposed algorithm gives results that are close to the results in literatures. If $\sigma_u = \sigma_y$, it leads to perfectly plastic material; if $\sigma_u \geq 2\sigma_y$, it leads to unbounded kinematic hardening material; otherwise, $\sigma_y < \sigma_u < 2\sigma_y$, we have bounded kinematic hardening material.

Let α_{el}, $\alpha_{\text{sd}}^{\text{pp}}$, and $\alpha_{\text{sd}}^{\text{blkh}}$ denote respectively elastic limit, shakedown limit for elastic perfectly plastic and shakedown limit for bounded kinematic hardening material, respectively, then:

$$\alpha_{\text{sd}}^{\text{pp}} \leq \alpha_{\text{sd}}^{\text{blkh}} \leq \frac{\sigma_u}{\sigma_y} \alpha_{\text{sd}}^{\text{pp}} \leq 2\alpha_{\text{el}}.$$

In the preceding expression, the left equality occurs if the subsequent yield surface translates inside the bounding surface, the middle equality occurs if the subsequent yield surface fixed on the bounding surface and the last equality occurs when yield surface translates unboundedly. If the structure shakes down in alternating plasticity mode, then there is no difference between perfectly plastic and kinematic hardening models.

Competing interests
The authors declare that they have no competing interests.

Author details
[1]Faculty of Civil Engineering, Hanoi Architectural University, Nguyen Trai Street, Thanh Xuân District, Hanoi, Vietnam. [2]Faculty of Medical Engineering and Technomathematics, Aachen University of Applied Science, Jülich Campus, Heinrich-Mußmann-Str. 1Jülich 52428, Germany.

References

1. Melan E (1938) Zur Plastizität des räumlichen Kontinuums. Ing-Arch 8:116–126
2. Prager W (1956) A new method of analyzing stress and strain in work hardening plastic solids. J Appl Mech ASME 23:493–496
3. Maier GA (1973) Shakedown matrix theory allowing for work hardening and second-order geometric effects. In: Sawczuk A (ed) Foundations of plasticity. Springer, North-Holland, Amsterdam, pp 417–433
4. Ponter ARS (1975) A general shakedown theorem for elastic plastic bodies with work hardening. In: Proc. SMiRT-3, paper L5/2
5. Gokhfeld DA, Cherniavsky OF (1980) Limit analysis of structures at thermal cycling. Sijthoff & Noordhoff, The Netherlands
6. Stein E, Huang YJ (1995) Shakedown for systems of kinematic hardening materials. In: Weichert D, Doroz S, Mróz Z (ed) Inelastic behaviour of structures under variables loads. Kluwer Academic Publishers, Springer, Netherlands, pp 33–50
7. Weichert D, Groß-Weege J (1988) The numerical assessment of elastic-plastic sheets under variable mechanical and thermal loads using a simplified two-surface yield condition. Int J Mech Sci 30:757–767
8. Bodovillé G, de Saxcé G (2001) Plasticity with non-linear kinematic hardening–modelling and shakedown analysis by the bipotential approach. Eur J Mech A/Solids 20:99–112
9. Pham DC (2005) Shakedown static and kinematic theorems for elastic-plastic limited linear kinematic-hardening solids. Eur J Mech A/Solids 24:35–45
10. Pham DC (2007) Shakedown theory for elastic plastic kinematic hardening bodies. Int J Plast 23:1240–1259
11. Nguyen QS (2003) On shakedown analysis in hardening. J Mech Phys Solids 51:101–125
12. Staat M, Heitzer M (2002) The restricted influence of kinematic hardening on shakedown loads. Proceedings of WCCM V, 5th World Congress on Computational Mechanics, Vienna, Austria. http://opus.bibliothek.fh-aachen.de/opus/volltexte/2005/79/
13. Staat M, Heitzer M (ed) (2003) Numerical Methods for Limit and Shakedown analysis–Deterministic and Probabilistic Problems. NIC Series, vol 15. John von Neumann Institute for Computing, Jülich. http://webarchiv.fz-juelich.de/nic-series/volume15/volume15.html
14. Stein E, Zhang G (1992) Theoretical and numerical shakedown analysis for kinematic hardening materials. In: Owen DRJ, Oñate E, Hinton E (ed) Proc. 3rd Int. Conf. on Computational Plasticity (COMPLAS 3), CIMNE. Pineridge Press, Barcelona, Spain, pp 1–25
15. Yan AM, Nguyen Dang H (2000) Direct finite element kinematical approaches in limit and shakedown analysis of shells and elbows. In: Inelastic Analysis of Structures under variable Loads, Theory and Engineering Applications. Kluwer Academic Publishers, Springer, Netherlands, pp 233–254
16. Yan AM, Nguyen Dang H (2001) Kinematical shakedown analysis with temperature-dependent yield stress. Int J Num Mech Engng 50:1415–1168

17. Yan AM, Khoi VD, Nguyen Dang H (2003) Kinematical formulation of limit and shakedown analysis. In: Numerical Methods for Limit and Shakedown Analysis–Deterministic and Probabilistic Problems. NIC Series, vol 15. John von Neumann Institute for Computing, Jülich. http://webarchiv.fz-juelich.de/nic-series/volume15/volume15.html
18. Nguyen Dang H, König J (1976) A finite element formulation for shakedown problems using a yield criterion of the mean. Comp Appl Mech Eng 1(Nr. 2):179–182
19. Nguyen Dang H, Palgen L (1980-81) Shakedown analysis by displacement method and equilibrium finite element. Transac CSME 6(Nr. 1):32–39
20. Vu DK, Yan AM, Nguyen Dang H (2003) A dual form for discretized kinematic formulation in shakedown analysis. Int J Solids Struct 41(1):267–277
21. Vu DK, Yan AM, Nguyen Dang H (2004) A primal-dual algorithm for shakedown analysis of structures. Comp Methods Appl Mech Eng (Elsevier) 193(42–44):4663–4674
22. Yan AM, Vu DK, Nguyen Dang H (2004) Dual in kinematical approaches of limit and shakedown analysis of structures. In: David Y (ed) Complimentarily, duality and symmetry in nonlinear mechanics, vol 6. Gao, Kluwer Academic Publishers, Springer, Netherlands, pp 127–148
23. Vu DK (2001) Dual Limit and Shakedown analysis of structures. PhD Thesis. Université de Liège, Belgium
24. Phạm PT, Staat M (2013) An upper bound algorithm for limit and shakedown analysis of bounded linearly kinematic hardening bodies. In: De Saxcé G et al. (ed) Direct Methods. Springer, Netherlands
25. Garcea G, Armentano G, Petrolo S, Casciaro R (2005) Finite element shakedown of two-dimensional structures. Int J Numer Mech Engng 63:1174–1202
26. Tran TN, Liu GR, Nguyen XH, Nguyen TT (2010) An edge-based smoothed finite element method for primal-dual shakedown analysis of structures. Int J Numer Engng 82:917–938

Hydraulic fracturing and its peculiarities

Stefano Secchi[1] and Bernhard A Schrefler[2*]

* Correspondence: bernhard.schrefler@dicea.unipd.it
[2]Department of Civil, Environmental and Architectural Engineering, University of Padua, 9 via Marzolo, Padua 35123, Italy
Full list of author information is available at the end of the article

Abstract

Background: Simulation of pressure-induced fracture in two-dimensional (2D) and three-dimensional (3D) fully saturated porous media is presented together with some peculiar features.

Methods: A cohesive fracture model is adopted together with a discrete crack and without predetermined fracture path. The fracture is filled with interface elements which in the 2D case are quadrangular and triangular elements and in the 3D case are either tetrahedral or wedge elements. The Rankine criterion is used for fracture nucleation and advancement. In a 2D setting the fracture follows directly the direction normal to the maximum principal stress while in the 3D case the fracture follows the face of the element around the fracture tip closest to the normal direction of the maximum principal stress at the tip. The procedure requires continuous updating of the mesh around the crack tip to take into account the evolving geometry. The updated mesh is obtained by means of an efficient mesh generator based on Delaunay tessellation. The governing equations are written in the framework of porous media mechanics and are solved numerically in a fully coupled manner.

Results: Numerical examples dealing with well injection (constant inflow) in a geological setting and hydraulic fracture in 2D and 3D concrete dams (increasing pressure) conclude the paper. A counter-example involving thermomecanically driven fracture, also a coupled problem, is included as well.

Conclusions: The examples highlight some peculiar features of hydraulic fracture propagation. In particular the adopted method is able to capture the hints of Self-Organized Criticality featured by hydraulic fracturing.

Keywords: Hydraulic fracturing; Cohesive model; Fluid lag; Finite elements

Background

Fluid-driven fracture propagating in porous media is widely used in geomechanics to improve the permeability of reservoirs in oil and gas recovery or of geothermal wells. Another application of importance is related to the overtopping stability analysis of dams. In the case of reservoir engineering, water is forced under high pressure deep into the ground by injection into a well. The fluid, usually mixed with sand and some chemicals, penetrates in the reservoir rock, opening long cracks (fracking). Horizontal drilling together with hydraulic fracturing makes the extraction of tightly bound natural gas from shale formations economically feasible [1]. In the field, it is unfortunately rather difficult to obtain direct information about the evolution of the crack in the ground, and very little data are known or accessible. Two types of measurements are mainly performed: monitoring of pressure fluctuations at the injection pump and registration of acoustic emissions at the surface [2]. Fracking can also induce small earthquakes [3]. Pressure-induced fracture propagation presents some peculiar features such as pressure peaks and stepwise advancement, which have been discovered only recently and need further investigation. It is recalled that differently from tensile experiments where the crack surfaces are stress free, in hydraulic fracturing, these surfaces are loaded by a pressure distribution resulting from the invading fluid or gas [2]. Simulation is an extremely useful tool to obtain more insight into the problem. The paper addresses this issue.

Contributions to the mathematical modelling of fluid-driven fractures have been made continuously since the 1960s, beginning with Perkins and Kern [4]. These authors made various simplifying assumptions, for instance, regarding fluid flow, fracture shape and velocity leakage from the fracture. For other analytical solutions in the frame of linear fracture mechanics, assuming the problem to be stationary, see [5-9]. They suffer the limits of an analytical approach, in particular the inability to represent an evolutionary problem in a domain with a real complexity. An analysis of solid and fluid behaviour near the crack tip can be found in [10,11]. Boone and Ingraffea [12] present a numerical model in the context of linear fracture mechanics which allows for fluid leakage in the medium surrounding the fracture and assumes a moving crack depending on the applied loads and material properties. Tzschichholz and Herrmann [2] used a two-dimensional (2D) lattice model for constant injection rate and homogeneous and heterogeneous material which only breaks under tension. Carter et al. [13] show a fully three-dimensional (3D) hydraulic fracture model which neglects the fluid continuity equation in the medium surrounding the fracture. A discrete fracture approach with remeshing in an unstructured mesh and automatic mesh refinement is used by Schrefler et al. [14]. An element threshold number (number of elements over the cohesive zone) was identified to obtain mesh-independent results. This approach has been extended to 3D situation in [15]. Extended finite elements (XFEM) have been applied to hydraulic fracturing in a partially saturated porous medium by Réthoré et al. [16] in a 2D setting. In this case, a two-scale model has been developed for the fluid flow: in the cohesive crack, Darcy's equation is used for flow in a porous medium, and identities are derived that couple the local momentum and mass balances to the governing equations for the unsaturated medium at macroscopic level. As an example, the rupture of a saturated square plate (0.25 × 0.25 m) in plane strain conditions is investigated under a prescribed fixed vertical velocity $v = 2.35 \times 10^{-2}$ μm/s in the opposite direction at the top and bottom of the plate (tensile loading). The mesh used consists of 20 × 20 quadrilateral elements (12.5 × 12.5 mm each) with bilinear shape functions, and the time step size is 1 s. In the cracked region, the elements are further divided in four triangles. Mohammadnejad and Khoei [17] solve the same problem also with XFEM, using full two-phase flow throughout the region. Darcy flow is assumed within the crack. Finer meshes are used as above (smallest element size 4.5 × 4.5 mm) and much lower time steps (0.25 to 0.125 s). Cavitation is found in both papers, also due to the impervious boundary conditions chosen. Partition of unity finite elements (PUFEM) are used for 2D mode I crack propagation in saturated ionized porous media by Kraaijeveldt et al. [18]. A pull test, a delamination test and an osmopolarity test are simulated with rather fine regular meshes (quadrangular elements with side length of the order of 2 mm and lower) and time step size down to 0.1 s. The time and space discretizations, including the element threshold number used for the solutions, are extremely important for catching the phenomena described next.

We address now the peculiar behaviour of hydraulic fracture propagation which has been observed only by a minority of the above-mentioned authors, but has been confirmed experimentally. Tzschichholz and Herrmann [2] have evidenced with their lattice model and constant injection rate a drop in pressure in time and oscillations on short time scales. These authors explain this by the fact that at the beginning high pressures are needed to push the fluid into the crack. The crack is enlarged and the pressure drops because the enlarged crack can now be opened much more easily than before. The pressure goes down although additional fluid has been added to the crack in the time step. If the pressure drops too much, the stresses at the crack tip fall below their cohesion value and the crack cannot grow at the next time step. By injecting more fluid into the crack, the pressure increases linearly in time until the cohesion forces can be overcome again. Using arguments from continuum mechanics, the authors show that the obtained value for pressure decline in the long term agrees acceptably with their numerical results. The short-term deviations are due the lattice model and the ensuing pressure drops. Oscillations are also obtained for the stored lattice energy. The breaking process is discontinuous in time with time intervals of quiescence where all beams on the crack surface are stressed below their cohesion thresholds and the acting pressure increases linearly in time. Tzschichholz and Herrmann [2] also find a temporal clustering of the breaking events, calling such a sequence bursts (avalanche behaviour). The bursts are unevenly distributed in time and occur relatively often for small times and become rarer later. There is resemblance between the obtained data and magnitude records of earthquakes or of acoustic emission records from laboratory experiments. We have shown with our porous media mechanics model in a 2D setting [14] that in the case of hydraulic fracturing the fracture advances stepwise. Two types of mesh refinement in space and refinement in time were used, but the stepwise advancement did not disappear. Such steps do not appear in other coupled solutions involving cohesive fracture, as e.g. the thermo-elastic one of [19] where the crack surfaces are stress free. The stepwise advancement and flow jumps were also found by Kraaijeveld [20] with a strong and a weak discontinuity model for flow. In [18], the stepwise advancement in mode I crack propagation is difficult to see because a continuous pressure profile across the crack is used. However, continuous pressure profile only works for sufficiently fine meshes. If the mesh is sufficiently fine, then the discretization can resolve the steep pressure gradients along the crack, but the advantage of PUFEM which allows keeping the mesh pretty rough all over the continuum is lost. Hence, dealing with the stepwise progression of the crack in this mode I model is only possible with a finer mesh than the one used (JM Huyghe, personal communication). This is why the authors state that the physical phenomenon challenges the numerical scheme. In mode II, as shown in [20,21], this problem does not appear because a discontinuous pressure across the crack is accounted for. There it is not attempted to resolve the steep pressure gradient, but this gradient is reconstructed afterwards, using the Terzaghi analytical solution for pressure diffusion. This two-step procedure allows using a rough mesh and still handling a realistic pressure gradient. Stepwise crack advancement can clearly be observed in the crack length histories of Figure four of [17], while it does not appear in the solution for the same problem in [16]. The cohesive fracture length for this problem is estimated with Barenblatt's expression (see Equation 22) [22] to be about 136 mm. Hence, there are about 10 elements over the cohesive zone in [16] and 30 elements in [17]. The first value is probably below the element threshold number for this type of problem, even with XFEM (see also the large time steps used), while the second one is sufficient even for standard elements. While both use XFEM, the two-step procedure and the large time step size and coarse mesh in [16] hide the problem.

Finally, stepwise advancement and flow are also mentioned in [23], where PUFEM is used for 2D poroelastic media. Their method still suffers from mesh dependence because the crack propagates through one element each time step. Hence, their conclusions are not definite. However, Pizzocolo et al. [24] confirmed stepwise advancement experimentally with a test on a small hydrogel disk. The duration of the pause Δt between steps is found to be inversely related to the hydraulic permeability K according to $\Delta t = \Delta x^2 \ / \ KE$ with E Young's modulus and Δx length of the step. A possible explanation for the stepwise behaviour observed in [20,21,24] put forward in [24] is that an incompressible fluid consolidation comes into play which prevents tip advancement until the overpressures due to the last advancement have been dissipated, and the stress has been transferred again to the solid phase. This implies the existence of pressure peaks after each advancement stage. During the period of quiescence, the effective stress is below the breaking threshold. Consolidation as a possible explanation for the stepwise advancement needs further investigation in the case of fluid injection, because for some permeability values the tip pressure goes down to zero as shown below on an example. The existence of periods of quiescence is in line with the findings of [2]. We will show that this phenomenon is not only relevant for small structures, where it has been observed experimentally, but also for large structures such as underground soil masses and dams. In that case, the fracture length is much larger, but the phenomenon is still there and the bursts can be felt at great distances compared to the crack length.

Methods

The first subsection presents the fracture model, the second subsection summarizes the governing equations and their numerical solution by means of the finite element method and the third subsection explains the adopted fracture advancement procedure and the required refinements necessary to obtain mesh-independent results.

The fracture model

We use a discrete crack model for a situation depicted in Figure 1: Ω is the domain, Γ_e is the boundary of the fully saturated porous material surrounding the crack, Γ' is the crack boundary and $\bar{\Omega}$ is the domain inside the crack filled with fluid only. There is fluid exchange between the crack and the surrounding porous medium. The mechanical behaviour of the solid phase at a distance from the process zone is assumed to obey a Green elastic or hyperelastic material behaviour [14].

For the fracture itself, we use a cohesive fracture model. Between the real fracture apex which appears at macroscopic level and the apex of a fictitious fracture, there is a

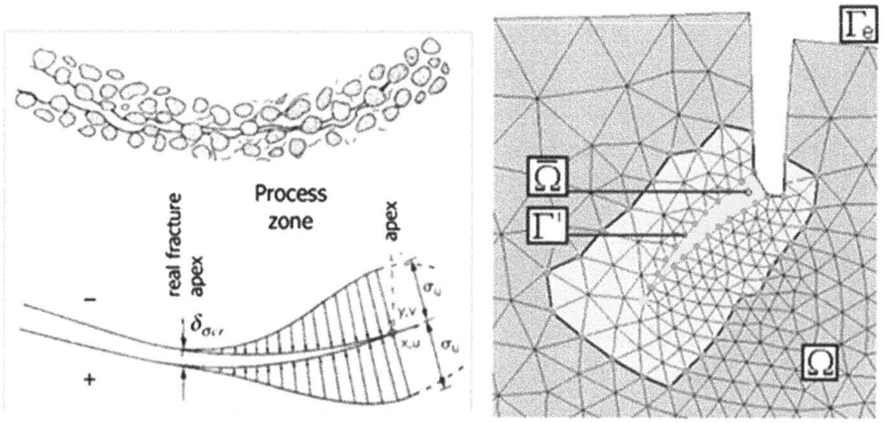

Figure 1 Hydraulic fracture domain and cohesive crack geometry. Definition of the hydraulic fracture domain, reprinted from [15], Copyright (2012), with permission from Springer, and the cohesive crack geometry, reprinted from [14], Copyright (2006), with permission from Elsevier.

process zone where cohesive forces act (see Figure 1). Following [22,25,26], the cohesive law for mode I crack opening with monotonically increasing opening is

$$\sigma = \sigma_0\left(1 - \frac{\delta_\sigma}{\delta_{\sigma\mathrm{cr}}}\right) \tag{1}$$

σ_0 being the maximum cohesive traction (closed crack), δ_σ the current relative displacement normal to the crack, $\delta_{\sigma\mathrm{cr}}$ the maximum opening with exchange of cohesive tractions and $G_c = \sigma_0 \times \delta_{\sigma\mathrm{cr}}\ /\ 2$ the fracture energy. If after some opening $\delta_{\sigma 1} < \delta_{\sigma\mathrm{cr}}$, the crack begins to close and tractions obey a linear unloading as

$$\sigma = \sigma_0\left(1 - \frac{\delta_{\sigma 1}}{\delta_{\sigma\mathrm{cr}}}\right)\frac{\delta_\sigma}{\delta_{\sigma 1}} \tag{2}$$

When the crack reopens, Equation 2 is reversed until the opening $\delta_{\sigma 1}$ is recovered; then, tractions obey again Equation 1.

When tangential relative displacements of the sides of a fracture in the process zone cannot be disregarded, mixed mode crack opening takes place. This is often the case of a crack moving along an interface separating two solid components. In fact, whereas the crack path in a homogeneous medium is governed by the principal stress direction, the interface has an orientation that is usually different from the principal stress direction. The mixed cohesive mechanical model involves the simultaneous activation of normal and tangential displacement discontinuity and corresponding tractions. For the pure mode II, the relationship between tangential tractions and displacements is

$$\tau = \tau_0\frac{\delta_\sigma}{\delta_{\sigma\mathrm{cr}}}\frac{\delta_\tau}{|\delta_\tau|} \tag{3}$$

τ_0 being the maximum tangential stress (closed crack), δ_τ the relative displacement parallel to the crack and $\delta_{\sigma\mathrm{cr}}$ the limiting value opening for stress transmission. The unloading/loading from/to some opening $\delta_{\sigma 1} < \delta_{\sigma\mathrm{cr}}$ follows the same behaviour as for mode I.

For the mixed mode crack propagation, the interaction between the two cohesive mechanisms is treated as in [27]. By defining an equivalent or effective opening displacement δ and the scalar effective traction t as

$$\delta = \sqrt{\beta^2 \delta_\tau^2 \delta_\sigma^2}, \quad t = \sqrt{\beta^{-2}\tau^2 + \sigma^2} \tag{4}$$

the resulting cohesive law is

$$\mathbf{t} = \frac{t}{\delta}\left(\beta^2 \boldsymbol{\delta}_\tau + \boldsymbol{\delta}_\sigma\right) \tag{5}$$

β being a suitable material parameter that defines the ratio between the shear and the normal critical components. For more details, see [14].

Governing equations and their discretization in space and time

Taking into account the cohesive forces and the symbols of Figure 1, the linear momentum balance of the mixture, discretized in space with finite elements according to the standard Galerkin procedure [28] is written as

$$\mathbf{M}\dot{\mathbf{v}} + \int_\Omega \mathbf{B}^T \boldsymbol{\sigma}'' \, d\Omega - \mathbf{Q}\mathbf{p} - \mathbf{f}^{(1)} - \int_{\Gamma'} (\mathbf{N}^u)^T \mathbf{c} \, d\Gamma' = \mathbf{0} \tag{6}$$

where $\mathbf{c}$ is the cohesive traction on the process zone as defined above.

The fully saturated medium surrounding the fracture has constant absolute permeability, while for the permeability within the crack, the Poiseuille or cubic law is assumed. This permeability does not depend on the rock type or stress history but is defined by crack aperture only. Deviation from the ideal parallel surface conditions causes only an apparent reduction in flow and can be incorporated into the cubic law, which reads as [29]

$$k_{ij} = \frac{1}{f}\frac{w^2}{12} \tag{7}$$

w being the fracture aperture and f a coefficient in the range 1.04 to 1.65 depending on the solid material. In the following, this parameter will be assumed as constant and equal to 1.0. Incorporating the Poiseuille law into the weak form of water mass balance equation within the crack and discretizing in space by means of the finite element method results in

$$\tilde{\mathbf{H}}\mathbf{p} + \tilde{\mathbf{S}}\dot{\mathbf{p}} + \int_{\Gamma'} (\mathbf{N}^p)^T \mathbf{q}^w \, d\Gamma' = \mathbf{0} \tag{8}$$

With

$$\tilde{\mathbf{H}} = \int_{\bar{\Omega}} (\nabla \mathbf{N}^p)^T \frac{w^2}{12\mu_w} \nabla \mathbf{N}^p \, d\bar{\Omega} \tag{9}$$

$$\tilde{\mathbf{S}} = \int_{\bar{\Omega}} (\mathbf{N}^p)^T \frac{1}{K_f} \mathbf{N}^p \, d\bar{\Omega} \tag{10}$$

μ_w is the dynamic viscosity and K_f the bulk modulus of the fluid. The last term of (8) represents the leakage flux into the surrounding porous medium across the fracture borders and is of paramount importance in hydraulic fracturing techniques. This term can be represented by means of Darcy's law using the medium permeability and pressure gradient generated by the application of water pressure on the fracture lips. No particular simplifying hypotheses are hence necessary for this term. This equation can be directly assembled at the same stage as the mass balance Equation 11 for the saturated medium surrounding the crack, because both have the same structure: only the parameters have to be changed in the appropriate elements depending whether they belong to the fracture or to the surrounding medium.

The discretized mass balance equation for the porous medium surrounding the fracture is

$$\mathbf{Q}^T\dot{\mathbf{u}} + \mathbf{Hp} + \mathbf{S}\dot{\mathbf{p}} - \mathbf{f}^{(2)} - \int_{\Gamma'} (\mathbf{N}^p)^T \mathbf{q}^w d\Gamma' = \mathbf{0} \tag{11}$$

where $\mathbf{q}^w$ represents the water leakage flux along the fracture toward the surrounding medium of Equation 7. This term is defined along the entire fracture, i.e. the open part and the process zone. It is worth mentioning that the topology of the domains Ω and $\bar{\Omega}$ changes with the evolution of the fracture. In particular, the fracture path, the position of the process zone and the cohesive forces are unknown and must be regarded as products of the mechanical analysis.

Discretization in time is then performed with time discontinuous Galerkin approximation following [30,31]. Denoting with $I_n = (t_n^-, t_{n+1}^+)$ a typical incremental time step of size $\Delta t = t_{n+1} - t_n$, the weighted residual forms are

$$\begin{aligned}\int_{I_n} \delta\mathbf{v}^T\left(\mathbf{M}\dot{\mathbf{v}} + \mathbf{Ku} - \mathbf{Qp} - \mathbf{f}^{(1)}\right)\mathrm{dt} + \int_{I_n} \delta\mathbf{u}^T\mathbf{K}(\dot{\mathbf{u}} - \mathbf{v})\mathrm{dt} + \\ + \delta\mathbf{u}^T\big|_{t_n}\mathbf{K}\left(\mathbf{u}_n^+ - \mathbf{u}_n^-\right)\mathrm{dt} + \delta\mathbf{v}^T\big|_{t_n}\mathbf{M}\left(\mathbf{v}_n^+ - \mathbf{v}_n^-\right) = \mathbf{0}\end{aligned} \tag{12}$$

$$\begin{aligned}\int_{I_n} \delta\mathbf{p}^T\left(\mathbf{Q}^T\mathbf{v} + \mathbf{Ss} + \mathbf{Hp} - \mathbf{f}^{(2)}\right)\mathrm{dt} + \int_{I_n} \delta\mathbf{p}^T\mathbf{S}(\dot{\mathbf{p}} - \mathbf{s})\mathrm{dt} + \\ + \delta\mathbf{p}^T\big|_{t_n}\mathbf{S}\left(\mathbf{p}_n^+ - \mathbf{p}_n^-\right)\mathrm{dt} = \mathbf{0}\end{aligned} \tag{13}$$

with the constraint conditions

$$\begin{aligned}\dot{\mathbf{u}} - \mathbf{v} = \mathbf{0} \\ \dot{\mathbf{p}} - \mathbf{s} = \mathbf{0}\end{aligned} \tag{14}$$

Subscripts −/+ indicate quantities immediately before and after the generic time station. Field variables and their first time derivatives at time $t \in [t_n, t_{n+1}]$ are interpolated by linear time shape functions, and the following discretized equations are obtained

$$\begin{aligned}\mathbf{u}_n &= \mathbf{u}_n^- + \frac{\Delta t}{2}\left(\mathbf{v}_n^+ - \mathbf{v}_{n+1}^-\right) \\ \mathbf{u}_{n+1} &= \mathbf{u}_n^- + \frac{\Delta t}{2}\left(\mathbf{v}_n^+ + \mathbf{v}_{n+1}^-\right) \\ \mathbf{s}_n &= \frac{1}{\Delta t}\left(\mathbf{p}_{n+1} + 3\mathbf{p}_n - 4\mathbf{p}_n^-\right) \\ \mathbf{s}_{n+1} &= \frac{1}{\Delta t}\left(\mathbf{p}_{n+1} + 3\mathbf{p}_n + 2\mathbf{p}_n^-\right)\end{aligned} \tag{15}$$

$$
\begin{aligned}
&\left(\frac{1}{2}\mathbf{M}-\frac{5}{36}\Delta t^2\mathbf{K}\right)\mathbf{v}_n+\left(\frac{1}{2}\mathbf{M}+\frac{1}{36}\Delta t^2\mathbf{K}\right)\mathbf{v}_{n+1}+\frac{\Delta t}{3}\mathbf{Q}\mathbf{p}_n+\\
&\qquad+\frac{\Delta t}{6}\mathbf{Q}\mathbf{p}_{n+1}=-\frac{\Delta t}{2}\mathbf{K}\mathbf{u}_n^-+\mathbf{M}\mathbf{v}_n^-+\int_{I_n}N_1(t)\,\mathbf{f}^{(1)}\,\mathrm{dt}\\
&\left(-\frac{1}{2}\mathbf{M}-\frac{7}{36}\Delta t^2\mathbf{K}\right)\mathbf{v}_n+\left(\frac{1}{2}\mathbf{M}+\frac{5}{36}\Delta t^2\mathbf{K}\right)\mathbf{v}_{n+1}+\frac{\Delta t}{3}\mathbf{Q}\mathbf{p}_n+\\
&\qquad+\frac{\Delta t}{3}\mathbf{Q}\mathbf{p}_{n+1}=-\frac{\Delta t}{2}\mathbf{K}\mathbf{u}_n^-+\int_{I_n}N_2(t)\,\mathbf{f}^{(1)}\,\mathrm{dt}\\
&\frac{\Delta t}{3}\mathbf{Q}^T\mathbf{v}_n\frac{\Delta t}{6}\mathbf{Q}^T\mathbf{v}_{n+1}+\left(\frac{1}{2}\mathbf{S}+\frac{\Delta t}{3}\mathbf{H}\right)\mathbf{p}_n+\left(\frac{1}{2}\mathbf{S}+\frac{\Delta t}{6}\mathbf{H}\right)\mathbf{p}_{n+1}=\\
&\qquad=\mathbf{S}\mathbf{p}_n^-+\int_{I_n}N_1(t)\,\mathbf{f}^{(2)}\,\mathrm{dt}\\
&\frac{\Delta t}{6}\mathbf{Q}^T\mathbf{v}_n\frac{\Delta t}{3}\mathbf{Q}^T\mathbf{v}_{n+1}+\left(-\frac{1}{2}\mathbf{S}+\Delta t\mathbf{H}\right)\mathbf{p}_n+\left(\frac{1}{2}\mathbf{S}+\frac{\Delta t}{3}\mathbf{H}\right)\mathbf{p}_{n+1}=\int_{I_n}N_1(t)\,\mathbf{f}^{(2)}\,\mathrm{dt}
\end{aligned}
\tag{16}
$$

The nodal displacement, velocity and pressure, $\mathbf{u}_n^-$, $\mathbf{v}_n^-$ and $\mathbf{p}_n^-$, respectively, for the current step coincide with the unknowns at the end of the previous one, hence are known in the time marching scheme and coincide with the initial condition for the first time step. The system of algebraic equations is solved with a monolithic approach using an optimized non-symmetric sparse matrix algorithm. The number of unknowns is doubled with respect to the traditional trapezoidal method.

In a quasistatic situation, adopted for the examples, the submatrices of the above equations are the usual ones of soil consolidation [28], except for

$$
\dot{\mathbf{f}}^{(1)}=\int_{\Omega}(\mathbf{N}^u)^T\rho\dot{\mathbf{b}}\,d\Omega+\int_{\Gamma_t}(\mathbf{N}^u)^T\dot{\mathbf{t}}\,d\Gamma+\int_{\Gamma'}(\mathbf{N}^u)^T\dot{\mathbf{c}}\,d\Gamma'
\tag{17}
$$

where $\dot{\mathbf{c}}$ is the cohesive traction rate and is different from zero only if the element has a side on the lips of the fracture Γ'. Given that the liquid phase is continuous over the whole domain, leakage flux along the opened fracture lips is accounted for through the **H** matrix together with the flux along the crack. Finite elements are in fact present along the crack (not shown in Figure 1), which account only for the pressure field and have no mechanical stiffness. In the present formulation, non-linear terms arise through cohesive forces in the process zone and permeability along the fracture.

Fracture advancement and refinement strategy

Because of the continuous variation of the domain as a consequence of the propagation of the cracks, also the boundary Γ' and the related mechanical conditions change. Along the formed crack edges and in the process zone, boundary conditions are the direct result of the field equations, while the mechanical parameters have to be updated. The following remeshing techniques account for all these changes [15,32].

For the fracture nucleation and advancement, the Rankine criterion is used. More than one crack can open and fractures can also branch. Fracture forms and advances if the maximum principal stress exceeds in a point the fixed threshold. The fracture advancement procedure differs for 2D and 3D situations: in 2D, the fracture follows directly the direction normal to the maximum principal stress, while in 3D, the fracture follows the face of the element around the fracture tip which is closest to the normal direction of the maximum principal stress. In this last case, the fracture tip becomes a curve in space (front). The advancement of a fracture creates new nodes: in 2D, the resulting new elements for the filler at the front are triangles, while in 3D situation, they are tetrahedral. If an internal node along the process zone advances in a 3D setting, a new wedge element results in the filler [15].

At each time station t_n, j successive tip (front) advancements are possible until the Rankine criterion is satisfied (Figure 2). Their number in general depends on the chosen time step increment Δt, the adopted crack length increment Δs and the variation of the applied loads. This requires continuous remeshing with a consequent transfer of nodal vectors from the old to the continuously updated mesh by a suitable operator $\mathbf{v}_m(\Omega_{m+1}) = \aleph(\mathbf{v}_m(\Omega_m))$. For momentum and energy conservation, the solution is repeated with the quantities of mesh m but re-calculated on the new mesh $m + 1$ before advancing the crack tip [33].

Three types of refinement are needed to obtain satisfactory results: the refinement in space in general, the satisfaction of an element threshold number over the process zone and a refinement in time. For refinement and de-refinement in space, the Zienkiewicz-Zhu error estimator is used [34]. Fluid lag, i.e. negative fluid pressures at the crack tip, may arise in the case of injection if the speed at which the crack tip advances is sufficiently high so that for a given permeability water cannot flow in fast enough to fill the created space. This as well as mesh-independent results can be obtained numerically only if an *element threshold number* is satisfied over the process zone. This number is given by the ratio of elements over the process zone and its length and can be estimated in advance from the problem at hand and the expected process zone. The number of elements over the process zone is of paramount importance and has not received sufficient attention by many authors. It is a sort of object-oriented refinement and is extensively dealt with in [14]. Adaptivity in time is obtained by means of the adopted discontinous Galerkin method in the time domain (DGT) [33]. The error of the time-integration procedure can be defined through the jump of the solution

$$\begin{aligned} \langle \mathbf{u}_n \rangle &= \mathbf{u}_n - \mathbf{u}_n^- \\ \langle \mathbf{v}_n \rangle &= \mathbf{v}_n - \mathbf{v}_n^- \\ \langle \mathbf{p}_n \rangle &= \mathbf{p}_n - \mathbf{p}_n^- \end{aligned} \tag{18}$$

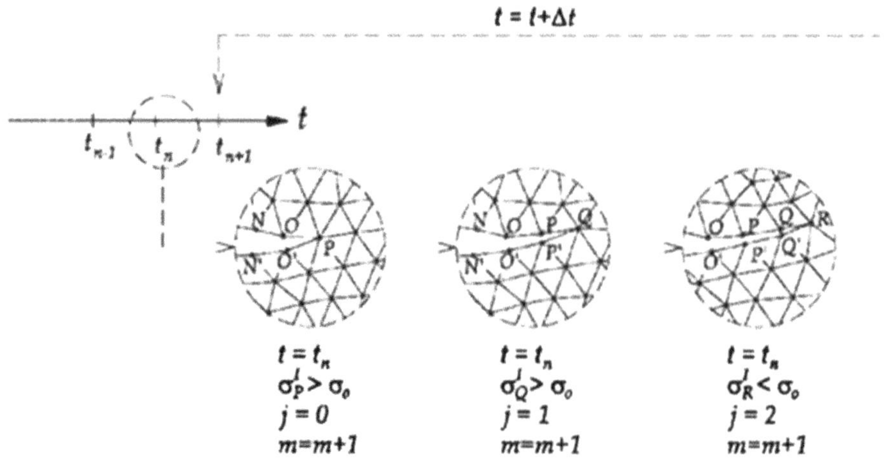

Figure 2 Multiple advancing fracture step at the same time station. Reprinted from [15], Copyright (2012), with permission from Springer.

at each time station, i.e. the difference between the final point of time step $n-1$ and the first point of time step n. By adopting the total energy norms as error measure, we define the following terms:

$$\begin{aligned}
\|\mathbf{e}_u\|_n &= \left(\langle\mathbf{v}_n\rangle^T\mathbf{M}\langle\mathbf{v}_n\rangle + \langle\mathbf{u}_n\rangle^T\mathbf{K}\langle\mathbf{u}_n\rangle\right)^{1/2}\\
\|\mathbf{e}_{u,p}\|_n &= \left(\langle\mathbf{u}_n\rangle^T\mathbf{Q}\langle\mathbf{p}_n\rangle\right)^{1/2}\\
\|\mathbf{e}_p\|_n &= \left(\langle\mathbf{p}_n\rangle^T\mathbf{Q}^T\langle\mathbf{u}_n\rangle + \langle\mathbf{p}_n\rangle^T\mathbf{H}\langle\mathbf{p}_n\rangle\Delta t + \langle\mathbf{p}_n\rangle^T\mathbf{P}^T\langle\mathbf{p}_n\rangle\right)^{1/2}\\
\|\mathbf{e}\|_n &= \max\left\{\|\mathbf{e}_u\|_n, \|\mathbf{e}_{u,p}\|_n, \|\mathbf{e}_p\|_n\right\}
\end{aligned} \tag{19}$$

Error measures defined in Equation 19 account at the same time for the cross effects among the different fields and the ones between space and time discretizations.

The relative error is defined as in [30]

$$\eta_n = \frac{\|\mathbf{e}\|_n}{\|\mathbf{e}\|_{\max}} \tag{20}$$

where $\|\mathbf{e}\|_{\max}$ is the maximum total energy norm $\|\mathbf{e}\|_{\max} = \max\left(\|\mathbf{e}\|_i\right), 0 < i < n$

When $\eta > \eta_{\text{toll}}$, the time step Δt_n is modified and a new $\Delta t_n^{'} < \Delta t_n$ is obtained according to

$$\Delta t_n^{'} = \left(\frac{\theta\,\eta_{\text{toll}}}{\eta}\right)^{1/3}\Delta t_n \tag{21}$$

where $\theta < 1.0$ is a safety factor. If the error is smaller than a defined value $\eta_{\text{toll,min}}$, the step is increased using a rule similar to Equation 21.

As it stands, the refinements in space and time are carried out sequentially, starting with the space refinement, followed by the element threshold number and then the refinement in time. An eye is kept on the satisfaction of the discrete maximum principle [35] which states that it is not possible to refine in time below a certain limit depending on the material properties without also refining in space. A proper functional would be needed to link all the three refinements. A flow chart of the numerical procedure is given in the 'Appendix'.

Results and discussion

First, we show for comparison purposes the results of cohesive fracture propagation in a thermo-elastic medium, a coupled problem solved with the method for fracture advancement outlined above [19]. The method itself of the crack tip advancement does not introduce steps, once mesh-independent results are achieved. This was also found in static problems (not shown here) such as the three-point bending test, the four-point shear test and the case of a plate with a circular hole. The problem shown here evidences also the importance of the element threshold number, i.e. the number of elements over the process zone. A three-point bending test is performed on a bimaterial specimen subjected to a thermo-mechanical loading [36]. One part of the sample is made of aluminium 6061 and the other of polymethylmethacrylate (PMMA), bonded with methacrylate adhesive. The geometry is presented in Figure 3: the sample has a notch with a sharp tip of 1-mm width and 30-mm height shifted 3 mm from the interface in the PMMA zone. The two materials present very different Young's moduli and

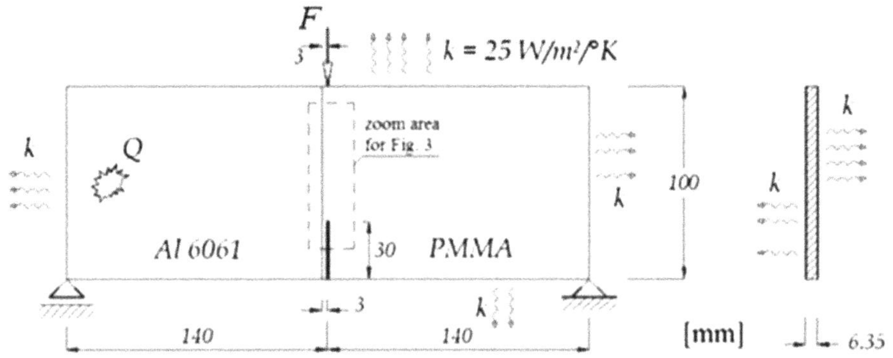

Figure 3 Geometry of the three-point bending test for a bimaterial specimen. Reprinted from [19], Copyright (2004), with permission from Elsevier.

thermal expansion coefficients, so that, when the system is subjected to heat, stresses arise near the interface as a result of the mismatch in thermal expansion.

Two different experiments are reported in [36]. In the first, at a room temperature of 25°C, a load was applied 3 mm from the interface in the PMMA zone (Figure 3) to trigger the fracture process. The loading rate was very low and the resulting speed of crack propagation at the initial stages was also quite slow, so that quasistatic conditions can be assumed. The crack path was individuated, and stresses near the crack tip in the PMMA were measured using a shearing interferometer.

In the second experiment, the same operations were performed when the temperature of the aluminium was 60°C in steady state conditions. To reach these conditions, a cartridge heater (Q in Figure 3) was inserted into the aluminium part near the external vertical side. The variation in time of the PMMA temperature was checked before the fracture test, which was performed when steady state conditions were reached. The temperature of PMMA was recorded at the crack tip location, at 5 and 7 mm from the interface. Also in this case, the crack path was spotted. From the differences between the two situations, the authors gathered the thermal effects, which were independent of the magnitude of the applied mechanical load.

In the two experiments, the crack propagation trajectories differ as shown in Figure 4a,b where a zoom of the fractured specimens in correspondence of the notch is presented. In particular, the crack path is closer to the interface when the temperature is higher. The numerical results are shown in Figure 4c. The agreement is remarkable, see also [19].

Application of Barenblatt's theory [22] for calculation of characteristic cohesive zone size l yields for PMMA

$$\ell = \frac{\pi E G_c}{8(1-\nu^2)\sigma_0^2} \cong 0.75 \text{ mm} \tag{22}$$

Our numerical results (0.8 mm) are in good accordance with this value. From this value, the choice of the crack tip advancement length can be estimated. It should be such that the heuristically determined element threshold number is satisfied (five elements in the thermo-mechanical case). Using linear elements of decreasing size, the value of the force F (Figure 3), corresponding to an applied vertical displacement on

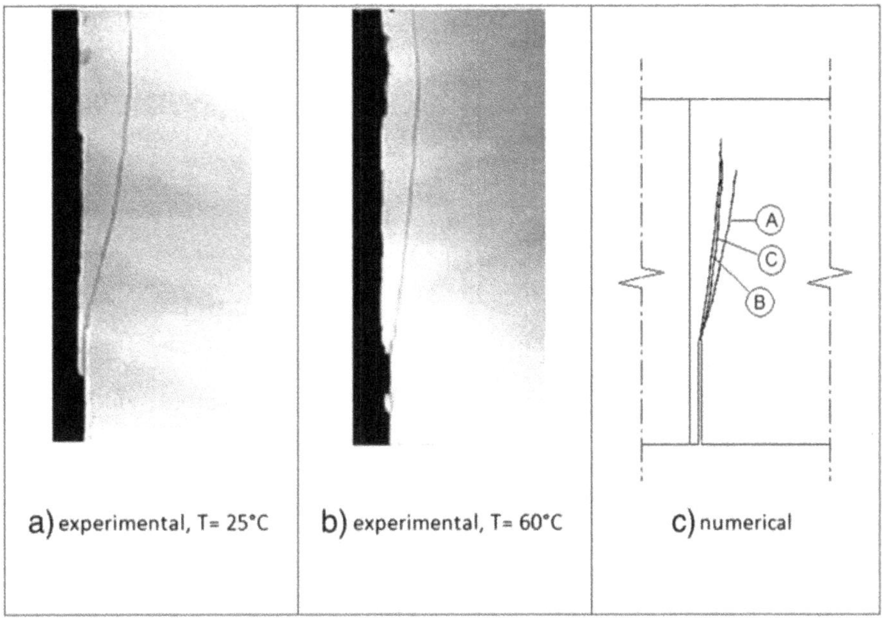

Figure 4 Zoom of the notch of the specimen with crack path trajectories. (a, b) Experimental results (reproduced from [36]). **(c)** Numerical results: case A, uniform temperature (25°C); case B, thermal load with E, σ_0, $\delta_{\sigma cr}$ varying with temperature; and case C, thermal load with $E = E(25°C)$, $\sigma_0 = \sigma_0(25°C)$, $\delta_{\sigma cr} = \delta_{\sigma cr}(25°C)$. Reprinted from [19], Copyright (2004), with permission from Elsevier.

the same point, is calculated. Results are summarized in Figure 5. The peak of the external load and the softening branch are mesh independent once the process zone is subdivided into at least five elements with edges of 0.15 mm or smaller. This situation is handled by the mesh generator simply by locating an element source [32] at the crack tip. Its weight may be *a priori* stated and/or can be *a posteriori* updated during the adaptive remeshing procedure once the length of the process zone has been determined. What is important here is that the diagrams in this coupled problem are smooth reasonably once mesh-independent results are obtained.

The next application deals with a hydraulically driven fracture due to fluid pumped at constant flow rate Q into a well in 2D conditions (plane strain) [14]. Figure 6 shows the geometry of the problem together with the initial finite element discretization. A notch with a sharp tip is present along the symmetry axis of the analyzed area.

The effects of combined spatial/temporal discretizations are clearly seen in Figure 7, where the crack length is drawn versus time for different tip advancements, Δs, and time step increments, Δt. The correct time history (case E) is obtained by simultaneously reducing these two parameters, whereas the reduction of only one discretization parameter leads to errors (about ±20%) even using small tip advancement, if compared to the crack length. Again, the importance of the element threshold number is evident for the choice of Δs (the length of the process zone according to Equation 22 is 0.8 m, and about 30 elements are needed over it). It clearly appears that the crack tip velocity is very mesh sensitive. Hence, the element threshold number must be satisfied to obtain mesh-independent results.

A lower number of elements results in wrong crack tip velocity, and the possible development of fluid lag may be missed [14]. Fluid lag corresponds to negative pressure

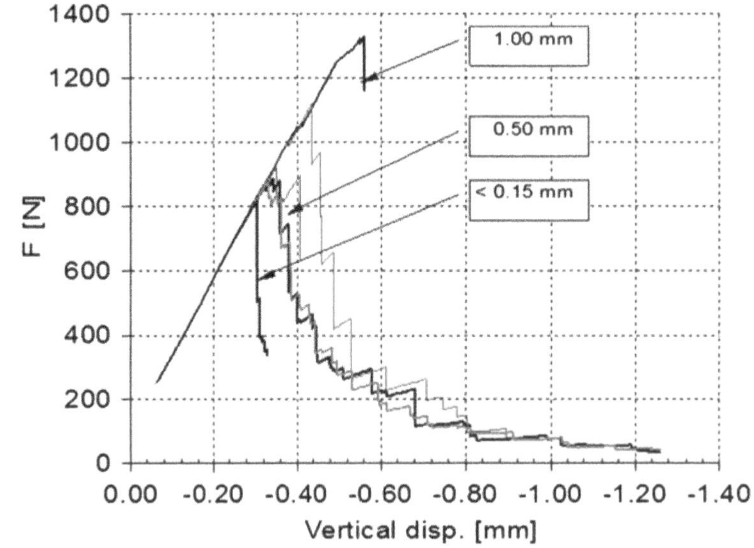

Figure 5 External force vs. vertical displacement and mesh size. Reprinted from [19], Copyright (2004), with permission from Elsevier.

in the process zone and determines hence different body forces (see Equation 6). The distribution of the pressure over the fracture length at time station 10 min is shown in Figure 8 for the following three combinations of dynamic viscosity and injection rate: $\mu_w = 1 \times 10^{-9}$ MPa s, $Q = 0.0001$ m^3/s; $\mu_w = 1 \times 10^{-11}$ MPa s, $Q = 0.0001$ m^3/s; and $\mu_w = 1 \times 10^{-9}$ MPa s, $Q = 0.0002$ m^3/s. The fracture length clearly varies with the chosen data. For the first combination, the pressure at the fracture tip goes almost to zero, while for lower values of μ_w, the pressure is almost constant. For high μ_w and doubled injection rate, cavitation occurs.

The third case deals with the benchmark exercise A2 proposed by ICOLD [37]. The benchmark consists in the evaluation of failure conditions as a consequence of overtopping wave acting on a concrete gravity dam. Contrarily to the previous example here, we have increasing pressure. The geometry of the dam is shown in Figure 9 together

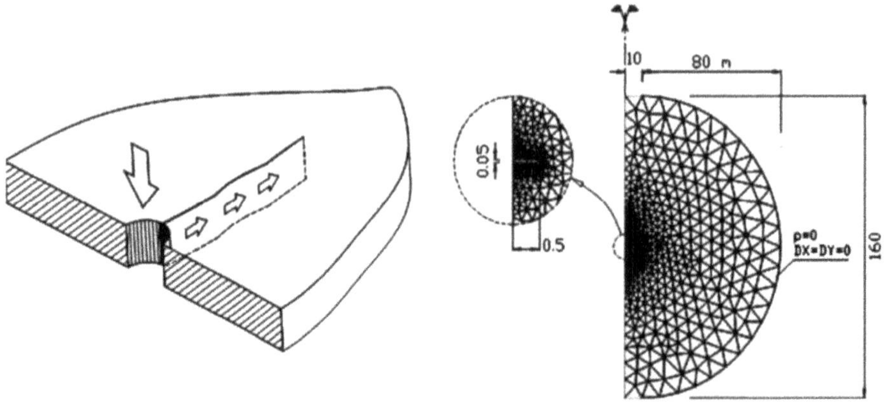

Figure 6 Problem geometry for water injection benchmark and overall discretization. Reprinted from [14], Copyright (2006), with permission from Elsevier.

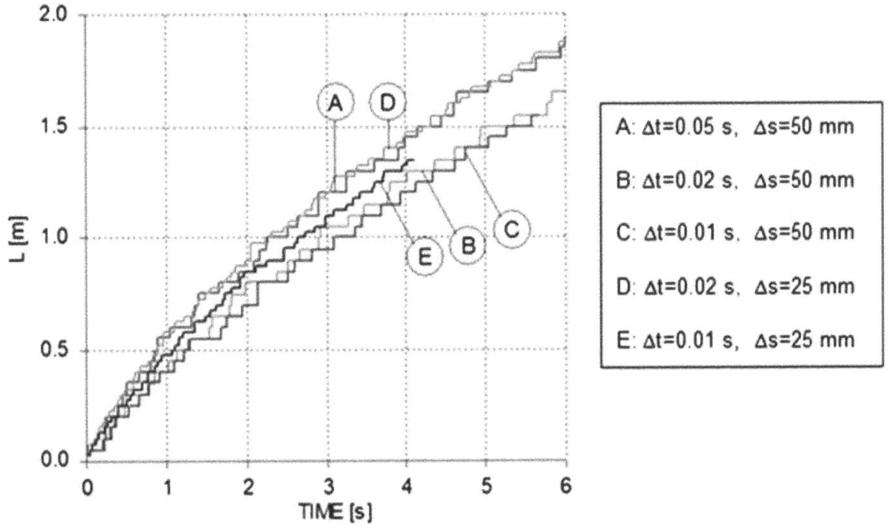

Figure 7 Crack length time history for $\mu_w = 1 \times 10^{-9}$ MPa s and $Q = 0.0001$ m^3/s. Reprinted from [14], Copyright (2006), with permission from Elsevier.

with boundary conditions and an intermediate discretization. Differently from the original benchmark, the dam concrete foundation is also considered, which has been assumed homogeneous with the dam body. In such a situation, the crack path is unknown. On the contrary, when a rock foundation is present, the crack naturally develops at the interface between the dam and foundation. In Figure 9 also, the influence of the viscosity on the crack direction is evidenced (circle).

The initial condition is obtained under self-weight and the hydrostatic pressure due to water in the reservoir up to a level of 52 m. From this point, the water level increases until the overtopping level is reached (higher than the dam crest [14]). The increase of water level in the reservoir is specified in days according to the benchmark.

For an intermediate situation, the principal stress contours and the cohesive forces are shown on Figure 10. Also, fluid lag has been obtained for this situation, not shown in the picture (see [14]). The crack mouth opening displacement versus days is depicted in Figure 11 for different values of the crack tip advancement. The smallest value corresponds to the proper element threshold number. Clearly, stepwise advancement can be observed with some clustering of the steps.

The effects of the stepwise advancement can also be felt at great distance from the actual crack: the horizontal displacements on the dam crest are effected, as can be seen from Figure 12. Only the diagram for the purely elastic solution (no crack) is smooth. Note that here the vertical scale is logarithmic and in the abscissa appear the time steps, not the actual time. This is the reason why the diagram for the elastic case is above the others.

For a similar problem, a 3D solution has been obtained in [15]. In Figure 13, the mesh, the fracture, the process zone and the stress contours are shown when the fracture length is about 15 m corresponding to an intermediate step of the analysis when the water level is 80 m. The horizontal displacement of the dam crest is drawn versus time in Figure 14. The following situations are considered: no fracture at all (elastic);

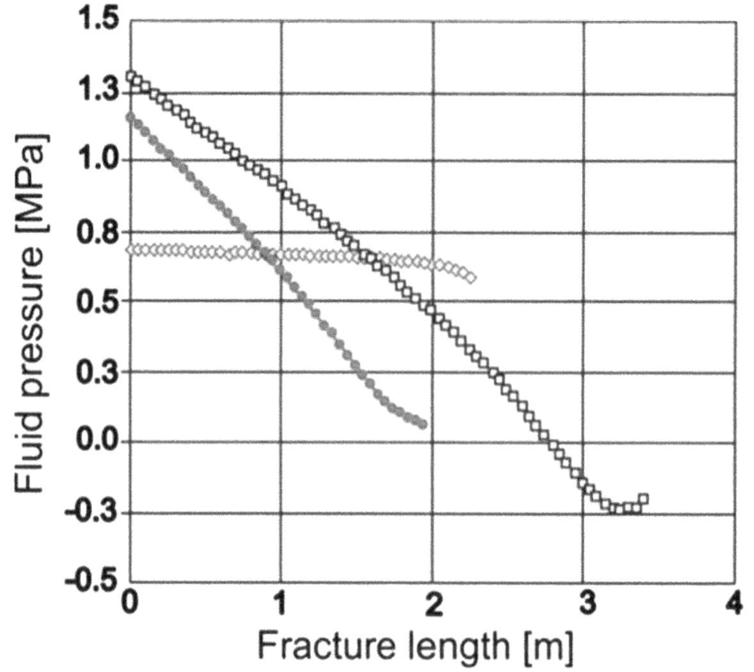

Figure 8 Distribution of the fluid pressure over the fracture length. At time station 10 min for the combinations of dynamic viscosity and injection rate: $\mu_w = 1 \times 10^{-9}$ MPa s, $Q = 0.0001$ m^3/s (red circles); $\mu_w = 1 \times 10^{-11}$ MPa s, $Q = 0.0001$ m^3/s (green diamonds); and $\mu_w = 1 \times 10^{-9}$ MPa s, $Q = 0.0002$ m^3/s (white squares).

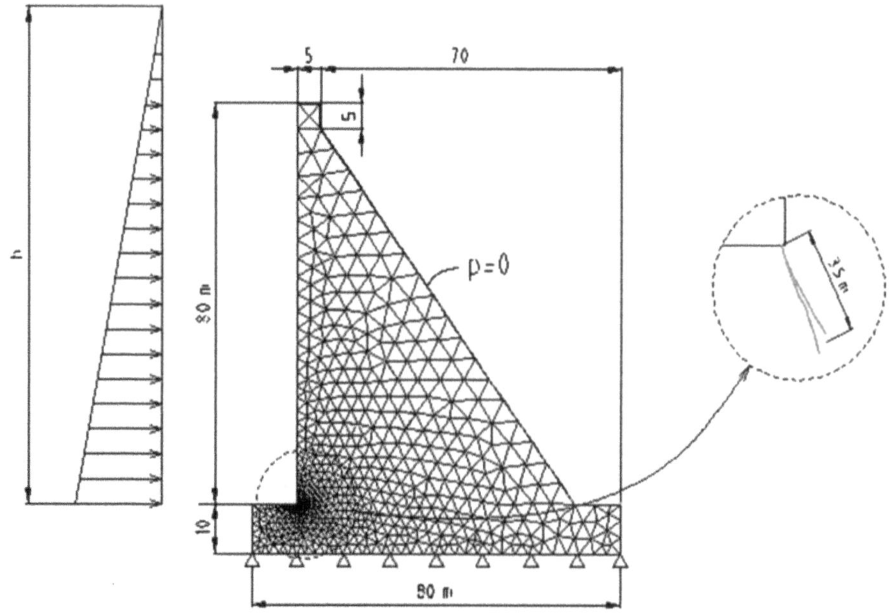

Figure 9 Problem geometry for ICOLD benchmark and calculated crack positions. Reprinted from [14], Copyright (2006), with permission from Elsevier.

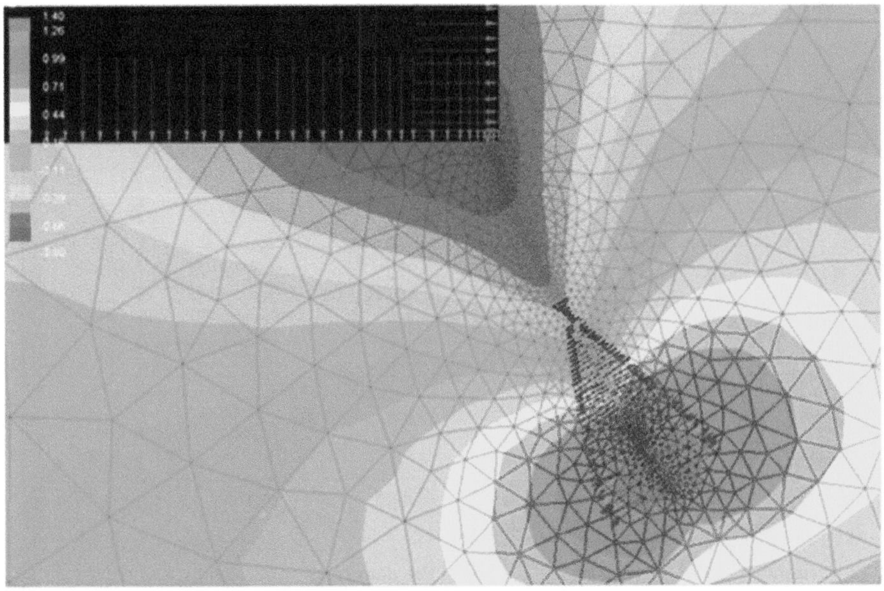

Figure 10 Zoom near the fracture on maximum principal stress contour and cohesive forces. Reprinted from [14], Copyright (2006), with permission from Elsevier.

dry fracture (fracture), i.e. water pressure acts only on the dam, not on the crack lips; hydrostatic water pressure in the crack, constant over the crack length (hydraulic fracture); and fully coupled solution with water pressure varying over the crack length (**u**-*p*). The last one has fluid exchange between the crack and surroundings. The results for the last case correspond to an intermediate value between the others because the pressure is diminishing towards the crack tip, reaching even negative values there (cavitation).

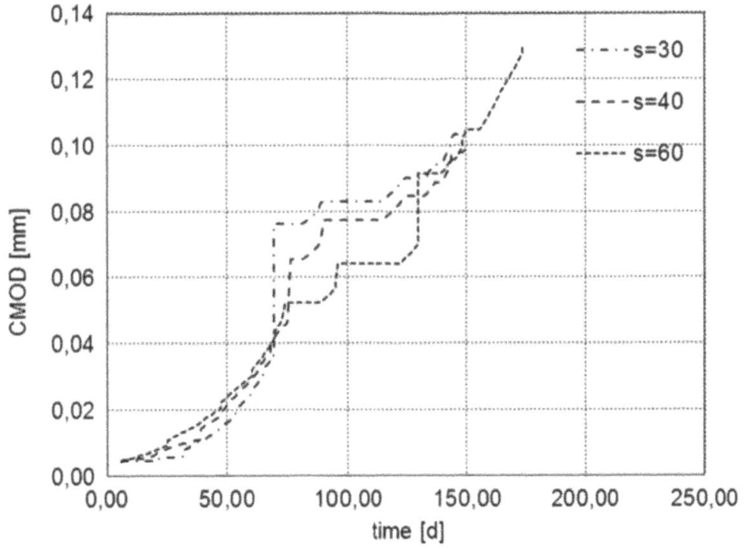

Figure 11 Crack mouth opening displacement versus time (days) for different values of the crack tip advancements (mm).

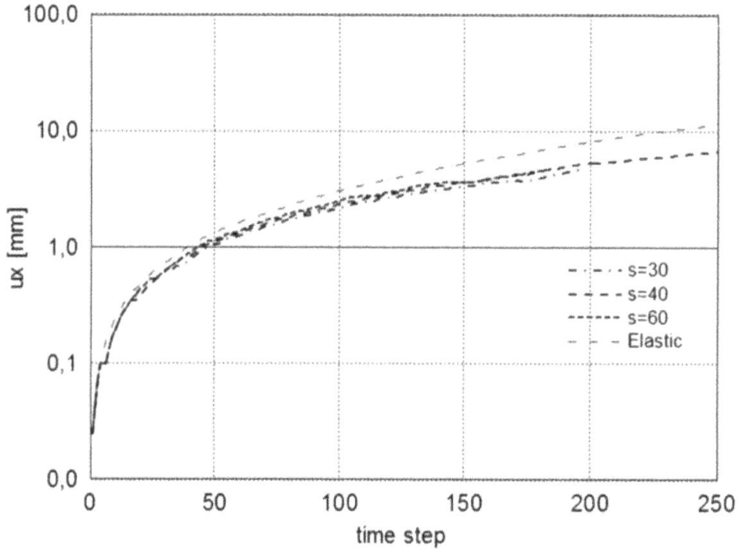

Figure 12 Horizontal displacements versus time step of the dam crest. For different values of the crack tip advancements (mm) and without fracture (elastic).

The relative variations of the horizontal crest displacements according to

$$\|u\| = \left(\frac{u_i}{u_{\mathrm{el}}}-1\right)\cdot 100 \tag{23}$$

with u_i referring to the studied cases and u_{el} to the elastic solution, are drawn in Figure 15. The largest steps correspond to the situations where fluid is present in the crack and may have pressure exchange (consolidation) with the material surrounding

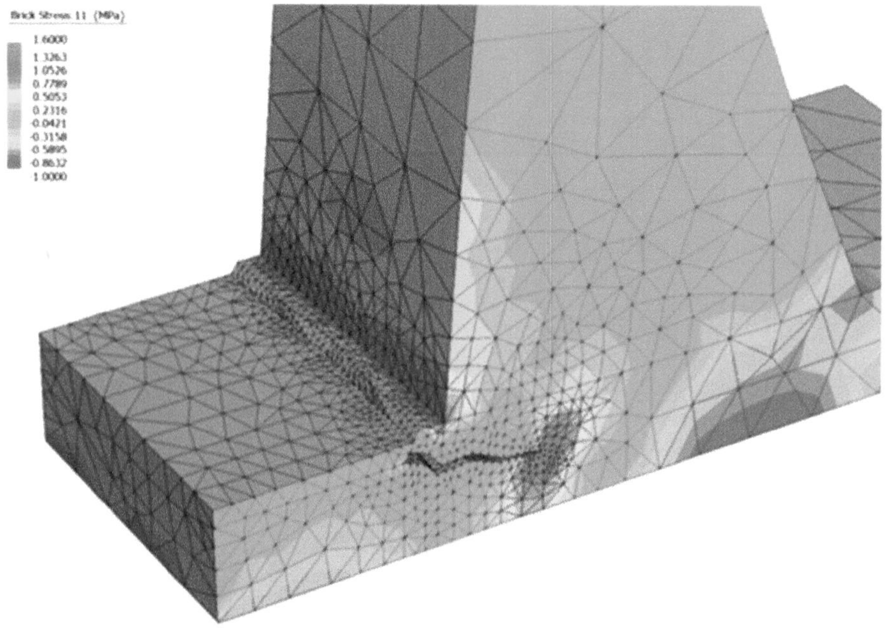

Figure 13 Mesh, fracture, process zone and stress contours. With a fracture length of about 15 m corresponding to an intermediate step of the analysis when the water level is 80 m. Reprinted from [15], Copyright (2012), with permission from Springer.

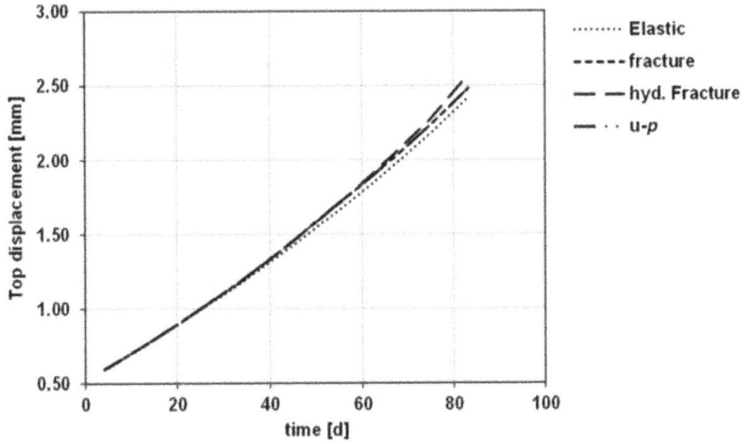

Figure 14 Horizontal displacement of the dam crest versus time. No fracture at all (elastic); dry fracture (fracture), i.e. water pressure acts only on the dam, not on the crack lips; hydrostatic water pressure in the crack, constant over the crack length (hydraulic fracture); and fully coupled solution with water pressure varying over the crack length and fluid exchange between the crack and surroundings (**u**-*p*).

the process zone. Note that these variations are felt on the dam crest, while the pressure-induced fracturing happens on the bottom of the dam. The 3D results have however only qualitative value because the element threshold number would require finer meshes over the cohesive zone which makes the solution very expensive (elements of about 300 mm minimum side length and time steps of a mean value of 4 days were used).

In all three examples of hydraulic fracturing, the fracture site is not easily accessible. However, the fact that the effects of the stepwise advancement can be felt also at distance as shown in two examples would make them possible to be monitored remotely. Field data and experimental evidence on reservoir rocks and large bodies are still missing. Data could possibly come from fracking sites or from some fracking-induced earthquakes [3].

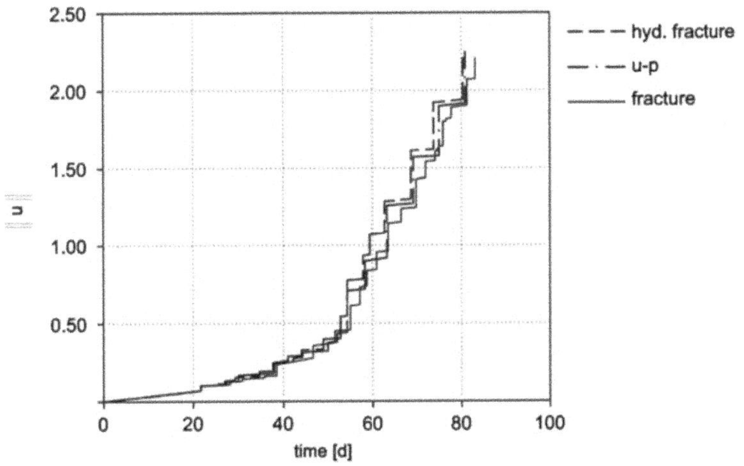

Figure 15 Relative displacements versus time at the dam crest.

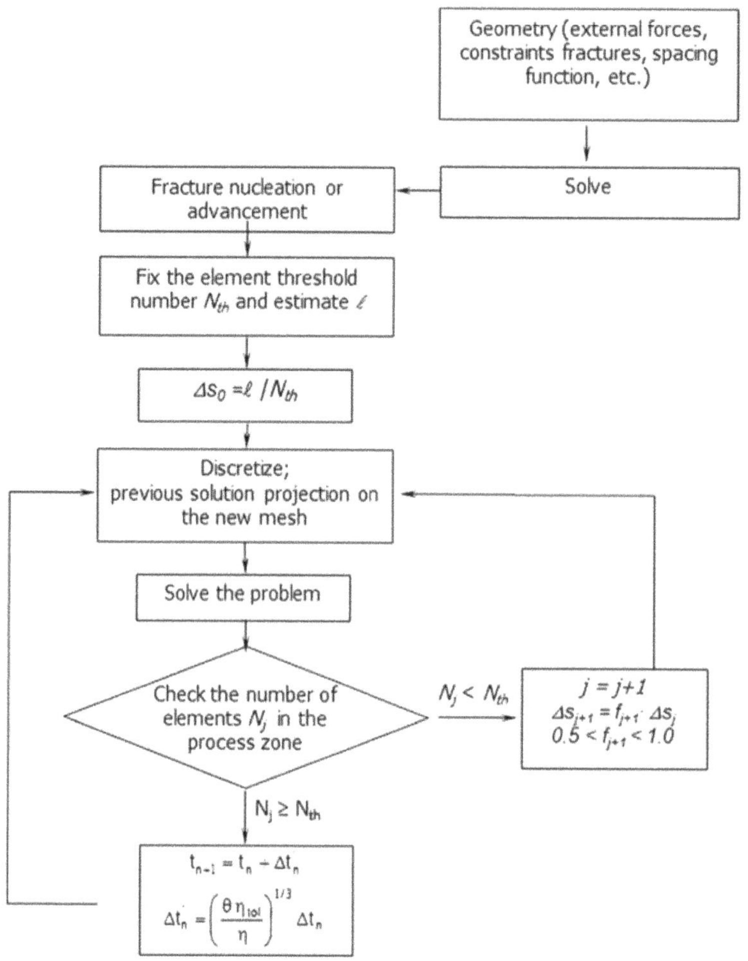

Figure 16 Flow chart.

Conclusions

A fully coupled model for pressure-induced cohesive fracture in a saturated porous medium and its solution by the finite element method has been shown. The model is of the discrete crack type and requires continuous updating of the mesh as the crack tip advances. This is achieved with powerful mesh generators. Three types of refinement are necessary to obtain mesh-independent results: a refinement over the domain of the Zienkiewicz-Zhu type, an element threshold number over the process zone and a refinement in time, here with DGT. The results show that in case of pressure induced fracture with pressure exchange and flow between the fracture and the surrounding medium the crack tip advances stepwise. This was found also by few other authors. Smooth diagrams are found on the contrary in a thermo-elastic fracture which is a coupled problem but with stress-free fracture surfaces. From a comparison of results obtained with different methods by other authors, it appears that in some situations a particular adopted method hides the problems discussed in this paper because the required refinements clash with the *raison d'être* of such methods like XFEM or PUFEM (adoption of rough meshes). This is the reason why 'the physical phenomenon challenges the numerical scheme' [18] and why several authors dealing with hydraulic fracturing have not noticed the peculiar behaviour shown here. Also, two-step procedures may introduce some bias in the solution. Two different explanations are found in the literature for the discussed phenomena: one invokes pressure drop [2] and the other pressure peak [24] after crack advancement. The respective loading conditions are different, but the question deserves further scrutiny. Finally, the stepwise advancement may be relevant for earthquake engineering, see e.g. the resemblance between the obtained data of [2] and magnitude records of earthquakes. In many earthquake-prone regions, there is plenty of water available at the level where the rupture takes place [38,39]. The problem solved in [17] has been solved again with XFEM and finer mesh in 40] and the steps in the fracture advancement featured in [17] disappeared. This implies that XFEM yields a smooth solution for a phenomenon which in nature is not smooth: as shown in [2] hydraulic fracturing exhibits avalanche behaviour and hints of Self-Organized Criticality.

Appendix

The flow chart of Figure 16 shows the numerical procedure adopted with particular emphasis on the refinement part.

Competing interests

The authors declare that they have no competing interests.

Authors' contribution

SS developed the code, devised the crack tip advancement procedure and carried out the simulations BS drafted the manuscript and explained the results in light of new findings in literature. All authors read and approved the final manuscript.

Author details

[1]Institute of system science ISIB – CNR, corso Stati Uniti 4, Padua 35127, Italy. [2]Department of Civil, Environmental and Architectural Engineering, University of Padua, 9 via Marzolo, Padua 35123, Italy.

References

1. Vidic RD, Brantley SE, Vandenbossche JM, Joxtheimer D, Abad JD (2013) Impact of shale gas development on regional water quality. Science 340:826–836
2. Tzschichholz F, Herrmann HJ (1995) Simulations of pressure fluctuations and acoustic emission in hydraulic fracturing. Phys Rev E 5:1961–1970
3. Ellsworth WL (2013) Injection induced earthquakes. Science 341:142–150
4. Perkins TK, Kern LR (1961) Widths of hydraulic fractures. SPE J 222:937–949
5. Rice JR, Cleary MP (1976) Some basic stress diffusion solutions for fluid saturated elastic porous media with compressible constituents. Rev Geophs Space Phys 14:227–241
6. Cleary MP (1978) Moving singularities in elasto-diffusive solids with applications to fracture propagation. Int J Solids Struct 14:81–97
7. Huang NC, Russel SG (1985) Hydraulic fracturing of a saturated porous medium—I: general theory. Theor Appl Fract Mech 4:201–213
8. Huang NC, Russel SG (1985) Hydraulic fracturing of a saturated porous medium—II: special cases. Theor Appl Fract Mech 4:215–222
9. Detournay E, Cheng AH (1991) Plane strain analysis of a stationary hydraulic fracture in a poroelastic medium. Int J Solids Struct 27:1645–1662
10. Advani SH, Lee TS, Dean RH, Pak CK, Avasthi JM (1997) Consequences of fluid lag in three-dimensional hydraulic fracture. Int J Num Anal Methods Geomech 21:229–240
11. Garagash D, Detournay E (2000) The tip region of a fluid-driven fracture in an elastic medium. J Appl Mech 67:183–192
12. Boone TJ, Ingraffea AR (1990) A numerical procedure for simulation of hydraulically driven fracture propagation in poroelastic media. Int J Num Ana Methods Geomech 14:27–47
13. Carter BJ, Desroches J, Ingraffea AR, Wawrzynek PA (2000) Simulating fully 3-D hydraulic fracturing. In: Zaman M, Booker JR, Gioda G (ed) Modeling in geomechanics. Wiley, Chichester, pp 525–567
14. Schrefler BA, Secchi S, Simoni L (2006) On adaptive refinement techniques in multifield problems including cohesive fracture. Comp Methods Appl Mech Engrg 195:444–461
15. Secchi S, Schrefler BA (2012) A method for 3-D hydraulic fracturing simulation. Int J Fracture 178:245–258
16. Réthoré J, de Borst R, Abellan MA (2008) A two-scale model for fluid flow in an unsaturated porous medium with cohesive cracks. Comput Mech 42:227–238

17. Mohammadnejad T, Khoei AR (2013) Hydromechanical modelling of cohesive crack propagation in multiphase porous media using extended finite element method. Int J Numer Anal Meth Geomech 37:1247–1279
18. Kraaijeveldt F, Huyghe JM, Remmers JJC, de Borst R (2013) 2-D mode one crack propagation in saturated ionized porous media using partition of unity finite elements. J Appl Mech 80:020907-1-12
19. Secchi S, Simoni L, Schrefler BA (2004) Cohesive fracture growth in a thermoelastic bi-material medium. Comput Struct 82:1875–1887
20. Kraaijeveld F (2009) Propagating discontinuities in ionized porous media, Dissertation. Eindhoven University of Technology
21. Kraaijeveldt F, Huyghe JM, Remmers JJC, de Borst R, Baaijens FPT (2014) Shearing in osmoelastic fully saturated media: a mesh-independent model. Engineering Fracture Mechanics. in press
22. Barenblatt GI (1959) The formation of equilibrium cracks during brittle fracture: general ideas and hypotheses: axially-symmetric cracks. J Appl Math Mech 23:622–636
23. Remij EW, Pizzoccolo F, Remmers JJ, Smeulders D, Huyghe JM (2013) Nucleation and mixed-mode crack propagation in porous material. ASCE, Poromechanics V, pp 2260–2269. doi:10.1061/9780784412992.247
24. Pizzocolo F, Hyughe JM, Ito K (2013) Mode I crack propagation in hydrogels is stepwise. Eng Fract Mech 97:72–79
25. Dugdale DS (1960) Yielding of steel sheets containing slits. J Mech Phys Solids 8:100–104
26. Hilleborg A, Modeer M, Petersson PE (1976) Analysis of crack formation and crack growth in concrete by means of fracture mechanics and finite elements. Cem Concr Res 6:773–782
27. Camacho GT, Ortiz M (1996) Computational modelling of impact damage in brittle materials. Int J Solids Struct 33:2899–2938
28. Lewis RW, Schrefler BA (1998) The finite element method in the static and dynamic deformation and consolidation of porous media. Wiley, Chichester
29. Witherspoon PA, Wang JSY, Iwai KJE, Gale JE (1980) Validity of cubic law for fluid flow in a deformable rock fracture. Water Resour Res 16:1016–1024
30. Li XD, Wiberg NE (1998) Implementation and adaptivity of a space-time finite element method for structural dynamics. Comp Methods Appl Mech Engrg 156:211–229
31. Secchi S, Simoni L, Schrefler BA (2008) Numerical difficulties and computational procedures for thermo-hydro-mechanical coupled problems of saturated porous media. Comput Mech 43:179–189
32. Secchi S, Simoni L (2003) An improved procedure for 2-D unstructured Delaunay mesh generation. Adv Eng Softw 34:217–234
33. Secchi S, Simoni L, Schrefler BA (2007) Numerical procedure for discrete fracture propagation in porous materials. Int J Num Anal Methods Geomech 31:331–345
34. Zhu JZ, Zienkiewic OC (1988) Adaptive techniques in the finite element method. Com Appl Num Methods 4:197–204
35. Rank E, Katz C, Werner H (1983) On the importance of the discrete maximum principle in transient analysis using finite element methods. Int J Num Methods Engng 19:1771–1782
36. Bae JS, Krishnaswamy S (2001) Subinterfacial cracks in bimaterial systems subjected to mechanical and thermal loading. Eng Fract Mech 68:1081–1094
37. ICOLD (1999) Fifth international benchmark workshop on numerical analysis of dams. Theme A2, Denver, Colorado
38. Doglioni C, Barba S, Carminati E, Riguzzi F (2013) Fault on-off fluids response. Geoscience Frontiers, pp 1–14. doi.org/10.1016/j.gsf.2013.08.004
39. Kelbert A, Schultz A, Egbert G (2009) Global electromagnetic induction constraints on transition-zone water content variations. Nature 460:1003–1006. doi:10.1038/nature08257
40. Mohammadnejad T, Khoei AR (2013) An extended finite element method for hydraulic fracture propagation in deformable porous media with the cohesive crack model. Finite Elements in Analysis and Design 73:77–95

7

Grain scale simulation of local deformation behavior

Tung Van Phan[1,2]

Correspondence:
phanvantung@dtu.edu.vn
[1] R&D Institute, Duy Tan University, 25/K7 Quang Trung, Da Nang 55000, Vietnam
[2] Department of Civil and Environmental Engineering, Faculty of Engineering, National University of Singapore, 1 Engineering Drive 2, Singapore 117576, Singapore

Abstract

In this work, a full-field finite element simulation of a heterogeneous DC04 steel microstructure identified from two-dimensional (2D) electron backscatter diffraction (EBSD) data is performed under a macroscopic tensile deformation. After discretization procedure by finite elements, the EBSD microstructure is subjected to homogeneous displacement boundary conditions approximately describing a large strain uniaxial tensile test. A crystal plasticity model applied on integration points of FE method is used to simulate the deformation behavior and the grain orientation evolution. The simulated grain orientation fields are compared to experimental measurements of the specimen after the tensile test at different deformation levels.

Background

Most of the metals used in industrial processes are polycrystalline materials. They are aggregates of approximately single crystals in grains with different crystal orientations. The anisotropic plasticity of polycrystalline materials is mainly caused by non-uniform distributions of crystal orientations [1]. Therefore, the analysis of the crystallographic texture, i.e., preferred crystal orientations, plays an important role when investigating the macroscopic material behavior. Crystallographic texture data allow for the characterization and prediction of the anisotropic plasticity in heterogeneous materials by using statistical models. Some representative studies of different polycrystalline materials with focus on the texture evolution are given, e.g., by [2-10]. In the intensive increase of computer powerful tool, modelling and simulation have contributed to predict the mechanical behavior and to facilitate the material design with particular properties. This issue often requires a computational framework based on the linking between the constitutive law describing physical phenomenon and the experimental information at the mesoscopic and microscopic level. The experimental electron backscatter diffraction (EBSD) technique, known as scanning electron microscope (SEM)-based technique, has become a major tool in measuring crystal orientations from a polycrystalline structure. A common application is the use of orientation data at every Gauss integration point in finite element (FE) simulations of crystal plasticity models. Hence, a grain scale simulation of the polycrystalline structure could be performed to describe the grain orientation evolution.

In this paper, a heat-treated DC04 steel microstructure identified from two-dimensional (2D) EBSD data is considered. A grain structure model is constructed based on the DC04 steel microstructure identified by a Matlab toolbox MTEX. After discretized by finite elements with one element over thickness, a grain scale simulation of the polycrystalline DC04 steel sample cut from a tensile specimen is performed within the finite strain crystal plasticity framework. The crystal plasticity model accounting for specified grain orientations is applied at Gauss integration points of finite elements of the corresponding grains simultaneously. The experimentally observed local grain orientations and reorientations in the polycrystalline sample will be predicted and evaluated at different deformation states. Subsequently, the simulated grain reorientation fields are compared to experimental measurements of the DC04 sample after the tensile test at different deformation levels.

Notation. Throughout the text, a second-order tensor and a fourth-order tensor are $\boldsymbol{A} = A_{ij}\boldsymbol{e}_i \otimes \boldsymbol{e}_j$ and $\mathbb{A} = A_{ijkl}\boldsymbol{e}_i \otimes \boldsymbol{e}_j \otimes \boldsymbol{e}_k \otimes \boldsymbol{e}_l$, respectively, where $\{\boldsymbol{e}_i\}$ represents an orthonormal basis of the three-dimensional (3D) Euclidean space. Symmetric and traceless tensors are designated by a prime, e.g., $\boldsymbol{A}'$. The set of proper orthogonal second-order tensors is specified by $SO(3)$. The scalar product, the dyadic product, and the Frobenius norm are denoted by $\boldsymbol{A} \cdot \boldsymbol{B} = \mathrm{tr}(\boldsymbol{A}^\top \boldsymbol{B}) = \mathrm{tr}(\boldsymbol{A}\boldsymbol{B}^\top)$, $\boldsymbol{A} \otimes \boldsymbol{B}$, and $\|\boldsymbol{A}\| = (\boldsymbol{A} \cdot \boldsymbol{A})^{1/2}$, respectively. Here, $\mathrm{tr}(\cdot)$ represents the trace of a second-order tensor. A linear mapping of second-order tensors is written as $\boldsymbol{A} = \mathbb{C}[\boldsymbol{B}]$.

Methods

The first subsection introduces the constitutive equations of a crystal plasticity material model applied at Gauss integration points of FE model. The constitutive model is described via an ABAQUS user subroutine UMAT allowing to define the mechanical behavior of material. The EBSD measurement technique to obtain the crystallographic texture data set is discussed in the second subsection. By using this experimental EBSD technique, the different EBSD data sets representing the deformation states of a tensile specimen of the heat-treated DC04 steel are shown. In addition, a Matlab toolbox MTEX allowing to import the EBSD data formats and to obtain an image of the grain structure is introduced. In the third subsection, the microstructural image of the tensile specimen at the initial state is discretized by finite elements. The FE mesh is used as an input data for performing crystal plasticity simulations on the grain scale into the ABAQUS/CAE software.

Constitutive model on a single crystal

Elastic law

An elastoviscoplastic constitutive model on a single crystal is introduced. The model is described in the context of large strain theory. Conceptually, the model is relied on the assumption of small elastic strains, finite plastic strains, and rotations. Plastic deformation is assumed to be the result from distinct slip mechanisms on specific crystallographic planes. The theory was developed in the works of [2,4]. The deformation gradient is decomposed multiplicatively into an elastic part $\boldsymbol{F}_e$ and a plastic part $\boldsymbol{F}_p$ [11,12]

$$\boldsymbol{F} = \boldsymbol{F}_e \boldsymbol{F}_p. \tag{1}$$

The plastic deformation $\boldsymbol{F}_p$ is the plastic contribution from crystallographic slips. The elastic deformation $\boldsymbol{F}_e$ accounts for the lattice distortion, which is inherently elastic. As the elastic strains are assumed to be small, a linearized relation between a conjugate pair of stress and strain measures is applicable for the description of the elastic behavior. Here, the elastic law is assumed to be given by

$$\boldsymbol{\tau} = \boldsymbol{F}_e \tilde{\mathbb{C}}[\boldsymbol{E}_e] \boldsymbol{F}_e^T. \tag{2}$$

The Kirchhoff stress tensor is given by $\boldsymbol{\tau} = \det(\boldsymbol{F})\boldsymbol{\sigma}$, with $\boldsymbol{\sigma}$ being the Cauchy stress tensor. Green's strain tensor is defined by

$$\boldsymbol{E}_e = (\boldsymbol{C}_e - \boldsymbol{I})/2, \tag{3}$$

with $\boldsymbol{I}$ being the second-order unit tensor and the right (elastic) Cauchy-Green tensor

$$\boldsymbol{C}_e = \boldsymbol{F}_e^{\mathrm{T}} \boldsymbol{F}_e. \tag{4}$$

The reference stiffness tensor $\tilde{\mathbb{C}}$ with respect to the orthonormal basis $\boldsymbol{B}_\alpha$ is given by

$$\tilde{\mathbb{C}} = \tilde{C}_{\alpha\beta} \boldsymbol{B}_\alpha \otimes \boldsymbol{B}_\beta = \begin{bmatrix} C_{1111} & C_{1122} & C_{1122} & 0 & 0 & 0 \\ & C_{1111} & C_{1122} & 0 & 0 & 0 \\ & & C_{1111} & 0 & 0 & 0 \\ & & & 2C_{1212} & 0 & 0 \\ & \text{sym.} & & & 2C_{1212} & 0 \\ & & & & & 2C_{1212} \end{bmatrix} \boldsymbol{B}_\alpha \otimes \boldsymbol{B}_\beta. \tag{5}$$

The components $\tilde{C}_{\alpha\beta}$ are defined by $\tilde{C}_{\alpha\beta} = \boldsymbol{B}_\alpha \cdot \tilde{\mathbb{C}}\left[\boldsymbol{B}_\beta\right]$. The orthonormal base tensors $\boldsymbol{B}_\alpha$ used are given by [13]. Due to the cubic material under consideration, the stiffness tensor $\tilde{\mathbb{C}}$ has three independent elastic constants.

Flow rule and hardening law

A rate-dependent flow rule specifies the time evolution of the plastic part $\boldsymbol{F}_p$ of $\boldsymbol{F}$

$$\dot{\boldsymbol{F}}_p \boldsymbol{F}_p^{-1} = \sum_\alpha \dot{\gamma}_\alpha \tilde{\boldsymbol{M}}_\alpha, \quad \dot{\gamma}_\alpha = \dot{\gamma}_0 \operatorname{sgn}(\tau_\alpha) \left| \frac{\tau_\alpha}{\tau^C} \right|^m, \tag{6}$$

where the exponent m quantifies the strain rate sensitivity of the material, $\dot{\gamma}_0$ is a reference rate, and $\tilde{\boldsymbol{M}}_\alpha$ is the Schmid tensor. τ^C denotes the critical resolved shear stress. A rate-dependent Kocks-Mecking hardening model see, e.g., [7,14]

$$\dot{\tau}^C\left(\tau_\alpha, \tau^C\right) = \Theta_0 \left(1 - \frac{\tau^C}{\tau_V^C\left(\tau_\alpha, \tau^C\right)}\right) \dot{\gamma}\left(\tau_\alpha, \tau^C\right) \tag{7}$$

is used, where the critical Voce stress is specified by

$$\tau_V^C\left(\tau_\alpha, \tau^C\right) = \tau_{V0}^C \left(\frac{\dot{\gamma}\left(\tau_\alpha, \tau^C\right)}{\dot{\gamma}_0}\right)^{\frac{1}{n}} \tag{8}$$

with the asymptotic critical resolved shear stress τ_{V0}^C and the initial hardening modulus Θ_0. The rate of the accumulated plastic slip is computed by

$$\dot{\gamma} = \sum_\alpha \left| \dot{\gamma}_\alpha \left(\tau_\alpha, \tau^C\right) \right|. \tag{9}$$

The resolved shear stress is defined by

$$\tau_\alpha = \boldsymbol{T}_e' \cdot \tilde{\boldsymbol{M}}_\alpha, \tag{10}$$

where

$$\boldsymbol{T}_e = \boldsymbol{C}_e \boldsymbol{S}_e^{\mathrm{2PK}} \tag{11}$$

denotes the Mandel stress tensor. The second Piola-Kirchhoff in the undistorted state is given by $\boldsymbol{S}_e^{2PK} = J\boldsymbol{F}_e^{-1}\boldsymbol{\tau}\boldsymbol{F}_e^{-\top}$. $J = \det(\boldsymbol{F}_e)$ is the determinant of $\boldsymbol{F}_e$. The Schmid or slip system tensors are rank-one tensors, which are defined in terms of the slip direction $\tilde{\boldsymbol{d}}_\alpha$ and slip plane normal $\tilde{\boldsymbol{n}}_\alpha$ in the undistorted configuration

$$\tilde{\boldsymbol{M}}_\alpha = \tilde{\boldsymbol{d}}_\alpha \otimes \tilde{\boldsymbol{n}}_\alpha. \tag{12}$$

The initial conditions for the ordinary differential equation are $\boldsymbol{F}_e(0) = \boldsymbol{Q}(t=0) \in SO(3)$ and the initial critical resolved shear stress $\tau^C(0) = \tau_0^C$. The crystal orientation is given by a proper orthogonal tensor $\boldsymbol{Q}(t) = \boldsymbol{g}_i(t) \otimes \boldsymbol{e}_i$, where the vectors $\boldsymbol{g}_i$ and $\boldsymbol{e}_i$ denote the orthonormal lattice vectors and the fixed orthonormal basis, respectively. The initial orientation of the single crystal $\boldsymbol{Q}(t=0) = \boldsymbol{g}_i(0) \otimes \boldsymbol{e}_i$ is defined in terms of the orthonormal lattice vectors $\boldsymbol{g}_i(0)$ at the time $t = 0$. As shown in [15], intrinsic characteristics of body-centered cubic (BCC) crystals are revealed by using a proper parameter identification method. The authors applied a BCC crystal plasticity model to perform uniaxial tension simulations at the material point level for different types of BCC single crystals and compare these with experiments. The results indicate that {110} and {112} planes are identified as intrinsic slip systems of BCC crystals, but not the {123} plane. Therefore, in this work, the attention is focused on a combination of {110}⟨111⟩ and {112}⟨111⟩ slip system families (Figure 1). There are two slip directions in each of the slip planes along the main diagonals of the cube. In total, there are 24 slip systems shown in Tables 1 and 2.

Experimental identification based on EBSD data of DC04 steel tensile samples

EBSD measurement

In recent years, EBSD has become an important technique for the quantitative characterization of different microstructural properties such as the grain size, the grain boundary structure, and the orientation distribution (see, e.g., [17-19]). The main objective of the technique is to obtain spatially resolved crystallographic information by a SEM. For every point analyzed on a sample, the position, the phase, and the orientation information are stored. The stored data set is a database of measurements produced by scanning the beam in a regular grid over the sample. The data format is shown in Figure 2 (left) for the microstructure sample of the mentioned DC04 steel at the initial state. Each row is a measurement point in the map, and each column is one of the several measured parameters. In the first column, each match unit contains the information necessary to model the EBSD pattern produced by the expected phase in the sample. The phase values 1 indicate the expected phases of ferrite, while the phase values 0 correspond to measurement errors.

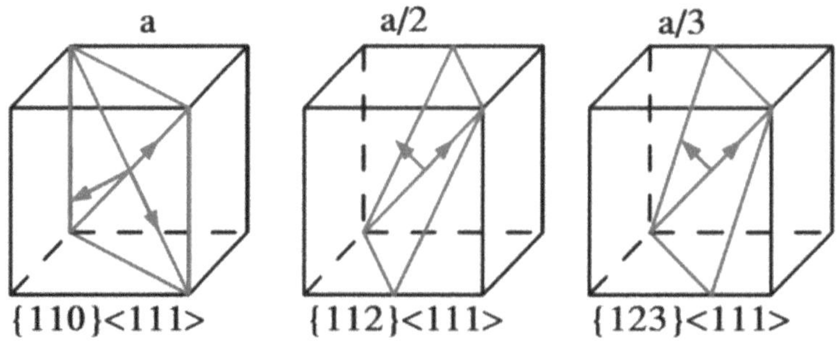

Figure 1 BCC slip systems of the unit cell (cubic crystal).

Table 1 12 BCC slip systems of {110}⟨111⟩ [16]

	Slip system (α)					
	1	2	3	4	5	6
$\sqrt{2}\left[\tilde{n}_i^\alpha\right]$	[1, −1, 0]	[1, −1, 0]	[1, 0, −1]	[1, 0, −1]	[0, 1, −1]	[0, 1, −1]
$\sqrt{3}\left[\tilde{d}_i^\alpha\right]$	[1, 1, 1]	[1, 1, −1]	[1, 1, 1]	[1, −1, 1]	[1, 1, 1]	[−1, 1, 1]
	7	8	9	10	11	12
$\sqrt{2}\left[\tilde{n}_i^\alpha\right]$	[1, 1, 0]	[1, 1, 0]	[1, 0, 1]	[1, 0, 1]	[0, 1, 1]	[0, 1, 1]
$\sqrt{3}\left[\tilde{d}_i^\alpha\right]$	[−1, 1, 1]	[1, −1, 1]	[−1, 1, 1]	[1, 1, −1]	[1, −1, 1]	[1, 1, −1]

The second and third column are the X and Y positions of the measurement points. Their dimensional unit is micrometer [μm]. The rotation is commonly parameterized by a triple of Euler angles ϕ_1, Φ, ϕ_2 and is described through a 3×3 orthogonal matrix given by

$$Q_{ij} = \begin{bmatrix} \cos\phi_1 & -\sin\phi_1 & 0 \\ \sin\phi_1 & \cos\phi_1 & 0 \\ 0 & 0 & 1 \end{bmatrix} \begin{bmatrix} 1 & 0 & 0 \\ 0 & \cos\Phi & -\sin\Phi \\ 0 & \sin\Phi & \cos\Phi \end{bmatrix} \begin{bmatrix} \cos\phi_2 & -\sin\phi_2 & 0 \\ \sin\phi_2 & \cos\phi_2 & 0 \\ 0 & 0 & 1 \end{bmatrix} \quad (13)$$

$$= \begin{bmatrix} \cos\phi_1\cos\phi_2 - \sin\phi_1\cos\Phi\sin\phi_2 & -\cos\phi_1\sin\phi_2 - \sin\phi_1\cos\Phi\cos\phi_2 & \sin\Phi\sin\phi_1 \\ \sin\phi_1\cos\phi_2 + \cos\phi_1\cos\Phi\sin\phi_2 & -\sin\phi_1\sin\phi_2 + \cos\phi_1\cos\Phi\cos\phi_2 & -\sin\Phi\cos\phi_1 \\ \sin\Phi\sin\phi_2 & \sin\Phi\cos\phi_2 & \cos\Phi \end{bmatrix}, \quad (14)$$

where the three Euler angles ϕ_1, Φ, and ϕ_2, shown schematically [20] in Figure 2 (right), are used to describe the crystallographic orientation of the crystals in relation to a reference coordinate system. In the database, these three Euler angles are recorded in the fourth, fifth, and sixth columns, respectively. The other parameters are neglected for the consideration.

Identification of microstructures and orientation information

An experimental tensile specimen of heat-treated low-carbon DC04 steel [21] is discussed here. The specimen geometry is width $w = 5$ mm, gauge length $L_0 = 15$ mm, and thickness $t = 1$ mm. From such specimen, a tiny sample was cut by laser rays with the same thickness. Through the EBSD technique in the scanning electron microscope, an initial raw database of such a sample is obtained.

Recently, a software package MTEX [22,23], a Matlab toolbox developed since 1997, is used for the quantitative analysis of experimental textures. The obtained EBSD database has been processed by MTEX to identify the grains and their boundaries. The EBSD sample database is then imported into the MTEX toolbox to identify the corresponding

Table 2 12 BCC slip systems of {112}⟨111⟩ [15]

	Slip system (α)					
	1	2	3	4	5	6
$\sqrt{6}\left[\tilde{n}_i^\alpha\right]$	[1, 1, 2]	[−1, 1, 2]	[1, −1, 2]	[1, 1, −2]	[1, 2, 1]	[−1, 2, 1]
$\sqrt{3}\left[\tilde{d}_i^\alpha\right]$	[1, 1, −1]	[1, −1, 1]	[−1, 1, 1]	[1, 1, 1]	[1, −1, 1]	[1, 1, −1]
	7	8	9	10	11	12
$\sqrt{6}\left[\tilde{n}_i^\alpha\right]$	[1, −2, 1]	[1, 2, −1]	[2, 1, 1]	[−2, 1, 1]	[2, −1, 1]	[2, 1, −1]
$\sqrt{3}\left[\tilde{d}_i^\alpha\right]$	[1, 1, 1]	[−1, 1, 1]	[−1, 1, 1]	[1, 1, 1]	[1, 1, −1]	[1, −1, 1]

Phase	X	Y	Euler1	Euler2	Euler3	MAD	BC	BS	Bands	Error	Index
0	0	0	0.0000	0.0000	0.0000	0.0000	89	153	0	3	1.0000
1	2	0	57.574	9.9495	30.985	0.2763	89	253	7	0	0.0000
1	4	0	58.866	10.229	29.698	0.3906	93	242	7	0	0.0000
⋮	⋮	⋮	⋮	⋮	⋮	⋮	⋮	⋮	⋮	⋮	⋮
⋮	⋮	⋮	⋮	⋮	⋮	⋮	⋮	⋮	⋮	⋮	⋮
1	926	468	246.20	43.831	44.345	0.3089	118	238	7	0	0.0000
1	928	468	246.12	43.781	44.340	0.4902	118	238	7	0	0.0000
1	930	468	246.15	43.786	44.487	0.4097	116	241	7	0	0.0000
⋮	⋮	⋮	⋮	⋮	⋮	⋮	⋮	⋮	⋮	⋮	⋮
⋮	⋮	⋮	⋮	⋮	⋮	⋮	⋮	⋮	⋮	⋮	⋮
1	998	764	329.37	41.729	34.829	0.4954	102	255	7	0	0.0000
1	1000	764	329.34	41.658	34.866	0.5155	98	249	7	0	0.0000
1	1002	764	329.40	41.797	34.753	0.4293	107	255	7	0	0.0000

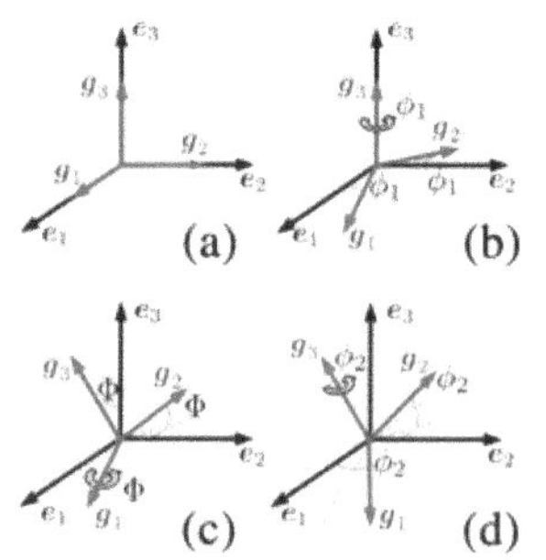

Figure 2 The file format and Euler angles. File format of the raw EBSD data set of the experimental sample at the initial state including 105,000 rows and 7 columns (left) and definition of Euler angles (right).

microstructure. Figure 3 shows an EBSD sample microstructure considered at the initial state. A strain rate of 10^{-3} s^{-1} is applied to the tensile specimen in loading direction. During the tensile test, several EBSD databases have been determined experimentally, and thereby, the evolution of the crystallographic texture is measured at different elongation states (5%, 10%, 15%, and 20%).

By using the MTEX toolbox, these raw EBSD databases are imported to obtain 2D images of grain structures. Two microstructural images of both the raw EBSD data and the clustered EBSD data are shown in Figure 4a,b, repectively, for the initial state of the sample. The grains consisting only of 1 pixel are eliminated in the clustering process of the MTEX toolbox. A clustered EBSD database which consists of identified grains and corresponding point sets is obtained. This database represents the X and Y positions (in μm) and three Euler angles (in degree) of the measurement points. In addition, the grain

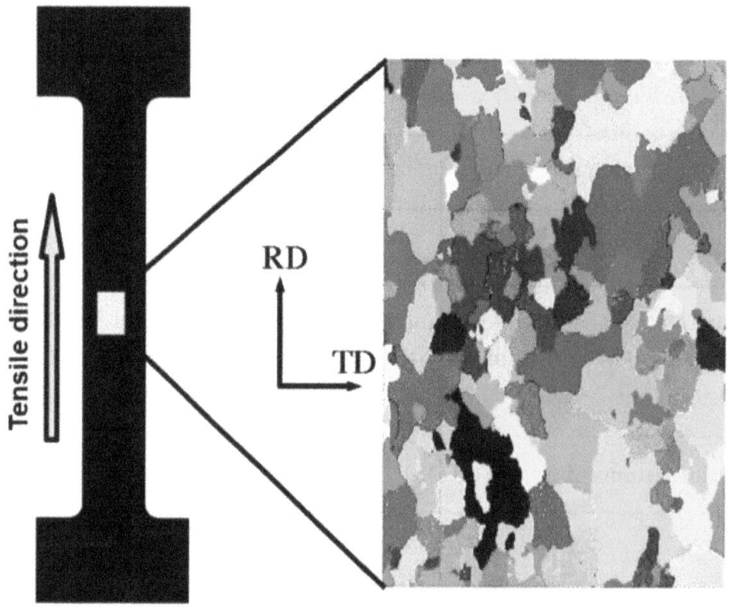

Figure 3 A raw microstructural image of the tiny DC04 steel sample. Raw EBSD microstructural image of a heterogeneous sample cut parallel to rolling direction from a DC04 steel specimen at the initial state. RD, rolling direction; TD, transverse direction. (For interpretation of the references to color in the text, the reader is referred to the web version of the article).

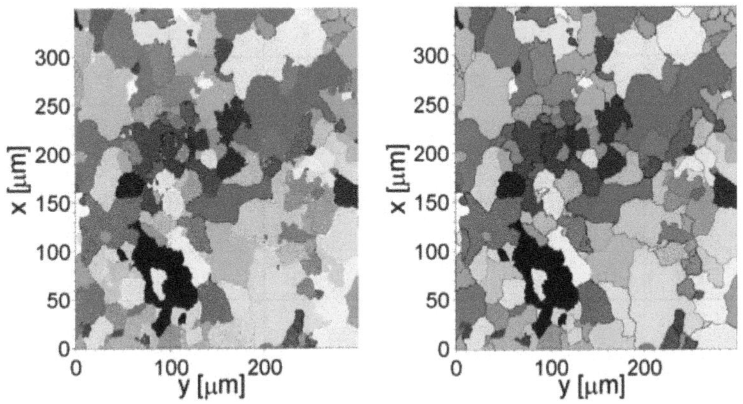

(a) Raw EBSD data set. (b) Clustered EBSD data set.

Figure 4 Microstructural images at the initial state. (a) Raw EBSD data set. **(b)** Clustered EBSD data set.

to which the measurement points belong is indicated in the database. The order numbering of grains and the identification of 574 grains are shown in Figure 5 at the initial state. Additionally, 2D images of the raw EBSD data at different strain states (5%, 10%, 15%, and 20%) are shown in Figure 6. In all microstructural images, each color indicates the lattice orientation in each grain at different states.

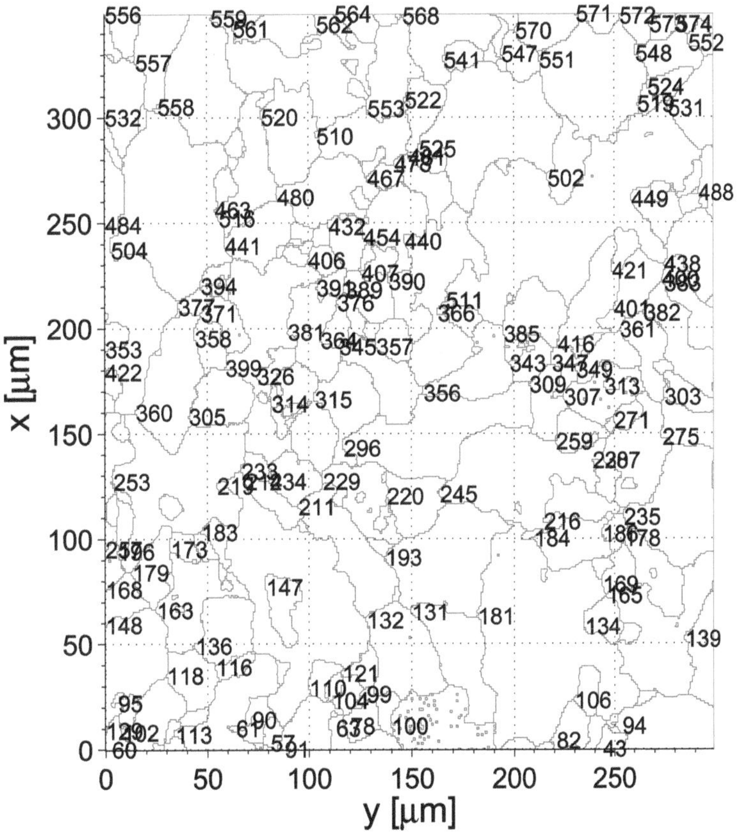

Figure 5 Identification and numbering of grains. Identification and numbering of 574 grains in the microstructural image of clustered data set at the initial state.

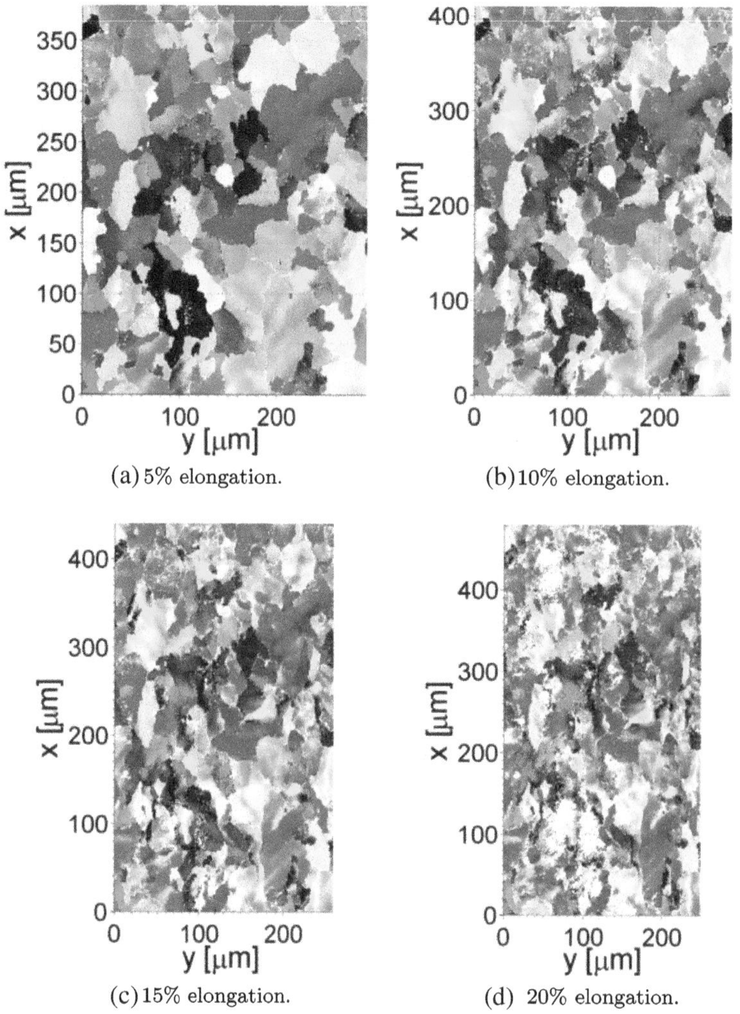

Figure 6 Microstructural images of raw EBSD data sets at different states. (a) 5% elongation. **(b)** 10% elongation. **(c)** 15% elongation. **(d)** 20% elongation.

Some conclusive descriptions of the raw EBSD data are summarized. In the raw EBSD database of the initial state, the total number of columns and rows is 7 and 105,000, respectively. After neglecting measurement errors, in such an EBSD database remain 103,671 rows (or the number of pixels) and 7 columns. The number of measurement errors is 1,329 pixels, i.e., approximately 1.26% of the area fraction. The map size of the raw grain structure in Figure 4a is 349 $\times$ 299 μm. The area of one measurement point is 1 μm^2. For the subsequent strain states, the measurement errors correspond to area fractions of 3.6%, 8.5%, 9.4%, and 18.5%, respectively.

FE modeling and full-field simulation

In this subsection, the microstructural image of the tensile specimen at the initial state shown in Figure 7 (left) is used as input data for performing crystal plasticity simulations on the grain scale. The sample picture is imported into a commercial software Simpleware to construct a computable grain structure model as shown in Figure 7 (right). Simpleware offers two important options for processing and meshing 2D or 3D image data. The

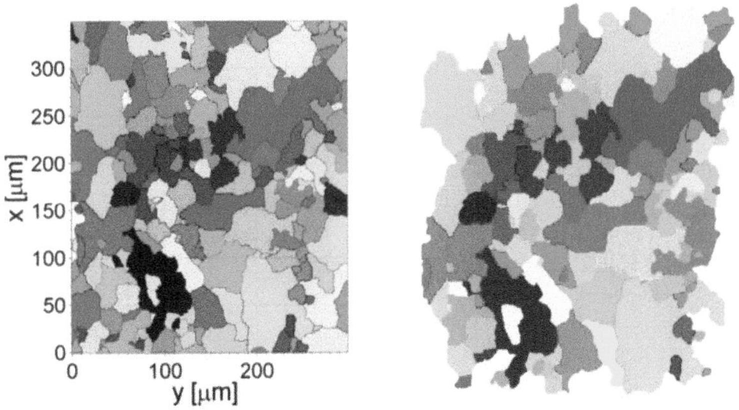

Figure 7 Microstructural image of the tensile specimen at the initial state. Microstructure of heat-treated DC04 steel at the initial state obtained from the clustering process by MTEX toolbox (left) and a microstructure including complete grains constructed by Simpleware software (right).

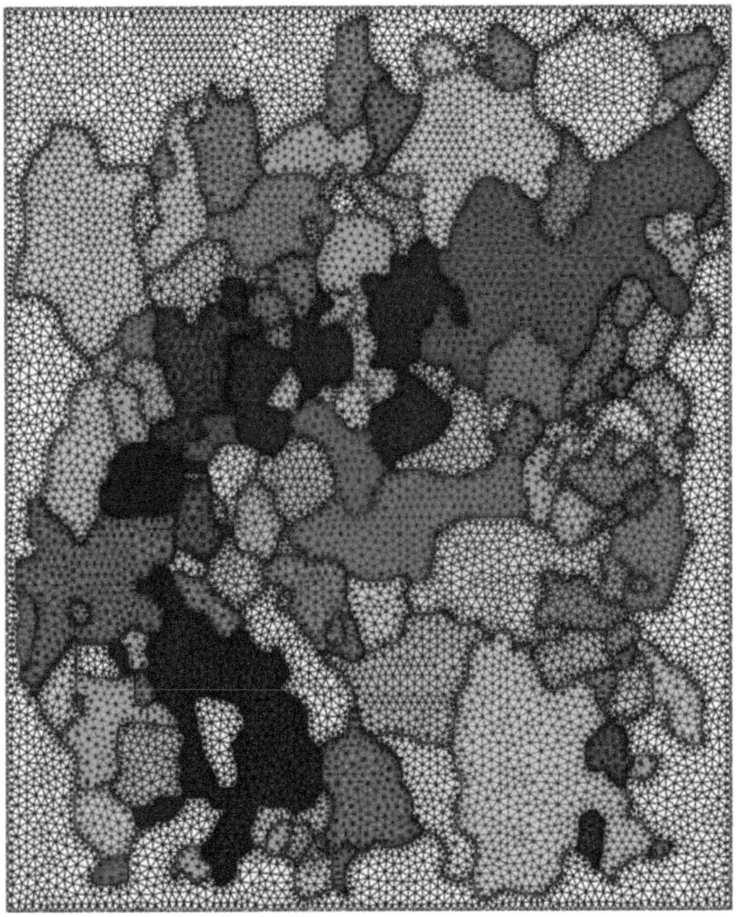

Figure 8 FE model of the microstructure at the initial state.

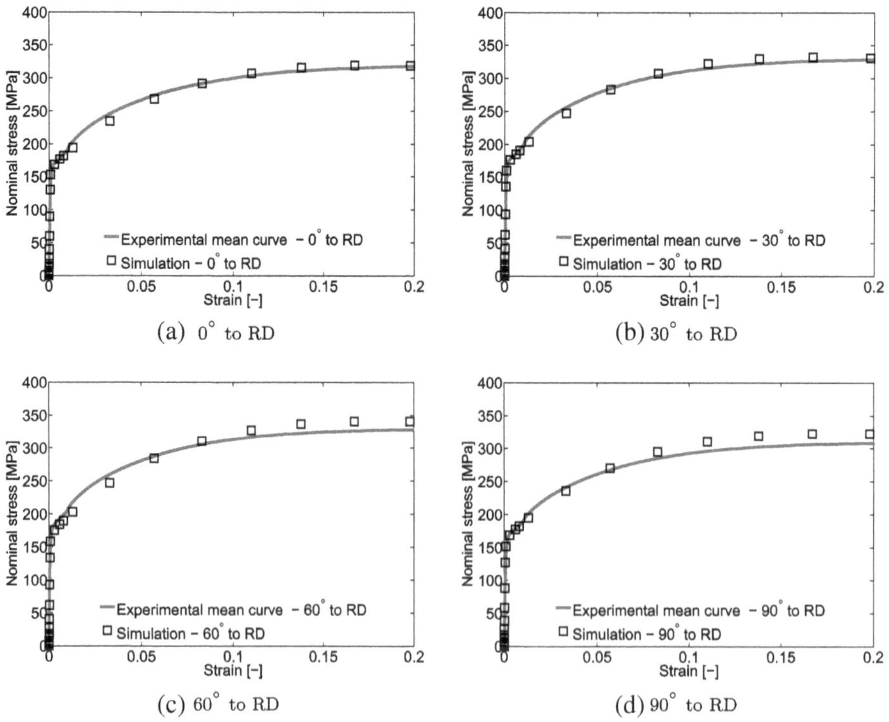

Figure 9 Stress-strain curves in comparison to experimental curves. Numerically determined stress-strain curves in comparison to experimental curves of the Institute of Forming Technology and Lightweight IUL (TU Dortmund University) for different angles to RD [25]. **(a)** 0° to RD. **(b)** 30° to RD. **(c)** 60° to RD. **(d)** 90° to RD.

first one is ScanIP, which is the platform for the image processing, and the second one is ScanFE, which is a fully integrated meshing module for the conversion of masks (or grains) to 2D or 3D FE meshes. The type of elements used in the FE mesh are linear and quadratic hexahedral elements. Details of the software can be found in [24]. Note that the color distribution of grains in Figure 7 (left) is not equal to the one in Figure 7 (right) due to the different conventions of colors between the MTEX and Simpleware software. After the processing steps in ScanIP, a FE output data containing the set of nodes, the set of hexahedral elements, and the set of tetrahedral elements is obtained. The data can be exported in the ABAQUS format with the FE mesh shown in Figure 8. Different colors indicate different crystal orientations of the grains. The white region around the grains

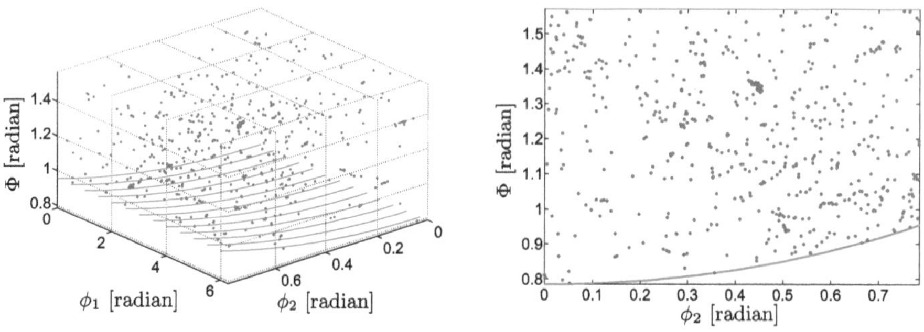

Figure 10 Initial grain orientations in the 3D (left) and 2D (right) fundamental zone $\phi_2 - \Phi$.

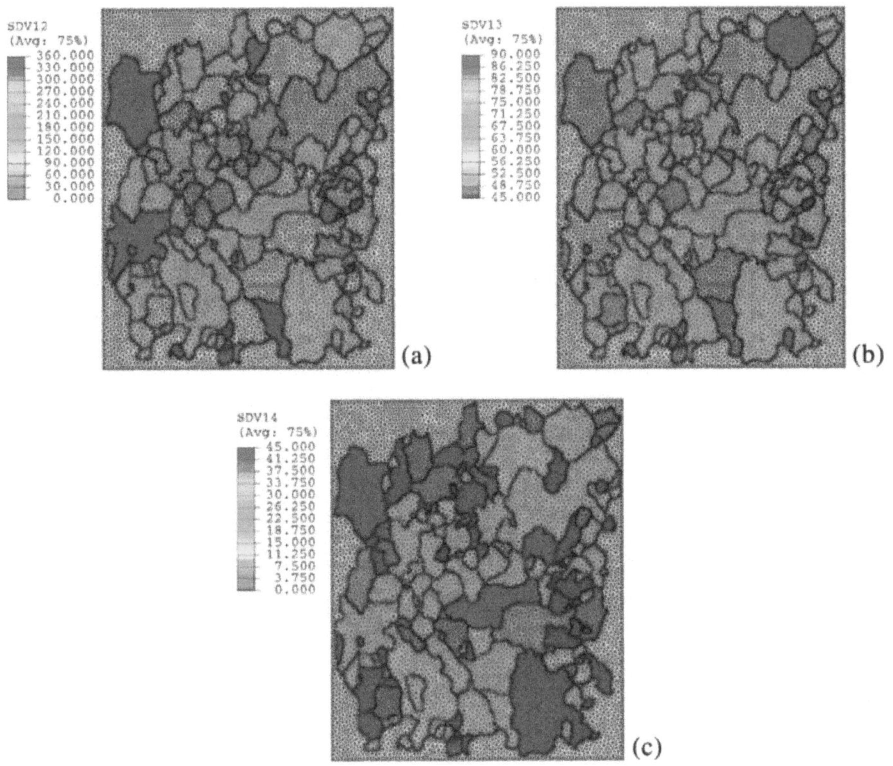

Figure 11 Initial Euler angle distribution [°] in the FE simulation. (a) Angle ϕ_1, **(b)** angle Φ, and **(c)** angle ϕ_2 in the fundamental zone.

was assumed to show an ideal behavior according to the von Mises plasticity model. The elastic properties of steel with Young's modulus ($E = 200$ GPa) and Poisson's ratio ($\nu = 0.3$) are assigned to the ideal von Mises plastic region. For the plastic behavior, the flow parameters $\sigma_{F0} = 180$ MPa, $\sigma_{F\infty} = 303$ MPa, describing the linear hardening, are estimated from the experimental tensile stress-strain curve for 0° to the RD (Figure 9a).

In order to uniquely define the evolution of grains during the FE simulation, initial Euler angles of 45 chosen complete grains are transformed into the cubic fundamental zone. The triple of Euler angles restricted in the cubic fundamental zone is given by

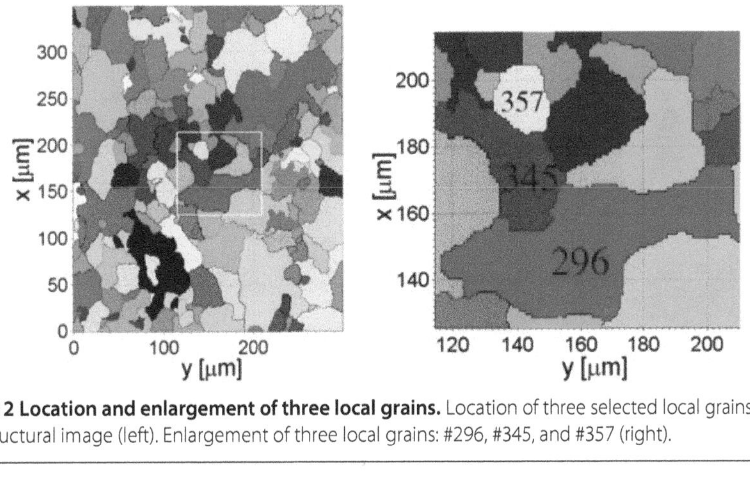

Figure 12 Location and enlargement of three local grains. Location of three selected local grains in the microstructural image (left). Enlargement of three local grains: #296, #345, and #357 (right).

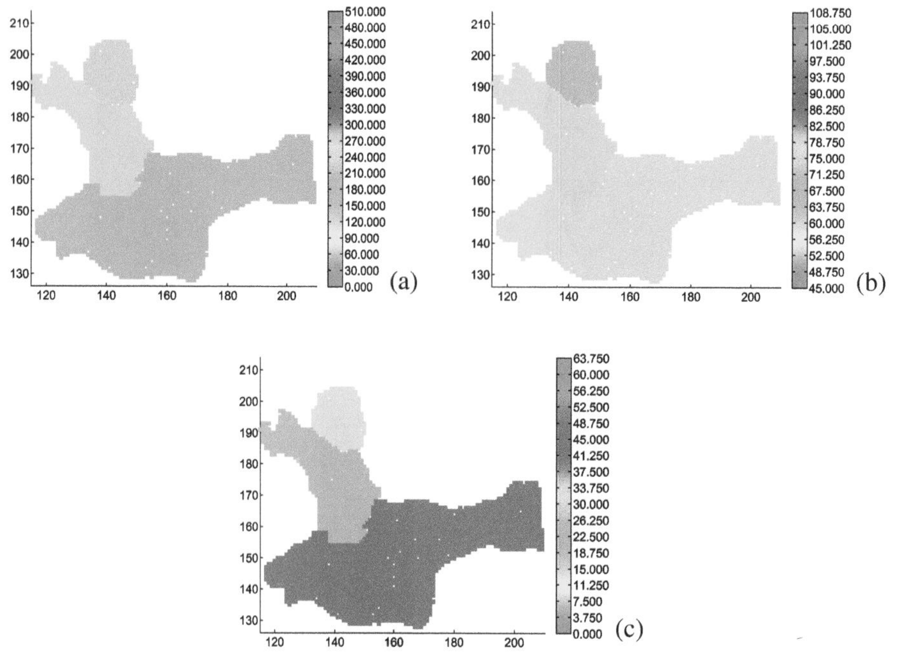

Figure 13 Initial Euler angles of three selected local grains. Using a local analysis for the reduced experiment data set, the initial Euler angles of three selected local grains are as follows: **(a)** angle ϕ_1, **(b)** angle Φ, and **(c)** angle ϕ_2 in the fundamental zone. The unit of Euler angles is [°].

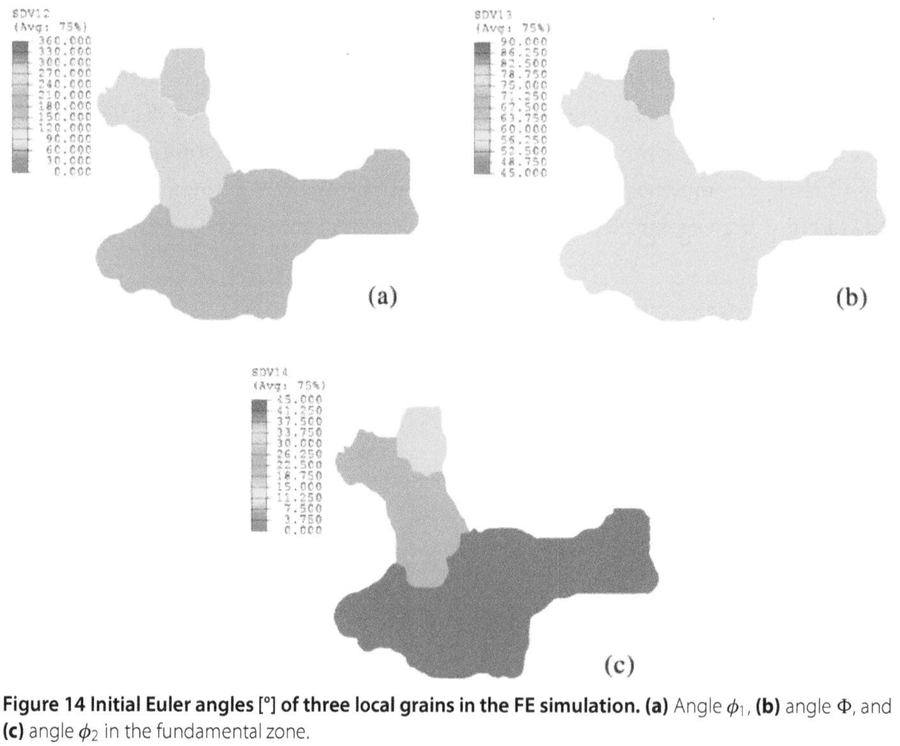

Figure 14 Initial Euler angles [°] of three local grains in the FE simulation. (a) Angle ϕ_1, **(b)** angle Φ, and **(c)** angle ϕ_2 in the fundamental zone.

Table 3 Set of material parameters

	Value
Elastic constants of DC04 steel [27]	
C_{1111}[GPa]	231.5
C_{1122}[GPa]	135.0
C_{1212}[GPa]	116.0
Material parameters for flow and hardening rule [25]	
τ_0^C[MPa]	67 ± 6
τ_{V0}^C[MPa]	130 ± 3
Θ_0[MPa]	755 ± 105
m	20
$\dot{\gamma}_0\left[s^{-1}\right]$	0.001
n	5

$$\phi_1 \in [0, 2\pi) \tag{15}$$

$$\Phi \in \left[f(\phi_2), \pi/2\right] \tag{16}$$

$$\phi_2 \in [0, \pi/4) \tag{17}$$

$$f(\phi_2) = \arccos\left(\frac{\cos(\phi_2)}{\sqrt{1+\cos(\phi_2)^2}}\right). \tag{18}$$

The detailed explanation of the fundamental zone could be found in [10,26]. In Figure 10, the initial crystal orientations of the grains transformed in the fundamental zone are shown. In FE simulation, initial Euler angles of the aforementioned 45 grains are depicted in Figure 11. For the comparison about the grain orientation and reorientation between simulated results and experimental results, three local grains are chosen. Figure 12 shows the location of three local grains and their enlargement in the experimental microstructure. The experimental identification of three initial Euler angles of these three local grains is shown in Figure 13 after transformed in the fundamental zone. It can be seen that the initial Euler angles of these local grains are explicitly shown in the FE simulation (Figure 14) when compared to the identified experimental ones in the same scale color (RGB). The simulation is carried out by using the implicit Euler scheme for time integration and the user subroutine UMAT defining the constitutive law of the crystals introduced in the first subsection. The material parameters shown in Table 3 are used for

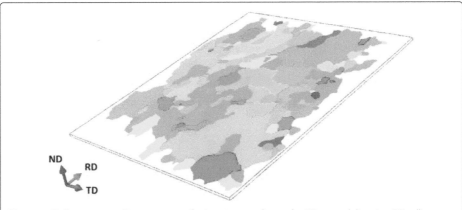

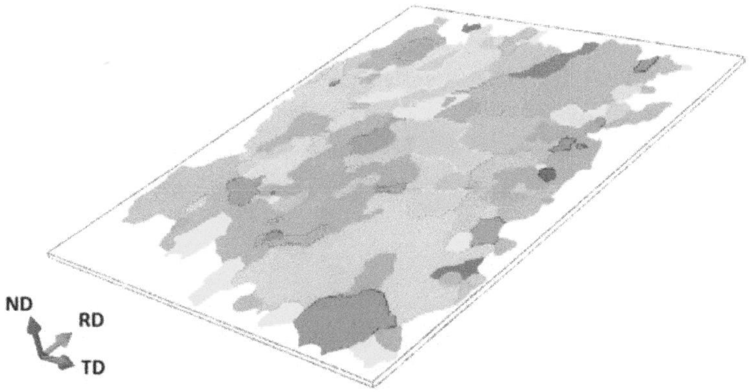

Figure 15 Reference coordinate system of microstructural sample. ND, normal direction; RD, rolling direction; TD, transverse direction.

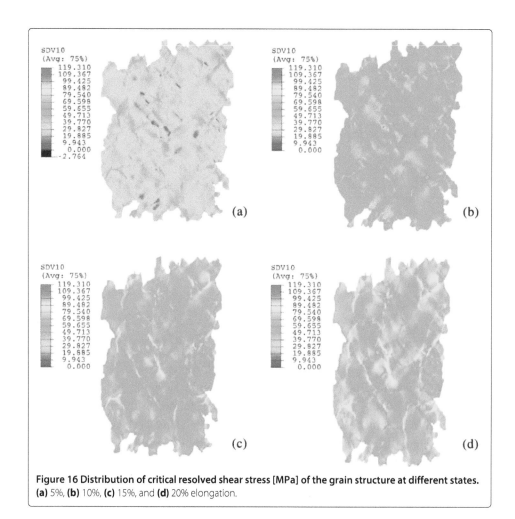

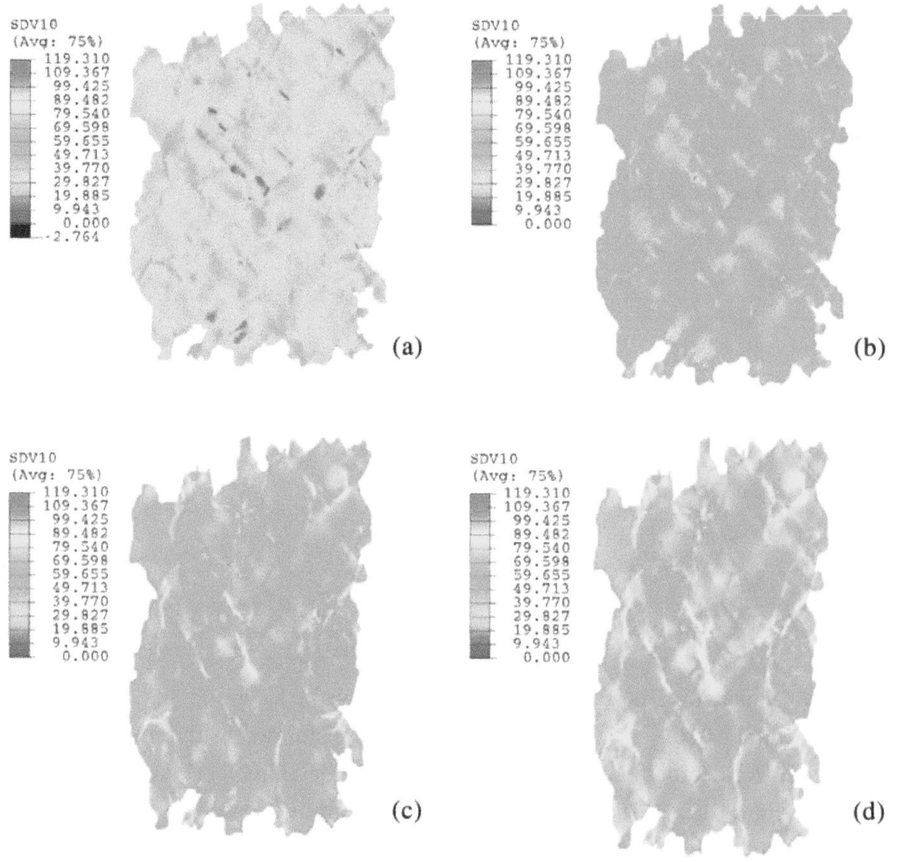

Figure 16 Distribution of critical resolved shear stress [MPa] of the grain structure at different states. **(a)** 5%, **(b)** 10%, **(c)** 15%, and **(d)** 20% elongation.

performing the grain scale simulation. The set of these material parameters are identified by [25] by using tensile stress-strain curves at different angles to RD. The stress-strain curves are shown in Figure 9. For the slip mechanism, the grain scale simulation accounts for the combination of $\{110\}\langle 111\rangle + \{112\}\langle 111\rangle$ slip systems.

Considering in the reference coordinate system of microstructural sample (Figure 15), homogeneous displacement boundary conditions at the outer boundary of the RD-TD plane are applied. The strain in the normal direction (ND) is assumed to be zero. Furthermore, a plane strain state is assumed. The boundary conditions are defined by the ABAQUS subroutine DISP. The displacement vector and the displacement gradient are given by

$$\boldsymbol{u}(\boldsymbol{X}, t) = \boldsymbol{x} - \boldsymbol{X} \tag{19}$$

and

$$\boldsymbol{H} = \mathrm{Grad}(\boldsymbol{u}(\boldsymbol{X}, t)), \tag{20}$$

respectively, where $\boldsymbol{X}$ is the reference position of the material points and $\boldsymbol{x} = \chi_{\kappa}(\boldsymbol{X}, t)$ is the current position at time t. The displacement gradient $\boldsymbol{H}$ can be given in terms of the deformation gradient $\boldsymbol{F}$

$$\boldsymbol{H} = \mathrm{Grad}\ (\boldsymbol{u}(\boldsymbol{X}, t)) = \mathrm{Grad}\ (\boldsymbol{x}) - \boldsymbol{I} = \boldsymbol{F} - \boldsymbol{I} \tag{21}$$

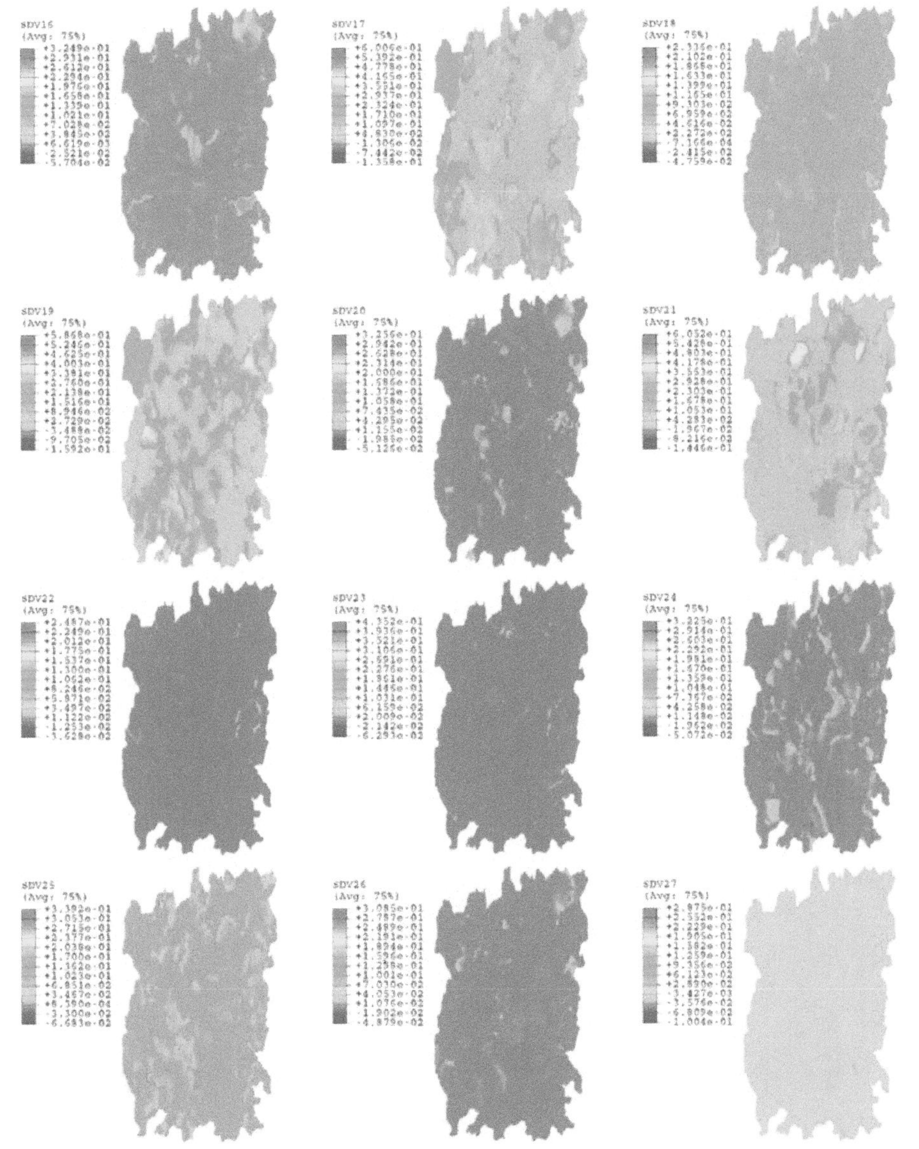

Figure 17 Plastic slip on 12 slip systems {110}⟨111⟩ at 20% elongation. The unit is per second $\left[\mathrm{s}^{-1}\right]$.

assuming the constant velocity gradient for plane strain compression is given by

$$\boldsymbol{L} = \dot{\varepsilon}_0 \begin{bmatrix} \frac{-1}{\sqrt{2}} & 0 & 0 \\ 0 & \frac{1}{\sqrt{2}} & 0 \\ 0 & 0 & 0 \end{bmatrix} \boldsymbol{e}_i \otimes \boldsymbol{e}_j. \tag{22}$$

The deformation gradient is given by the exponential form

$$\boldsymbol{F}(t) = \exp(\boldsymbol{L}t)\boldsymbol{F}(0), \tag{23}$$

with $\boldsymbol{F}(0) = \boldsymbol{I}$. The constant strain rate is set to $\dot{\varepsilon}_0 = 10^{-3}\ \mathrm{s}^{-1}$. The special form of the velocity gradient implies a displacement in the X-Y plane in the reference configuration

Figure 18 Plastic slip of 12 slip systems {112}⟨111⟩ at 20% elongation. The unit is per second $\left[s^{-1}\right]$.

and a constant volume during the simulation. From Equation 20, the displacement on the boundary is obtained

$$\boldsymbol{u}(\boldsymbol{X},t) = \boldsymbol{H}\boldsymbol{X} = \boldsymbol{H}\boldsymbol{F}^{-1}\boldsymbol{x}. \tag{24}$$

By combining this equation with Equation 21, the prescribed displacement is defined in the subroutine DISP at the time t in terms of the deformation gradient in Equation 23, so that the displacement becomes

$$\boldsymbol{u}(\boldsymbol{X},t) = \left(\boldsymbol{I} - \boldsymbol{F}^{-1}\right)\boldsymbol{x}. \tag{25}$$

The total time in FE simulation is 260 s corresponding to 20% elongation. The FE results are evaluated at different total times such as 65, 130, and 195 s corresponding to 5%, 10%, and 15% elongation, respectively. The field of critical resolved shear stress τ_c is depicted in

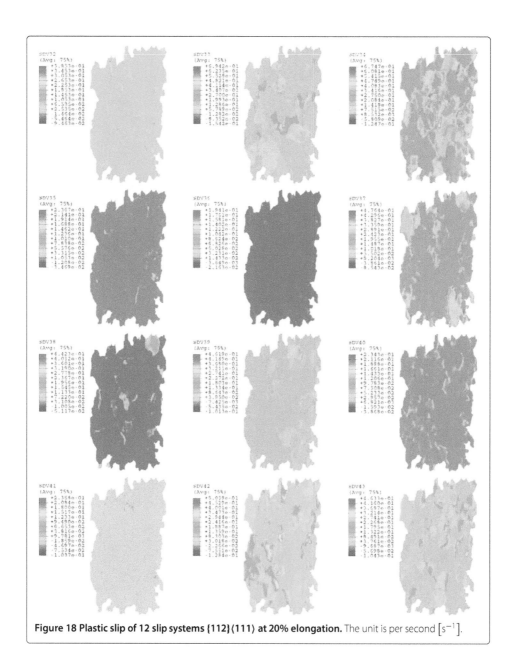

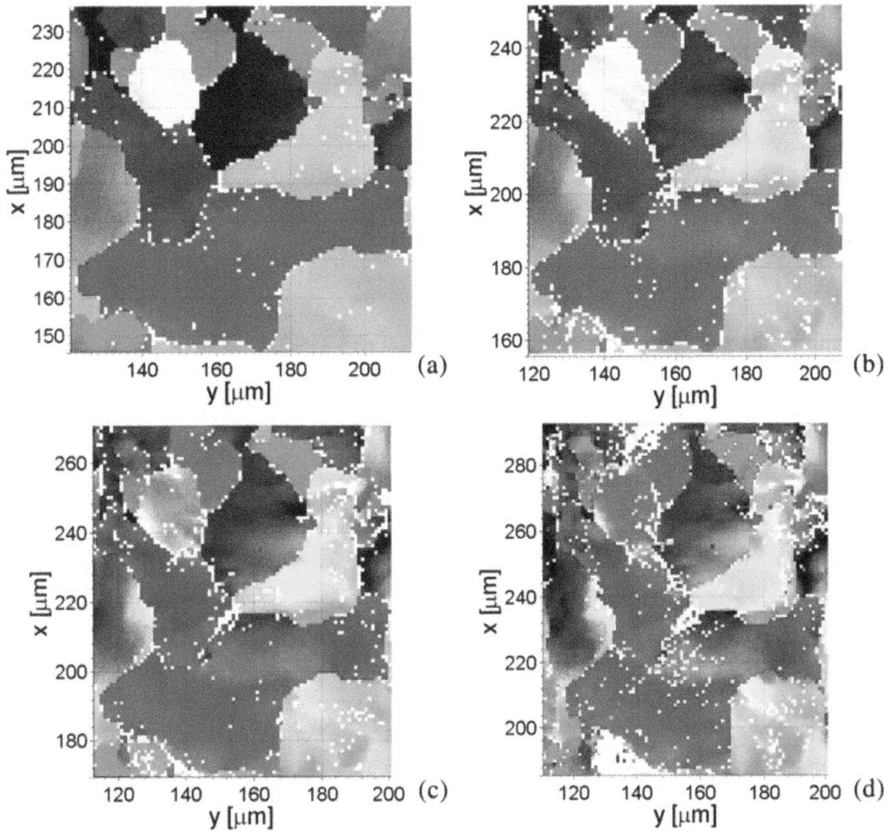

Figure 19 Microstructural images of local grains identified by MTEX at different states. **(a)** 5%, **(b)** 10%, **(c)** 15%, and **(d)** 20% elongation.

Figure 16 at the aforementioned different states of the FE simulation. These results show a strongly inhomogeneous field caused by the evolution of individual grain orientations in the microstructure during deformation.

In addition, the plastic slip of each slip system α ($\alpha = 1 \ldots 24$) in BCC slip systems $\{110\}\langle 111\rangle + \{112\}\langle 111\rangle$ is computed by integrating the slip rate $\dot{\gamma}_\alpha$ over the time during the grain scale simulation. The plastic slip is described as follows:

$$\gamma_\alpha = \int_0^t |\dot{\gamma}_\alpha| \, \mathrm{d}t. \tag{26}$$

Figures 17 and 18 represent the plastic slip in 24 slip systems at 20% elongation. It can be seen that the grain structure shows a very heterogeneous state of slip.

Results and discussion

This section aims to perform a comparison between the numerical results and the experimental data for three local grains. Numerical results at different tensile strains are compared to the corresponding experimental results. In order to obtain Euler angles and the reorientation in the three grains (Figure 19), post-processing steps have to be carried out. Firstly, the measured grain data set at each different state of deformation is transformed into the fundamental zone. Secondly, each triple of Euler angles of the measurement points is extracted at different states of deformation. A comparison of

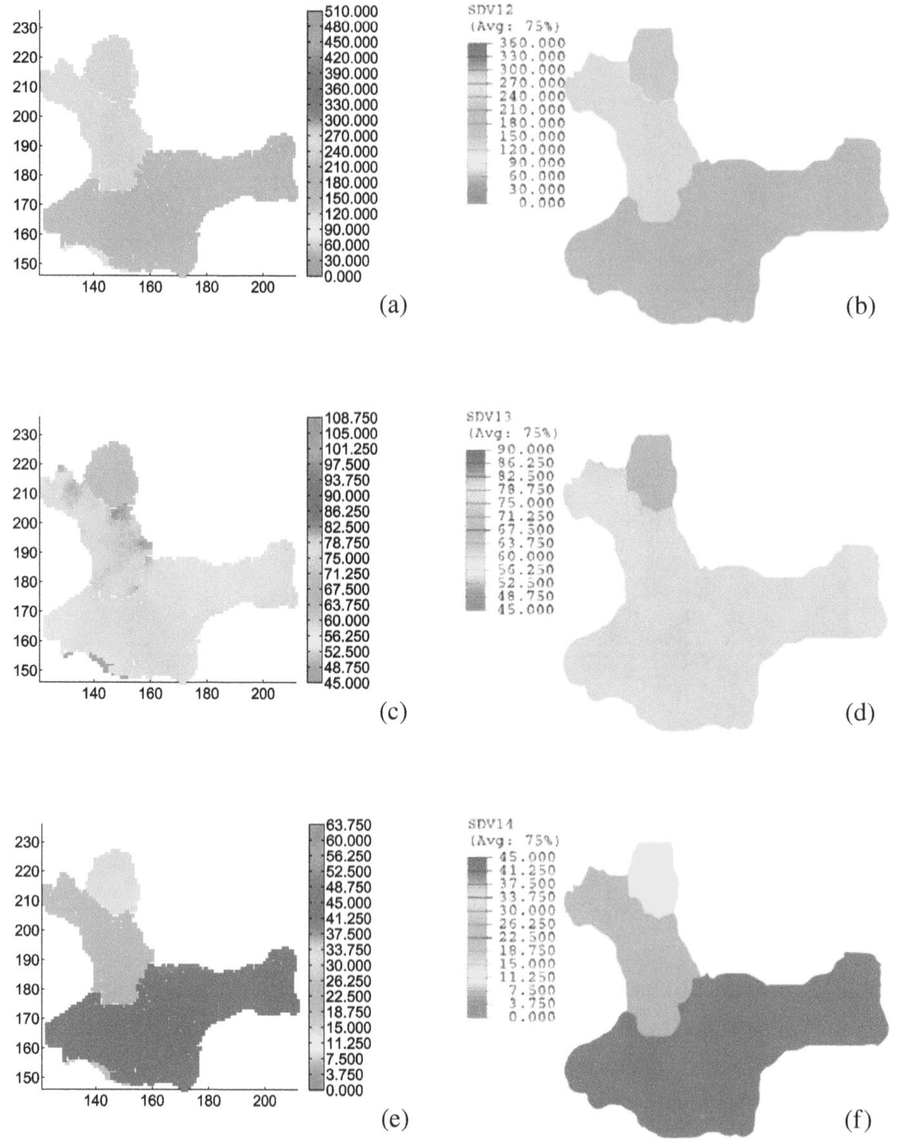

Figure 20 Comparison of Euler angles [°] between the experiment (left) and numerical results (right) at 5% elongation state. (a, b) Angle ϕ_1, **(c, d)** angle Φ, and **(e, f)** angle ϕ_2.

Euler angles between the experiment and the FE simulation is shown in Figures 20,21,22 and 23. The evolution of Euler angles in the numerical simulation is quite close to the experimental findings.

Thirdly, the reorientation of each measurement point is computed for each state of deformation. The formula to compute the angle of reorientation is given by

$$\omega = \left| \arccos\left(\frac{\mathrm{tr}\boldsymbol{Q}\boldsymbol{Q}_0^{\mathsf{T}} - 1}{2} \right) \right|, \tag{27}$$

where $\boldsymbol{Q}_0$ represents the crystal orientation at the initial state of deformation and $\boldsymbol{Q}$ represents the crystal orientation of the same point at different states of deformation. Both $\boldsymbol{Q}_0$ and $\boldsymbol{Q}$ are parameterized by Euler angles lying in the same fundamental zone.

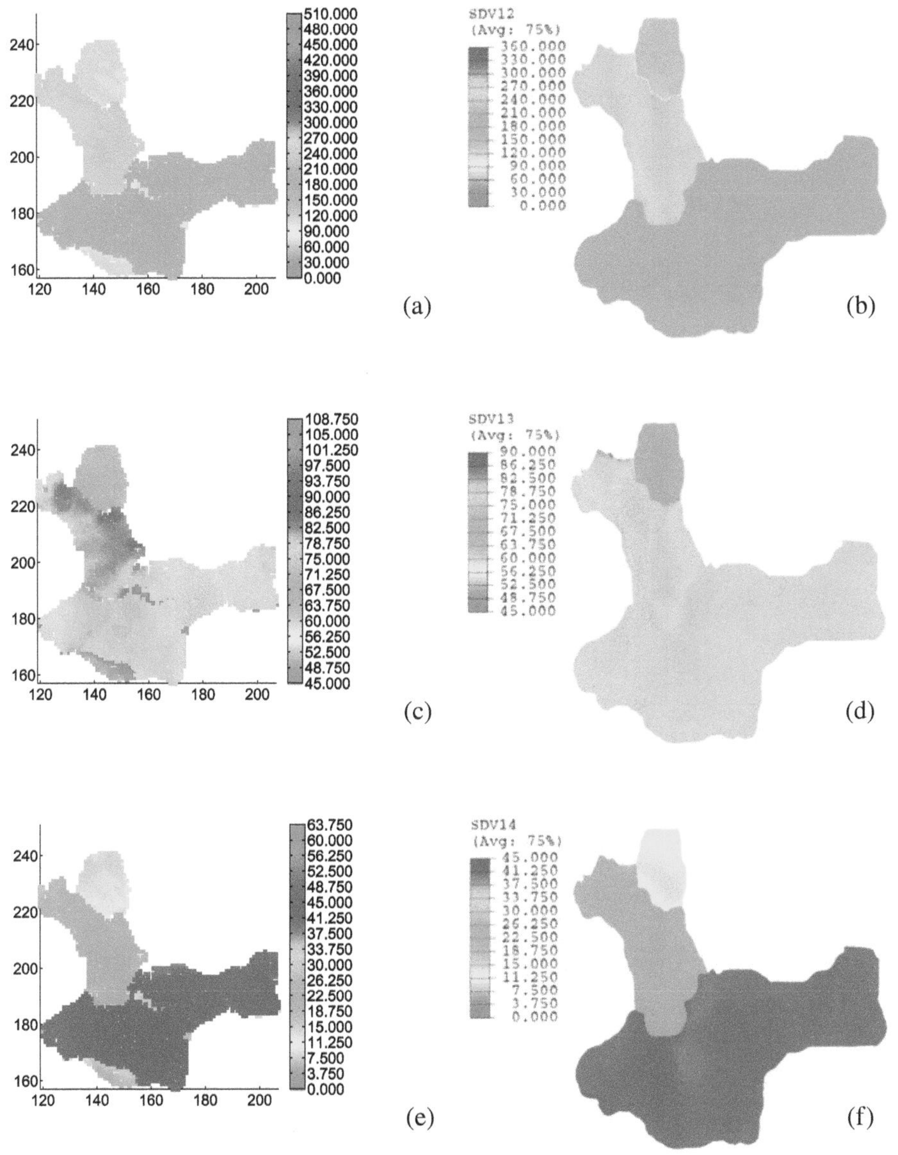

Figure 21 Comparison of Euler angles [°] between the experiment (left) and numerical results (right) at 10% elongation state. (a, b) Angle ϕ_1, **(c, d)** angle Φ, and **(e, f)** angle ϕ_2.

During the simulation, $\boldsymbol{Q}$ is extracted by the polar decomposition $\boldsymbol{F}_e = \boldsymbol{R}_e\boldsymbol{U}_e$, where $\boldsymbol{R}_e = \boldsymbol{Q}$ is the elastic rotation and $\boldsymbol{U}_e$ is the elastic stretch tensor. The computed reorientation is the minimum relative orientation distance between the initial and actual crystal orientation. By comparing the color distribution representing the values in the legend (Figure 24), the reorientations in the numerical simulations agree well with the experimental results. In addition, the computed reorientations of local grains #345 and #296 are in good agreement with the experiment. However, the computed reorientation of local grain #357 is lower than in the experiment. This can probably be explained by neglecting the beneath grain interaction in the ND due to the lack of the experimental 2D EBSD data.

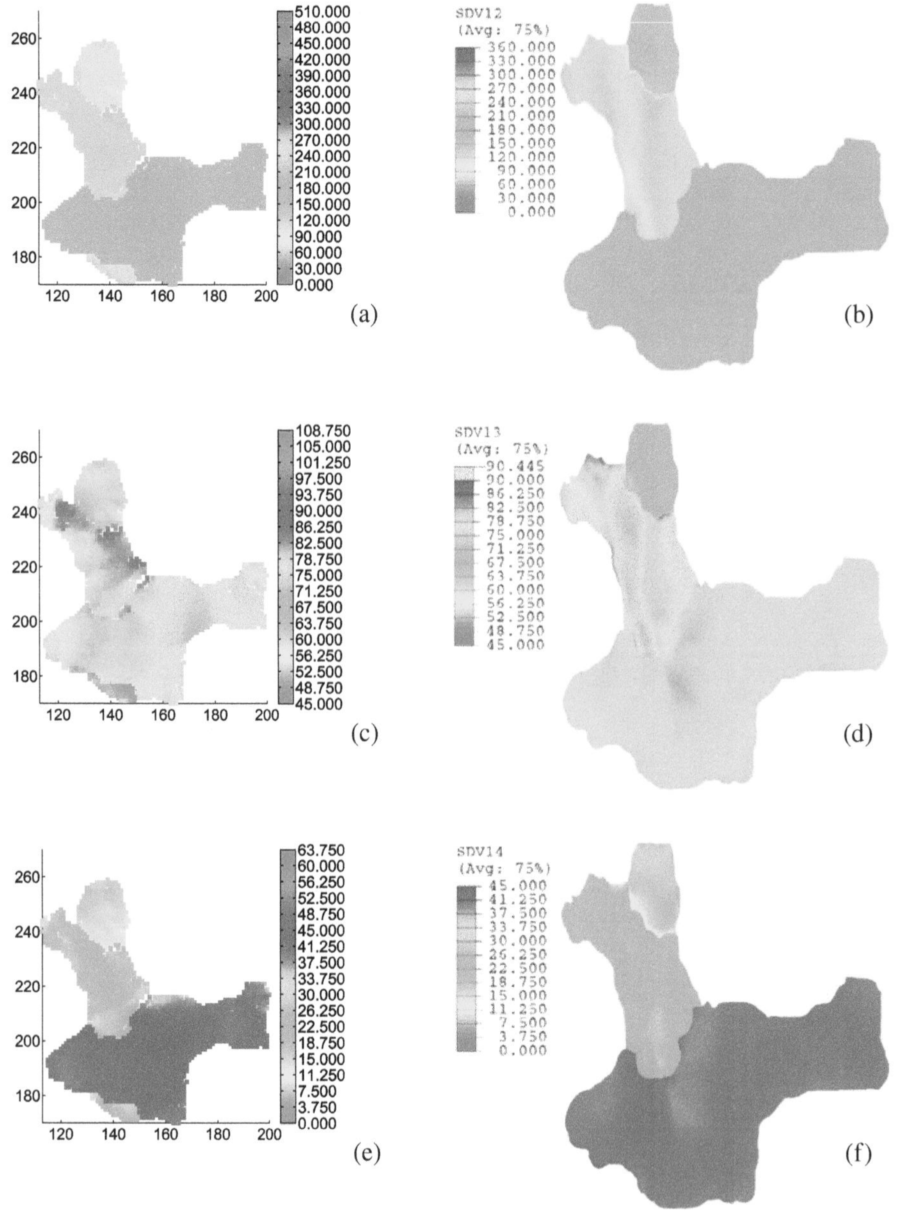

Figure 22 Comparison of Euler angles [°] between the experiment (left) and numerical results (right) at 15% elongation state. (a, b) Angle ϕ_1, **(c, d)** angle Φ, and **(e, f)** angle ϕ_2.

Conclusions

In the paper, a finite strain crystal plasticity model has been presented. The constitutive equations applied on the grain scale to model the elasto-viscoplastic behavior of BCC single crystals have been described in the context of large deformations. In particular, the crystal plasticity model is rate dependent and takes into account hardening effects on the microscale. The material parameters of the DC04 steel used in the crystal plasticity model were identified in the work of [25].

In addition, the experimental EBSD technique to obtain the microstructural information has been introduced. By using the EBSD measurement technique, a data set of a

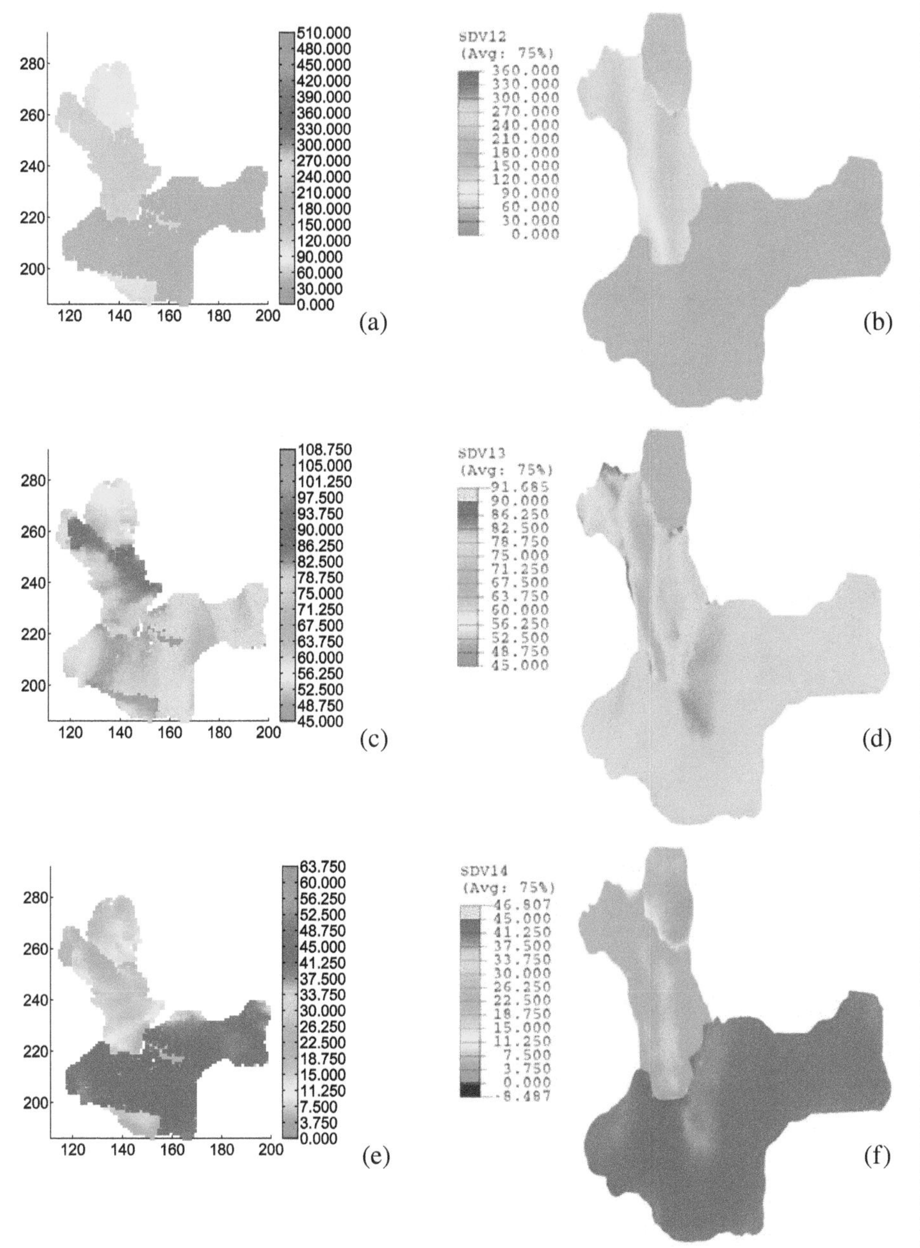

Figure 23 Comparison of Euler angles [°] between the experiment (left) and numerical results (right) at 20% elongation state. (a, b) Angle ϕ_1, **(c, d)** angle Φ, and **(e, f)** angle ϕ_2.

DC04 steel specimen in the cold formed and the heat-treated processes has been presented. In order to analyze and evaluate quantitatively the experimental texture data, a Matlab toolbox MTEX has been introduced and used. The MTEX allowed to import the different EBSD data formats and to obtain a 2D grain structure with corresponding crystal orientations. These EBSD data sets have been processed to identify the grain information and to obtain the clustered data.

A verification of the material model has been carried out. Based on EBSD data, the grain structure was modeled by a FE model. The FE mesh has been imported into the ABAQUS/CAE software for the performance of the grain scale simulation. This

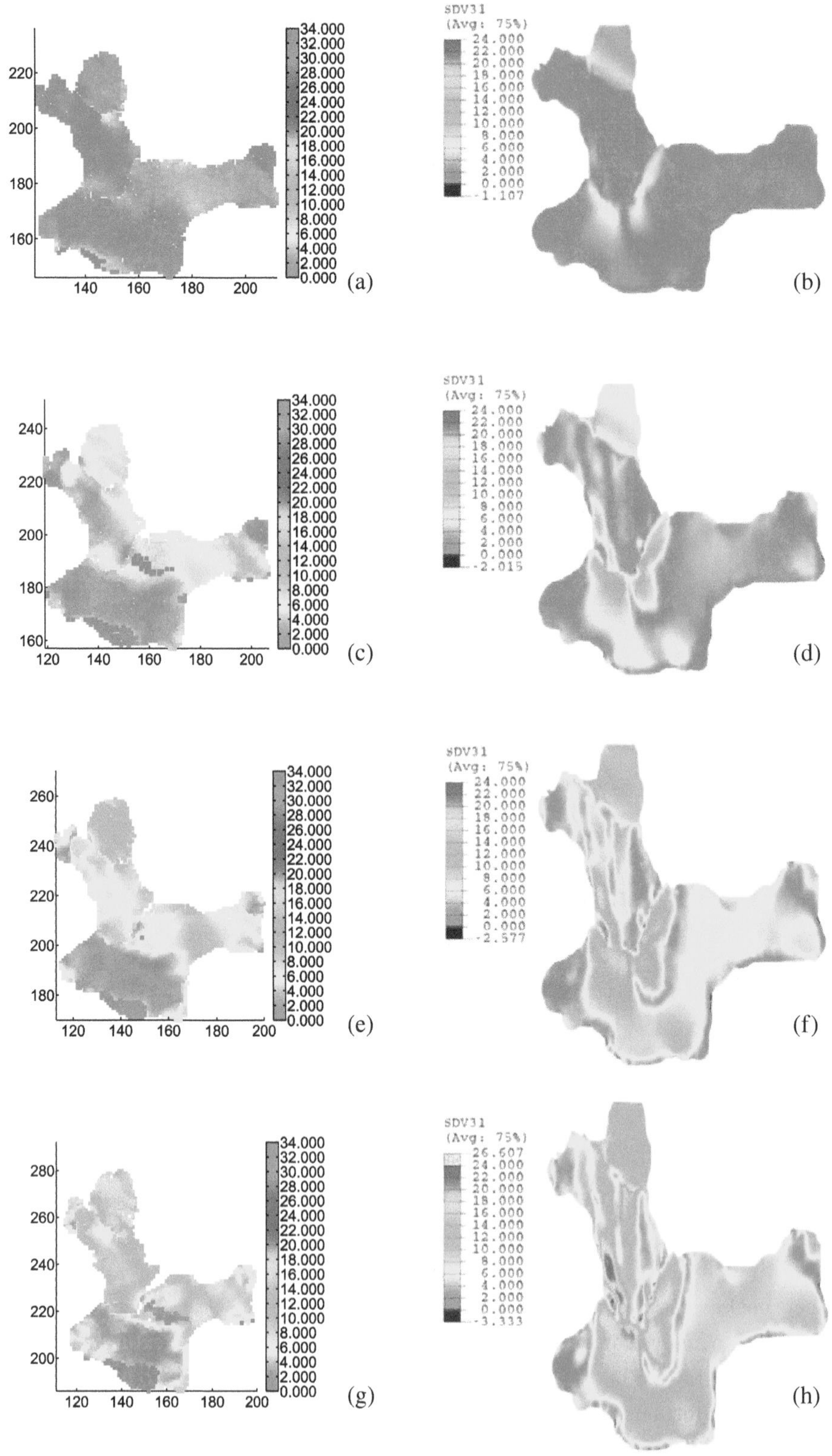

Figure 24 Comparison of reorientation [°] between the experiment (left) and numerical results (right) at different states. (a, b) 5%, **(c, d)** 10%, **(e, f)** 15%, and **(g, h)** 20% elongation.

FE simulation has been used for the identified DC04 steel material microparameters, and two families of the BCC slip systems were assumed to possibly act simultaneously, namely $\{110\}\langle 111\rangle + \{112\}\langle 111\rangle$. In addition, a procedure for mapping the initial grain orientations into the fundamental zone has been implemented. The micromechanical behavior was analyzed in terms of the evolution of grain orientations. The grain orientations and reorientations are compared to the experiment for a group of local grains. The numerical results of local grain reorientations seem to underestimate the heterogeneity compared to the experimental results. This issue can be probably explained by the neglect of the 3D microstructure and interaction of the beneath microstructure in the grain scale simulation. The influence of 3D interaction needs to be further investigated in further studies.

Competing interests
The author declares no competing interests.

Acknowledgements
The author acknowledges gratefully T. Böhlke (ITM, KIT) for his constructive contribution. The author also thanks S. Schreijäg and R. Mönig (IAM, KIT) for the supply of the EBSD data of DC04 steel in this research work.

References

1. Bunge H (1993) Texture analysis in materials science. Culliver Verlag, Göttingen
2. Asaro RJ, Needleman A (1985) Texture development and strain hardening in rate dependent polycrystals. Acta Materialia 33: 923–953
3. Mathur K, Dawson P (1989) On modeling the development of crystallographic texture in bulk forming processes. International Journal of Plasticity 5: 67–94
4. Bronkhorst CA, Kalidindi SR, Anand L (1992) Polycrystalline plasticity and the evolution of crystallographic texture in FCC metals. Philosophical Transactions of the Royal Society A 341: 443–477
5. Raabe D (1995) Simulation of rolling textures of b.c.c, metals considering grain interactions and crystallographic slip on 110, 112 and 123 planes. Materials Science and Engineering A 197: 31–37
6. Böhlke T (2000) Crystallographic texture evolution and elastic anisotropy: simulation, modeling, and application. Shaker Verlag GmbH, Aachen
7. Böhlke T, Risy G, Bertram A (2005) A texture component model for anisotropic polycrystal plasticity. Computational Materials Science 32: 284–293
8. Böhlke T, Glüge R, Klöden B, Skrotzki W, Bertram A (2007) Finite element simulation of texture evolution and swift effect in NiAl under torsion. Modelling and Simulation in Materials Science and Engineering 15: 619–637
9. Roters F, Eisenlohr P, Hantcherli L, Tjahjanto DD, Bieler TR, Raabe D (2010) Overview of constitutive laws, kinematics, homogenization and multiscale methods in crystal plasticity finite-element modeling: theory, experiments, applications. Acta Materialia 58: 1152–1211
10. Jöchen K, Böhlke T (2013) Representative reduction of crystallographic orientation data. Journal of Applied Crystallography 46: 960–971
11. Lee EH (1969) Elastic-plastic deformation at finite strains. ASME Journal of Applied Mechanics 36: 1–6
12. Asaro RJ, Rice JR (1977) Strain localization in ductile single crystals. Journal of the Mechanics and Physics of Solids 25: 309–338
13. Ting T (1996) Anisotropy elasticity: theory and applications. Oxford University Press, New York/Oxford
14. Kocks U, Mecking H (2003) Physics and phenomenology of strain hardening: the FCC case. Progress in Materials Science 48: 171–273
15. Yalcinkaya T, Brekelmans WAM, Geers MGD (2008) BCC single crystal plasticity modeling and its experimental identification. Modelling and Simulation in Materials Science and Engineering 16(8): 085007
16. Paquin A, Berbenni S, Favier V, Lemoine X, Berveiller M (2001) Micromechanical modeling of the elastic-viscoplastic behavior of polycrystalline steels. International Journal of Plasticity 17: 1267–1302
17. Maitland T (2004) Electron backscattered diffraction: an EBSD system added to an SEM is a valuable new tool in the materials characterization. Advanced Materials and Processes 162(5): 34–36
18. Maitland T, Sitzman S (2006) Scanning microscopy for nanotechnology. Chapter 2: Electron backscatter diffraction (EBSD) technique and material characterization examples. Springer, New York, pp. 41–75
19. Schwartz AJ, Kumar M, Adams BL, Field DP (2009) Electron backscatter diffraction in materials science. 2nd edn. Springer, New York
20. Bunge H (1982) Texture analysis and materials science. Butterworths, London
21. Schreijäg S (2013) Microstructure and mechanical behavior of deep drawing DC04 steel at different length scales. PhD thesis, KIT Scientific Publishing, Karlsruhe
22. Hielscher R (2010) MTEX Quantitative Texture Analysis Software. http://code.google.com/p/mtex/. 1 Sept 2009
23. Bachmann F, Hielscher R, Schaeben H (2011) Grain detection from 2D and 3D EBSD data–specification of the MTEX algorithm. Ultramicroscopy 111: 1720–1733

24. Simpleware (2000) Simpleware: converting 3D images into models. http://www.simpleware.com/. 15 Dec 2011
25. Phan VT (2012) Modeling the mesoscopic and macroscopic deformation behavior of the ferritic stainless steel DC04. PhD Thesis, Karlsruhe Institute of Technology, Karlsruhe
26. Gao X, Przybyla CP, Adams BL (2006) Methodology for recovering and analyzing two-point pair correlation functions in polycrystalline materials. Metallurgical and Materials Transactions A 37A: 2379–2387
27. Sudook AK, Ward LJ (2007) Elastic constants and internal friction of martensitic steel, ferritic-pearlitic steel, and alpha-iron. Materials Science and Engineering A 452–453: 633–639

8

Upper bound limit analysis of plates using a rotation-free isogeometric approach

Hung Nguyen-Xuan[1*], Chien Hoang Thai[2], Jeremy Bleyer[3] and Phu Vinh Nguyen[4]

*Correspondence:
hung.nx@vgu.edu.vn
[1] Department of Computational Engineering, Vietnamese-German University, Binh Duong New City, Vietnam
Full list of author information is available at the end of the article

Abstract

Background: This paper presents a simple and effective formulation based on a rotation-free isogeometric approach for the assessment of collapse limit loads of plastic thin plates in bending.

Methods: The formulation relies on the kinematic (or upper bound) theorem and namely B-splines or non-uniform rational B-splines (NURBS), resulting in both exactly geometric representation and high-order approximations. Only one deflection variable (without rotational degrees of freedom) is used for each control point. This allows us to design the resulting optimization problem with a minimum size that is very useful to solve large-scale plate problems. The optimization formulation of limit analysis is transformed into the form of a second-order cone programming problem so that it can be solved using highly efficient interior-point solvers.

Results and conclusions: Several numerical examples are given to demonstrate reliability and effectiveness of the present method in comparison with other published methods.

Keywords: Plate bending; Limit analysis; Rigid-perfect plasticity; NURBS; Isogeometric analysis; Second-order cone programming

Background

Accurate prediction of the load bearing capacity of plate structures plays an important role in many practical engineering problems. Traditional elastic designs cannot evaluate the actual load carrying capacity of plates and incremental elasto-plastic analyses can become cumbersome and present convergence issues for large-scale structures. Therefore, various limit analysis approaches have been devised to investigate the behavior of structures in the plastic region. Nowadays, limit analysis has become a well-known tool for assessing the safety load factor of engineering structures as an efficient direct method. Due to limitation of analytical methods, various numerical approaches such as finite element methods (FEM) [1-6], meshfree methods [7,8], and natural element method [9], just to mention a few, have therefore been developed.

It is also worth adding that mathematical programming is the other key issue in numerical assessment of limit analysis problem. Discrete upper bound limit analysis results in a minimization problem involving linear or nonlinear programming. Linear programming problems can be applied for piecewise linearization of yield criteria, but an important number of additional variables is often needed. However, most of the yield criteria for plates can be formed as an intersection of cones for which the limit analysis problem can be solved efficiently by the primal-dual interior point method [10,11] implemented in the MOSEK software package [12]. This algorithm was proved to be a very effective optimization tool for the limit analysis of structures [4,6,7,13-16], and therefore it will be used in our study.

Isogeometric approach (IGA) has been recently proposed by Hughes et al. [17] to unify the fields of Computer Aided Design (CAD) and Finite Element Analysis (FEA). The basic idea is that the IGA uses the same basis functions, namely B-splines or non-uniform rational B-splines (NURBS), to describe precisely the geometry, especially containing conic sections and to construct the finite approximation for analysis. It is well known that NURBS functions provide a flexible way to make refinement, de-refinement and degree elevation [18]. They enable to easily achieve continuity up to $C^{(p-1)}$, instead of C^0-continuity as it typically happens with traditional FEM. Hence, IGA naturally verifies the C^1-continuity of thin plates, which is interested in this study. The IGA has been well known and widely applied to various practical problems [19-27] and so on.

Among various plate theories [28], the classical plate theory (CPT) and the first-order shear deformation plate theory (FSDT) have been widely used in many numerical methods, especially finite elements. The first-order shear deformation plate theory assumes that transverse shear stresses are constants through the thickness and a shear correction factor (SCF) is needed to take into account the non-linear distribution of shear stresses. It is known in FSDT models that the FE approximation functions only require C^0-continuity across element boundaries. Such a construction is simple but leads to shear locking problems. In CPT, C^1-continuity of approximation fields across element boundaries is needed. Unfortunately, it is difficult to construct FE formulations with C^1-continuous approximation. Traditionally, the conforming FE approximation of the Kirchhoff plate model has in general 3 degrees of freedom per node. This is due to the continuity of the rotation solutions. It is also well known in the literature that non-conforming finite element models enable us to relax strict requirements of the continuity of the rotations. Attempts to eliminate the rotational degrees of freedom help us to reduce significantly the total number of degrees of freedom of problem without loss of accuracy of solution. As a result, such approaches promise more benefit for solving large-scale industrial problems [26,29,30]. For example, an efficient way of the rotation-free FE approaches for plate and shell analysis is to use C^0 basis functions via the so-called cell-centred and cell-vertex finite volume schemes [29-32]. The rotation-free isogeometric approach recently proposed is regarded as an alternative way for solving practical problems. The method is conformable to the thin plate/shell theory and the C^1-continuity is easily achieved using NURBS basis functions [33]. Several investigations on the rotation-free formulation can be found in the literature, e.g., Bernoulli-Euler beams [34], Poisson-Kirchhoff plates [35], multi-patch Kirchhoff-Love shells [23] and large deformation analysis with rotation-free [26]. It was demonstrated in the aforementioned references that the rotation-free isogeometric approach is a potential candidate for solving a wide range of practical problems. It therefore deserves for pursuing and developing this approach for limit analysis of thin plate structures.

This paper further exploits the advantage of a rotation-free isogeometric approach to the assessment of collapse limit loads of plastic thin plates in bending. The kinematic formulation relies on the displacement (deflection) approximation using NURBS, resulting in both exact geometric representation and high-order approximations. Only deflection degrees of freedom are involved in the underlying optimization problem. This enables us to design the resulting optimization problem with a minimum size and to reduce computational cost. We adopt a simple procedure to eliminate rotational degrees of freedom on essential boundary conditions related to the constraint of normal slopes. The resulting non-smooth optimization problem is then written in the form of minimizing a sum of Euclidean norms so that it can be solved using highly efficient interior-point solvers. Several numerical examples are provided to show the reliability and accuracy of the present formulation.

The paper is arranged as follows: a brief review of B-spline and NURBS surfaces is described in the next section. This is followed by a section stating a rotation-free NURBS-based isogeometric formulation for limit analysis of thin plate problems. The solution procedure is given in the fourth section. Several numerical examples are illustrated in the fifth section. Finally, we close our paper with some concluding remarks.

Methods

A brief review of NURBS basis functions and surfaces

Knot vectors and basis functions and surfaces

Let $\Xi = [\xi_1, \xi_2, \ldots, \xi_{n+p+1}]$ be a nondecreasing sequence of parameter values, $\xi_i \leq \xi_{i+1}, i = 1, \ldots, n+p$, where p is the polynomial order and n is the number of basis functions. The ξ_i are called knots, and Ξ is the set of coordinates in the parametric space. The knot vector is called uniform if all knots are equally spaced. If the first and the last knots are reduplicated $p+1$ times, the knot vector is known as open. A B-spline basis function is C^∞ continuous inside a knot span and C^{p-1} continuous at a single knot. A knot value can appear more than once and is then called a multiple knot. At a knot of multiplicity k, the continuity is C^{p-k}. Given a knot vector, the B-spline basis functions $N_{i,p}(\xi)$ of order $p = 0$ are defined as follows:

$$N_{i,0}(\xi) = \begin{cases} 1 & \xi_i \leq \xi < \xi_{i+1} \\ 0 & \text{otherwise} \end{cases} \tag{1}$$

The basis function of order $p > 0$ is defined by the following recursion formula [33]

$$N_{i,p}(\xi) = \frac{\xi - \xi_i}{\xi_{i+p} - \xi_i} N_{i,p-1}(\xi) + \frac{\xi_{i+p+1} - \xi}{\xi_{i+p+1} - \xi_{i+1}} N_{i+1,p-1}(\xi) \qquad \text{with } p = (1, 2, 3, \ldots) \tag{2}$$

For $p = 0$ and 1, the basis functions of isogeometric analysis are identical to those of standard piecewise constant and linear finite elements, respectively. Nevertheless, for $p \geq 2$, they are different [17]. Therefore, the present work will consider only basis functions with $p \geq 2$. Figures 1 and 2 illustrate a set of one-dimensional (1D) and two-dimensional (2D) quadratic and cubic B-spline basis functions for open uniform knot vectors $\Xi = \{0, 0, 0, \frac{1}{2}, 1, 1, 1\}$ and $\Xi = \{0, 0, 0, 0, \frac{1}{2}, 1, 1, 1, 1\}$, respectively.

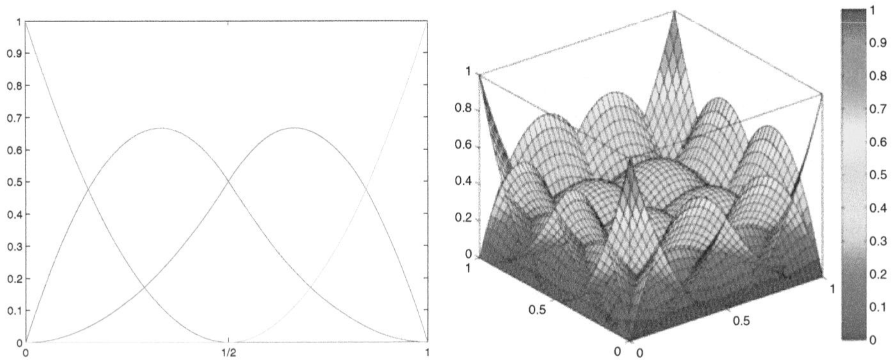

Figure 1 1D and 2D quadratic B-spline basis functions.

NURBS surfaces

A B-spline curve is defined as

$$\mathbf{C}(\xi) = \sum_{i=1}^{n} N_{i,p}(\xi)\, \mathbf{P}_i \tag{3}$$

where $\mathbf{P}_i$ are the control points, n denotes the number of control points and $N_{i,p}(\xi)$ is the pth-degree B-spline basis function defined on the open knot vector.

Given two knot vectors $\Xi = \{\xi_1, \xi_2, \ldots, \xi_{n+p+1}\}$ and $\mathscr{H} = \{\eta_1, \eta_2, \ldots, \eta_{m+q+1}\}$ and a control net $\mathbf{p}_{i,j}$, a tensor-product B-spline surface is defined as

$$\mathbf{S}(\xi, \eta) = \sum_{i=1}^{n} \sum_{j=1}^{m} N_{i,p}(\xi)\, M_{j,q}(\eta)\, \mathbf{p}_{i,j} \tag{4}$$

where $N_{i,p}(\xi)$ and $M_{j,q}(\eta)$ are the B-spline basis functions defined on the knot vectors Ξ and $\mathscr{H}$, respectively.

In a finite element context, we identify the logical coordinates (i, j) of B-spline surfaces with the traditional notation of a 'node' I [24] and rewrite Equation 4 as follows:

$$\mathbf{S}(\xi, \eta) = \sum_{I}^{n \times m} N_I^b(\xi, \eta)\, \mathbf{P}_I \tag{5}$$

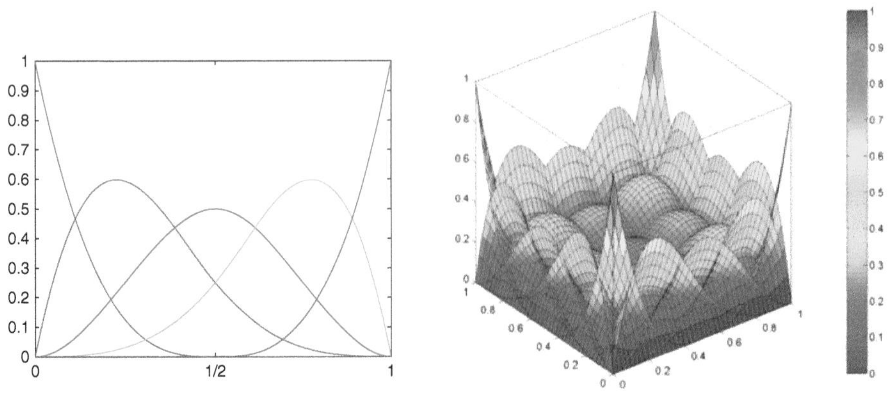

Figure 2 1D and 2D cubic B-spline basis functions.

where $N_I^b(\xi,\eta) = N_{i,p}(\xi)\,M_{j,q}(\eta)$ is the shape function associated with a node I. The superscript b indicates that $N_I^b(\xi,\eta)$ is a B-spline shape function.

Non-uniform rational B-splines (NURBS) are obtained by augmenting every point in the control mesh $\mathbf{P}_I$ with the control weight ζ_I. The weighting function is constructed as follows:

$$\zeta_g(\xi,\eta) = \sum_{I=1}^{n\times m} N_I^b(\xi,\eta)\,\zeta_I \tag{6}$$

The NURBS surfaces are then defined by

$$\mathbf{S}(\xi,\eta) = \frac{\sum_{I=1}^{n\times m} N_I^b(\xi,\eta)\,\zeta_I\mathbf{P}_I}{\zeta_g(\xi,\eta)} = \sum_{I=1}^{n\times m} N_I(\xi,\eta)\mathbf{P}_I \tag{7}$$

where $N_I(\xi,\eta) = N_I^b(\xi,\eta)\,\zeta_I/\zeta_g(\xi,\eta)$ are NURBS basis functions. An example of a quadratic NURBS surface with 4×4 elements is indicated in Figure 3.

Rotation-free isogeometric formulation for upper bound limit analysis of plates

A background on limit analysis theorems of thin plates

Let $\Omega \subset \mathbb{R}^2$ be the mid-plane of a plate and $\dot{w}$ be the transversal displacement velocity (or deflection velocity) in the z direction. Further, let us consider a kinematical boundary $\Gamma_1 = \Gamma_w \cup \Gamma_{w_n}$ and a static boundary $\Gamma_2 = \Gamma_m \cup \Gamma_{m_n}$, where the subscript $\mathbf{n}$ stands for the outward normal vector. The general relations for thin Kirchhoff plates are described as follows.

Equilibrium

Collecting the bending moments in the vector $\mathbf{m}^T = \left[m_{xx}, m_{yy}, m_{xy}\right]$, the equilibrium equation can be written as

$$(\nabla^2)^T\mathbf{m} + \lambda\bar{q} = 0 \tag{8}$$

where $\bar{q}$ is the transverse load, λ is the collapse load multiplier and the differential operator ∇^2 is defined by $\nabla^2 = \left[\frac{\partial^2}{\partial x^2}\ \frac{\partial^2}{\partial y^2}\ 2\frac{\partial^2}{\partial x \partial y}\right]^T$.

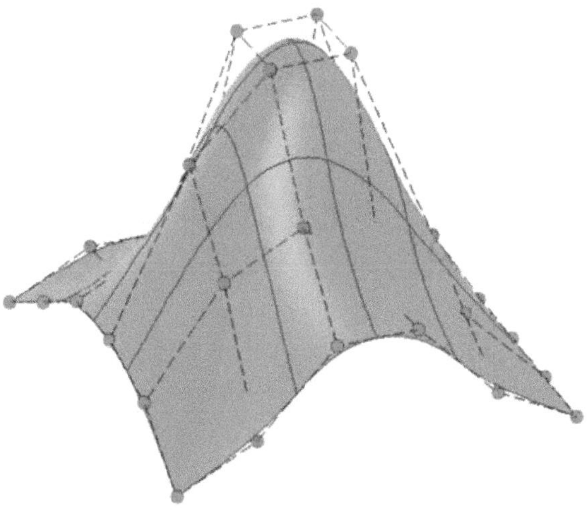

Figure 3 Physical mesh and control points of a quadratic NURBS surface.

Compatibility

If w denotes the transverse displacement velocity, the curvature rates can be expressed by the following relation

$$\dot{\boldsymbol{\kappa}} = \left[\dot{\kappa}_{xx}, \dot{\kappa}_{yy}, 2\dot{\kappa}_{xy}\right]^T = \nabla^2 \dot{w} \tag{9}$$

Flow rule and yield condition

In the framework of a limit analysis problem, only plastic strains are considered and are assumed to obey the normality rule $\dot{\boldsymbol{\kappa}} = \dot{\mu}\frac{\partial \psi}{\partial \mathbf{m}}$, where the plastic multiplier $\dot{\mu}$ is non-negative and the yield function $\psi(\mathbf{m})$ is convex. In this study, the von Mises failure criterion in the space of moment components is used

$$\psi(\mathbf{m}) = \sqrt{\mathbf{m}^T\ \mathbf{P}\ \mathbf{m}} - m_p \leq 0 \tag{10}$$

where $m_p = \sigma_0 t^2/4$ is the plastic moment of resistance per unit width of a plate of uniform thickness t, σ_0 is the yield stress and

$$\mathbf{P} = \frac{1}{2}\begin{bmatrix} 2 & -1 & 0 \\ -1 & 2 & 0 \\ 0 & 0 & 6 \end{bmatrix} \tag{11}$$

The dissipation rate

The internal dissipation power of the two-dimensional plate domain can be written as a function of the curvature rates as

$$D_p(\dot{\boldsymbol{\kappa}}) = \int_\Omega \int_{-t/2}^{t/2} \sigma_0 \sqrt{\dot{\boldsymbol{\epsilon}}^T \boldsymbol{\Theta} \dot{\boldsymbol{\epsilon}}}\ \mathrm{d}z\ \mathrm{d}A = m_p \int_\Omega \sqrt{\dot{\boldsymbol{\kappa}}^T \boldsymbol{\Theta}\ \dot{\boldsymbol{\kappa}}}\, \mathrm{d}\Omega \tag{12}$$

where

$$\dot{\boldsymbol{\epsilon}} = \begin{bmatrix} \dot{\epsilon}_{xx} \\ \dot{\epsilon}_{yy} \\ \dot{\gamma}_{xy} \end{bmatrix} = z\dot{\boldsymbol{\kappa}} \tag{13}$$

and

$$\boldsymbol{\Theta} = \mathbf{P}^{-1} = \frac{1}{3}\begin{bmatrix} 4 & 2 & 0 \\ 2 & 4 & 0 \\ 0 & 0 & 1 \end{bmatrix} \tag{14}$$

Details on the derivation of the dissipation for plate problems can be found in [2]. Let it be pointed out that, here, the velocity fields are supposed to be C^1-continuous. In fact, more general fields presenting discontinuities of the normal rotation are possible. In this case, the expression of the dissipation power includes a supplementary term. For more details on this aspect, we refer to [6].

Let $\mathcal{V}$ denote a space of kinematically admissible velocity field:

$$\mathcal{V} = \left\{\dot{w} \in H^2(\Omega)\right\} \cap B \tag{15}$$

and $\boldsymbol{\Sigma}$ be an appropriate space of symmetric stress tensors and B is a set of essential boundary conditions defined in subsection 'Essential boundary conditions'. More details on the mathematical formulations for limit analysis can be found in [36]. The external work rate of a transversal force $\bar{q}$ associated with a virtual plastic flow $\dot{w} \in \mathcal{V}$ is expressed in the linear form as

$$W_{\mathrm{ex}}(\dot{w}) = \int_\Omega \bar{q}\dot{w}\, \mathrm{d}\Omega \tag{16}$$

The internal work rate for sufficiently smooth stresses (or moments) **m** and velocity field $\dot{w}$ is given by the bilinear form

$$W_{\text{in}}(\mathbf{m}, \dot{w}) = \int_{\Omega} \mathbf{m}^T \kappa(\dot{w})\, \mathrm{d}\Omega \tag{17}$$

The equilibrium equation is then described in the form of virtual work rate as follows:

$$W_{\text{in}}(\mathbf{m}, \dot{w}) = W_{\text{ex}}(\dot{w}), \forall \dot{w} \in \mathscr{V} \tag{18}$$

Furthermore, the stresses **m** must satisfy the yield condition for the assumed material. This stress field belongs to a convex set, $\mathscr{B}$, obtained from the used field condition. For the von Mises criterion, one writes

$$\mathscr{B} = \left\{\mathbf{m} \in \mathbf{\Sigma};\, |\, m_{xx}^2 - m_{xx}m_{yy} + m_{yy}^2 + 3m_{xy}^2 \leq m_p^2\right\} \tag{19}$$

If defining $\mathscr{C} = \{\dot{w} \in \mathscr{V} \mid W_{\text{ex}}(\dot{w}) = 1\}$, the exact collapse multiplier λ_{exact} can be determined by solving any of the following optimization problems [36]:

$$\lambda_{\text{exact}} = \max\{\lambda \mid \exists \mathbf{m} \in \mathscr{B}:\ W_{\text{in}}(\mathbf{m}, \dot{w}) = \lambda W_{\text{ex}}(\dot{w}), \forall \dot{w} \in \mathscr{V}\} \tag{20}$$

$$= \max_{\mathbf{m}\in\mathscr{B}} \min_{\dot{w}\in\mathscr{C}} W_{in}(\mathbf{m}, \dot{w}) \tag{21}$$

$$= \min_{\dot{w}\in\mathscr{C}} \max_{\mathbf{m}\in\mathscr{B}} W_{in}(\mathbf{m}, \dot{w}) \tag{22}$$

$$= \min_{\dot{w}\in\mathscr{C}} D_p(\dot{w}) \tag{23}$$

Problems (20) and (23) are known as static and kinematic principles of limit analysis, respectively. The limit load of both approaches converges to the exact solution. Herein, a saddle point $(\mathbf{m}^*, \dot{w}^*)$ exists such that both the maximum of all lower bounds λ^- and the minimum of all upper bounds λ^+ coincide and are equal to the exact value λ_{exact}. In this work, we only focus on the kinematic formulation. Hence, problem (23) will be used to evaluate an upper-bound limit load factor using a NURBS-based isogeometric approach.

NURBS-based approximate formulation

Using the same NURBS basis functions, both the description of the geometry (or the physical point) and the velocity of the displacement field are expressed as

$$\mathbf{x}(\xi, \eta) = \sum_{I}^{n\times m} N_I(\xi, \eta)\mathbf{P}_I, \quad \dot{w}^h(\mathbf{x}(\xi, \eta)) = \sum_{I}^{n\times m} N_I(\xi, \eta)\dot{w}_I \tag{24}$$

where $n \times m$ represent the number of basis functions, $\mathbf{x}^T = (x, y)$ is the physical coordinates vector, $N_I(\xi, \eta)$ is the NURBS basis function and $\dot{w}_I$ is the nodal value of $\dot{w}^h$ at the control point I, respectively.

The curvature rates are written as

$$\dot{\kappa} = \sum_{I} \mathbf{B}_I \dot{w}_I \tag{25}$$

where

$$\mathbf{B}_I = \left[\, N_{I,xx}\ N_{I,yy}\ 2N_{I,xy} \,\right]^T \tag{26}$$

The plastic dissipation power (Equation 12) of the perfectly rigid plastic body is computed over all patches:

$$D_p^h = m_p \int_{\Omega} \sqrt{\dot{\kappa}^T \mathbf{\Theta} \dot{\kappa}}\, \mathrm{d}\Omega = m_p \sum_{e=1}^{\text{nel}} \int_{\Omega^e} \sqrt{\dot{\kappa}^T \mathbf{\Theta} \dot{\kappa}}\, \mathrm{d}\Omega \tag{27}$$

where nel denotes the total number of elements. The integration $\int_{\Omega^e} \sqrt{\dot{\boldsymbol{\kappa}}^T \boldsymbol{\Theta} \dot{\boldsymbol{\kappa}}}\, d\Omega$ in Equation 27 is approximated using the Gaussian quadrature rule [17] which allows Equation 27 to be rewritten as

$$D_p^h \approx m_p \sum_{i=1}^{\mathrm{NG}} \bar{\omega}_i \, |\mathbf{J}_i| \sqrt{\dot{\boldsymbol{\kappa}}_i^T \boldsymbol{\Theta} \, \dot{\boldsymbol{\kappa}}_i} \tag{28}$$

where $NG = nel \times nG$ is the total number of Gauss points of the problem, nG is the number of Gauss points in each element, $\bar{\omega}_i$ is the weight value at the Gauss point i and $|\mathbf{J}_i|$ is the determinant of the Jacobian matrix computed at the Gauss point i.

The curvature rate $\dot{\boldsymbol{\kappa}}$ is now evaluated at Gauss points as

$$\dot{\boldsymbol{\kappa}}_i = \mathbf{B}_i \dot{\mathbf{w}} \quad \forall i = \overline{1, \mathrm{NG}} \tag{29}$$

where $\mathbf{B}_i$ is defined as the global deformation matrix and $\dot{\mathbf{w}}^T = [\dot{w}_1, \dot{w}_2, \ldots, \dot{w}_{\mathrm{nCP}}]$ is the global displacement velocity vector, in which nCP is the total control points of the problem. The external work rate given in Equation 16 is also computed at Gauss points as

$$W_{\mathrm{ext}}(\dot{w}) = \sum_{i=1}^{\mathrm{NG}} \bar{q} \bar{\omega}_i \, |\mathbf{J}_i| \, \mathbf{N}(\bar{\xi}_i, \bar{\eta}_i) \dot{\mathbf{w}} = 1 \tag{30}$$

where $\mathbf{N} = [N_1(\bar{\xi}_i, \bar{\eta}_i), N_2(\bar{\xi}_i, \bar{\eta}_i), \ldots, N_{\mathrm{nCP}}(\bar{\xi}_i, \bar{\eta}_i)]$ is the global basic function vector and $(\bar{\xi}_i, \bar{\eta}_i)$ is the Gaussian quadrature point in a bi-unit parent element.

Finally, the optimization problem (23) associated with the IGA can now be rewritten as

$$\lambda^+ = \min \; m_p \sum_{i=1}^{\mathrm{NG}} \bar{\omega}_i \, |\mathbf{J}_i| \sqrt{\dot{\boldsymbol{\kappa}}_i^T \boldsymbol{\Theta} \, \dot{\boldsymbol{\kappa}}_i}$$

$$\text{s.t} \begin{cases} \dot{\boldsymbol{\kappa}}_i = \mathbf{B}_i \dot{\mathbf{w}}, \quad \forall i = \overline{1, \mathrm{NG}} \\ \dot{w} = 0 \text{ and } \dot{w}_n = 0 \text{ on } \Gamma_1 \\ W_{\mathrm{ext}}(\dot{w}) = \sum_{i=1}^{\mathrm{NG}} \bar{q} \omega_i \, |\mathbf{J}_i| \, \mathbf{N}(\bar{\xi}_i, \bar{\eta}_i) \dot{\mathbf{w}} = 1 \end{cases} \tag{31}$$

Since integral Equation 27 is not calculated exactly, it cannot be said that the formulation yields a strict upper bound using this formula. Nevertheless, the optimal velocity field is still kinematically admissible and corresponding compatible strain are obtained using the $\mathbf{B}_i$ matrix so that a strict upper bound can be obtained provided that the dissipation is computed exactly *a posteriori*. However, in practice, there is practically no difference and the computed values can be considered as upper bounds.

Essential boundary conditions

In this part, we show how to impose essential boundary conditions of the isogeometric approach. For the sake of simplicity, we consider the following several Dirichlet boundary conditions (BCs):

- Simply supported plates with curved boundaries

$$B = \{\dot{w}(\mathbf{x}_D) = 0 \text{ on } \Gamma_1\} \tag{32}$$

- Clamped plates

$$B = \{\dot{w}(\mathbf{x}_D) = 0 \text{ and } \dot{w}_n(\mathbf{x}_D) = 0 \text{ on } \Gamma_1\} \tag{33}$$

where $\dot{w}_n(\mathbf{x}_D)$ is the normal rotation constraint and $\mathbf{x}_D$ are control points that define the essential boundary.

It is well known that the enforcement of Dirichlet BCs on $\dot{w}$ is treated as in the standard FEM. This procedure involves only control points that define the essential boundary. However, for the normal rotation $\dot{w}_n$ occurred in (32), the enforcement of Dirichlet BCs can be solved in a special way reported in [23,37]. The idea for a clamped case, i.e, $\dot{w}_n(\mathbf{x}_D) = 0$ is to impose zero values of deflection velocity variables, i.e., $\dot{w} = 0$, at both control points $\mathbf{x}_D = \{\mathbf{x}_{D_1}, \ldots, \mathbf{x}_{D_d}\}$ and $\mathbf{x}_A = \{\mathbf{x}_{A_1}, \ldots, \mathbf{x}_{A_d}\}$ adjacent to the boundary control points $\mathbf{x}_D$ as shown in Figure 4. It be can seen that enforcing essential boundary conditions using this way in the isogeometric approach is very simple and efficient when comparing with other numerical methods.

The second and third constraints (31) can be written as a standard linear equality constraint (ec):

$$\mathbf{B}^{ec}\dot{\mathbf{q}} = \mathbf{b}^{ec} \tag{34}$$

where the matrix $\mathbf{B}^{ec}$ and vector $\mathbf{b}^{ec}$ of Equation 34 are given by

$$\mathbf{B}^{ec} = \left[\begin{array}{ccc} \sum\limits_{i=1}^{NG} \bar{\omega}_i \, |\mathbf{J}_i| \, N_1(\bar{\xi}_i, \bar{\eta}_i) & \cdots & \sum\limits_{i=1}^{NG} \bar{w}_i \, |\mathbf{J}_i| \, N_{\mathrm{nCP}}(\bar{\xi}_i, \bar{\eta}_i) \\ \hline & \mathbf{B}^{ec}_{IJ} & \\ \hline & \mathbf{B}^{ec}_{IJ} & \end{array}\right]_{(2d+1)\times \mathrm{nCP}} \tag{35}$$

$$\mathbf{b}^{ec\mathrm{T}} = \left[\, 1 \; \overbrace{0 \cdots 0}^{d} \; \overbrace{0 \cdots 0}^{d} \,\right] \tag{36}$$

where row 1, row 2 to $d+1$ and row $d+2$ to $2d+1$ in $\mathbf{B}^{ec}$ matrix stand for the number of constraints related to an external work rate, the boundary control points and control points adjacent to the boundary, respectively, and $\mathbf{B}^{ec}_{IJ}$ is described as

$$\mathbf{B}^{ec}_{IJ} = \begin{cases} 1 & \text{each } I \in \{1, 2, \ldots d\} \text{ with respect to each } J \in \mathscr{D} \\ 0 & \text{otherwise} \end{cases} \tag{37}$$

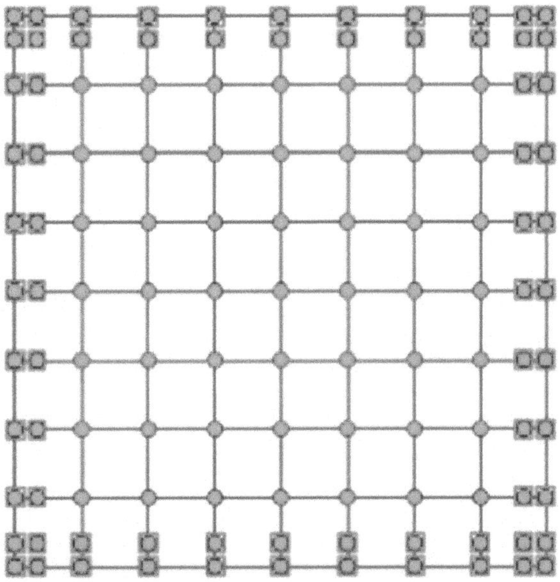

Figure 4 Clamped boundary conditions in a rotation-free IGA formulation.

where d denotes the number of control points defining the Dirichlet boundary with respect to a set of boundary control points $\mathscr{D} = \{n_1, n_2, \ldots n_d\}$.

Note that first $d + 1$ rows in (35) are indeed used for limit analysis of plates with the only prescribed deflection on Γ_1. In addition, when the symmetric boundary conditions are employed, as illustrated in Figure 5, we enforce the constraint of same deflections into the boundary control points and control points adjacent to the symmetric boundary, (i.e. along the symmetry lines, the normal rotation is fixed which can be achieved by enforcing the deflection of two rows of control points that define the tangent of the plate to have the same value [22]). A matrix storing such constraints will be added to the extensive rows of $\mathbf{B}^{ec}$.

It be can observed that the enforcement of essential boundary conditions using the rotation-free approach is simple and efficient in comparison with other numerical methods. For instance, readers can find more details on the advantages of this procedure in [22,23,25,26]. In addition, IGA based on the Lagrange multiplier, penalty and collocation methods (see [7]) can be also used to enforce essential boundary conditions for the thin plate.

Solution procedure of the discrete problem

Second-order cone programming

The above limit analysis problem is a non-linear optimization problem with equality constraints. It can be solved using a general non-linear optimization solver such as a sequential quadratic programming (SQP) algorithm (which is a generalization of Newton's method for unconstrained optimization), a direct iterative algorithm [38]. In particular, the optimization problem can be reduced to the problem of minimizing a sum of norms by Andersen et al. [39] due to the specific choice of the von Mises criterion and can be reformed as a second-order cone programming (SOCP) problem and solved

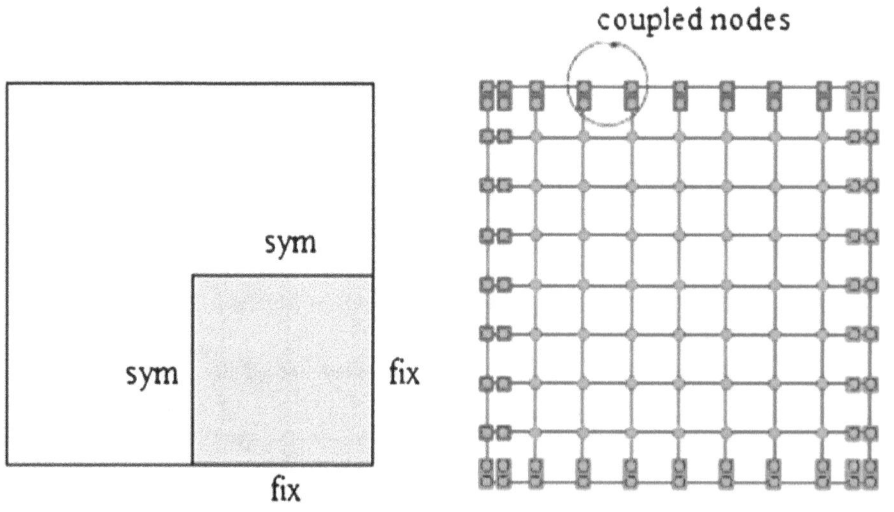

(a) Symmetric conditions (b) Coupled nodes

Figure 5 A fully clamped square plate: a quarter of plate is modeled: (a) symmetric conditions; (b) coupled nodes.

using an interior point method [12]. The general form of a SOCP problem with N_{cs} sets of constraints has the following form

$$\min \sum_{i=1}^{NG} c_i t_i$$

$$\text{s. t.} \quad \|\mathbf{H}_i \mathbf{t} + \mathbf{v}_i\| \leq \mathbf{y}_i^T \mathbf{t} + z_i \quad \text{for } i = 1, \ldots, N_{cs} \tag{38}$$

where $t_i \in \mathbb{R}$, $i = \overline{1, NG}$ or $\mathbf{t} \in \mathbb{R}^{NG}$ are optimization variables, and the coefficients are $c_i \in \mathbb{R}$, $\mathbf{H}_i \in \mathbb{R}^{m_{\dim} \times NG}$, $\mathbf{v}_i \in \mathbb{R}^{m_{\dim}}$, $\mathbf{y}_i \in \mathbb{R}^{NG}$, and $z_i \in \mathbb{R}$. For optimization problems in 2D or 3D Euclidean space, $m_{\dim} = 2$ or $m_{\dim} = 3$, respectively. When $m_{\dim} = 1$, the SOCP problem reduces to a linear programming problem.

Solution procedure using second-order cone programming

The limit analysis problem, Equation 31, is a non-linear optimization problem with equality constraints. As stated before, the problem can be reduced to the problem of minimizing a sum of norms following the procedure described by Andersen et al. [39].

Since $\mathbf{\Theta}$ is a positive definite matrix, the objective or the internal plastic dissipation function in Equation 31 can be straightforwardly rewritten in a form involving a sum of norms as

$$W_{\text{int}} \approx m_p \sum_{i=1}^{NG} \bar{\omega}_i \, |\mathbf{J}_i| \left|\left| \mathbf{C}^T \, \dot{\boldsymbol{\kappa}}_i \right|\right| \tag{39}$$

where $\|\cdot\|$ denotes the Euclidean norm appearing in the plastic dissipation function, i.e., $\|\mathbf{v}\| = (\mathbf{v}^T\mathbf{v})^{1/2}$, $\mathbf{C}$ is the so-called Cholesky factor of $\mathbf{\Theta}$ which is given by

$$\mathbf{C} = \frac{1}{\sqrt{3}} \begin{bmatrix} 2 & 0 & 0 \\ 1 & \sqrt{3} & 0 \\ 0 & 0 & 1 \end{bmatrix} \tag{40}$$

For convenience, a vector of additional variables $\boldsymbol{\rho}_i$ is introduced as

$$\boldsymbol{\rho}_i = \begin{bmatrix} \rho_1 & \rho_2 & \rho_3 \end{bmatrix}^T = \mathbf{C}^T \, \dot{\boldsymbol{\kappa}}_i \tag{41}$$

Hence, Equation 39 becomes

$$W_{\text{int}} = m_p \sum_{i=1}^{NG} \bar{\omega}_i \, |\mathbf{J}_i| \, ||\boldsymbol{\rho}_i|| \tag{42}$$

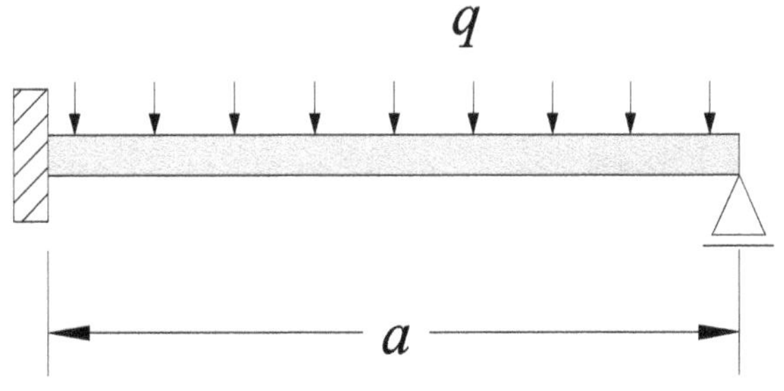

Figure 6 Clamped - supported beam model.

Table 1 A comparison of the limit load factor $\left(\frac{\bar{q}a^2}{m_p}\right)$ of beams with $m_p = \sigma_0 bt^2/4$

Methods	SS	CS	CC
Present (p = 2)	8.0007 (66 Dofs)	11.703 (514 Dofs)	16.063 (258 Dofs)
Present (p = 3)	8.0004 (67 Dofs)	11.687 (515 Dofs)	16.042 (259 Dofs)
Analytical	8.0	11.657	16.0

Now the optimization problem (31) becomes a problem of minimizing a sum of norms as

$$\lambda^+ = \min\ m_p \sum_{i=1}^{NG} \bar{\omega}_i \left|\mathbf{J}_i\right| \left|\left|\boldsymbol{\rho}_i\right|\right|$$
$$\text{s.t} \begin{cases} \boldsymbol{\rho}_i = \mathbf{C}^T\,\mathbf{B}_i\dot{\mathbf{w}} & \forall i = \overline{1,\text{NG}} \\ \mathbf{B}^{\text{ec}}\dot{\mathbf{w}} = \mathbf{b}^{\text{ec}} \end{cases} \tag{43}$$

In fact, a problem of this sort can be reformed as a SOCP problem by introducing auxiliary variables $t_1,\ t_2,\ \ldots,\ t_{\text{NG}}$

$$\lambda^+ = \min\ m_p \sum_{i=1}^{NG} \bar{\omega}_i \left|\mathbf{J}_i\right| t_i$$
$$\text{s.t} \begin{cases} \left|\left|\boldsymbol{\rho}_i\right|\right| \le t_i & \forall i = \overline{1,\text{NG}} \\ \boldsymbol{\rho}_i = \mathbf{C}^T\,\mathbf{B}_i\dot{\mathbf{w}} & \forall i = \overline{1,\text{NG}} \\ \mathbf{B}^{\text{ec}}\dot{\mathbf{w}} = \mathbf{b}^{\text{ec}} \end{cases} \tag{44}$$

where the first constraint in Equation 44 represents quadratic cones. The total number of variables of the optimization problem is $N_{\text{var}} = \text{NoDofs} + 4 \times \text{NG}$ where NoDofs is the total number of the degrees of freedom (DOFs) of the underlying problem. As a result, the optimization problem defined by Equation 44 can be effectively solved by the academic version of the Mosek optimization package [12].

Results and discussion

In this section, we examine the performance of the present approach through the limit analysis of beams and plates. The computations are performed on a desktop computer

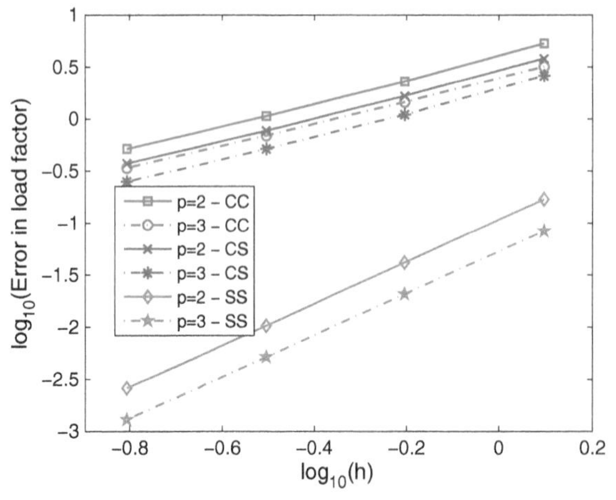

Figure 7 Convergence rate of limit load factors of beams.

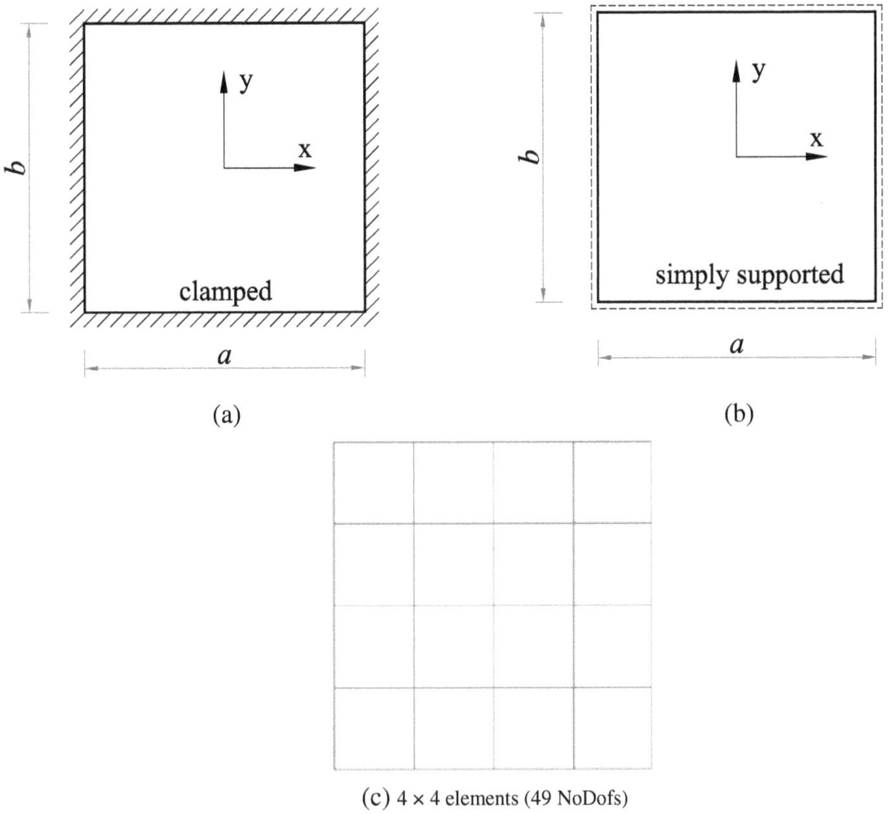

Figure 8 Full model of square plates and an illustration of uniform mesh: (a) fully clamped; (b) simply supported; (c) coarse mesh.

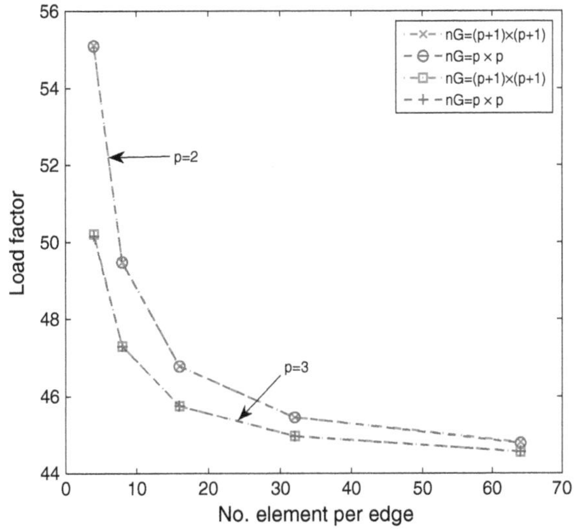

Figure 9 Comparison of numerical results of the clamped square plate using two Gaussian rules.

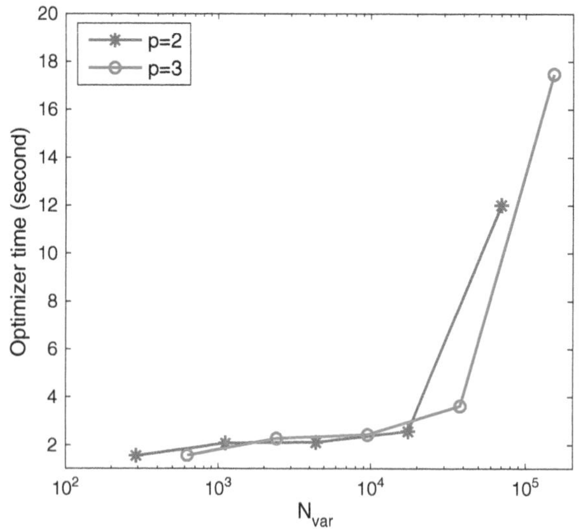

Figure 10 Comparison of computational times of the clamped square plate using quadratic and cubic elements.

with ADM Phenom II X6 (2.8GHz CPU, 16G RAM). For purpose of comparison with other published methods in the literature, we will restrict our interest to simply supported and clamped plates, which are the most frequently found case in practice. As shown in [17], the standard Gaussian quadrature rule (or nG $= (p+1) \times (p+1)$ Gauss points) is used to evaluate the integrals of NURBS elements of p degree. Just a precision, this is valid only for evaluating stiffness matrices and load vector for elastoplastic analyses, but here the dissipation involving a square root cannot be evaluated exactly using Gauss rules. However, we also can utilize this quadrature rule for limit analysis problem without much loss of accuracy of solution. It also is worth mentioning that the computational cost increases significantly when higher-order elements are used. This was pointed out that using the Gauss quadrature rule for NURBS elements is far from optimal. Hence, a simple and efficient quadrature algorithm [40,41] for NURBS-based isogeometric analysis will be recommended for our future research. For the limit problem of thin plates, we in this study employ only nG $= p \times p$ Gauss points[a] to compute the integral in Equation 27. We also exploit the so-called k-refinement approach, which is a unique characteristic of IGA as a flexible way for refinement and degree elevation for limit analysis problems. Note that with the same number of elements, the total number of DOFs of IGA is less than that of FEM. For all the examples, the von Mises criterion and perfectly rigid plastic material are used.

Table 2 The convergence of the limit load factor ($\bar{q}a^2/m_p$) for a clamped square plate

Authors	Mesh			
	8 x 8	**16 x 16**	**32 x 32**	**64 x 64**
Present (Quadratic)	49.487	46.784	45.456	44.781
Present (Cubic)	47.302	45.760	44.963	44.556
Hodge and Belytschko [1]	-	-	-	49.25/42.86

Reference solution [1]: upper/lower bounds.

Table 3 The convergence of the limit load factor ($\bar{q}a^2/m_p$) for a simply supported square plate

Authors	Mesh			
	4 x 4	8 x 8	16 x 16	32 x 32
Present (Quadratic)	25.295	25.089	25.037	25.023
Present (Cubic)	25.064	25.022	25.019	25.018
Hodge and Belytschko [1]	-	-	-	26.54/24.86

Reference solution [1]: upper/lower bounds.

Beams

We restrict the present formulation to a 1D beam case and verify its performance for the Euler beam of length a and thickness t. Without loss of generality, beams of rectangular cross section ($b \times t$) are considered and subjected to a uniform load and various boundary conditions at the ends, as shown in Figure 6. For computation, a symmetry model is applied to the simply supported and clamped beams whilst the clamped simply supported beam uses a full model.

Table 1 shows limit load factors of the beam with various boundary conditions. It can be seen that the numerical results are in very good agreement with analytical solutions. The convergence rates are plotted in Figure 7. They verify the theoretically expected values of 1:1 for the clamped beam and 1:2 for the simply supported beam. Being different from the regularity of the convergence rate in elastic problems [17], the convergence rates obtained do not change significantly when increasing the degree of basis functions of the approximate solution. This is due to the appearance of plastic hinges in the beam. More importantly, the accuracy of solution is improved with increasing the degree of basis functions.

Rectangular plates

We next consider a square plate of length a and thickness t with clamped and simply supported boundary conditions subjected to a uniform load, as shown in Figure 8. Here, we use a symmetric model and a coarsely uniform mesh is given in Figure 8c.

Similar to FEM, Gauss quadrature can be utilized for integration on element level, although it was proved that such a Gauss quadrature is far from optimal with NURBS

Table 4 A comparison of the limit load factor ($\bar{q}a^2/m_p$) for a square plate

Authors	Methods	Bounds	Simply supported	Clamped
Hodge and Belytschko [1]	Quadratic field (nonconforming)	UB	26.54	49.25
Capsoni and Corradi [2]	BFS (conforming)	UB	25.02	45.29
Le et al. [4]	HCT (conforming)	UB	25.01	45.12
Bleyer and de Buhan [6]	T6b (nonconforming)	UB	-	45.036
Bleyer and de Buhan [6]	H3 (nonconforming)	UB	-	44.287
Zhou et al. [9]	C^1-NEM	UB	25.07	45.18
Le et al. [7]	EFG	QUB	25.01	45.07
Le et al. [16]	EFG	QLB	24.98	43.86
Le et al. [4]	Enhanced Morley (EM)	LB	24.93	43.454
Present ($p = 2$)	IGA	UB	25.023	44.803
Present ($p = 3$)	IGA	UB	25.018	44.556

UB, upper bound; QUB, quasi-upper bound; QLB, quasi-lower bound; LB, lower bound.

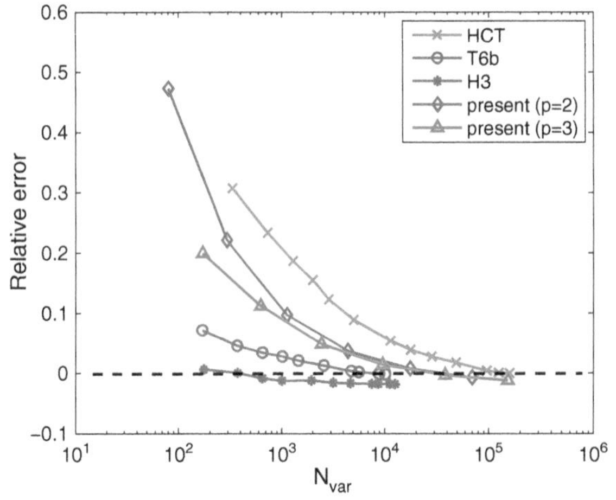

Figure 11 Relative error to the reference upper bound of the clamped square plate.

basis functions [40,41]. Herein, discussion focuses on using a right reduction of the number of Gauss points without loss of accuracy of solution. Figure 9 shows that two Gaussian quadrature rules produce the same results while the number of optimization variables using $p \times p$ Gauss points reduces very significantly, approximately $N_{\mathrm{var}}/3$ less than those using the full integration.

For the computational cost, it is estimated based on N_{var} versus total optimization steps (Mosek times). Results are plotted in Figure 10. It is seen that the total number of variables increases quickly when increasing the degree of basis functions. Optimization problems solved using the Mosek academic software show very fast convergence in about 13 to 16 step iterations with computing times ranging from 2 to 18 s only.

Although the analytical solution is unknown, this benchmark has been investigated by many authors. The earliest numerical performance of the upper and lower bounds was proposed by Hodge and Belytschko [1]. Tables 2 and 3 show the convergence of

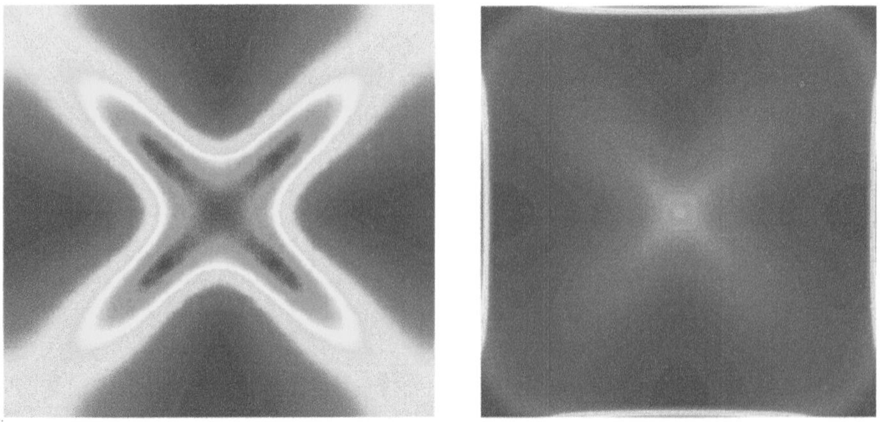

(a) (b)

Figure 12 The plastic dissipation of a square plate: (a) SSSS; (b) CCCC.

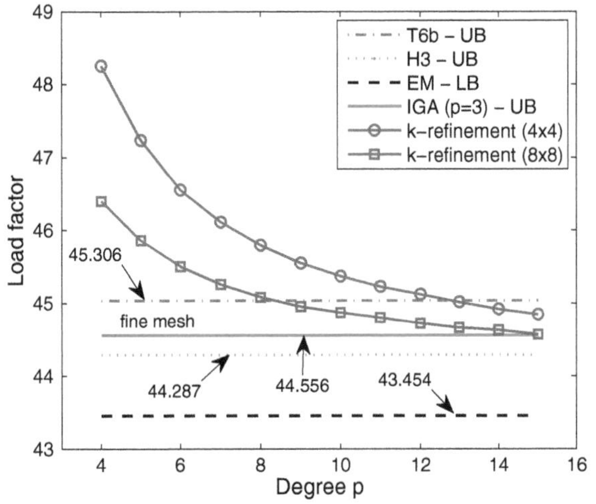

Figure 13 Convergence of the limit load factor ($\bar{q}ab^2/m_p$) of a clamped square plate using *k*-refinement.

the present solutions using quadratic and cubic elements versus elemental meshes. The present solutions fall between lower and upper bound published ones.

Table 4 compares the present results with the upper bound solutions [1,2,4,6,9], the quasi-upper bound [7] and the (quasi-) lower bound [4,16]. As seen, the limit load factor using the rotation-free IGA approach is more accurate than that of several published solutions. The improved upper bound solution of 45.036 and 44.287 derived with respect to T6b and H3 elements is provided by Bleyer and de Buhan [6] for the clamped square plate problem. The present results agree well with the most recent upper bounds; one has a value of 44.560 for the cubic B-splines element (between 1% and 0.6% with respect to T6b and H3). Figure 11 illustrates several reference upper bound solutions of the clamped square plate and proves the reliability of the present solutions.

In addition, Figure 12 depicts the plastic dissipation of simply supported and clamped square plates. It is seen that the rotation-free IGA approach can reproduce properly the plastic dissipation (or yield line mechanism). Even the failure mechanism can be reproduced exactly using a lower number of DOFs.

Furthermore, to prove the flexibility of the present method, we study its performance using *k*-refinement (higher order and higher continuity). In this case, two slightly coarse mesh of 4 × 4 and 8 × 8 B-spline elements are illustrated. We know that one of the main advantages of IGA is to increase easily the order of basis functions. Especially, *k*-refinement algorithm in IGA can produce easily C^1-continuity between elements while *p*-refinement (in the *p*-version FEM) achieves only C^0 continuity. The limit load factor of

Table 5 The limit load factor ($\bar{q}ab/m_p$) for a rectangular plate with $a/b = 2$ and various condition boundaries

Authors	SSSS	CCCC	CCCsF	CCClF	CCsFF
Le et al. [7]	29.88	54.61	43.86	-	-
Zhou et al. [9]	28.90	55.09	45.18	18.82	40.39
Melosh [42]	29.88	57.26	46.31	19.74	40.28
Present (p = 2)	29.93	54.95	45.19	19.61	39.40
Present (p = 3)	29.88	54.65	44.91	19.44	38.55

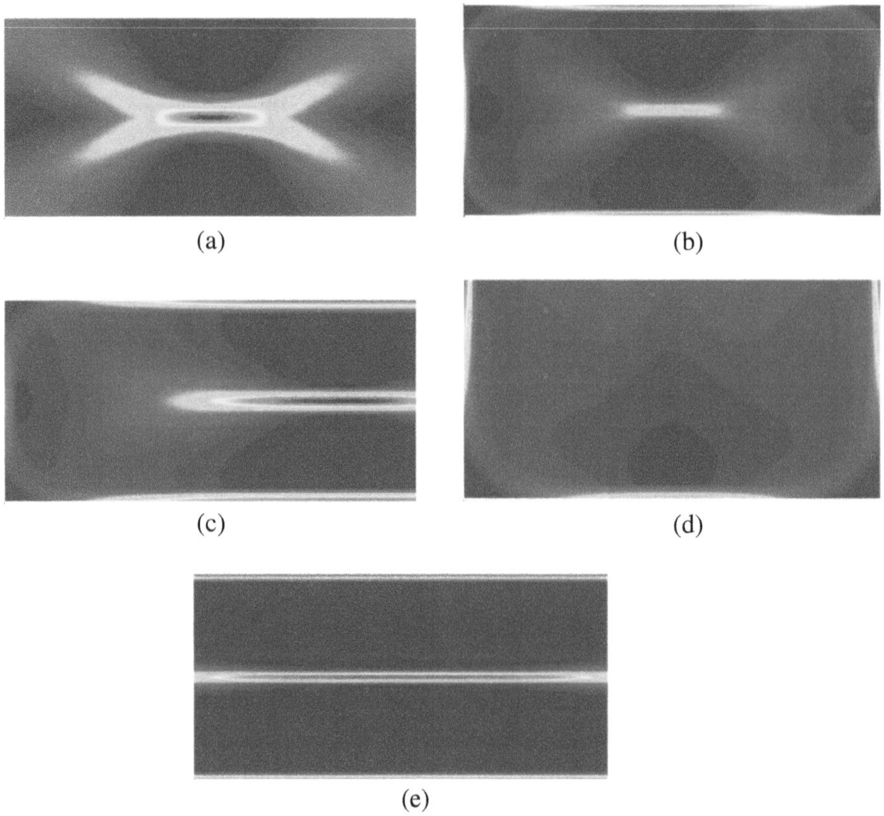

Figure 14 The plastic dissipation of a rectangular plate: (a) SSSS; (b) CCCC; (c) CCCsF; (d) CCClF; (e) CCsFF.

the clamped square plate using the k-refinement algorithm is shown in Figure 13. Numerical results indicate that the rotation-free isogeometric approach with k-refinement improves very well the convergence of solution.

Next, let us consider the rectangular plate (length-to-width ratio $a/b = 2$) with various boundary conditions. We compare the present results with other published ones such

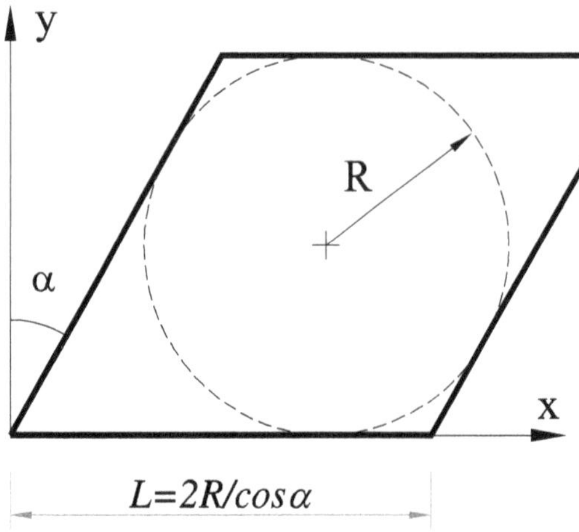

Figure 15 Geometry of a rhombic plate.

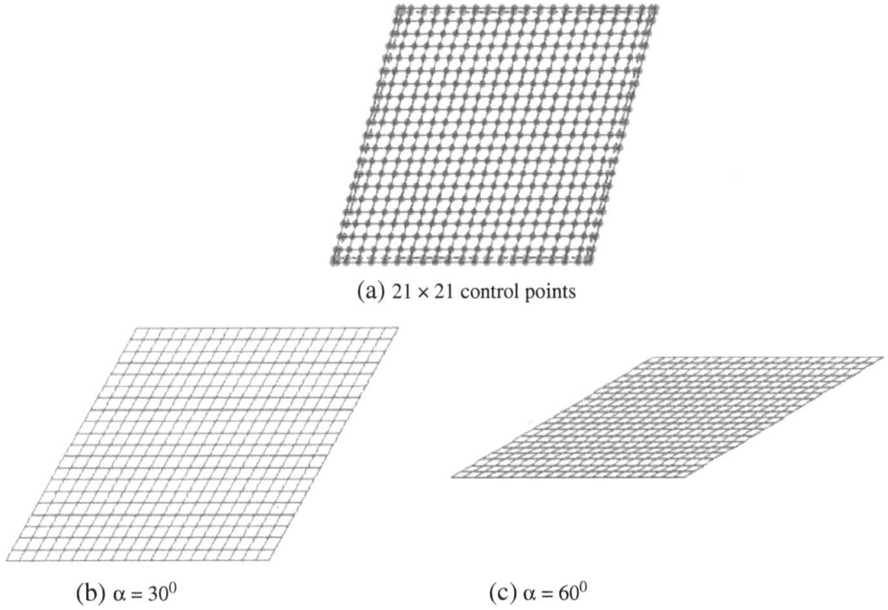

Figure 16 Meshes of B-spline elements: (a) control points; (b) α=30°; (c) α=60°.

as the EFG method [7], the rectangular non-deforming plate element (ACM) [42] and the C^1 natural element method [9]. Table 5 summarizes the limit load multipliers of a rectangular plate with various boundary conditions such as simply supported (SSSS), fully clamped (CCCC), three-clamped and one-short free sides (CCCsF), three-clamped and one-long free sides (CCClF), and two-clamped and two-short free sides (CCsFF). It is again observed that the results obtained are in good accordance with other published ones. Figure 14 shows the plastic dissipation with very good smoothness using the cubic B-spline basis functions.

Rhombic plate

A rhombic plate with varying skewness angles α as shown in Figure 15 is subjected to a uniform load. For comparison, the rhombic plate is modeled by 20 × 20 B-spline elements, as shown in Figure 16. Simply supported and fully clamped boundary conditions are considered. In the numerical calculation, the radius of the circular in Figure 16 is

Table 6 Results of the limit load factor ($\bar{q}R^2/m_p$) for the rhombic plate

α^0	Boundaries	Capsoni and Silva [44]	Zhou et al. [9]	Present (p = 2)	Present (p = 3)
0	SSSS	6.278	6.267	6.267	6.255
15		6.197	6.186	6.230	6.166
30		5.966	5.916	5.942	5.901
45		5.609	5.447	5.570	5.475
60		5.140	4.808	5.090	4.89
0	CCCC	12.062	11.296	12.100	11.674
15		11.893	11.065	11.928	11.506
30		11.394	10.781	11.423	11.010
45		10.596	9.939	10.615	10.195
60		9.575	8.901	9.602	9.077

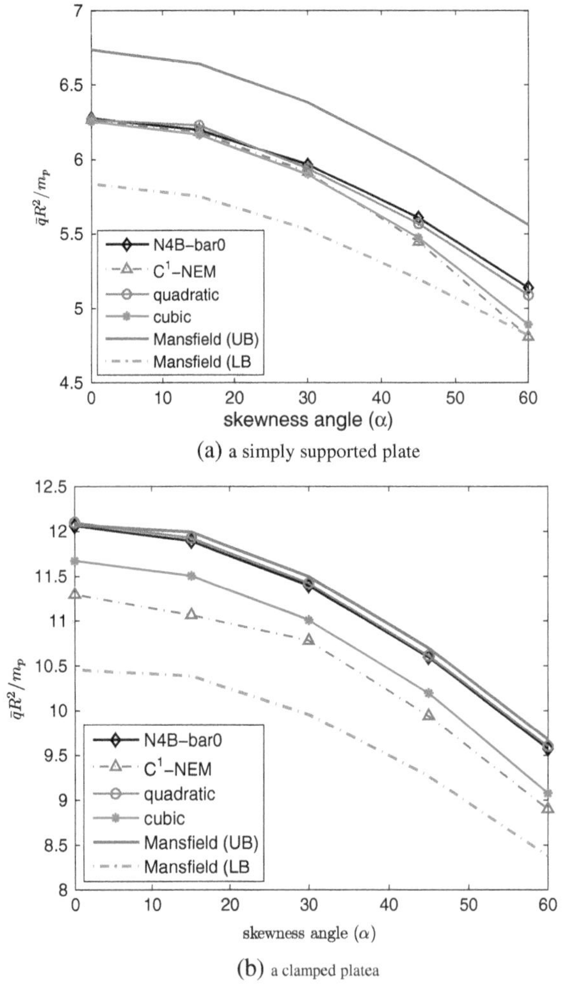

Figure 17 Limit load factor of a skew plate: (a) simply supported; (b) fully clamped.

chosen as $R = 0.5$ and the plate thickness is fixed at $t = 0.02$. The results of the collapse limit factor with varying skewness angle are listed in Table 6. The obtained result is compared with the analytical solution given by Mansfield [43], the Mindlin plate finite element (N4$\bar{\text{B}}$0) proposed by Capsoni and Silva [44] and C^1 natural element method (C^1-NEM) based on Kirchhoff plate model by Zhou et al. [9]. For this problem, an analytical

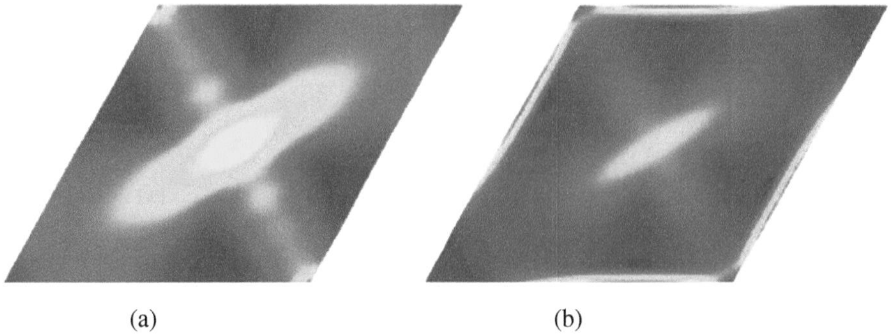

Figure 18 Plastic dissipation of a rhombic plate with α=30°: (a) simply supported plate, (b) clamped plate.

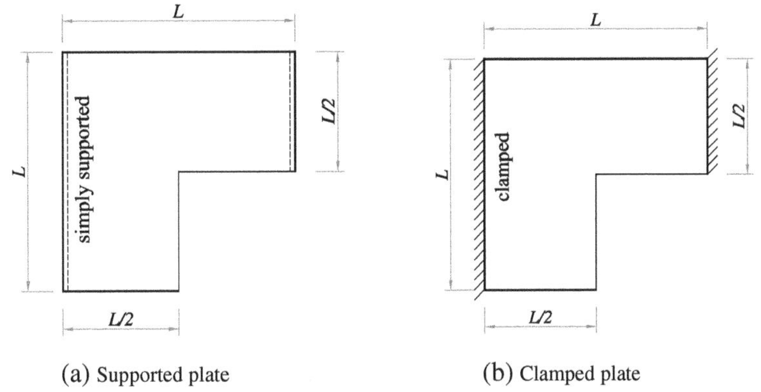

Figure 19 L-shaped plate models: (a) supported plate; (b) clamped plate.

approach into lower bound (LB) and upper bound solutions using the square yield criterion were proposed by Mansfield [43]. Note that an upper bound (UB) solution using the square yield criterion can be obtained by multiplying the lower bound value with a factor of $2/\sqrt{3}$. Figure 17 depicts the collapse limit factor with respect to various skewness angles. It is observed that the result of the quadratic element matches well with that of

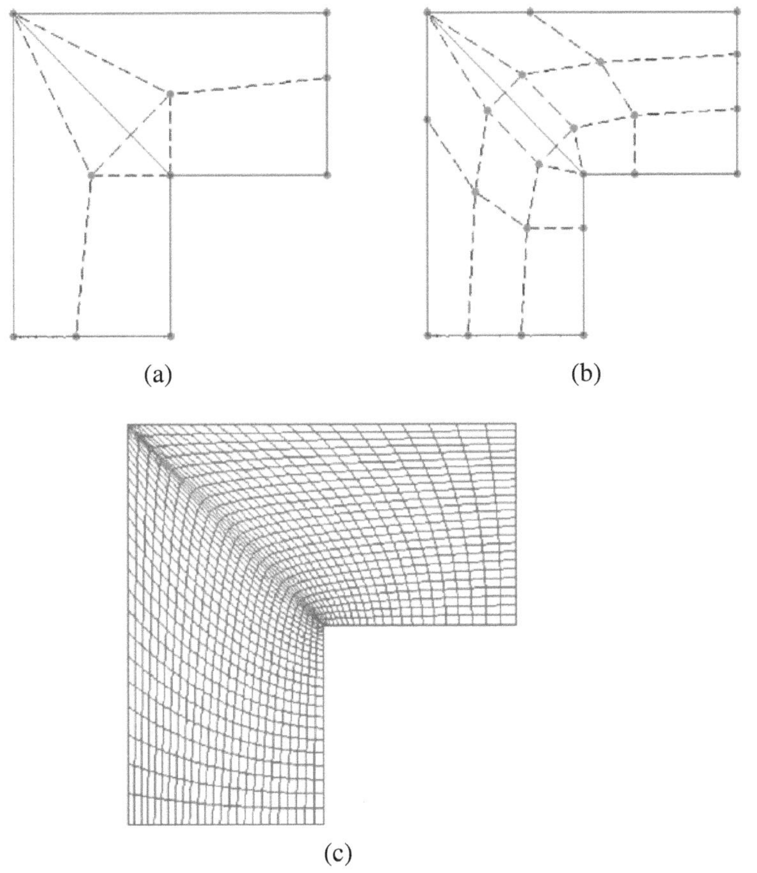

Figure 20 Control net, coarse mesh and fine mesh of an L-shaped plate: (a) quadratic, (b) cubic, (c) 50 × 25 B-splines elements.

Table 7 The limit load factor ($\bar{q}L^2/m_p$) for an L-shaped plate

Authors	Methods	SSSS	CCCC
Le et al. [7]	QUB	6.298	-
Le et al. [4]	UB/LB	6.288/6.065	-
Bleyer and de Buhan [6]	UB -T6b	6.44	-
Bleyer and de Buhan [6]	UB -H3	6.24	-
Present (p = 2)	UB	6.298	16.146
Present (p = 3)	UB	6.174	15.621
Reference [6]		6.16	-

the N4$\bar{B}$0 element. The cubic element produces higher accuracy solutions than the N4$\bar{B}$0 element and is competitive to the C^1-NEM. When increasing skewness angle, the limit load factor value decreases. Figure 18 shows the plastic dissipation energy of 60°-rhombic plates using the cubic element. It is clear that the present method is reliable for predicting collapse mechanism compared to other published ones [9,44].

L-shaped plate

We consider an L-shaped plate subjected to a uniform load. The plate geometry is shown in Figure 19. Control net, coarse mesh and fine mesh are detailed in Figure 20. Knot vectors and control data are given in the Appendix ('L-shaped plate'). This problem involves a singular behaviour at the obtuse vertices. Simply supported and fully clamped boundary conditions are used. The plate is modeled by 50 × 25 B-spline elements of 1,512 nodes ($N_{\text{var}} = 21,512$ for $p = 2$, and $N_{\text{var}} = 46513$ for $p = 3$). The obtained results are compared with those of the quasi-upper approach based on the element-free method [7] and the dual FEM approach [4] based on the conforming HCT and enhanced equilibrium Morley (EM) element using the finest mesh of 6,426 nodes (or $N_{\text{var}} = 105,264$ for HCT). Table 7 summarizes the collapse limit load factor. The present elements provide strict upper bound solutions and produce load factor values lower than EFG and HCT elements. Note that the HCT element has 3 Dofs per node resulting in a larger number of DOFs than the present elements. Also, for comparison,

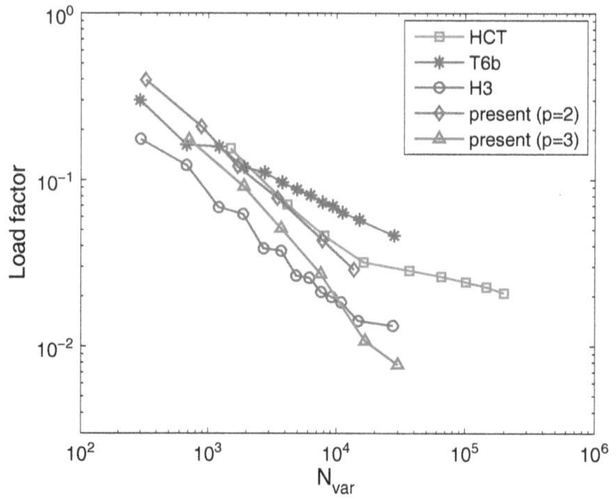

Figure 21 Relative error to the reference upper bound of a simply supported L-shape plate.

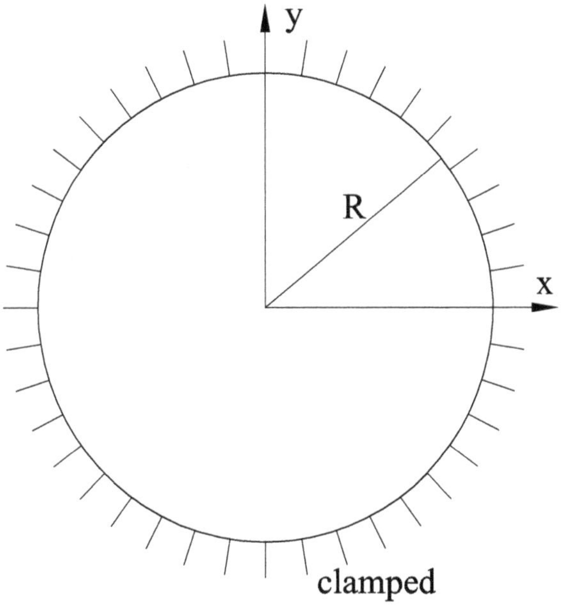

Figure 22 Geometry of a clamped circular plate.

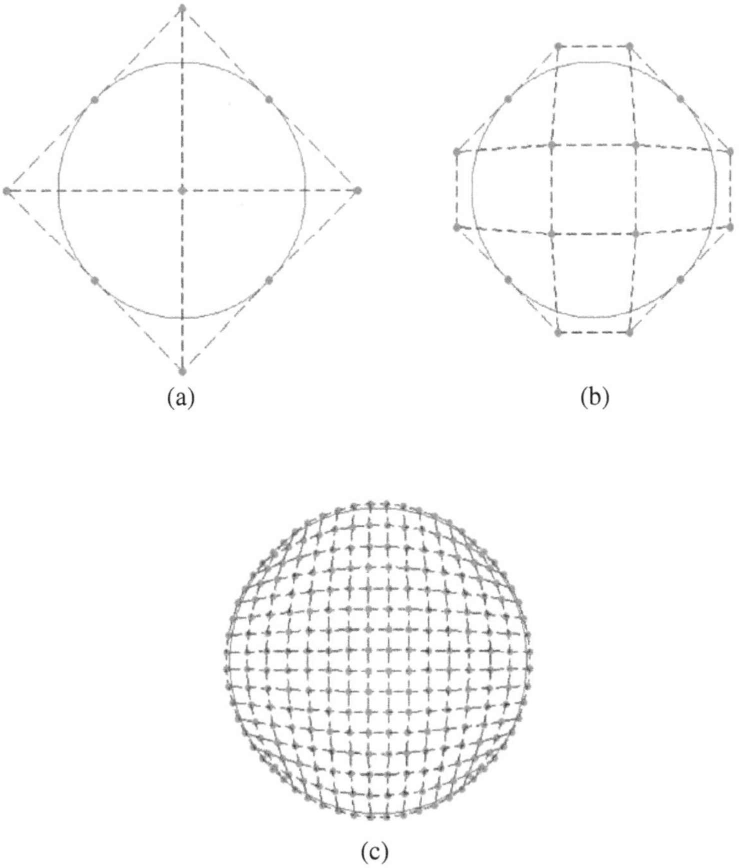

Figure 23 Coarse mesh and control points of a circular plate with various degrees: (a) $p = 2$, (b) $p = 3$ and (c) $p = 15$.

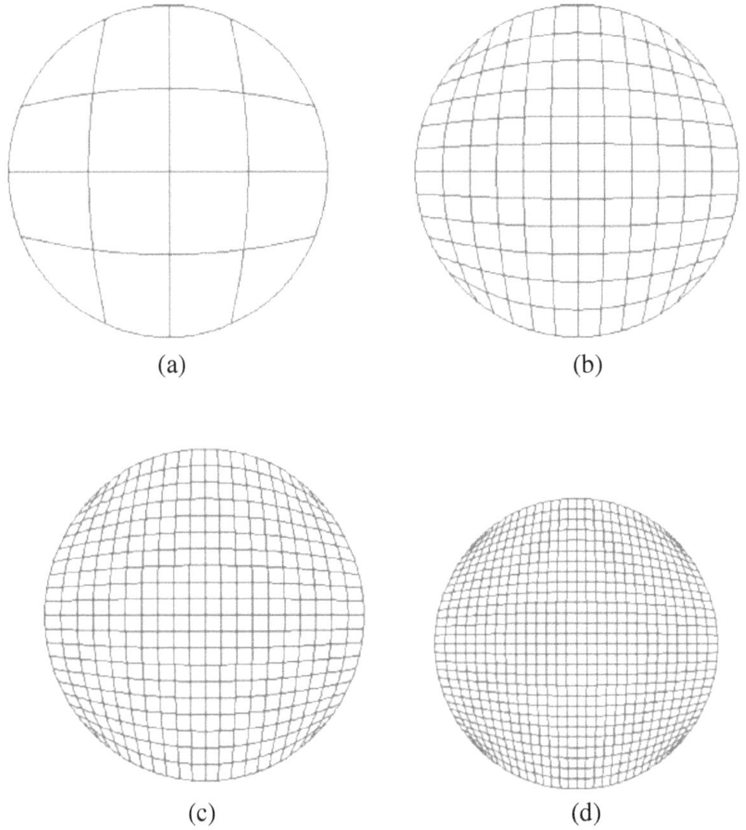

Figure 24 Element meshes of a circular plate: (a) 4 x 4; (b) 12 x 12; (c) 20 x 20; (d) 28 x 28.

the EFG requires 3,816 nodes (or 3,816 NoDofs) while the cubic element has only 1,024 nodes.

The accuracy of the present method in comparison with HCT element is also shown in Figure 21. It is clear that the performance of the present elements is better than that of the HCT.

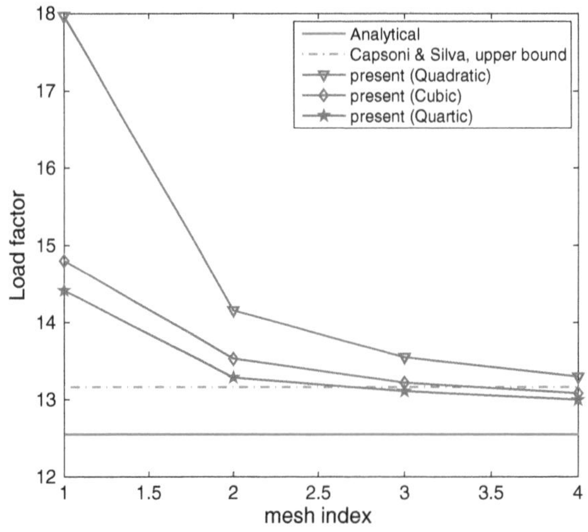

Figure 25 Convergence of the limit load factor ($\bar{q}R^2/m_p$) of a circular plate.

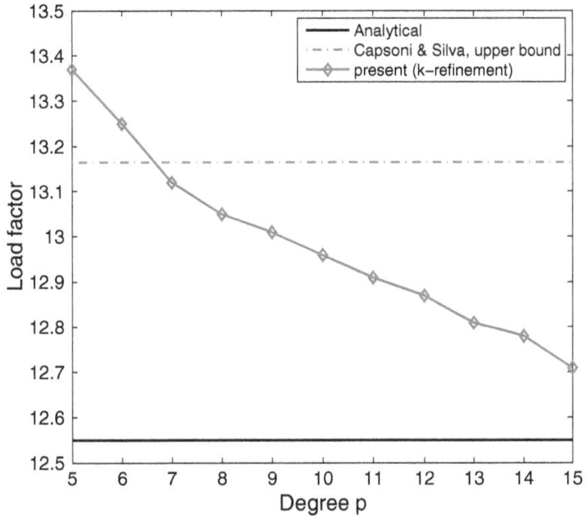

Figure 26 Convergence of the limit load factor ($\bar{q}R^2/m_p$) of a circular plate using k-refinement.

Circular plate

Circular plate subjected to uniform transverse loading

In this example, we consider a fully clamped circular plate under uniform transverse loading as illustrated in Figure 22. The circular plate has a radius to thickness ratio of 100 ($R/t = 100$). A rational quadratic basis is enough to model exactly the circular geometry. Knot vectors and control data of the circular plate are given in the Appendix ('Circular plate'). Coarse mesh and control net of the plate with respect to quadratic, cubic, quartic and fifteenth elements are illustrated in Figure 23. To investigate the convergence of the limit load factor, different meshes of 4×4, 12×12, 20×20 and 28×28 NURBS elements are displayed in Figure 24. The results of the limit load factor are provided in Figure 25. The obtained solution is compared with that of the analytical approach [45] and the numerical formulation presented in Capsoni and Silva [44]. It can be seen that the present results converge well to the analytical value and are much better than those of the N4$\bar{\text{B}}$0 element.

The k-refinement algorithm is now used to calculate the limit load factor of the clamped circular plate. Figure 26 shows the limit load factor of various degrees of NURBS functions (from 5 to 15) based on a mesh of 6×6 NURBS elements. The obtained result converges well to the best reference value given in the literature.

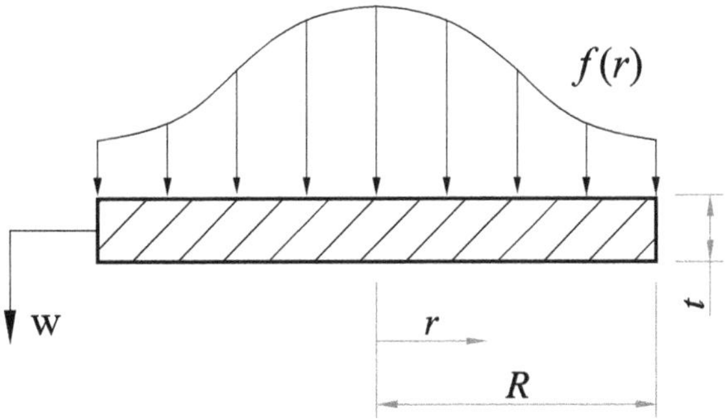

Figure 27 An illustration of a circular plate subjected to a non-uniform load.

Table 8 The limit load factor λ_{cr}/m_p for a clamped circular plate subjected to a linear load

a_2	Tresca(UB)	Square(UB)	Quadratic	Cubic
−3	8.404	9.238	8.554	8.402
−2	6.412	6.928	6.639	6.485
−1	5.174	5.543	5.414	5.270
0	4.334	4.619	4.567	4.446
1	3.727	3.959	3.948	3.8926
2	3.269	3.464	3.475	3.363
3	2.911	3.080	3.074	3.000

Circular plate subjected to non-uniform transverse loading

Finally, we study a clamped circular plate subjected to non-uniform (linear and parabolic) load as shown in Figure 27. The parabolic load can be written as follows [43]:

$$f(r) = a_1 + a_2 r + a_3 r^2 \tag{45}$$

where a_1, a_2 and a_3 are predefined constants. In the numerical calculation, the constants a_1, a_2 and a_3 are chosen in such a way that a_1 is fixed at value of 3 ($a_1 = 3$) and a_2, a_3 vary. The geometry and material parameters are as given in the previous case. For illustration, we use a slightly fine mesh of 17 × 17 NURBS elements for quadratic and cubic elements.

For a varying load case, the analytically upper bound value based on the square yield criterion is $\lambda_{cr} = 12\sqrt{3}m_p/\left((2a_1 + a_2R)\,R^2\right)$ [43]. Table 8 compares the present solutions and the analytical values using both the Tresca and square yield criteria reported by Ghorashi [43]. As expected, the present results almost vary between the upper bound solutions using the Tresca and square yield criteria.

For a parabolic load case, the constants are chosen such as $a_1 = 3, a_2 = 2$ and various a_3 values. The limit load factor is given in Table 9. Again, the present solutions are bounded by the upper bound values reported in [43].

Conclusions

We have for the first time presented a rotation-free isogeometric finite element approach for upper bound limit analysis of thin plate structures. The method was derived from the kinematic theorem and isogeometric finite elements. The underlying optimization formulation of limit analysis was transformed into the form of a second-order cone programming, and it was then solved by highly efficient interior-point solvers. The performance of the method is validated through benchmark problems of plastic thin plates. Through the examples tested, some concluding remarks can be given as follows:

Table 9 The limit load factor λ_{cr}/m_p for a clamped circular plate subjected to a parabolic load

a_3	Tresca(UB)	Square(UB)	Quadratic	Cubic
−3	4.172	4.469	4.358	4.244
−2	3.821	4.074	4.019	3.904
−1	3.524	3.744	3.728	3.644
1	3.037	3.222	3.254	3.144
2	2.854	3.002	3.059	2.952
3	2.684	2.827	2.886	2.781

Table 10 Control points and weights for a disk of radius 0.5

i	1	2	3	4	5	6	7	8	9
x_i	$-\sqrt{2}/4$	$-\sqrt{2}/2$	$-\sqrt{2}/4$	0	0	0	$\sqrt{2}/4$	$\sqrt{2}/2$	$\sqrt{2}/4$
y_i	$\sqrt{2}/4$	0	$-\sqrt{2}/4$	$\sqrt{2}/2$	0	$-\sqrt{2}/2$	$\sqrt{2}/4$	0	$-\sqrt{2}/4$
w_i	1	$\sqrt{2}/2$	1	$\sqrt{2}/2$	1	$\sqrt{2}/2$	1	$\sqrt{2}/2$	1

- Only deflection degrees of freedom were needed in the optimization problem. Thus, the method requires less variables than N4$\bar{B}$0 element (or C^0-FEM), HCT element (or C^1-FEM) and C^1 natural element (C^1-NEM). As a result, it is promising to provide an effective way to solve large-scale plate problems.
- The essential boundary conditions are easily imposed in the context of the rotation-free isogeometric approach.
- Beyond h-and p-refinement schemes currently available in the traditional FEM, the present approach was found to be more efficient with k-refinement type for limit analysis of thin plates.
- Numerical results showed that the present method provides upper bound estimates of collapse limit loads, that proves the stability of the method. Also, the proposed method exhibited very good agreement with several published results in the literature for different benchmark problems. It seems, in particular, very efficient for the L-shaped plate problem which presents a singularity near the corner.

In present work, only benchmark problems were used to show the performance of the proposed formulation. However, we believe that the methodology is generalizable for large-scale plate problems in practice. Although the present method achieved high reliability, its computational cost is still significant due to an excessive overhead of control points for very uniformly refined meshes. It would therefore be interesting to associate the present method with adaptive local refinement procedures [25,46]. This is a work in progress and our findings will be devoted in a forthcoming paper.

Endnotes

[a]This helps to reduce the size of the optimization problem without loss of accuracy of solution as it will be shown later.

Appendix

Knot vectors and control points for NURBS objects

Circular plate

A circular plate is shown in Figure 22. A rational quadratic basis is used to exactly describe the geometry of the circular plate. Knot vectors $\Xi \times \mathscr{H}$ of the coarsest mesh with one element is defined as follows: $\Xi = \{0, 0, 0, 1, 1, 1\}$; $\mathscr{H} = \{0, 0, 0, 1, 1, 1\}$. Data of the circular plate are given in Table 10.

Table 11 Control points for the L-shaped plate

i	$P_{i,1}$	$P_{i,2}$	$P_{i,3}$
1	(0, 1)	(0, 2.5)	(0, 4)
2	(1, 1)	(1, 2.5)	(4, 4)
3	(1, 1)	(2.5, 1)	(4, 4)
4	(1, 0)	(2.5, 0)	(4, 0)

L-shaped plate

An L-shaped plate is illustrated in Figure 20. As stated previously, a rational quadratic basis is used to describe an L-shaped plate. Knot vectors $\Xi \times \mathscr{H}$ of the coarsest mesh with two elements are defined as follows: $\Xi = \{0, 0, 0, 0.5, 1, 1, 1\}$; $\mathscr{H} = \{0, 0, 0, 1, 1, 1\}$. Control points of the L-shaped plate are given in Table 11. Note that all control points have unit weights.

Acknowledgments
This research is funded by Vietnam National Foundation for Science and Technology Development (NAFOSTED) under grant number 107.02-2014.24. The support is gratefully acknowledged.

Competing interests
The authors declare that they have no competing interests.

Authors' contributions
HXN provided an original idea of further developing the rotation-free isogeometric approach in upper bound limit analysis of plates, developed the code, and revised the manuscript. CHT carried out the numerical examples and drafted the manuscript. JB revised the manuscript. PVN provided the source code of isogeometric analysis and revised the manuscript. All authors read and approved the final manuscript.

Author details
[1]Department of Computational Engineering, Vietnamese-German University, Binh Duong New City, Vietnam. [2]Division of Computational Mechanics, Ton Duc Thang University, HCMC, Vietnam. [3]Université Paris-Est, Laboratoire Navier, Ecole des Ponts ParisTech-IFSTTAR-CNRS (UMR 8205), 6-8 av Blaise Pascal, Cité Descartes, 77455 Champs-sur-Marne, France. [4]Institute of Mechanics and Advanced Materials, School of Engineering, Cardiff University, Queen's Buildings, The Parade, Cardiff CF24 3AA, UK.

References

1. Hodge PG, Belytschko T (1968) Numerical methods for the limit analysis of plates. J Appl Mech 35(4):795–802
2. Capsoni A, Corradi L (1999) Limit analysis of plates - a finite element formulation. Struct Eng Mech 8:325–341
3. Le CV, Nguyen-Xuan H, Nguyen-Dang H (2006) Dual limit analysis of plate bending. In: Collection of papers (modeling in mechanical and civil engineering) from Prof. Nguyen-Dang Hung's former students. Vietnam National University Ho Chi Minh City Publishing House, Ho Chi Minh, pp 476–494
4. Le CV, Nguyen-Xuan H, Nguyen-Dang H (2010) Upper and lower bound limit analysis of plates using FEM and second-order cone programming. Comput Struct 88:65–73
5. Tran TN (2011) A dual algorithm for shakedown analysis of plate bending. Int J Numer Meth Eng 86(7):862–875
6. Bleyer J, Buhan P (2013) On the performance of non-conforming finite elements for the upper bound limit analysis of plates. Int J Numer Meth Eng 94:308–330
7. Le CV, Gilbert M, Askes H (2009) Limit analysis of plates using the EFG method and second-order cone programming. Int J Numer Meth Eng 78(13):1532–1552
8. Le CV, Askes H, Gilbert M (2010) Adaptive element-free Galerkin method applied to the limit analysis of plates. Comput Meth Appl Mech Eng 199:2487–2496
9. Zhou S, Liu Y, Chen S (2012) Upper bound limit analysis of plates utilizing the C^1 natural element method. Comput Mech 50:543–561
10. Andersen KD, Christiansen E, Overton ML (2001) An efficient primal-dual interior-point method for minimizing a sum of Euclidean norms. SIAM J Sci Comput 22:243–262
11. Andersen ED, Roos C, Terlaky T (2003) On implementing a primal-dual interior-point method for conic quadratic programming. Math Program 95:249–277
12. Mosek (2009) The MOSEK optimization toolbox for MATLAB manual. Mosek ApS, version 5.0 edition. http://www.mosek.com.
13. Ciria H, Peraire J, Bonet J (2008) Mesh adaptive computation of upper and lower bounds in limit analysis. Int J Numer Meth Eng 75:899–944
14. Makrodimopoulos A, Martin CM (2006) Upper bound limit analysis using simplex strain elements and second-order cone programming. Int J Numer Anal Meth Geomech 31:835–865
15. Munoz JJ, Bonet J, Huerta A, Peraire J (2009) Upper and lower bounds in limit analysis: adaptive meshing strategies and discontinuous loading. Int J Numer Meth Eng 77:471–501
16. Le CV, Gilbert M, Askes H (2010) Limit analysis of plates and slabs using a meshless equilibrium formulation. Int J Numer Meth Eng 83:1739–1758
17. Hughes TJR, Cottrell JA, Bazilevs Y (2005) Isogeometric analysis: CAD, finite elements, NURBS, exact geometry and mesh refinement. Comput Methods Appl Mech Eng 194(39–41):4135–4195
18. Cottrell J, Hughes TJR, Reali A (2007) Studies of refinement and continuity in isogeometric analysis. Comput Methods Appl Mech Eng 196:4160–4183
19. Cottrell JA, Reali A, Bazilevs Y, Hughes TJR (2006) Isogeometric analysis of structural vibrations. Comput Methods Appl Mech Eng 195(41–43):5257–5296

20. Elguedj T, Bazilevs Y, Calo V, Hughes T (2008) B and F projection methods for nearly incompressible linear and non-linear elasticity and plasticity using higher-order NURBS elements. Comput Methods Appl Mech Eng 197:2732–2762
21. Wall WA, Frenzel MA, Cyron C (2008) Isogeometric structural shape optimization. Comput Methods Appl Mech Eng 197(33–40):2976–2988
22. Kiendl J, Bletzinger KU, Linhard J, Wüchner R (2009) Isogeometric shell analysis with Kirchhoff–Love elements. Comput Methods Appl Mech Eng 198(49–52):3902–3914
23. Kiendl J, Bazilevs Y, Hsu MC, Wüchner R, Bletzinger KU (2010) The bending strip method for isogeometric analysis of Kirchhoff–Love shell structures comprised of multiple patches. Comput Methods Appl Mech Eng 199(37–40):2403–2416
24. Benson DJ, Bazilevs Y, Hsu MC, Hughes TJR (2010) Isogeometric shell analysis: the Reissner–Mindlin shell. Comput Methods Appl Mech Eng 199(5–8):276–289
25. Nguyen-Thanh N, Kiendl J, Nguyen-Xuan H, Wuchner R, Bletzinger KU, Bazilevs Y, Rabczuk T (2011) Rotation free isogeometric thin shell analysis using PHT-splines. Comput Methods Appl Mech Eng 200(47–48):3410–3424
26. Benson DJ, Bazilevs Y, Hsu MC, Hughes TJR (2011) A large deformation, rotation-free, isogeometric shell. Comput Methods Appl Mech Eng 200(13–16):1367–1378
27. Simpson RN, Bordas SPA, Trevelyan J, Rabczuk T (2012) A two-dimensional isogeometric boundary element method for elastostatic analysis. Comput Methods Appl Mech Eng 209–212:87–100
28. Reddy JN (2007) Theory and analysis of elastic plates and shells. CRC Press, Taylor and Francis Group, Boca Raton
29. Oñate E, Zarate F (2000) Rotation-free triangular plate and shell elements. Int J Numer Meth Eng 47:557–603
30. Oñate E, Flores FG (2005) Advances in the formulation of the rotation-free basic shell triangle. Comput Methods Appl Mech Eng 194:2406–2443
31. Flores FG, Estrada CF (2007) A rotation-free thin shell quadrilateral. Comput Methods Appl Mech Eng 196:2631–2646
32. Flores FG, Oñate E (2007) Wrinkling and folding analysis of elastic membranes using an enhanced rotation-free thin shell triangular element. Comput Methods Appl Mech Eng 196:2631–2646
33. Piegl LA, Tiller W (1997) The NURBS book. Springer Verlag, Heidelberg
34. Cottrell JA, Reali A, Bazilevs Y, Hughes TJR (2006) Isogeometric analysis of structural vibrations. Comput Methods Appl Mech Eng 195:5257–5297
35. Cottrell JA, Hughes TJR, Bazilevs Y (2009) Isogeometric analysis toward integration of CAD and FEA. Wiley, New York
36. Christiansen E (1996) Limit analysis of collapse states. In: Handbook of numerical analysis, vol IV, chapter II. North-Holland, Amsterdam, pp 193–312
37. Auricchio F, Beirao da Veiga L, Buffa A, Lovadina C, Reali A, Sangalli G (2007) A fully locking-free isogeometric approach for plane linear elasticity problems: a stream function formulation. Comput Methods Appl Mech Eng 197:160–172
38. Capsoni A, Corradi L (1997) A finite element formulation of the rigid-plastic limit analysis problem. Int J Numer Meth Eng 40:2063–2086
39. Andersen KD, Christiansen E, Overton ML (1998) Computing limit loads by minimizing a sum of norms. SIAM J Sci Comput 19:1046–1062
40. Hughes TJR, Reali A, Sangalli G (2010) Efficient quadrature for NURBS-based isogeometric analysis. Comput Methods Appl Mech Eng 199:301–313
41. Auricchio F, Calabroo F, Hughes TJR, Reali A, Sangalli G (2012) A simple algorithm for obtaining nearly optimal quadrature rules for NURBS-based isogeometric analysis. Comput Methods Appl Mech Eng 249–252:15–27
42. Melosh RJ (1963) Basis for derivation of matrices for the direct stiffness method. J Am Inst Aeronaut Astronautics 1(7):1631–1637
43. Ghorashi M (1994) Limit analysis of circular plates subjected to arbitrary rotational symmetric loadings. Int J Mech Sci 36(2):87–94
44. Capsoni A, Silva MV (2011) A finite element formulation of Mindlin plates for limit analysis. Int J Numerical Methods Biomed Eng 27(1):143–156
45. Cinquini C, Zanon P (1985) Limit analysis of circular and annular plates. Ingenier - Archiv 55:157–175
46. Bazilevs Y, Calo VM, Cottrell JA, Evans JA, Hughes TJR, Lipton S, Scott MA, Sederberg TW (2010) Isogeometric analysis using T-splines. Comput Methods Appl Mech Eng 199(5–8):229–263

A limit analysis of Mindlin plates using the cell-based smoothed triangular element CS-MIN3 and second-order cone programming (SOCP)

Nguyen-Thoi Trung[1,2*], Phung-Van Phuc[1] and Le-Van Canh[3]

* Correspondence:
nguyenthoitrung@tdt.edu.vn
[1]Division of Computational Mathematics and Engineering (CME), Institute for Computational Science (INCOS), Ton Duc Thang University, Hochiminh City, Viet Nam
[2]Department of Mechanics, Faculty of Mathematics and Computer Science, VNUHCM University of Science, Hochiminh City, Viet Nam
Full list of author information is available at the end of the article

Abstract

Background: The paper presents a numerical procedure for kinematic limit analysis of Mindlin plate governed by von Mises criterion.

Methods: The cell-based smoothed three-node Mindlin plate element (CS-MIN3) is combined with a second-order cone optimization programming (SOCP) to determine the upper bound limit load of the Mindlin plates. In the CS-MIN3, each triangular element will be divided into three sub-triangles, and in each sub-triangle, the gradient matrices of MIN3 is used to compute the strain rates. Then the gradient smoothing technique on whole the triangular element is used to smooth the strain rates on these three sub-triangles. The limit analysis problem of Mindlin plates is formulated by minimizing the dissipation power subjected to a set of constraints of boundary conditions and unitary external work. For Mindlin plates, the dissipation power is computed on both the middle plane and thickness of the plate. This minimization problem then can be transformed into a form suitable for the optimum solution using the SOCP.

Results and Conclusions: The numerical results of some benchmark problems show that the proposal procedure can provide the reliable upper bound collapse multipliers for both thick and thin plates.

Keywords: Limit analysis; Upper bound; Mindlin plates; Cell-based smoothed three-node Mindlin plate element (CS-MIN3); Smoothed finite element methods (S-FEM); Second-order cone programming (SOCP)

Background

Limit analysis is a branch of plasticity analysis and plays an important role in determining the limit loads of a structure. The fundamental theorems of limit analysis ignore the evolutive elastoplastic computations but focus to determine the upper or lower bound loads which cause the plastic collapse of structures.

Using analytical methods and different yield criteria such as the maximum principal stress criterion, Tresca criterion, and von Mises criterion, many scholars derived the analytical solutions for the limit loads of plates. Some systematic and comprehensive summaries can be found in the monographs of Hodge [1], Save and Massonnet [2], Zyczkowski [3], Xu and Liu [4], Lubliner [5], Yu et al. [6], etc. Using numerical methods, some early works for the limit loads of plates can be mentioned such as those by Hodge and Belytschko [7] and Nguyen [8]. However, due to the lack of efficient optimization algorithms and the limit of the computing power, the numerical limit analysis of plates seems to be ignored for a certain times.

Recently, the interest of scientists in numerical limit analysis [9-15] has been resurged, principally thanks to the rapid development of efficient optimization algorithms and the continuous improvement in computer facilities. Current research is focusing on developing numerical limit analysis tools which are efficient and robust for the practice usage of engineers. In the numerical limit analysis, once the stress or displacement/velocity fields are approximated and the bound theorems are applied, the limit analysis becomes a problem of optimization involving either linear programing (LP) or nonlinear programming (NLP) which can be solved respectively by the available LP or NLP algorithms [16-23].

For the LP algorithms, some significant contributions have been published such as the active set LP algorithm by Sloan [16], the bespoke interior-point algorithm for LP by Andersen and Christiansen [17], and the commercial LP code XA by Pastor et al. [18]. For the NLP algorithms, some recently important contributions can be mentioned such as the algorithm based on feasible directions by Zouain et al. [10] or by Lyamin and Sloan [19], the algorithm based on the interior-point method by Andersen et al. [20] or by Krabbenhoft and Damkilde [21], and the general-purpose NLP codes CONOPT and MINOS by Tin-Loi and Ngo [22]. Recently, one of the most efficient NLP algorithms based on the primal-dual interior-point method was proposed by Andersen et al. [23]. The algorithm can be applied to von Mises-type yield functions and can handle problems with any nonlinear yield functions. The algorithm is implemented in second-order cone programming (SOCP) [24] of the commercial software MOSEK [25] and has been applied for the limit loads of some limit analysis problems [26,27].

Using such LP and NLP algorithms for the numerical limit analyses of plate structures, many significant researches have been published. For the Kirchhoff plates, we can list the works by Christiansen and Larsen [28], Turco and Caracciolo [29], Corradi and Vena [30], Corradi and Panzeri [31], Tran et al. [32], Le et al. [33-35], and Zhou et al. [36]. For the Mindlin plates, we can list the works by Capsoni and Corradi [37] and Capsoni and Vicente da Silva [38]. In comparison, it is seen that many studies in the literature are concerned with the limit analysis of Kirchhoff plates, while the literature related to those of Mindlin plates is somehow still limited. This paper hence aims to further contribute a numerical limit analysis of Mindlin plates by using a Mindlin plate element proposed recently together with the SOCP.

In the other front of the development of numerical methods, Liu and Nguyen Thoi [39] have integrated the strain smoothing technique [40] into the finite element method (FEM) to create a series of smoothed FEMs (S-FEMs) such as cell/element-based smoothed FEM (CS-FEM) [41-43], node-based smoothed FEM (NS-FEM) [44-46], edge-based smoothed FEM (ES-FEM) [47,48], face-based smoothed FEM (FS-FEM) [49], and a group of alpha-FEM [50-53]. Each of these smoothed FEMs has different properties and has been used to produce desired solutions for a wide class of benchmark and practical mechanics problems. Several theoretical aspects of the S-FEM models have been provided in [54,55]. The S-FEM models have also been further investigated and applied to various problems such as plates and shells [56-68], piezoelectricity [69,70], fracture mechanics [71], visco-elastoplasticity [72-74], limit and shakedown analysis for solids [75-77], and some other applications [78,79].

Among these S-FEM models, the CS-FEM [39,41] shows some interesting properties in solid mechanics problems. Extending the idea of the CS-FEM to plate structures, Nguyen-Thoi et al. [80] have recently formulated a cell-based smoothed three-node Mindlin plate element (CS-MIN3) for static and free vibration analyses of isotropic Mindlin plates by incorporating the CS-FEM with the original MIN3 element [81]. In the CS-MIN3, each triangular element will be divided into three sub-triangles, and in each sub-triangle, the MIN3 is used to compute the strains. Then, the strain smoothing technique on whole the triangular element is used to smooth the strains on these three sub-triangles. The numerical results showed that the CS-MIN3 is free of shear locking and achieves high accuracy compared to the exact solutions and other existing elements in the literature.

In this paper, the CS-MIN3 is further extended to the kinematic limit analysis of Mindlin plates governed by the von Mises criterion. The CS-MIN3 is combined with a SOCP to determine the limit load of the plates. The limit analysis problem of Mindlin plates is formulated by minimizing the dissipation power subjected to a set of constraints of boundary conditions and unitary external work. For Mindlin plates, the dissipation power is computed on both the middle plane and the thickness of the plate. This minimization problem can then be transformed into a form suitable for the optimum solution using the SOCP. The accuracy and reliability of the proposed method are verified by comparing its numerical solutions with those of other available numerical results.

Methods

Limit analysis of Mindlin plates-kinematic formulation

We now consider a rigid-perfectly plastic plate identified by its middle plane Ω, the thickness h, and the boundary $\Gamma = \Gamma_u \cup \Gamma_t$ where Γ_t is the boundary subjected to a surface traction $\lambda\bar{\mathbf{t}}$ and Γ_u is the constrained boundary. Let w be the transverse displacement (deflection) and $\boldsymbol{\beta}^T = \begin{bmatrix}\beta_x & \beta_y\end{bmatrix}$ be the vector of rotations, in which β_x and β_y are the rotations of the middle plane around the y-axis and x-axis, respectively, with the positive directions defined as shown in Figure 1.

The unknown vector of three independent field variables at any point in the problem domain of the Mindlin plates can be written as

$$\mathbf{u}^T = \begin{bmatrix} w & \beta_x & \beta_y \end{bmatrix} \tag{1}$$

The curvature of the deflected plate $\boldsymbol{\kappa}$ and the shear strains $\boldsymbol{\gamma}$ are defined, respectively, as

$$\boldsymbol{\kappa} = \begin{bmatrix} \kappa_x \\ \kappa_y \\ \gamma_{xy} \end{bmatrix} = \mathbf{L}_d\boldsymbol{\beta} \;;\; \boldsymbol{\gamma} = \begin{bmatrix} \gamma_{xz} \\ \gamma_{yz} \end{bmatrix} = \nabla w + \boldsymbol{\beta} \tag{2}$$

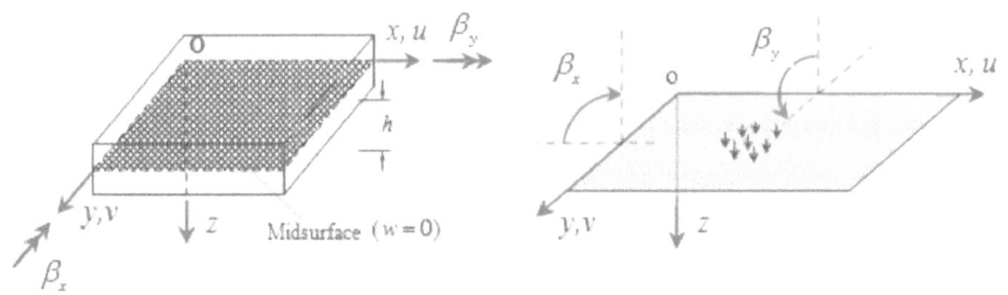

Figure 1 Mindlin plate and positive directions of the displacement w and two rotations β_x and β_y.

where $\nabla = [\partial/\partial x \quad \partial/\partial y]^T$ and $\mathbf{L}_d$ is a differential operator matrix defined by

$$\mathbf{L}_d = \begin{bmatrix} \partial/\partial x & 0 \\ 0 & \partial/\partial y \\ \partial/\partial y & \partial/\partial x \end{bmatrix} \tag{3}$$

Because the material in the limit analysis is assumed to be rigid-perfectly plastic, the bending stress $\boldsymbol{\sigma}$ and transverse shear $\boldsymbol{\tau}$ are confined within the convex domain $\boldsymbol{\Phi}(\boldsymbol{\sigma}, \boldsymbol{\tau}) \leq 0$, where $\boldsymbol{\Phi}(\boldsymbol{\sigma}, \boldsymbol{\tau})$ is the yield function. If von Mises's criterion is adopted, we have

$$\boldsymbol{\Phi}(\boldsymbol{\sigma}, \boldsymbol{\tau}) = \sqrt{(\boldsymbol{\sigma}^T \mathbf{P}_b \boldsymbol{\sigma} + \boldsymbol{\tau}^T \mathbf{P}_s \boldsymbol{\tau})} - \sigma_0 \leq 0 \tag{4}$$

where σ_0 is the yield stress and

$$\mathbf{P}_b = \frac{1}{2}\begin{bmatrix} 2 & -1 & 0 \\ -1 & 2 & 0 \\ 0 & 0 & 6 \end{bmatrix} \qquad \mathbf{P}_s = \begin{bmatrix} 3 & 0 \\ 0 & 3 \end{bmatrix} \tag{5}$$

Deformations cannot occur as long as $\boldsymbol{\Phi}(\boldsymbol{\sigma}, \boldsymbol{\tau}) < 0$, while plastic flow may develop when $\boldsymbol{\Phi}(\boldsymbol{\sigma}, \boldsymbol{\tau}) = 0$. In this case, strain rates $\dot{\boldsymbol{\varepsilon}}$ and $\dot{\boldsymbol{\gamma}}$ obey the normality flow rule as

$$\dot{\boldsymbol{\varepsilon}} = \dot{\lambda}\frac{\partial \Phi}{\partial \boldsymbol{\sigma}}, \quad \dot{\boldsymbol{\gamma}} = \dot{\lambda}\frac{\partial \Phi}{\partial \boldsymbol{\tau}}, \quad \dot{\lambda} \geq 0 \tag{6}$$

Equation 6 might impose restrictions on strain rates, by confining them within a convex domain $\Psi(\dot{\boldsymbol{\varepsilon}}, \dot{\boldsymbol{\gamma}})$, the sub-space spanned by the outward normals to the yield surface.

Let $(\tilde{\boldsymbol{\sigma}}, \tilde{\boldsymbol{\tau}})$ represent the admissible stresses contained within the convex yield surface and $(\hat{\boldsymbol{\sigma}}, \hat{\boldsymbol{\tau}})$ represent the stress point on the limit surface associated to any given strain rate $(\dot{\boldsymbol{\varepsilon}}, \dot{\boldsymbol{\gamma}})$ through the plasticity condition, then the plastic dissipation power $\hat{d}(\dot{\boldsymbol{\varepsilon}}, \dot{\boldsymbol{\gamma}})$ (per unit volume) is defined by Hill's maximum principle as

$$\hat{d}(\dot{\boldsymbol{\varepsilon}}, \dot{\boldsymbol{\gamma}}) = \max_{\Phi(\tilde{\boldsymbol{\sigma}}, \tilde{\boldsymbol{\varepsilon}}) \leq 0} \tilde{\boldsymbol{\sigma}}^T \dot{\boldsymbol{\varepsilon}} + \tilde{\boldsymbol{\tau}}^T \dot{\boldsymbol{\gamma}} = \hat{\boldsymbol{\sigma}}^T \dot{\boldsymbol{\varepsilon}} + \hat{\boldsymbol{\tau}}^T \dot{\boldsymbol{\gamma}} \tag{7}$$

The plastic dissipation power is a uniquely defined function of strain rates, and its explicit expression is available for a number of yield criteria [5]. If von Mises's criterion is adopted, one has [37]

$$\hat{d}(\dot{\boldsymbol{\varepsilon}}, \dot{\boldsymbol{\gamma}}) = \sigma_0 \sqrt{\dot{\boldsymbol{\varepsilon}}^T \Gamma_b \dot{\boldsymbol{\varepsilon}} + \dot{\boldsymbol{\gamma}}^T \Gamma_s \dot{\boldsymbol{\gamma}}} \tag{8}$$

with

$$\boldsymbol{\Gamma}_b = \mathbf{P}_b^{-1} = \frac{1}{3}\begin{bmatrix} 4 & 2 & 0 \\ 2 & 4 & 0 \\ 0 & 0 & 1 \end{bmatrix} \qquad \boldsymbol{\Gamma}_s = \mathbf{P}_s^{-1} = \frac{1}{3}\begin{bmatrix} 1 & 0 \\ 0 & 1 \end{bmatrix} \tag{9}$$

Using the relation $\boldsymbol{\varepsilon} = z\boldsymbol{\kappa}$ between the membrane strain $\boldsymbol{\varepsilon}$ with the curvature $\boldsymbol{\kappa}$, Equation 8 can be rewritten as

$$\hat{d}(\dot{\boldsymbol{\kappa}}, \dot{\boldsymbol{\gamma}}) = \sigma_0 \sqrt{z^2 c_b + c_s} \quad c_b = \dot{\boldsymbol{\kappa}}^T \boldsymbol{\Gamma}_b \dot{\boldsymbol{\kappa}} \;\; ; \;\; c_s = \dot{\boldsymbol{\gamma}}^T \boldsymbol{\Gamma}_s \dot{\boldsymbol{\gamma}} \tag{10}$$

The internal dissipation power for the two-dimensional plate domain Ω with the thickness h is now expressed as

$$D(\dot{\boldsymbol{\kappa}}, \dot{\boldsymbol{\gamma}}) = \int_{\Omega}\int_{-h/2}^{h/2} \hat{d}\, \mathrm{d}z\, \mathrm{d}\Omega = \int_{\Omega}\int_{-h/2}^{h/2} \sigma_0 \sqrt{z^2 c_b + c_s} \mathrm{d}z\, \mathrm{d}\Omega \tag{11}$$

The limit analysis of the Mindlin plate considers a rigid-perfectly plastic plate subjected to body forces $\lambda \mathbf{b} = [\lambda p \quad 0 \quad 0]^T$ on its middle plane Ω and to surface tractions $\lambda \bar{\mathbf{t}}$ on the boundary Γ_t. The constrained boundary Γ_u is fixed. Loads now are defined as basic values $\mathbf{b}$ and $\bar{\mathbf{t}}$, affected by a load multiplier λ. Then, the kinematic theorem of limit analysis states that the limit value λ^+ (collapse multiplier) of λ is the optimal value of the minimization problem [37]

$$\boldsymbol{\lambda}^+ = \min_{\dot{w}, \dot{\theta}} D(\dot{\boldsymbol{\kappa}}, \dot{\boldsymbol{\gamma}}) \tag{12}$$

subject to

$$\begin{cases} \dot{\mathbf{u}}\left(\dot{w}, \dot{\theta}\right) = \mathbf{0} \quad \text{on } \Gamma_u & \text{(a)} \\ c_b = \dot{\boldsymbol{\kappa}}^T \boldsymbol{\Gamma}_b \dot{\boldsymbol{\kappa}} \;;\; c_s = \dot{\boldsymbol{\gamma}}^T \boldsymbol{\Gamma}_s \dot{\boldsymbol{\gamma}} & \text{(b)} \\ \text{where } \dot{\boldsymbol{\kappa}} = \mathbf{L}_d \dot{\boldsymbol{\beta}} \text{ and } \dot{\boldsymbol{\gamma}} = \nabla \dot{w} + \dot{\boldsymbol{\beta}} & \\ W_{\text{ext}}(\dot{\mathbf{u}}) = \int_{\Omega} \mathbf{b}^T \dot{\mathbf{u}}\, \mathrm{d}\Omega + \int_{\Gamma_t} \bar{\mathbf{t}}^T \dot{\mathbf{u}}\, \mathrm{d}\Gamma = 1 & \text{(c)} \end{cases} \tag{13}$$

Equations 13(a) and 13(b) express the compatibility of the constrained boundary and the strain rate with a velocity field $\dot{\mathbf{u}}$, respectively, and Equation 13(c) denotes the power of basic loads, which is normalized to unity.

Note that in Equation 11, the dissipation power $D(\dot{\boldsymbol{\kappa}}, \dot{\boldsymbol{\gamma}})$ is a positively homogeneous function of degree 1 in the strain rates and not differentiable at strain rate zero. Equations 13(a) to 13(c) hence bring the computation of the collapse multiplier to the search of the minimum of a convex but not everywhere differentiable functional. The functional minimized in Equation 12 is only differentiable in the region Ω_p where plastic flow develops, but not so in the remaining portion Ω_r of the plate, which keeps rigid in the mechanism, and hence, the minimum does not correspond to a stationary point.

Brief on kinematic formulation of CS-MIN3 for Mindlin plates

Kinematic formulation of the MIN3 for Mindlin plates

In the original MIN3 [81], the rotations are assumed to be linear through the rotational degrees of freedom (DOFs) at three nodes of the elements, and the deflection is initially assumed to be quadratic through the deflection DOFs at six nodes (three nodes of the elements and three mid-edge points). Then, by enforcing continuous shear constraints at every element edge, the deflection DOFs at three mid-edge points can be removed and the deflection is now approximated only by vertex DOFs at three nodes of the elements. The MIN3 element can hence overcome shear locking and produces convergent solutions. In this paper, we just brief on the kinematic formulation of the MIN3 which is necessary for the kinematic formulation of the CS-MIN3.

Using a mesh of three-node triangular elements, the approximation of displacement flow $\dot{\mathbf{u}}^h = \begin{bmatrix} \dot{w} & \dot{\beta}_x & \dot{\beta}_y \end{bmatrix}^T$ for an element Ω_e shown in Figure 2 can be written as

$$\dot{\mathbf{u}}_e^h = \sum_{I=1}^{3} \underbrace{\begin{bmatrix} N_I(\mathbf{x}) & 0 & 0 \\ 0 & N_I(\mathbf{x}) & 0 \\ 0 & 0 & N_I(\mathbf{x}) \end{bmatrix}}_{\mathbf{N}_I(\mathbf{x})} \dot{\mathbf{d}}_{eI} = \sum_{I=1}^{3} \mathbf{N}_I(\mathbf{x}) \dot{\mathbf{d}}_{eI} \tag{14}$$

where $\dot{\mathbf{d}}_{eI} = \begin{bmatrix} \dot{w}_I \, \dot{\beta}_{xI} \, \dot{\beta}_{yI} \end{bmatrix}^T$, $I = 1, 2, 3$, is the flow vector of the nodal degrees of freedom of $\dot{\mathbf{u}}_e^h$ associated to node I and $N_I(\mathbf{x})$, $I = 1, 2, 3$, are linear shape functions at node I.

The curvature rates of the deflection flow in an element are then defined by

$$\dot{\boldsymbol{\kappa}}^h = \mathbf{B}\dot{\mathbf{d}}_e \tag{15}$$

where $\dot{\mathbf{d}}_e = \begin{bmatrix} \dot{\mathbf{d}}_{e1} & \dot{\mathbf{d}}_{e2} & \dot{\mathbf{d}}_{e3} \end{bmatrix}^T$ is the vector of nodal displacement flow of the element and $\mathbf{B}$ contains the constants which are derived from the derivatives of the shape functions as

$$\mathbf{B} = \begin{bmatrix} 0 & 0 & \mathbf{N}_{,x} \\ 0 & \mathbf{N}_{,y} & 0 \\ 0 & \mathbf{N}_{,x} & \mathbf{N}_{,y} \end{bmatrix} \tag{16}$$

in which $\mathbf{N}_{,x}$ and $\mathbf{N}_{,y}$ are the matrices of derivatives of the shape functions in the x-direction and y-direction, respectively.

The shear strain rates of the deflection flow in an element are then defined by

$$\dot{\boldsymbol{\gamma}}^h = \mathbf{S}\dot{\mathbf{d}}_e \tag{17}$$

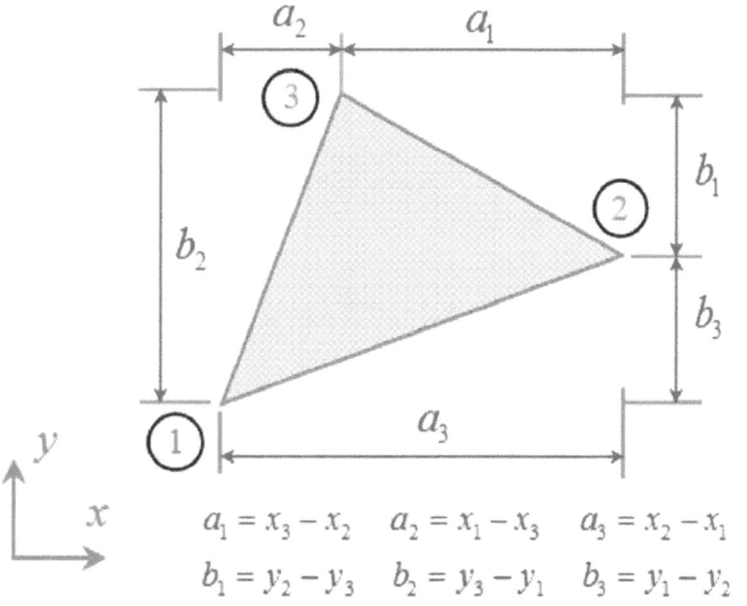

Figure 2 Three-node triangular plate element in the MIN3.

where

$$\mathbf{S} = \begin{bmatrix} \mathbf{N}_{,x} & \mathbf{L}_{,x} + \mathbf{N} & \mathbf{H}_{,x} \\ \mathbf{N}_{,y} & \mathbf{L}_{,y} & \mathbf{H}_{,y} + \mathbf{N} \end{bmatrix} \tag{18}$$

in which $\mathbf{L}_{,x}$, $\mathbf{L}_{,y}$, $\mathbf{H}_{,x}$, and $\mathbf{H}_{,y}$ are the matrices of derivatives of the shape functions in the x-direction and y-direction, respectively, and $\mathbf{L} = [L_1 \quad L_2 \quad L_3]$ and $\mathbf{H} = [H_1 \quad H_2 \quad H_3]$ are the vectors of shape functions, with L_I and H_I, $I = 1, 2, 3$, given by

$$L_1 = \frac{1}{2}(b_3N_1N_2 - b_2N_3N_1); L_2 = \frac{1}{2}(b_1N_2N_3 - b_3N_1N_2); L_3 = \frac{1}{2}(b_2N_3N_1 - b_1N_2N_3) \tag{19}$$

$$H_1 = \frac{1}{2}(a_2N_3N_1 - a_3N_1N_2); H_2 = \frac{1}{2}(a_3N_1N_2 - a_1N_2N_3); H_3 = \frac{1}{2}(a_1N_2N_3 - a_2N_3N_1) \tag{20}$$

in which a_i and b_i $(i = 1 \div 3)$ are the geometric distances as shown in Figure 2.

Kinematic formulation of CS-MIN3

In the CS-MIN3 [80], the domain discretization is the same as that of the MIN3 using N_n nodes and N_e triangular elements. However, in the formulation of the CS-MIN3, each triangular element Ω_e is further divided into three sub-triangles Δ_1, Δ_2, and Δ_3 by connecting the central point O of the element to three field nodes as shown in Figure 3.

In the CS-MIN3, we assume that the vector of displacement flow $\dot{\mathbf{d}}_{eO}$ at the central point O is the simple average of three vectors of displacement flow $\dot{\mathbf{d}}_{e1}$, $\dot{\mathbf{d}}_{e2}$, and $\dot{\mathbf{d}}_{e3}$ of three field nodes as

$$\dot{\mathbf{d}}_{eO} = \frac{1}{3}(\dot{\mathbf{d}}_{e1} + \dot{\mathbf{d}}_{e2} + \dot{\mathbf{d}}_{e3}) \tag{21}$$

On the first sub-triangle Δ_1 (triangle O-1-2), the linear approximation $\dot{\mathbf{u}}_e^{\Delta_1} = \begin{bmatrix} \dot{w}_e & \dot{\beta}_{ex} & \dot{\beta}_{ey} \end{bmatrix}^T$ is constructed by

$$\dot{\mathbf{u}}_e^{\Delta_1} = N_1^{\Delta_1}(\mathbf{x})\dot{\mathbf{d}}_{eO} + N_2^{\Delta_1}(\mathbf{x})\dot{\mathbf{d}}_{e1} + N_3^{\Delta_1}(\mathbf{x})\dot{\mathbf{d}}_{e2} = \mathbf{N}^{\Delta_1}(\mathbf{x})\dot{\mathbf{d}}^{\Delta_1} \tag{22}$$

where $\dot{\mathbf{d}}^{\Delta_1} = \begin{bmatrix} \dot{\mathbf{d}}_{eO} & \dot{\mathbf{d}}_{e1} & \dot{\mathbf{d}}_{e2} \end{bmatrix}^T$ is the vector of displacement flow of nodal degrees of freedom of the sub-triangle Δ_1 and $\mathbf{N}^{\Delta_1} = \begin{bmatrix} N_1^{\Delta_1} & N_2^{\Delta_1} & N_3^{\Delta_1} \end{bmatrix}$ is the vector containing the linear shape functions at nodes O, 1, 2 of the sub-triangle Δ_1.

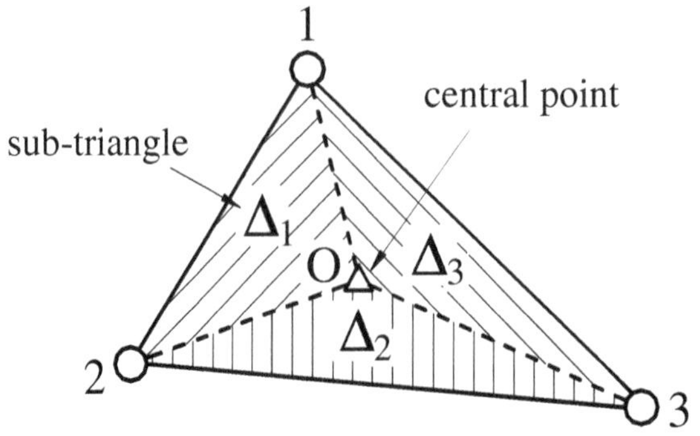

Figure 3 **Three sub-triangles (Δ_1, Δ_2, and Δ_3) created from the triangle 1-2-3 in the CS-MIN3.**

The curvature rates of the deflection flow $\dot{\boldsymbol{\kappa}}^{\Delta_1}$ and the altered shear strain rates $\dot{\boldsymbol{\gamma}}^{\Delta_1}$ in the sub-triangle Δ_1 are then obtained by

$$\dot{\boldsymbol{\kappa}}^{\Delta_1} = \underbrace{\begin{bmatrix} \mathbf{b}_1^{\Delta_1} & \mathbf{b}_2^{\Delta_1} & \mathbf{b}_3^{\Delta_1} \end{bmatrix}}_{\mathbf{b}^{\Delta_1}} \begin{bmatrix} \dot{\mathbf{d}}_{eO} \\ \dot{\mathbf{d}}_{e1} \\ \dot{\mathbf{d}}_{e2} \end{bmatrix} = \mathbf{b}^{\Delta_1}\dot{\mathbf{d}}^{\Delta_1} \tag{23}$$

$$\dot{\boldsymbol{\gamma}}^{\Delta_1} = \underbrace{\begin{bmatrix} \mathbf{s}_1^{\Delta_1} & \mathbf{s}_2^{\Delta_1} & \mathbf{s}_3^{\Delta_1} \end{bmatrix}}_{\mathbf{s}^{\Delta_1}} \begin{bmatrix} \dot{\mathbf{d}}_{eO} \\ \dot{\mathbf{d}}_{e1} \\ \dot{\mathbf{d}}_{e2} \end{bmatrix} = \mathbf{s}^{\Delta_1}\dot{\mathbf{d}}^{\Delta_1} \tag{24}$$

where $\mathbf{b}^{\Delta_1}$ and $\mathbf{s}^{\Delta_1}$ are respectively computed similarly as the matrices $\mathbf{B}$ and $\mathbf{S}$ of the MIN3 in Equations 16 and 18 but with two following changes: (1) the coordinates of three-node $\mathbf{x}_i = [x_i \quad y_i]^T$, $i = 1, 2, 3$, are replaced by $\mathbf{x}_O$, $\mathbf{x}_1$, and $\mathbf{x}_2$, respectively, and (2) the area A_e is replaced by the area A_{Δ_1} of sub-triangle Δ_1.

Substituting $\dot{\mathbf{d}}_{eO}$ in Equation 21 into Equations 23 and 24, and then rearranging, we obtain

$$\dot{\boldsymbol{\kappa}}^{\Delta_1} = \underbrace{\begin{bmatrix} \frac{1}{3}\mathbf{b}_1^{\Delta_1} + \mathbf{b}_2^{\Delta_1} & \frac{1}{3}\mathbf{b}_1^{\Delta_1} + \mathbf{b}_3^{\Delta_1} & \frac{1}{3}\mathbf{b}_1^{\Delta_1} \end{bmatrix}}_{\mathbf{B}^{\Delta_1}} \begin{bmatrix} \dot{\mathbf{d}}_{e1} \\ \dot{\mathbf{d}}_{e2} \\ \dot{\mathbf{d}}_{e3} \end{bmatrix} = \mathbf{B}^{\Delta_1}\dot{\mathbf{d}}_e \tag{25}$$

$$\dot{\boldsymbol{\gamma}}^{\Delta_1} = \underbrace{\begin{bmatrix} \frac{1}{3}\mathbf{s}_1^{\Delta_1} + \mathbf{s}_2^{\Delta_1} & \frac{1}{3}\mathbf{s}_1^{\Delta_1} + \mathbf{s}_3^{\Delta_1} & \frac{1}{3}\mathbf{s}_1^{\Delta_1} \end{bmatrix}}_{\mathbf{S}^{\Delta_1}} \begin{bmatrix} \dot{\mathbf{d}}_{e1} \\ \dot{\mathbf{d}}_{e2} \\ \dot{\mathbf{d}}_{e3} \end{bmatrix} = \mathbf{S}^{\Delta_1}\dot{\mathbf{d}}_e \tag{26}$$

Similarly, by using cyclic permutation, we easily obtain the curvature rates of the deflection flow $\dot{\boldsymbol{\kappa}}^{\Delta_j}$, the shear strains $\dot{\boldsymbol{\gamma}}^{\Delta_j}$, and matrices $\mathbf{B}^{\Delta_j}$ and $\mathbf{S}^{\Delta_j}$, $j = 2, 3$, for the second sub-triangle Δ_2 (triangle *O*-2-3) and third sub-triangle Δ_3 (triangle *O*-3-1), respectively.

Now, by applying the cell-based strain smoothing operation in the CS-FEM [39,41], the bending and shear strain rates $\dot{\boldsymbol{\kappa}}^{\Delta_j}$ and $\dot{\boldsymbol{\gamma}}^{\Delta_j}$, $j = 1, 2, 3$, are used to create the *smoothed* bending and *smoothed* shear strain rates $\dot{\tilde{\boldsymbol{\kappa}}}_e$ and $\dot{\tilde{\boldsymbol{\gamma}}}_e$, respectively, on the triangular element Ω_e, such as

$$\dot{\tilde{\boldsymbol{\kappa}}}_e = \int_{\Omega_e} \dot{\boldsymbol{\kappa}}^h \, \Phi_e(\mathbf{x}) \, d\Omega = \sum_{j=1}^{3} \dot{\boldsymbol{\kappa}}^{\Delta_j} \int_{\Delta_j} \Phi_e(\mathbf{x}) \, d\Omega \tag{27}$$

$$\dot{\tilde{\boldsymbol{\gamma}}}_e = \int_{\Omega_e} \dot{\boldsymbol{\gamma}}^h \, \Phi_e(\mathbf{x}) \, d\Omega = \sum_{j=1}^{3} \dot{\boldsymbol{\gamma}}^{\Delta_j} \int_{\Delta_j} \Phi_e(\mathbf{x}) \, d\Omega \tag{28}$$

where $\Phi_e(\mathbf{x})$ is a given smoothing function that satisfies the unity property $\int_{\Omega_e} \Phi_e(\mathbf{x}) \, d\Omega = 1$. Using the following constant smoothing function

$$\Phi_e(\mathbf{x}) = \begin{cases} 1/A_e & \mathbf{x} \in \Omega_e \\ 0 & \mathbf{x} \notin \Omega_e \end{cases} \tag{29}$$

where A_e is the area of the triangular element, the smoothed bending strain rate $\dot{\tilde{\boldsymbol{\kappa}}}_e$ and the smoothed shear strain rate $\dot{\tilde{\boldsymbol{\gamma}}}_e$ in Equations 27 and 28 become

$$\dot{\tilde{\boldsymbol{\kappa}}}_e = \frac{1}{A_e} \sum_{j=1}^{3} A_{\Delta_j} \dot{\boldsymbol{\kappa}}^{\Delta_j} \quad ; \quad \dot{\tilde{\boldsymbol{\gamma}}}_e = \frac{1}{A_e} \sum_{j=1}^{3} A_{\Delta_j} \dot{\boldsymbol{\gamma}}^{\Delta_j} \tag{30}$$

Substituting $\dot{\boldsymbol{\kappa}}^{\Delta_j}$ and $\dot{\boldsymbol{\gamma}}^{\Delta_j}$, $j = 1, 2, 3$, into Equation 30, the smoothed bending strain rate $\dot{\tilde{\boldsymbol{\kappa}}}_e$ and the smoothed shear strain rate $\dot{\tilde{\boldsymbol{\gamma}}}_e$ are expressed by

$$\dot{\tilde{\boldsymbol{\kappa}}}_e = \tilde{\mathbf{B}}_e \dot{\mathbf{d}}_e \quad ; \quad \dot{\tilde{\boldsymbol{\gamma}}}_e = \tilde{\mathbf{S}}_e \dot{\mathbf{d}}_e \tag{31}$$

where $\tilde{\mathbf{B}}_e$ and $\tilde{\mathbf{S}}_e$ are the smoothed bending and shear strain gradient matrices given by

$$\tilde{\mathbf{B}}_e = \frac{1}{A_e}\sum_{j=1}^{3} A_{\Delta_j}\mathbf{B}^{\Delta_j} \quad ; \quad \tilde{\mathbf{S}}_e = \frac{1}{A_e}\sum_{j=1}^{3} A_{\Delta_j}\mathbf{S}^{\Delta_j} \tag{32}$$

Discretization of kinematic formulation by CS-MIN3

In Equation 11, when c_s becomes small at the thin plate limit, the last term is very nearly singular and numerical integration is preferable. To avoid inaccuracies associated with the point $z = 0$, twice the integral over half thickness is considered, and Equation 11 can be rewritten as [37]

$$D(\dot{\boldsymbol{\kappa}}, \dot{\boldsymbol{\gamma}}) = 2\int_{\Omega}\int_{0}^{h/2} \sigma_0 \sqrt{z^2 c_b + c_s}\,\mathrm{d}z\,\mathrm{d}\Omega = \int_{\Omega} m_0 \sum_{g=1}^{n_G} \sqrt{W_g^2 (1+\zeta_g)^2 c_b + W_g^2 \frac{16}{h^2} c_s}\,\mathrm{d}\Omega \tag{33}$$

where $\zeta = 4z/h - 1$ and ζ_g and W_g are the usual Gauss integration point coordinates and weights, respectively; n_G is the number of Gauss integration points; $m_0 = \sigma_0 h^2/4$ is the plastic moment of resistance per unit width of the plate of thickness h.

By discretizing the domain Ω into n_e triangular plate elements such that $\Omega = \bigcup_{e=1}^{n_e} \Omega_e$ and $\Omega_i \cap \Omega_j = \emptyset$, $i \neq j$, and using the kinematic formulation of the CS-MIN3 as presented in the 'Brief on kinematic formulation of CS-MIN3 for Mindlin plates' section, the plastic dissipation in Equation 33 is expressed as

$$\begin{aligned} D^{\text{CS-DSG3}}_{(\dot{\boldsymbol{\kappa}},\dot{\boldsymbol{\gamma}})} &= \sum_{e=1}^{n_e}\sum_{g=1}^{n_G} A_e m_0 \sqrt{W_g^2 (1+\zeta_g)^2 \tilde{c}_b + W_g^2 \frac{16}{h^2}\tilde{c}_s} \\ &= \sum_{i=1}^{n_e \times n_G} A_i m_0 \sqrt{W_i^2 (1+\zeta_i)^2 \tilde{c}_b + W_i^2 \frac{16}{h^2}\tilde{c}_s} \end{aligned} \tag{34}$$

where $\tilde{c}_b = \dot{\tilde{\boldsymbol{\kappa}}}_e^T \boldsymbol{\Gamma}_b \dot{\tilde{\boldsymbol{\kappa}}}_e$ and $\tilde{c}_s = \dot{\tilde{\boldsymbol{\gamma}}}_e^T \boldsymbol{\Gamma}_s \dot{\tilde{\boldsymbol{\gamma}}}_e$ in which $\dot{\tilde{\boldsymbol{\kappa}}}_e = \left[\dot{\tilde{\kappa}}_x \dot{\tilde{\kappa}}_y \dot{\tilde{\gamma}}_{xy}\right]^T$ and $\dot{\tilde{\boldsymbol{\gamma}}}_e = \left[\dot{\tilde{\gamma}}_{xz} \dot{\tilde{\gamma}}_{yz}\right]^T$ are computed at the Gauss points by Equation 31.

Combining Equations 9 and 31, $\tilde{c}_b$ and $\tilde{c}_s$ are now expressed explicitly as

$$\tilde{c}_b = \frac{2}{3}\left[\left(\dot{\tilde{\kappa}}_x + \dot{\tilde{\kappa}}_y\right)^2 + \dot{\tilde{\kappa}}_x^{\,2} + \dot{\tilde{\kappa}}_y^{\,2}\right] + \frac{1}{3}\dot{\tilde{\gamma}}_{xy}^2 \;;\; \tilde{c}_s = \frac{1}{3}\dot{\tilde{\gamma}}_{xz}^2 + \frac{1}{3}\dot{\tilde{\gamma}}_{yz}^2 \tag{35}$$

The plastic dissipation in Equation 34 is hence expressed as

$$D^{\text{CS-DSG3}}_{(\dot{\boldsymbol{\kappa}},\dot{\boldsymbol{\gamma}})} = \sum_{i=1}^{n_e \times n_G} A_i m_0 \sqrt{z_{i1}^2 + z_{i2}^2 + z_{i3}^2 + z_{i4}^2 + z_{i5}^2 + z_{i6}^2} \tag{36}$$

where

$$\begin{cases} z_{i1} = \sqrt{2/3}\, W_i(1+\zeta_i)(\dot{\kappa}_x + \dot{\kappa}_y) \\ z_{i2} = \sqrt{2/3}\, W_i(1+\zeta_i)\dot{\kappa}_x \\ z_{i3} = \sqrt{2/3}\, W_i(1+\zeta_i)\dot{\kappa}_y \\ z_{i4} = \sqrt{2/3}\, W_i(1+\zeta_i)\dot{\gamma}_{xy} \\ z_{i5} = \sqrt{2/3}\,(4/h)W_i\dot{\gamma}_{xz} \\ z_{i6} = \sqrt{2/3}\,(4/h)W_i\dot{\gamma}_{yz} \end{cases} \tag{37}$$

Equation 37 can be rewritten in the matrix form as

$$\mathbf{H}_i^T\mathbf{y}_i - \mathbf{z}_i = \mathbf{0}, \quad i = 1, 2, ..., n_e \times n_G \tag{38}$$

where

$$\mathbf{H}_i^T = \sqrt{\frac{2}{3}}W_i \begin{bmatrix} (1+\zeta_i) & (1+\zeta_i) & 0 & 0 & 0 \\ (1+\zeta_i) & 0 & 0 & 0 & 0 \\ 0 & (1+\zeta_i) & 0 & 0 & 0 \\ 0 & 0 & (1+\zeta_i) & 0 & 0 \\ 0 & 0 & 0 & (4/h) & 0 \\ 0 & 0 & 0 & 0 & (4/h) \end{bmatrix} \tag{39}$$

and

$$\mathbf{y}_i = \left[\dot{\kappa}_x\, \dot{\kappa}_y \dot{\gamma}_{xy} \dot{\gamma}_{xz} \dot{\gamma}_{yz}\right]^T \text{ at the } i\text{th Gauss point} \tag{40}$$

$$\mathbf{z}_i = \begin{bmatrix} z_{i1} & z_{i2} & z_{i3} & z_{i4} & z_{i5} & z_{i6} \end{bmatrix}^T \tag{41}$$

Note that using Equations 31 and 32, the vector $\mathbf{y}_i$ in Equation 40 can be rewritten in the form of the discrete element displacement flow vector $\dot{\mathbf{d}}_i$

$$\mathbf{y}_i = \begin{bmatrix} \dot{\boldsymbol{\kappa}}_i \\ \dot{\boldsymbol{\gamma}}_i \end{bmatrix} = \mathbf{G}_i\dot{\mathbf{d}}_i \tag{42}$$

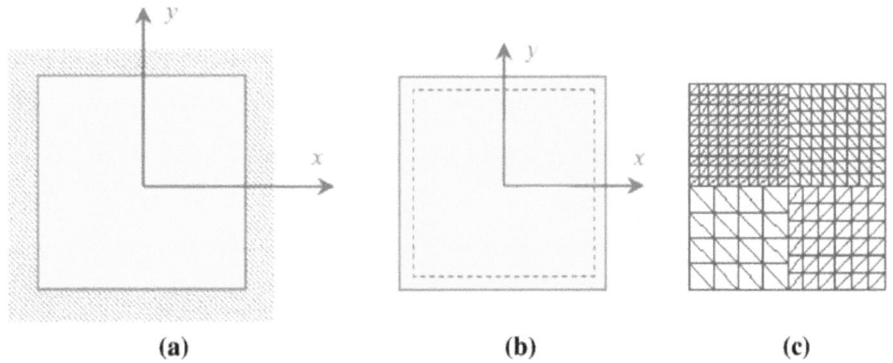

Figure 4 Square plate models and their discretizations using triangular elements. (a) Clamped plate. **(b)** Simply supported plate. **(c)** Four forms of discretization of the plate using triangular elements.

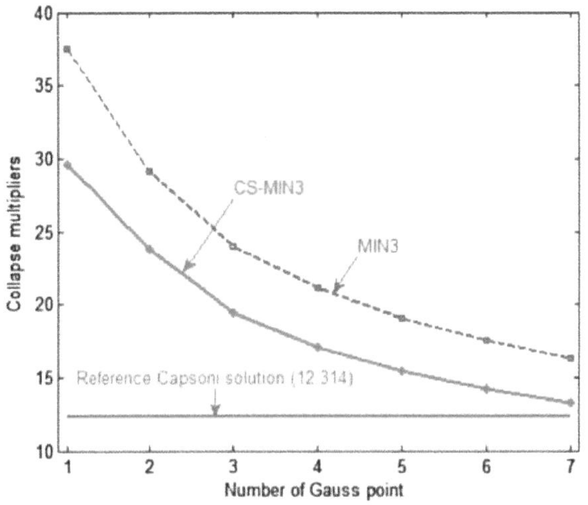

Figure 5 Convergence of collapse multipliers of the clamped square plate versus the number of Gauss points.

where

$$\mathbf{G}_i = \begin{bmatrix} 0 & \tilde{B}_{i11} & \tilde{B}_{i12} \\ 0 & \tilde{B}_{i21} & \tilde{B}_{i22} \\ 0 & \tilde{B}_{i31} & \tilde{B}_{i32} \\ \tilde{S}_{i11} & \tilde{S}_{i12} & 0 \\ \tilde{S}_{i21} & 0 & \tilde{S}_{i22} \end{bmatrix} \tag{43}$$

and $\tilde{B}_{ixx}$ and $\tilde{S}_{ixx}$ are the components extracted, respectively, from the matrices $\tilde{\mathbf{B}}_e$ and $\tilde{\mathbf{S}}_e$ in Equation 32.

Similarly, the external energy $W_{\text{ext}}(\dot{\mathbf{u}})$ in Equation 13(c) and the boundary condition of displacement flow Equation 13(a) can be combined and rewritten in the matrix form of the discrete system displacement flow vector $\dot{\mathbf{d}}$ as [33]

$$\mathbf{A}_{\text{eq}}\dot{\mathbf{d}} = \mathbf{b}_{\text{eq}} \tag{44}$$

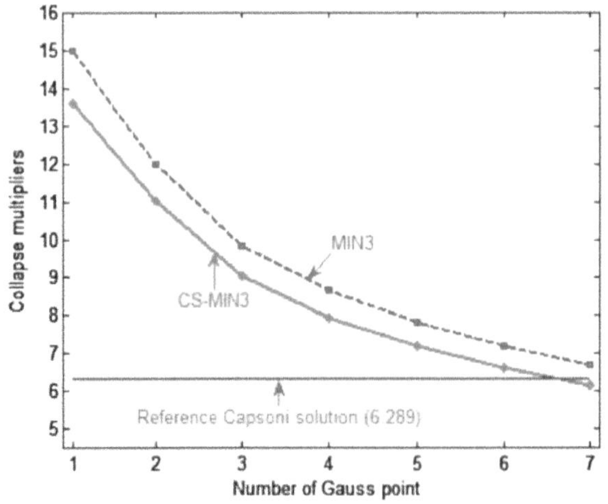

Figure 6 Convergence of collapse multipliers of the supported square plate versus the number of Gauss points.

Table 1 Convergence of collapse multipliers of clamped square plate subjected to uniform pressure versus various DOFs

Boundary condition	Method	Degrees of freedom					Reference solution [38] with 867 DOFs
		75	146	243	363	507	
Clamped	MIN3	67.2856	25.8273	17.7147	14.8945	13.5918	12.314
	CS-MIN3	29.0137	16.9008	14.2239	13.1852	12.6364	
Supported	MIN3	14.169	8.597	7.1727	6.6701	6.4414	6.289
	CS-MIN3	9.4622	7.1383	6.5829	6.3688	6.265	

Basic load $p = M_p/L^2$.

Combining Equations 36, 38, 42, and 44, the minimization problem (12) associated with the CS-MIN3 now becomes the problem of finding the optimal value λ^+ such that

$$\lambda^+ = \min \sum_{i=1}^{n_e \times n_G} A_i m_0 \|\mathbf{z}_i\| \tag{45}$$

subjected to the constraints

$$\begin{cases} \mathbf{H}_i^T \mathbf{G}_i \dot{\mathbf{d}}_i - \mathbf{z}_i = \mathbf{0}, \quad i = 1, 2, ..., n_e \times n_G & \text{(a)} \\ \mathbf{A}_{\text{eq}} \dot{\mathbf{d}} = \mathbf{b}_{\text{eq}} & \text{(b)} \end{cases} \tag{46}$$

The minimization problem (45) is a convex programming problem in which the objective function is a positively homogeneous function of degree 1 in the variables $\mathbf{z}_i$ (or in the strain rates) and is not differentiable at any points in the rigid domain which do not undergo plastic flow ($\|\mathbf{z}_i\| = 0$). The minimization problem (45) is also categorized into the group of the problems of minimizing a sum of Euclidean norms which has a natural dual maximization formulation [23].

For solving this group of problem, one of the well-known approaches used is to replace the terms $\|\mathbf{z}_i\|$ in the objective by the differentiable quantity $\sqrt{\|\mathbf{z}_i\|^2 + \mu^2}$, where μ is a fixed positive number. This method is robust but converges slowly as $\mu \to 0$ because some of the norms in the objective function have zero as their optimal value [23].

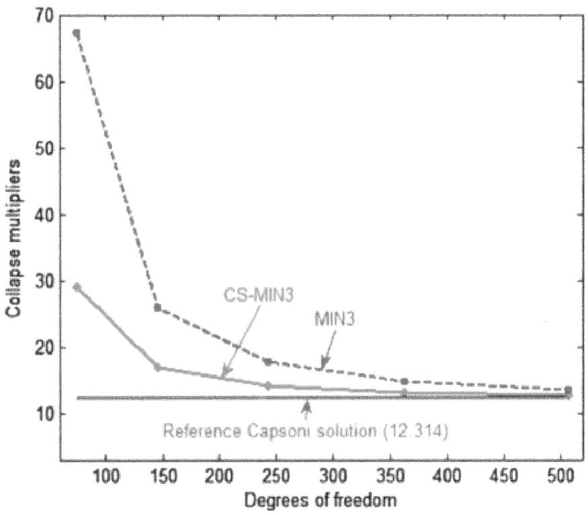

Figure 7 Convergence of collapse multipliers of the clamped square plate subjected to uniform pressure versus various DOFs.

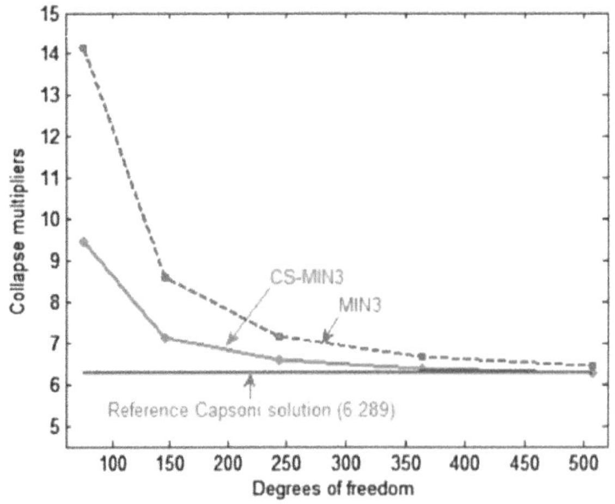

Figure 8 Convergence of collapse multipliers of the supported square plate subjected to uniform pressure versus various DOFs.

Recently, Andersen et al. [24] recently employed the aspect of duality of the problem to propose a primal-dual interior-point method for solving a homogeneous self-dual model of conic quadratic programming. In this method, the terms $\|\mathbf{z}_i\|$ are also replaced by $\sqrt{\|\mathbf{z}_i\|^2 + \mu^2}$, but the quantity μ is treated as an extra variable, whose value is determined by duality estimates. Using this method, the minimization problem (45) is now solved rapidly and accurately even if there are a large number of variables and many norms $\|\mathbf{z}_i\|$ are zero at a solution point. Also, the primal-dual interior-point method is recently integrated in an available general software (e.g., MOSEK [25]) which specializes second-order cone programming (SOCP) problems [24]. The limit analysis problem can hence be solved efficiently using such software.

The minimization problem (45) is hence rewritten in the form of a standard SOCP problem by introducing auxiliary variables t_i, $i = 1, 2, \ldots, n_e \times n_G$, such that

$$\lambda^+ = \min \sum_{i=1}^{n_e \times n_G} A_i m_0 t_i \tag{47}$$

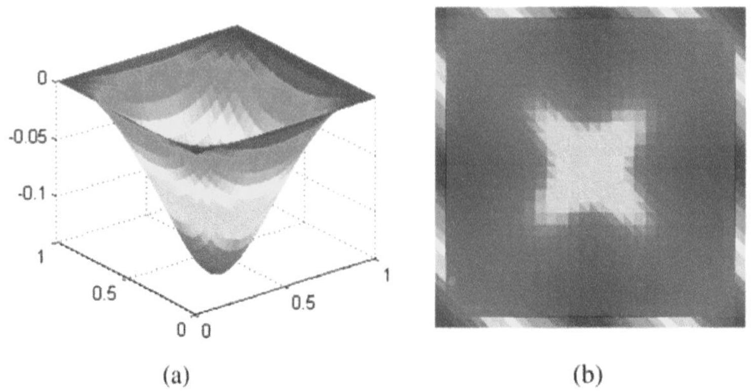

Figure 9 Patterns of displacement and plastic energy dissipation of the clamped square plate at collapse by CS-MIN3. (a) Displacement. **(b)** Plastic energy dissipation.

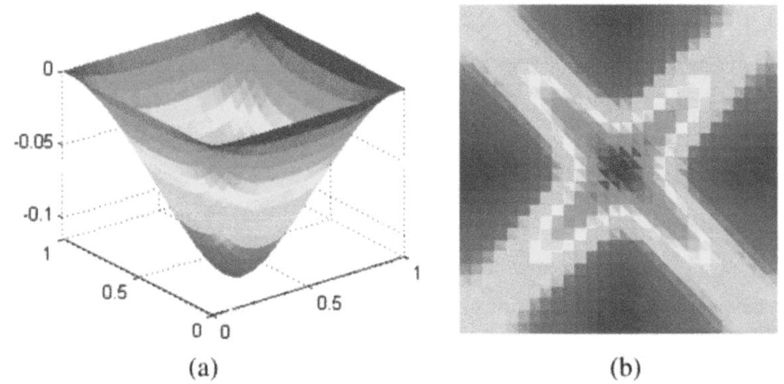

Figure 10 Patterns of displacement and plastic energy dissipation of the supported square plate at collapse by CS-MIN3. (a) Displacement. **(b)** Supported plate.

subjected to the constraints

$$\begin{cases} \mathbf{H}_i^T\mathbf{G}_i\dot{\mathbf{d}}_i - \mathbf{z}_i = \mathbf{0} & \text{(a)} \\ \mathbf{A}_{\text{eq}}\dot{\mathbf{d}} = \mathbf{b}_{\text{eq}} & \text{(b)} \\ t_i \geq \|\mathbf{z}_i\| & \text{(c)} \\ i = 1, 2, \ldots, n_e \times n_G \end{cases} \tag{48}$$

where Equation 48(c) represents quadratic cone constraints. With the form of standard SOCP problem, the minimization problem (47) for finding the collapse multipliers of the Mindlin plates can now be solved efficiently by using the software MOSEK.

Note that the formulation of the minimization problem of the plastic dissipation power in the form of standard SOCP problem was also presented in [33,35]; however, the form of standard SOCP problem in these references is only for Kirchhoff plates.

Also, note that in the kinematic limit analysis of plates, the ability to obtain the strict upper bound depends not only on the efficient solution of the arising optimization problem but also on the effectiveness of the elements employed. It is required that the flow rule needs hold throughout each element. For the C1-continuous elements, this requirement can be satisfied naturally. However, for the C0-continuous elements, it can

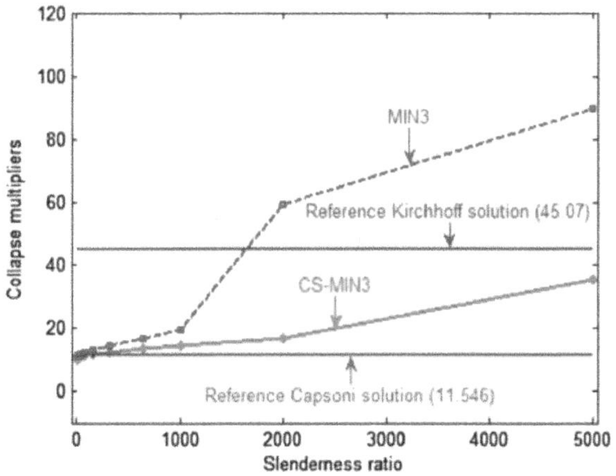

Figure 11 Convergence of collapse multipliers of the clamped square plate subjected to uniform pressure for various (*L*/*t*).

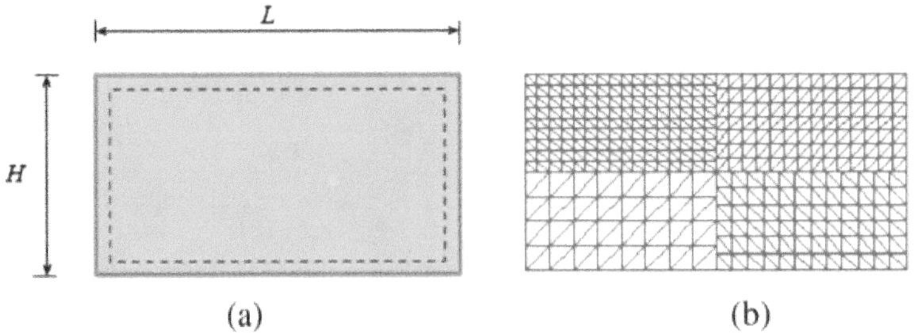

Figure 12 A rectangular plate and four forms of discretization. (a) A simply supported rectangular plate. **(b)** Four discretizations of a quarter of plate using triangular elements.

be violated due to the appearance of plastic hinge lines on boundaries of elements. In order to overcome this violation, the internal work dissipated in resulting hinge lines on boundaries of elements should be taken into account as done by Hodge and Belytschko [7] and Makrodimopoulos and Martin [82]. In this paper, the CS-MIN3 uses only three-node triangular plate elements and hence belongs to the C0-continuous elements. However, for the sake of simplicity of using the CS-MIN3 in the limit analysis of plates, we can ignore considering the internal work dissipated in resulting hinge lines on boundaries of elements. It is therefore no longer possible to guarantee that the solution obtained from the minimization problem (47) is a strict upper bound on the collapse multiplier. However, using the smoothed strain rates which are constant over elements, the flow rule only needs to be enforced at any point in each element, and it is guaranteed to be satisfied almost everywhere in the problem domain. Therefore, the computed collapse load obtained using the proposed method can still be reasonably considered as an upper bound on the actual value.

Results and discussion

The number performance of the proposed limit analysis will now be tested by examining a number of benchmark uniformly loaded or point-loaded plate problems for which numerical solutions have been published in the literature. For all the examples considered, the following were assumed: yield stress $\sigma_p = 250$ MPa and yield moment $M_p = \sigma_p t^2/4$.

Square plates

We now consider a square plate subjected to a uniform out-of-plane pressure loading (with basic load $p = M_p/L^2$) with two different boundary conditions: (1) clamped supports on all edges as shown in Figure 4a and (2) simply supported supports on all edges as shown in Figure 4b. For this problem, the full plate is considered and the upper

Table 2 Convergence of collapse multipliers of clamped rectangular plate subjected to uniform pressure versus various DOFs

Method	Degrees of freedom				Reference solution [33] with 1350 DOFs
	135	273	360	510	
MIN3	62.2853	39.4181	35.883	33.0316	29.88
CS-MIN3	42.2025	33.4743	31.9999	30.7917	

Basic load $p = M_p/(LH)$.

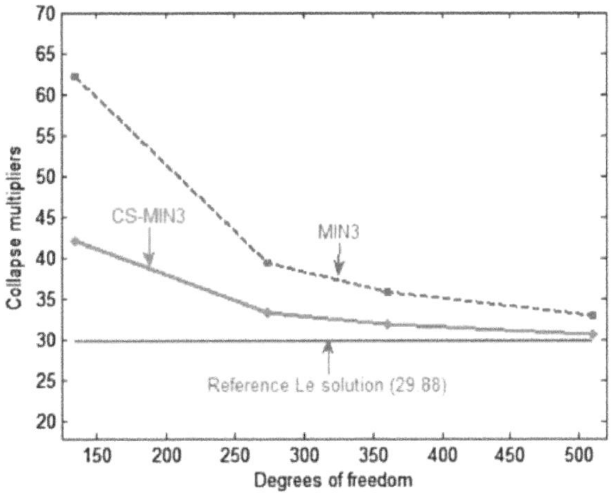

Figure 13 Convergence of collapse multipliers of the supported rectangular plate subjected to uniform pressure versus DOFs.

bound reference solution using quadrilateral elements with 867 degrees of freedom (DOFs) can be found in [37,38]. Figure 4c illustrates four forms of discretization of the plate using triangular elements.

In this example, firstly, the thickness of the plate is chosen such that the ratio $L/t = 10$ and the plate is discretized by the mesh 12×12 with 507 DOFs. We first consider the effect of the collapse multipliers when the number of Gauss points along the half of the thickness of the plate is changed from 1 point to 7 points. Figures 5 and 6 show the convergence of the collapse multipliers versus the different numbers of Gauss points for both cases of boundary conditions by MIN3 and CS-MIN3. The results show that both solutions of the CS-MIN3 and MIN3 converge to the upper bound reference solution [38] when the number of Gauss points increases, but those of the CS-MIN3 are more accurate than those of the MIN3. This hence implies that the CS-MIN3 can provide the reliable upper bound collapse multipliers for the Mindlin plates when a suitable number of Gauss points is used along the half of the thickness of the plate. In these analyses, it is seen that the usage of 6 Gauss points is the most suitable for both cases of boundary conditions and hence will be recommended for default employing in the CS-MIN3 (and also in the MIN3) for all numerical examples in this paper.

Next, the convergence of the collapse multipliers versus various degrees of freedom of the system is considered. The numbers of degrees of freedom of the system are now changed from 75 (corresponding to the mesh 4×4) to 507 (corresponding to the mesh

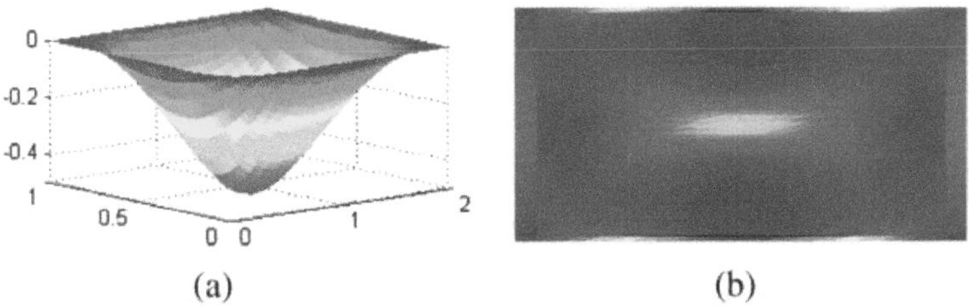

Figure 14 Patterns of displacement and plastic energy dissipation of the supported rectangular plate at collapse by CS-MIN3. (a) Displacement. **(b)** Plastic energy dissipation.

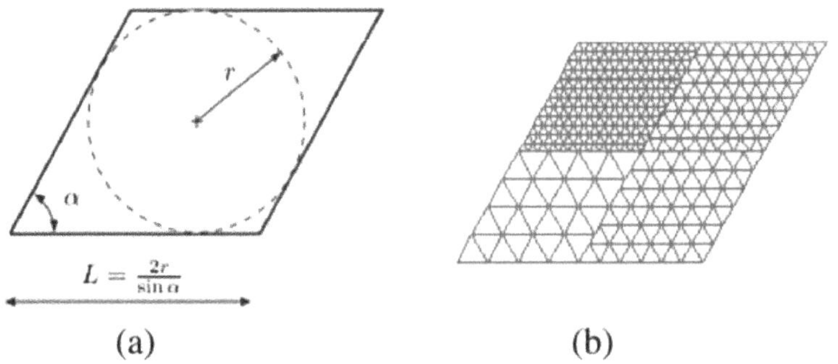

Figure 15 A rhombic plate and four forms of discretization. (a) A rhombic plate. **(b)** Four discretizations of a quarter of plate using triangular elements.

12 × 12). The results for both cases of boundary conditions by the CS-MIN3 and MIN3 are listed in Table 1 and plotted in Figures 7 and 8, respectively. The results show that both solutions of the CS-MIN3 and MIN3 converge to the reference solutions when the number of degrees of freedom increases. In addition, Figures 9 and 10 show the patterns of displacement and plastic energy dissipation at collapse for both cases of boundary conditions by using the CS-MIN3. It can be observed that the forms of the yield lines are clearly identified reasonably from these dissipation patterns. These results hence imply that the CS-MIN3 can provide the reliable upper bound collapse multipliers for the Mindlin plates when a suitable number of degrees of freedom is used. Note that in the above analyses, the results of the CS-MIN3 are more accurate than those of the MIN3, especially in the coarse meshes. This hence implies that the cell-based strain smoothing technique in the CS-MIN3 is very necessary to improve the accuracy of the MIN3 in the limit analysis of Mindlin plates.

Last, the analysis for the solutions of the thin plate by the CS-MIN3 and MIN3 is performed for the clamped square plate by changing the slenderness ratios (L/t) from 5 to 6,250 with the mesh 12 × 12. Convergence of the collapse multipliers of the clamped square plate versus various slenderness ratios (L/t) by the CS-MIN3 and MIN3 is plotted in Figure 11. The Kirchhoff reference results can be found in [33,37]. As expected,

Table 3 Convergence of collapse multipliers of clamped rhombic plate subjected to uniform pressure versus various DOFs

Skewness angle α	Method	Degrees of freedom					Reference solution [38] with 867 DOFs
		75	146	243	363	507	
30	CS-MIN3	20.5975	13.109	11.0884	10.2647	9.8309	9.852
	MIN3	36.1594	21.4943	16.6904	14.0769	12.4709	
45	CS-MIN3	23.8074	14.2608	12.3219	11.4793	11.0211	10.847
	MIN3	46.298	24.0417	17.946	14.7981	13.0246	
60	CS-MIN3	26.561	15.3363	13.2884	12.3919	11.8979	11.641
	MIN3	55.5217	25.6668	18.3164	15.0692	13.3652	
75	CS-MIN3	28.4641	16.2358	13.9159	12.9635	12.438	12.143
	MIN3	62.9974	26.2878	18.2042	15.0939	13.5819	
90	CS-MIN3	29.0137	16.9008	14.2239	13.1852	12.6364	12.314
	MIN3	67.2856	25.8273	17.7147	14.8945	13.5918	

Basic load $p = M_p/R^2$.

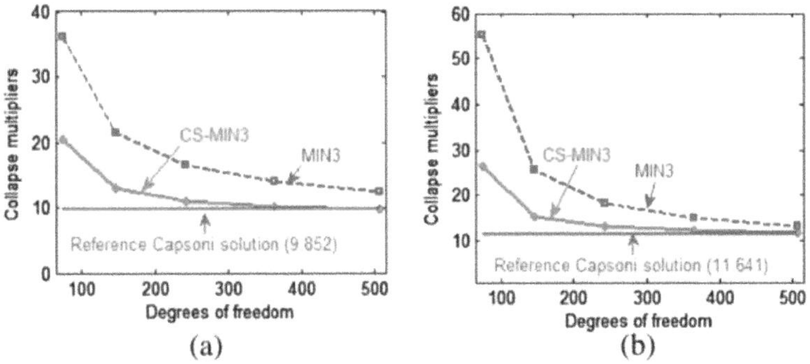

Figure 16 Convergence of collapse multipliers of clamped rhombic plate for two cases. (a) $\alpha = 30°$. **(b)** $\alpha = 60°$.

the solutions of the CS-MIN3 converge to the reference Kirchhoff solution [33] when the slenderness ratio is increased to the limit of the thin plate. This hence shows that the CS-MIN3 is free of shear locking in the limit analysis of thin plates. Also, note that the convergence of solutions of MIN3 is much higher than the expected value when the slenderness ratio is increased to the limit of the thin plate. This hence implies that the cell-based strain smoothing technique in the CS-MIN3 is very necessary to improve the instable behavior of the MIN3 in the limit analysis of thin plates.

Rectangular plate

We now consider a rectangular plate with simply supported supports on all edges and subjected to a uniform out-of-plane pressure loading (with basic load $p = M_p/(L.\ H)$) as shown in Figure 12a. For this problem, the full plate is considered and the upper bound reference solution using a meshfree method with 1,350 DOFs can be found in [33]. Figure 12b illustrates four forms of discretization using uniform meshes of triangular elements.

The convergence of collapse multipliers with respect to the number of degrees of freedom is considered by choosing the thickness of the plate $t = 0.01$ m, the width $L =$ 2 m, and the ratio $L/H = 2$. The results by the CS-MIN3 and MIN3 are listed in Table 2 and plotted in Figure 13. In addition, Figure 14 shows the patterns of displacement and plastic energy dissipation at collapse by the CS-MIN3. It is seen that the obtained comments from the square plates related to the convergence and accuracy of the CS-MIN3 in the limit analysis of Mindlin plates are confirmed for the rectangular plates.

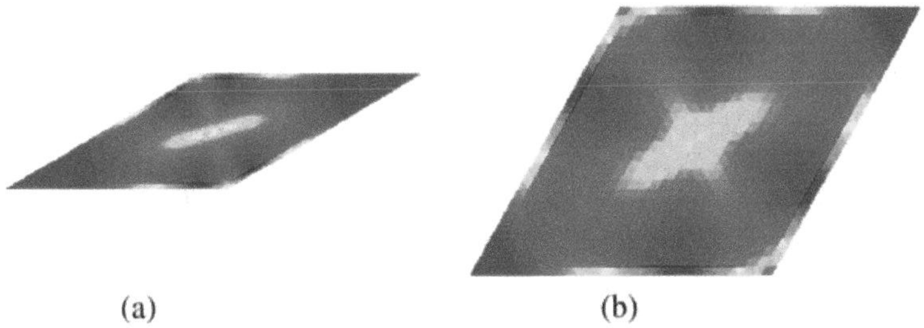

Figure 17 Patterns of plastic energy dissipation rate of clamped rhombic plate at collapse by CS-MIN3 for two cases. (a) $\alpha = 30°$. **(b)** $\alpha = 60°$.

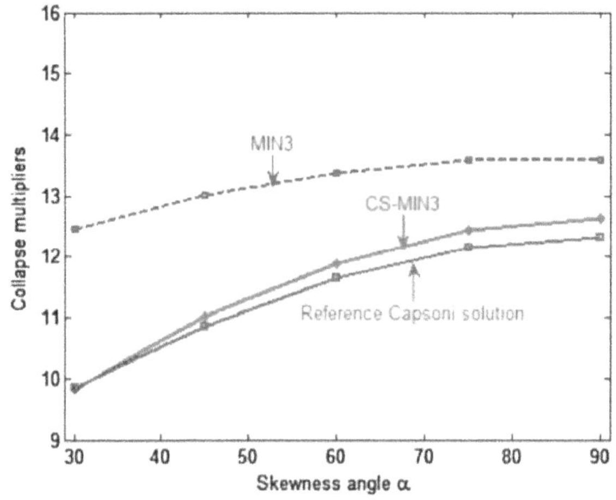

Figure 18 Collapse multipliers of clamped rhombic plate versus various skewness angles α by the CS-MIN3 and MIN3.

Rhombic plate

We now consider a clamped rhombic plate with the radius $R = 0.5$ m and the thickness $t = 0.02$ m subjected to a uniform out-of-plane pressure loading (with basic load $p = M_p/R^2$) as shown in Figure 15a. For this problem, the full plate is considered and the upper bound reference solutions using quadrilateral elements with 867 degrees of freedom can be found in [38]. Figure 15b illustrates four forms of discretization using uniform meshes of triangular elements.

The convergence of collapse multipliers of the clamped rhombic plate with respect to the number of degrees of freedom and various skewness angles α is listed in Table 3 and plotted in Figure 16 for two cases of $\alpha = 30°$ and $\alpha = 60°$. In addition, the patterns

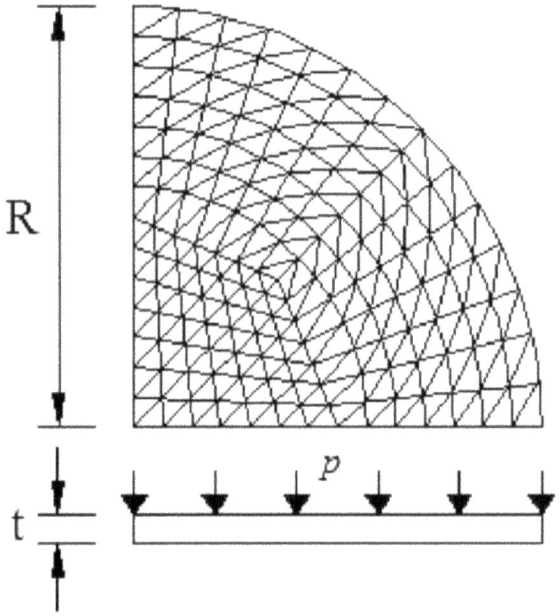

Figure 19 Discretization by 294 triangular elements of the upper right quadrant of the clamped circular plate. The plate was subjected to a uniform out-of-plane pressure loading.

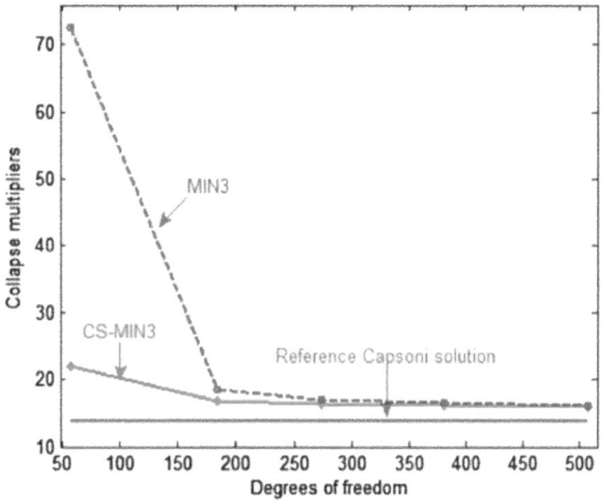

Figure 20 Convergence of collapse multipliers of clamped circular plate subjected to uniform pressure versus various DOFs.

of the plastic energy dissipation at collapse by the CS-MIN3 for two cases of $\alpha = 30°$ and $\alpha = 60°$ are shown in Figure 17. Again, it is seen that the comments obtained from two previous examples related to the convergence and accuracy of the CS-MIN3 in the limit analysis of Mindlin plates are confirmed for the rhombic plates.

In addition, an analysis of collapse multipliers of the clamped rhombic plate with respect to various skewness angles α by the CS-MIN3 and MIN3 is illustrated in Figure 18. It is observed that the results of the CS-MIN3 are very close to those of reference solutions, especially for small skewness angles α. These results hence imply that the CS-MIN3 can provide the reliable solutions in the limit analysis of skew Mindlin plates.

Circular plate

We now consider a clamped circular plate (radius $R = 1$m and thickness of plate $t = 0.01$ m) subjected to a uniform out-of-plane pressure loading (with basic load $p = M_p/R^2$). Due to its symmetry, only the upper right quadrant of the plate is discretized by

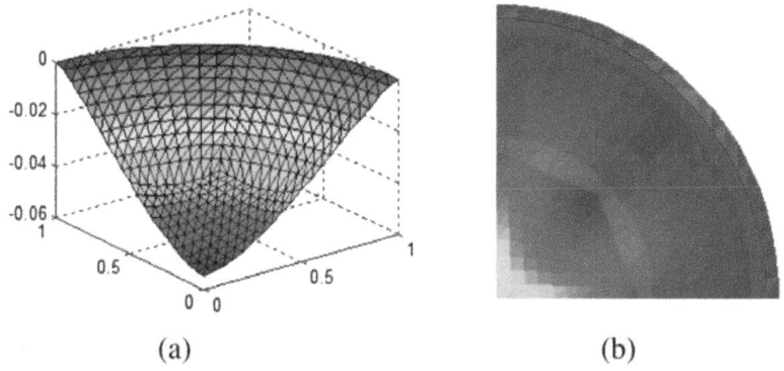

Figure 21 Patterns of displacement and plastic energy dissipation at collapse of clamped circular plate by CS-MIN3. The plate was subjected to uniform pressure. **(a)** Displacement. **(b)** Plastic energy dissipation.

Table 4 Convergence of collapse multipliers of clamped circular plate versus various slenderness ratios (2*R*/*t*) by CS-MIN3 and MIN3

2*R*/*t*	Methods		Reference solution [38] with 1,041 DOFs
	MIN3	CS-MIN3	
2	10.768	4.174	4.740
4	14.201	7.840	8.778
8	15.389	11.058	11.893
10	15.547	11.694	12.378
20	15.771	12.699	12.990
40	15.851	12.986	13.126
80	15.909	13.065	13.160
100	15.927	13.077	13.165
500	16.872	13.275	13.231

294 triangular elements (507 DOFs) as shown in Figure 19. The upper bound reference solutions using quadrilateral elements with 1,041 DOFs can be found in [38].

The convergence of collapse multipliers with respect to the number of degrees of freedom is plotted in Figure 20, and the patterns of displacement and the plastic energy dissipation at collapse by the CS-MIN3 are shown Figure 21. Again, it is seen that the comments obtained from three previous examples related to the convergence and accuracy of the CS-MIN3 in the limit analysis of Mindlin plates are confirmed for the circular plates.

Next, due to the availability of the thin plate reference solutions [38] (collapse multiplier = 13.231), we hence perform a convergent analysis of the collapse multipliers with respect to various slenderness ratios (2*R*/*t*) by the CS-MIN3 and MIN3. The results are listed in Table 4 and plotted in Figure 22. As expected, the solutions of the CS-MIN3 again converge to the reference solutions when the slenderness ratio is increased to the limit of the thin plate. This hence confirms again that the CS-MIN3 is free of shear locking in the limit analysis of thin plates. Also, note that the convergence of solutions of MIN3 is much higher than the expected value when the slenderness ratio is

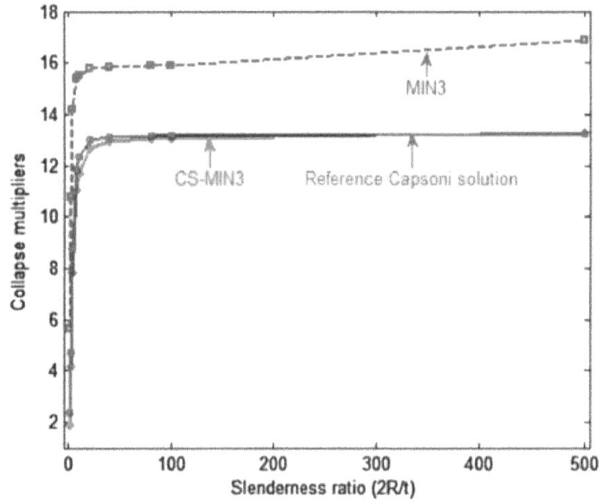

Figure 22 Convergence of collapse multipliers of clamped circular plate subjected to a uniform pressure versus various (2*R*/*t*).

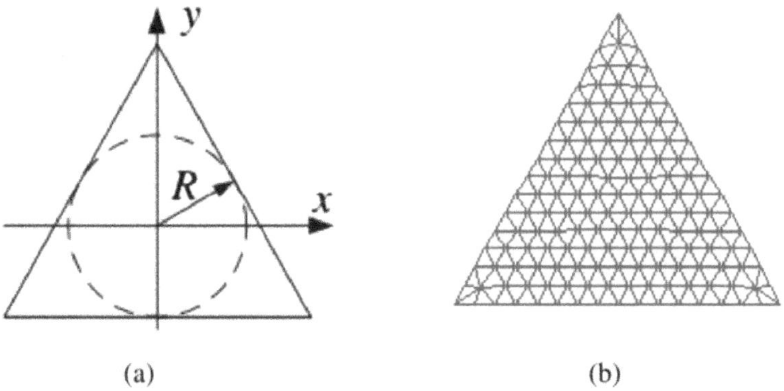

Figure 23 Equilateral triangle plate and discretization. (a) Equilateral triangle plate. **(b)** A discretization using triangular elements of the equilateral triangle plate.

increased to the limit of the thin plate. This hence confirms again that the cell-based strain smoothing technique in the CS-MIN3 is very necessary to improve the instable behavior of the MIN3 in the limit analysis of thin plates.

Equilateral triangle plate

We now consider an equilateral triangle plate as shown in Figure 23a with the assigned radius $R = 1\text{m}$ and thickness $t = 0.04\text{m}$. The plate is clamped on the boundary and subjected to a uniform out-of-plane pressure loading (with basic load $p = M_p/R^2$). For this problem, the full plate is considered and the upper bound reference solutions can be found in [38]. Figure 23b illustrates a discretization using uniform meshes of triangular elements.

The convergence of collapse multipliers with respect to the number of degrees is listed in Table 5 and plotted in Figure 24, and the patterns of displacement and the plastic energy dissipation at collapse by the CS-MIN3 are shown in Figure 25. Again, it is seen that the obtained comments from four previous examples related to the convergence and accuracy of the CS-MIN3 in the limit analysis of Mindlin plates are confirmed for the equilateral triangle plate.

Conclusions

The paper presents a numerical procedure for the kinematic limit analysis of thick plates governed by the von Mises criterion. The cell-based smoothed three-node Mindlin plate element (CS-MIN3) is combined with a second-order cone optimization programming (SOCP) to determine the upper bound limit load of the Mindlin plates. In the CS-MIN3, each triangular element is divided into three sub-triangles, and in each sub-triangle, the gradient matrices of MIN3 are used to compute the strain rates. Then,

Table 5 Convergence of collapse multipliers of clamped equilateral triangle plate subjected to uniform pressure versus various DOFs

Method	Degrees of freedom				Reference solution [83]
	162	273	360	459	
MIN3	15.8781	12.1345	11.1476	10.4487	9.61
CS-MIN3	11.5344	10.6225	10.1818	9.7984	

Basic load $p = M_p/R^2$.

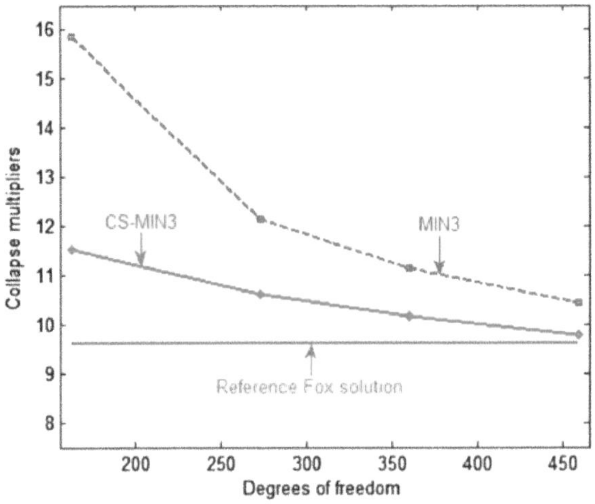

Figure 24 Convergence of collapse multipliers of clamped equilateral triangle plate subjected to uniform pressure versus various DOFs.

the gradient smoothing technique on whole the triangular element is used to smooth the strain rates on these three sub-triangles. The limit analysis problem of Mindlin plates is formulated by minimizing the dissipation power subjected to a set of constraints of boundary conditions and unitary external work. For Mindlin plates, the dissipation power is computed on both the middle plane and the thickness of the plate. This minimization problem can then be transformed into a form suitable for optimum solution using the SOCP. Through the formulation and numerical examples, some concluding remarks can be drawn as follows:

1. The CS-MIN3 uses only three-node triangular elements that are much easily generated automatically for arbitrary complex geometrical domains.
2. The CS-MIN3 can provide reliable upper bound collapse multipliers for both thick and thin plates.
3. The solutions of the CS-MIN3 converge from the upper bound, and the CS-MIN3 is free of shear locking in the limit analysis of thin plates.

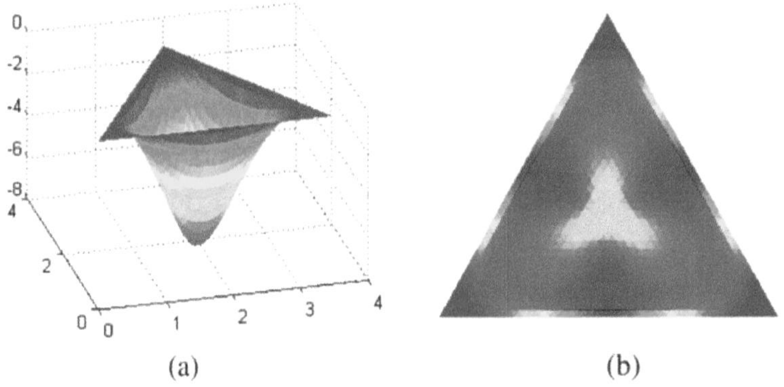

Figure 25 Patterns of displacement and plastic energy dissipation at collapse of clamped circular plate by CS-MIN3. The plate was subjected to a uniform pressure. **(a)** Displacement. **(b)** Plastic energy dissipation.

4. Compared to the MIN3, the CS-MIN3 is more accurate in the limit analysis of thick plates and more stable in the limit analysis of thin plates.
5. The forms of the yield lines by the CS-MIN3 are identified reasonably from the dissipation patterns.

In addition, the extension of the present CS-MIN3 for the limit analysis of flat shells using triangular elements is very promising.

Competing interests
The authors declare that they have no competing interests.

Authors' contributions
NTT proposed the main idea of extending the CS-MIN3 to the limit analysis of Mindlin plates, carriout out the theory model, numerical discretization model, and revising the manuscript. PVP carried out the numerical results and wrote the first draft of the manuscript. LVC carried out the source code of the limit analysis for Kirchhoff plates. All authors read and approved the final manuscript.

Acknowledgements
This work was supported by Vietnam National Foundation for Science & Technology Development (NAFOSTED), Ministry of Science & Technology, under the basic research program (Project No.: 107.02-2012.05).

Author details
[1]Division of Computational Mathematics and Engineering (CME), Institute for Computational Science (INCOS), Ton Duc Thang University, Hochiminh City, Viet Nam. [2]Department of Mechanics, Faculty of Mathematics and Computer Science, VNUHCM University of Science, Hochiminh City, Viet Nam. [3]Department of Civil Engineering, VNUHCM International University, Hochiminh City, Viet Nam.

References
1. Hodge PG (1963) Limit analysis of rotationally symmetric plates and shells. Prentice-Hall, Englewood Cliffs
2. Save MA, Massonnet CE (1972) Plastic analysis and design of plates, shells and disks. North-Holland, Amsterdam
3. Zyczkowski M (1981) Combined loadings in the theory of plasticity. Polish Scientific, PWN and Nijhoff, Wasarwa, Poland
4. Xu BY, Liu XS (1985) Plastic limit analysis of structures. China Architecture & Building Press, Beijing
5. Lubliner J (1990) Plasticity theory. Macmillan, New York
6. Yu MH, Ma GW, Li JC (2009) Structural plasticity limit, shakedown and dynamic plastic analyses of structures. Springer, New York
7. PhGJr H, Belytschko T (1968) Numerical methods for the limit analysis of plates. ASME J Appl Mech 35:796–802
8. Nguyen HD (1976) Direct limit analysis via rigid-plastic finite elements. Comput Methods Appl Mech Eng 8:81–116
9. Christiansen E, Kortanek KO (1991) Computation of the collapse state in limit analysis using the LP affine scaling algorithm. J Comput Appl Math 34:47–63
10. Zouain N, Herskovits J, Borges LA, Feijóo RA (1993) An iterative algorithm for limit analysis with nonlinear yield functions. Int J Solids Struct 30:1397–1417
11. Liu YH, Zen ZZ, Xu BY (1995) A numerical method for plastic limit analysis of 3-D structures. Int J Solids Struct 32:1645–1658
12. Capsoni A, Corradi L (1997) A finite element formulation of the rigid-plastic limit analysis problem. Int J Numer Methods Eng 40:2063–2086
13. Christiansen E, Andersen KD (1999) Computation of collapse states with von Mises type yield condition. Int J Numer Methods Eng 46:1185–1202
14. Corradi L, Panzeri N (2004) A triangular finite element for sequential limit analysis of shells. Adv Eng Software 35:633–643
15. Le VC, Nguyen-Xuan H, Askes H, Bordas S, Rabczuk T, Nguyen-Vinh H (2010) A cell-based smoothed finite element method for kinematic limit analysis. Int J Numer Methods Eng 83:1651–1674
16. Sloan SW (1988) A steepest edge active set algorithm for solving sparse linear programming problems. Int J Numer Methods Eng 26:2671–2685
17. Andersen KD, Christiansen E (1995) Limit analysis with the dual affine scaling algorithm. J Comput Appl Math 59:233–243
18. Pastor J, Thai TH, Francescato P (2003) Interior point optimization and limit analysis: an application. Commun Numer Methods Eng 19:779–785
19. Lyamin AV, Sloan SW (2002) Upper bound analysis using linear finite elements and non-linear programming. Int J Numer Anal Methods Geomech 26:181–216
20. Andersen KD, Christiansen E, Overton ML (1998) Computing limit loads by minimizing a sum of norms. SIAM J Sci Comput 19:1046–1062
21. Krabbenhoft K, Damkilde L (2003) A general non-linear optimization algorithm for lower bound limit analysis. Int J Numer Methods Eng 56:165–184
22. Tin-Loi F, Ngo NS (2003) Performance of the *p*-version finite element method for limit analysis. Int J Mech Sci 45:1149–1166

23. Andersen KD, Christiansen E, Overton ML (2001) An efficient primal-dual interior-point method for minimizing a sum of Euclidean norms. SIAM J Sci Comput 22:243–262
24. Andersen ED, Roos C, Terlaky T (2003) On implementing a primal-dual interior-point method for conic quadratic programming. Math Program 95:249–277
25. Mosek (2008) The MOSEK optimization toolbox for MATLAB manual. Mosek ApS. http://www.mosek.com
26. Krabbenhoft K, Lyamin AV, Sloan SW (2006) Formulation and solution of some plasticity problems as conic programs. Int J Solids Struct 44:1533–1549
27. Makrodimopoulos A, Martin CM (2007) Upper bound limit analysis using simplex strain elements and second-order cone programming. Int J Num Anal Methods Geomech 31:825–865
28. Christiansen E, Larsen S (1983) Computations in limit analysis for plastic plates. Int J Numer Methods Eng 19:169–184
29. Turco E, Caracciolo P (2000) Elasto-plastic analysis of Kirchhoff plates by high simplicity finite elements. Comput Methods Appl Mech Eng 10:691–706
30. Corradi L, Vena P (2003) Limit analysis of orthotropic plates. Int J Plast 19:1543–1566
31. Corradi L, Panzeri N (2003) Post-collapse analysis of plates and shells based on a rigid-plastic version of the TRIC element. Comput Methods Appl Mech Eng 192:3747–3775
32. Tran TN, Kreissig R, Staat M (2009) Probabilistic limit and shakedown analysis of thin plates and shells. Struct Saf 31:1–18
33. Le VC, Gilbert M, Askes H (2009) Limit analysis of plates using the EFG method and second-order cone programming. Int J Numer Methods Eng 78:1532–1552
34. Le VC, Askes H, Gilbert M (2010) Adaptive element-free Galerkin method applied to the limit analysis of plates. Comput Methods Appl Mech Eng 199:2487–2496
35. Le VC, Nguyen-Xuan H, Nguyen-Dang H (2010) Upper and lower bound limit analysis of plates using FEM and second-order cone programming. Comput Struct 88:65–73
36. Zhou S, Liu Y, Chen S (2010) Upper bound limit analysis of plates utilizing the C1 natural element method. Comput Mech. doi:10.1007/s00466-012-0688-8
37. Capsoni A, Corradi L (1999) Limit analysis of plates - a finite element formulation. Struct Eng Mech 8:325–341
38. Capsoni A, Vicente da Silva M (2011) A finite element formulation of Mindlin plates for limit analysis. Int J Num Methods Biomed Eng 27:143–156
39. Liu GR, Nguyen Thoi T (2010) Smoothed finite element methods. CRC Press, Taylor and Francis Group, New York
40. Chen JS, Wu CT, Yoon S, You Y (2001) A stabilized conforming nodal integration for Galerkin mesh-free methods. Int J Numer Methods Eng 50:435–466
41. Liu GR, Dai KY, Trung NT (2007) A smoothed finite element for mechanics problems. Comp Mech 39:859–877
42. Trung NT, Liu GR, Dai KY, Lam KY (2007) Selective smoothed finite element method. Tsinghua Sci Technol 12(5):497–508
43. Liu GR, Trung NT, Nguyen-Xuan H, Dai KY, Lam KY (2009) On the essence and the evaluation of the shape functions for the smoothed finite element method (SFEM). Int J Numer Methods Eng 77:1863–1869
44. Liu GR, Nguyen-Thoi T, Nguyen-Xuan H, Lam KY (2009) A node-based smoothed finite element method (NS-FEM) for upper bound solutions to solid mechanics problems. Comput Struct 87:14–26
45. Nguyen-Thoi T, Liu GR, Nguyen-Xuan H, Nguyen-Tran C (2011) Adaptive analysis using the node-based smoothed finite element method (NS-FEM). Commun Numer Methods Eng 27:198–218
46. Nguyen-Thoi T, Liu GR, Nguyen-Xuan H (2009) Additional properties of the node-based smoothed finite element method (NS-FEM) for solid mechanics problems. Int J Comp Methods 6:633–666
47. Liu GR, Nguyen-Thoi T, Lam KY (2009) An edge-based smoothed finite element method (ES-FEM) for static and dynamic problems of solid mechanics. J Sound Vib 320:1100–1130
48. Nguyen-Thoi T, Liu GR, Nguyen-Xuan H (2011) An *n*-sided polygonal edge-based smoothed finite element method (nES-FEM) for solid mechanics. Commun Numer Methods Eng 27:1446–1472
49. Nguyen-Thoi T, Liu GR, Lam KY, Zhang GY (2009) A face-based smoothed finite element method (FS-FEM) for 3D linear and nonlinear solid mechanics problems using 4-node tetrahedral elements. Int J Numer Methods Eng 78:324–353
50. Liu GR, Nguyen-Thoi T, Lam KY (2008) A novel alpha finite element method (αFEM) for exact solution to mechanics problems using triangular and tetrahedral elements. Comput Methods Appl Mech Eng 197:3883–3897
51. Liu GR, Nguyen-Thoi T, Lam KY (2009) A novel FEM by scaling the gradient of strains with factor α (αFEM). Comput Mech 43:369–391
52. Liu GR, Nguyen-Xuan H, Nguyen-Thoi T, Xu X (2009) A novel Galerkin-like weakform and a superconvergent alpha finite element method (SαFEM) for mechanics problems using triangular meshes. J Comput Phys 228:4055–4087
53. Liu GR, Nguyen-Xuan H, Nguyen-Thoi T (2011) A variationally consistent αFEM (VCαFEM) for solid mechanics problems. Int J Numer Methods Eng 85:461–497
54. Liu GR, Nguyen-Thoi T, Dai KY, Lam KY (2007) Theoretical aspects of the smoothed finite element method (SFEM). Int J Numer Methods Eng 71:902–930
55. Liu GR, Nguyen-Xuan H, Nguyen-Thoi T (2010) A theoretical study on NS/ES-FEM: properties, accuracy and convergence rates. Int J Numer Methods Eng 84:1222–1256
56. Nguyen-Xuan H, Nguyen-Thoi T (2009) A stabilized smoothed finite element method for free vibration analysis of Mindlin-Reissner plates. Int J Num Methods Biomed Eng 25:882–906
57. Cui XY, Liu GR, Li GY, Zhao X, Nguyen-Thoi T, Sun GY (2008) A smoothed finite element method (SFEM) for linear and geometrically nonlinear analysis of plates and shells. CMES-Comp Model Eng Sci 28:109–125
58. Nguyen-Xuan H, Rabczuk T, Nguyen-Thanh N, Nguyen-Thoi T, Bordas S (2010) A node-based smoothed finite element method (NS-FEM) with stabilized discrete shear gap technique for analysis of Reissner-Mindlin plates. Comput Mech 46(5):679–701
59. Nguyen-Xuan H, Loc TV, Chien TH, Nguyen-Thoi T (2012) Analysis of functionally graded plates by an efficient finite element method with node-based strain smoothing. Thin-Walled Struct 54:1–18
60. Thai-Hoang C, Loc T-V, Tran-Trung D, Nguyen-Thoi T, Nguyen-Xuan H (2012) Analysis of laminated composite plates using higher-order shear deformation plate theory and node-based smoothed discrete shear gap method. Appl Math Model 36:5657–5677

61. Nguyen-Xuan H, Tran-Vinh L, Nguyen-Thoi T, Vu-Do HC (2011) Analysis of functionally graded plates using an edge-based smoothed finite element method. Compos Struct 93(11):3019–3039
62. Phan-Dao HH, Nguyen-Xuan H, Thai-Hoang C, Nguyen-Thoi T, Rabczuk T (2013) An edge-based smoothed finite element method for analysis of laminated composite plates. Int J Comp Methods 10(1):1340005
63. Nguyen-Thoi T, Phung-Van P, Nguyen-Xuan H, Thai-Hoang H (2012) A cell-based smoothed discrete shear gap method using triangular elements for static and free vibration analyses of Reissner–Mindlin plates. Int J Numer Methods Eng 91(7):705–741
64. Trung NT, Bui-Xuan T, Phung-Van P, Nguyen-Hoang S, Nguyen-Xuan H (2013) An edge-based smoothed three-node Mindlin plate element (ES-MIN3) for static and free vibration analyses of plates. KSCE J Civ Eng. in press
65. Phung-Van P, Nguyen-Thoi T, Tran V, Nguyen-Xuan H (2013) A cell-based smoothed discrete shear gap method (CS-FEM-DSG3) based on the C^0-type higher-order shear deformation theory for static and free vibration analyses of functionally graded plates. Comput Mater Sci 79:857–872
66. Nguyen-Thoi T, Bui-Xuan T, Phung-Van P, Nguyen-Xuan H, Ngo-Thanh P (2013) Static, free vibration and buckling analyses of stiffened plates by CS-FEM-DSG3 using triangular elements. Comput Struct 125:100–113
67. Nguyen-Thoi T, Phung-Van P, Thai-Hoang C, Nguyen-Xuan H (2013) A cell-based smoothed discrete shear gap method (CS-FEM-DSG3) using triangular elements for static and free vibration analyses of shell structures. Int J Mech Sci 74:32–45
68. Nguyen-Xuan H, Liu GR, Thai-Hoang C, Nguyen-Thoi T (2009) An edge-based smoothed finite element method with stabilized discrete shear gap technique for analysis of Reissner-Mindlin plates. Comput Methods Appl Mech Eng 199:471–489
69. Nguyen-Xuan H, Liu GR, Nguyen-Thoi T, Nguyen-Tran C (2009) An edge-based smoothed finite element method (ES-FEM) for analysis of two-dimensional piezoelectric structures. Smart Mater Struct 18:1–12
70. Phung-Van P, Nguyen-Thoi T, Le-Dinh T, Nguyen-Xuan H (2013) Static, free vibration analyses and dynamic control of composite plates integrated with piezoelectric sensors and actuators by the cell-based smoothed discrete shear gap method (CS-FEM-DSG3). Smart Mater Struct 22:095026
71. Liu GR, Chen L, Nguyen-Thoi T, Zeng K, Zhang GY (2010) A novel singular node-based smoothed finite element method (NS-FEM) for upper bound solutions of cracks. Int J Numer Methods Eng 83:1466–1497
72. Nguyen-Thoi T, Liu GR, Vu-Do HC, Nguyen-Xuan H (2009) An edge-based smoothed finite element method (ES-FEM) for visco-elastoplastic analyses of 2D solids using triangular mesh. Comput Mech 45:23–44
73. Nguyen-Thoi T, Vu-Do HC, Rabczuk T, Nguyen-Xuan H (2010) A node-based smoothed finite element method (NS-FEM) for upper bound solution to visco-elastoplastic analyses of solids using triangular and tetrahedral meshes. Comput Methods Appl Mech Eng 199:3005–3027
74. Nguyen-Thoi T, Liu GR, Vu-Do HC, Nguyen-Xuan H (2009) A face-based smoothed finite element method (FS-FEM) for visco-elastoplastic analyses of 3D solids using tetrahedral mesh. Comput Methods Appl Mech Eng 198:3479–3498
75. Tran TN, Liu GR, Nguyen-Xuan H, Nguyen-Thoi T (2010) An edge-based smoothed finite element method for primal-dual shakedown analysis of structures. Int J Numer Methods Eng 82:917–938
76. Nguyen-Xuan H, Rabczuk T, Nguyen-Thoi T, Tran TN, Nguyen-Thanh N (2012) Computation of limit and shakedown loads using a node-based smoothed finite element method. Int J Numer Methods Eng 90:287–310
77. Le-Van C, Nguyen-Xuan H, Askes H, Rabczuk T, Nguyen-Thoi T (2013) Computation of limit load using edge-based smoothed finite element method and second-order cone programming. Int J Comp Methods 10(1):1340005
78. Nguyen-Thoi T, Phung-Van P, Rabczuk T, Nguyen-Xuan H, Le-Van C (2013) Free and forced vibration analysis using the *n*-sided polygonal cell-based smoothed finite element method (*n*CS-FEM). Int J Comp Methods 10(1):1340008
79. Nguyen-Thoi T, Phung-Van P, Rabczuk T, Nguyen-Xuan H, Le-Van C (2013) An application of the ES-FEM in solid domain for dynamic analysis of 2D fluid-solid interaction problems. Int J Comp Methods 10(1):1340003
80. Nguyen-Thoi T, Phung-Van P, Luong-Van H, Nguyen-Van H, Nguyen-Xuan H (2013) A cell-based smoothed three-node Mindlin plate element (CS-MIN3) for static and free vibration analyses of plates. Comput Mech 51:65–81
81. Tessler A, Hughes TJR (1985) A three-node Mindlin plate element with improved transverse shear. Comp Methods Appl Mech Eng 50:71–101
82. Makrodimopoulos A, Martin CM (2008) Upper bound limit analysis using discontinuous quadratic displacement fields. Commun Numer Methods Eng 24:911–927
83. Fox EN (1974) Limit analysis for plates: the exact solution for a clamped square plate of isotropic homogeneous material obeying square yield criterion and loaded by uniform pressure. Philos Trans Royal Soc A 277:121–155

10

Application of the duality in the finite element analysis of shell: self-dual metis planar shell elements

Nguyen Dang Hung[1,2]

Correspondence: hung.nd@vgu.edu.vn
[1]Vietnamese-German University, Binh Duong New City, Vietnam
[2]University of Liège, Liège B4000, Belgium

Abstract

In this paper, an application of the duality principle in finite element shell analysis is presented. It is based upon Lure (Prikl. Mat. Mekh, XIV 5, 1958) and Goldenveizer's (Theory of thin shells, Pergamon Press, 1961) theory of thin shells. For the finite element analysis of thin shells, using the stress function, the problem of finding a stress fields in equilibrium and expressing their continuity across the interfaces is shown to be identical to the problem of derivation of conforming displacement fields and vice versa. It appears that one may derive from this concept of duality a new family of shell finite elements: the auto-dual shell elements. In this paper, we consider a self-dual flat element for thin shell analysis. This element is based on the already developed and implemented in LTAS department, University of Liège. It was mixed hybrid elements called 'mixed métis'. Numerical efficiency is demonstrated by means of some examples: cylindrical shell roof simply supported by two diaphragms and submitted to its dead weight and cylinder loaded by two diametrically opposed point loads, clamped hyperbolic shell loaded by uniform normal pressure.

Keywords: Thin shell finite element; Hybrid and Métis Model; Duality in shell analysis; Stress and displacement element; Equilibrium element; Stress function

Background

Expanding from the analogy between flexure and extension of flat plates [1], Fraeys De Veubeke and Zienkiewicz [2] and, later, Elias Ziad [3] have pointed out the possibility of dual analysis of plates using equilibrium and conforming finite elements. The generalization of this duality to the case of curved shell from the finite element point of view has been presented by Nguyen Dang Hung [4]. These considerations are based on the static-geometric analogy due to Lure [5] and Goldenveizer [6]. In this paper, we discuss a further development of this duality by combining a hybrid stress and displacement model into a flat shell element.

This hybridmixed planar shell element is self-dual because the shape functions of the dual quantities (Airy's stress function for the membrane effect and the vertical deflection for the bending effect, on one hand, stretching displacement field and bending stress-function, on the other hand) are the same. The choice of the nodal connections is such that nodal displacements or mean displacements are the unknowns: the element can therefore be readily implemented into finite element algorithms based upon the displacement method.

Both the bending element and the membrane element which combine into the planar shell element belong to a special class of hybrid elements called 'metis element' [7,8]. The important advantages exhibited by these elements concerning speed of convergence and stability in stress calculation are expected in the present case.

A raw version about the existence of this element was presented long time ago in Madrid [9] but this present version is more detailed mostly about the detailed illustrations of the concept of self-dual finite elements.

Methods

Development of the element

Duality in the finite element analysis of shells

Lure [5] and Goldenveizer [6] have demonstrated that a perfect analogy does exist between the stress quantities and the strain quantities in the formulation of thin shell theory. Compatibility equations for strains and displacement components become equilibrium equations for stresses and stress function components when dual quantities are replaced by each other as follows:

$$|u, v, w, \varepsilon_1, \varepsilon_2, \omega_{12}, \omega_{21}, \kappa_1, \kappa_2, \tau_{12}, \tau_{21}| \tag{1}$$

$$|U, V, W, -M_2, -M_1, M_{12}, M_{21}, N_2, N_1, -N_{12}| \tag{2}$$

Where $d^T = |u, v, w|$ are the displacement components defined on the middle surface

$$\mathbf{a}^T = |-M_2, -M_1, M_{12}, M_{21}, N_2, N_1, -N_{21}, -N_{12}|$$

are the moments and membrane forces defined per unit length of middle surface as in the classical shell theory, see for example reference [10], U, V, and W are the stress functions.

It is shown that equilibrium and compatibility are exactly satisfied with the following definition of the strain and stress:

$$\varepsilon = \nabla d, \sigma = \nabla D \tag{3}$$

where $\mathbf{D}^T = |U, V, W|$ are the stress function components defined on the middle surface

$\tilde{N}^T$ a derivative operator of matrix form [3x8] (4)

$$\begin{aligned}
a1 &= \frac{1}{2R_1}\left(\frac{\partial}{A_2\partial\alpha_2} - \frac{1}{\rho_1}\right);\ \delta_1 = \frac{\partial}{A_1\partial\alpha_1}\left(\frac{1}{R_1}\right) + \frac{1}{2}\left(\frac{1}{R_1} + \frac{1}{R_2}\right)\frac{\partial}{A_1\partial\alpha_1} + \frac{1}{2R_1R_2}\left(R_1\frac{\partial}{A_1\partial\alpha_1} - \frac{R_2}{\rho_2}\right)\\
a_3 &= -\frac{\partial^2}{A_1\partial\alpha_1 A_2\partial\alpha_2} + \frac{\partial}{\rho_1 A_1\partial\alpha_1};\ \delta_2 = \frac{\partial}{A_2\partial\alpha_2}\left(\frac{1}{R_2}\right) + \frac{1}{2}\left(\frac{1}{R_1} + \frac{1}{R_2}\right)\frac{\partial}{A_2\partial\alpha_2} + \frac{1}{2R_1R_2}\left(R_2\frac{\partial}{A_2\partial\alpha_2} - \frac{R_1}{\rho_1}\right)\\
b_2 &= \frac{1}{2R_2}\left(\frac{\partial}{A_1\partial\alpha_1} - \frac{1}{\rho_2}\right);\ b_3 = -\frac{\partial^2}{A_2\partial\alpha_2 A_1\partial\alpha_1} + \frac{\partial}{\rho_2 A_2\partial\alpha_2}
\end{aligned}$$

α_1, α_2, orthogonal coordinate system

A_1, A_2, corresponding Lame's system

ρ_1, ρ_2, radius of geodesic curvature on the middle surface

Conformity and diffusivity

A displacement field satisfies conformity in a curved shell if the following continuity is insured along any edge of the shell element:

$$(u_n)^+ = (u_n)^-, (u_n)^+ = (u_s)^-, (w_n)^+ = (w_n)^-, \left(\frac{\partial w}{\partial n}\right)^+ = \left(\frac{\partial w}{\partial n}\right)^- \tag{5}$$

Where $\vec{n}$ and $\vec{s}$ are the middle surface normal and tangent to the edge, respectively. A stress resultant field satisfies diffusivity if the following quantities are continuously transmitted through the boundary of the element.

$$(N_n)^+ = (N_n)^-, (\bar{N}_s)^+ = (N_s + M_n s/R_s)^+ = (\bar{N}_s)^-, (M_n)^+ = (M_n)^- \tag{6}$$

$$(K_n)^+ = Q_n + (?M_n s)/?s = (K_n)^-$$

And the local jumps of the twisting moment at vertex k is as follows:

$$Z_k = (M_n s)_k^+ - (M_n s)_k^-$$

Nguyen Dang Hung [4] has presented a boundary duality theorem which states that: 'If displacements conformity is satisfied, stress resultants diffusivity is also satisfied when the same fields are used for displacement and stress functions'. In other words, let us choose a shape function for the displacement field d, making use of some appropriate connectors (nodal displacements) on the boundary, such that (5) is satisfied; if the same shape function is chosen for the stress function field D, that is similar assumptions on the field and corresponding connectors (nodal stress functions), then equilibrium conditions on the boundary (6) are automatically satisfied.

In the case of planar shell $\left(\frac{1}{R_1} = \frac{1}{R_2} = 0\right)$, there is no coupling between membrane stress components and bending moments and if Cartesian coordinates are used $\left(\frac{1}{\rho_1} = \frac{1}{\rho_2} = 0\right)$, the derivative operator ∇ is reduced to a simpler form:

$$\nabla^T = \begin{bmatrix} \frac{\partial}{\partial x} & 0 & \frac{\partial}{2\partial y} & 0 & 0 & 0 \\ 0 & \frac{\partial}{\partial y} & \frac{\partial}{2\partial x} & 0 & 0 & 0 \\ 0 & 0 & 0 & \frac{\partial^2}{\partial x^2} & \frac{\partial^2}{\partial y^2} & -2\frac{\partial^2}{\partial x \partial y} \end{bmatrix} \tag{7}$$

The dual quantities become

$$d^T = |u, v, \mathrm{w}|;\ \varepsilon^T = \left|\varepsilon_x, \varepsilon_y, \frac{\gamma_{xy}}{2}, \kappa_x, \kappa_y, \kappa_{xy}\right| \tag{8}$$

$$D^T = |U, V, -F|;\ \sigma^T = \left|-M_y, -M_x, M_{xy}, N_y, N_x, -N_{xy}\right| \tag{9}$$

Where we recognize U and V as Southwell's stress functions (for bending effects) and F as Airy's stress function (for the membrane part). The boundary duality theorem identifies the problem of finding stress functions U and V and of expressing their continuity across the interface with the problem encountered in the derivation of conforming displacement fields for membrane stretching [11]:

$$\text{(u, v) continuous entails (U, V) continuous i.e. force components } M_n,\ K_n \text{continuous and } Z_k = 0 \text{ at the vertex k.} \tag{10}$$

Conversely, according to the same theorem, the problem of finding a continuous stress field (*Nx, Ny, Nxy*) and expressing the continuity of the components (*Nn, Nns*) across the interface of a membrane element is the same as the problems of finding a conforming transversal displacement in plate bending.

$$(N_n, N_{ns},)\ \left(F, -\frac{\partial F}{\partial n}\right)\ \left(w, \frac{\partial w}{\partial n}\right) \text{Continuous} \tag{11}$$

Figure 1a presents a triangular element with quadratic displacement field along the edges; 12 nodal displacements are necessary to satisfy the conformity.

Figure 1b shows a bent plate finite element with 12 nodal stress functions as connectors; this triangle ensures continuity of the normal moment *Mn* (linear along an edge), the equivalent shear force *Kn* (constant along an edge) and the local jumps of twisting moment *Zk* at each corner. If forces are taken as nodal values rather than stress functions, the corresponding 12 connectors are those exhibited in Figure 1c.

This system of nodal forces is adopted in reference [12] for the formulation of an equilibrium model for plate bending with linear assumptions for the moment field.

Figure 2a represents a conforming element for plate bending with quadratic assumptions on the vertical deflection w along the edges.

Figure 2b shows the dual membrane element with nodal values of the Airy' stress function; it is equivalent to the element shown on Figure 2c where the resultants.

$R_x = \int (l.\ N_x + m.\ N_{xy})dx; \quad R_y = \int (m.\ N_y + l.\ N_{xy})dy$ have been chosen as nodal values.

(*l, m* are the components of the unit normal to the edge).

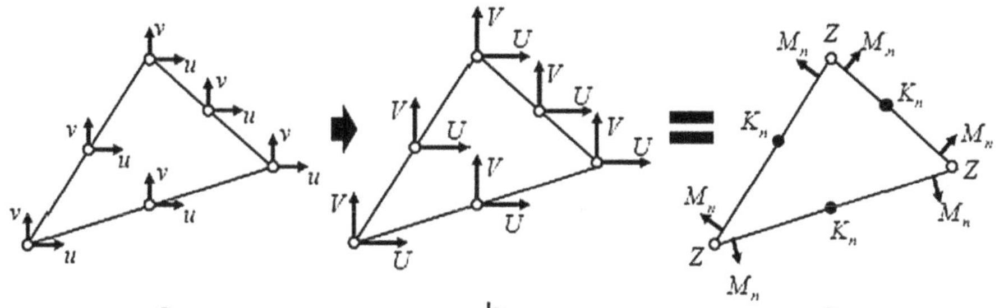

Figure 1 A triangular element with quadratic displacement field along the edges. (a) Membrane element with quadratic displacement field. Conformity is satisfied with 12 nodal connectors. **(b)** Dual element for plate bending with quadratic stress field. Boundary equilibrium (diffusivity) is satisfied with 12 stress connectors. **(c)** Corresponding element for plate bending with linear moment field. Boundary equilibrium (diffusivity) requires 12 nodal forces.

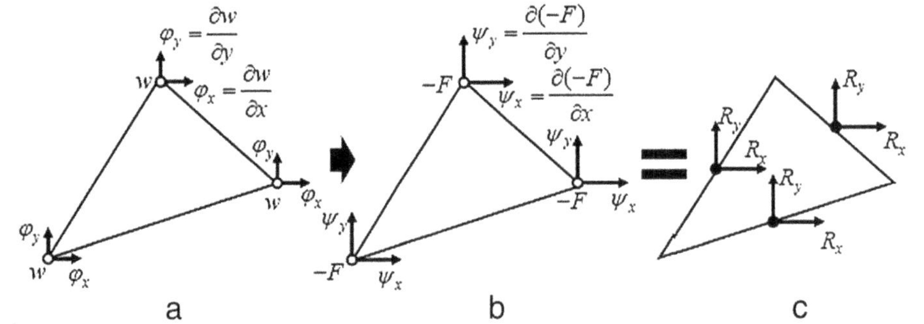

Figure 2 Elements of plate bending and membrane stretching. (a) Element of plate bending with quadratic deflection. Conformity requires 2 nodal displacements on each edge. **(b)** Dual element for membrane stretching with quadratic Airy's function. Diffusivity requires nine nodal stress function connectors. **(c)** Corresponding element for membrane stretching constant stress field. Boundary equilibrium (diffusivity) requires six nodal forces.

Hybrid finite elements and métis finite elements

Let us now consider the following mixed hybrid functional:

$$I = I_T + I_B \tag{12}$$

Where IT is the modified complementary energy functional for the membrane effect:

$$I_T = \sum_N \left(\int_{AN} \frac{1}{2} T_{ijkl}.N_{ij}N_{kl} \right) dA - \int_{\Gamma_N} n_j.N_{ij}\bar{u}_i\, ds + \int_{\Gamma_{\sigma N}} nj.\bar{N}_{ij}\bar{u}_i\, ds) \tag{13}$$

and IB is the modified potential energy functional for the bending effect:

$$I_B = \sum_N \left(\int_{A_N} \left(\frac{1}{2} Bi_{jkl}.K_{ij}K_{kl} - pw \right) dA + \int \Gamma_{u_N} \left[M_n \, \tilde{} \frac{\partial \bar{w}}{\partial n} - \tilde{K}_n \bar{w} + \frac{\partial}{\partial s}\left(\tilde{M}_{ns}\bar{w} \right) \right] ds \right.$$
$$\left. - \int_{\Gamma_N} \left[\tilde{M}_n \frac{\partial w}{an} - \tilde{K}_n w + \frac{\partial}{\partial s}\left(\tilde{M}_{ns} w \right) \right] ds \right) \tag{14}$$

In these expressions,

$Ti_{jkl} = [T] = \frac{1}{Eh}\begin{bmatrix} 1 & -\nu & 0 \\ -\nu & 1 & 0 \\ 0 & 0 & 2(1+\nu) \end{bmatrix}$ is the elastic compliance of the stretching effect

$B_{ijkl} = [B] = \frac{Eh^3}{12(1-\nu^2)}\begin{bmatrix} 1 & \nu & 0 \\ \nu & 1 & 0 \\ 0 & 0 & 2(1-\nu) \end{bmatrix}$ is the elastic compliance of the bending effect

AN, the domain of element

N, its boundary

Γ_{σ_N}, portion of where tensions $n_j\bar{N}_{ij} = \bar{T}_i$ are prescribed

p, normal pressure

h, thickness of the shell

One may notice that in (13) there are two unknown fields: the stress field Nij must be defined and in equilibrium over the domain AN.

The displacement field $\tilde{u}_i$ is defined on the boundary Γ_N in such a way that conformity (i.e., the two first relations of 5) is insured. This functional was first proposed by Pian [13,14] for a hybrid stress finite element formulation. On the other hand, functional (14) possesses two other unknown fields: the deflection w must be defined continuously in AN; the stress field $\left[\tilde{M}_n \quad \tilde{K}_n \quad \tilde{Z}\right]$ must be defined on the boundary Γ_N in such a way that diffusivity (i.e., three last relations of 6) is satisfied.

This functional is adopted by Jones [15] for a hybrid displacement finite element formulation.

Nguyen Dang Hung [7,8] has shown that if the boundary conforming field $\tilde{u}_i$ of (13) defined on the boundary Γ_N can be extended over AN in other words if the two unknown fields in (13) are well defined everywhere in the closed domain $\bar{A}_N$, the hybrid stress element belongs to a special class called 'mongrel displacement element' which leads to important advantage in energy convergence. In the same way, if the two unknown fields of functional (14) are well defined in the closed domain $\bar{A}_N$ (i.e., equilibrium boundary field $\left[\tilde{M}_n \quad \tilde{K}_n \quad \tilde{Z}\right]$ can be extended everywhere in $\bar{A}_N$), the corresponding hybrid displacement element for plate bending becomes a 'mongrel stress element' with the same properties concerning the convergence.

In this paper, such is the case for the mixed hybrid planar shell element described in this paper as well for membrane as for bending effects.

Self-dual metis planar shell element

Let us make the following assumptions concerning the four unknown fields of the hybrid mixed functional (12):

$$w = \sum_{m=0}^{M}\sum_{n=0}^{n}\beta_{mn}x^{m-n}y^{n}; -F = \sum_{m=0}^{M}\sum_{n=0}^{n}\beta'_{mn}x^{m-n}y^{n} \tag{15}$$

$$\begin{aligned} \tilde{u} &= \alpha_1 + \alpha_2 x + \alpha_3 y + \alpha_4 x^2 + \alpha_5 xy + \alpha_6 y^2 \\ \tilde{v} &= \alpha_7 + \alpha_8 x + \alpha_9 y + \alpha_{10} x^2 + \alpha_{11} xy + \alpha_{12} y^2 \\ \tilde{V} &= \alpha'_7 + \alpha'_8 x + \alpha'_9 y + \alpha'_{10} x^2 + \alpha'_{11} xy + \alpha'_{12} y^2 \\ \tilde{U} &= \alpha'_1 + \alpha'_2 x + \alpha'_3 y + \alpha'_4 x^2 + \alpha'_5 xy + \alpha'_6 y^2 \end{aligned} \tag{16}$$

Where β_{mn}, β'_{mn}, α_i, α'_i are the interpolation parameters,

M is the maximum degree of the polynomial (15).

Let us adopt for the membrane element the natural system of nodal displacements shown on Figure 1a and for the bending effect the natural system of nodal stress functions shown on Figure 1b. It appears that we will have a mongrel-mixed planar shell element. Assumptions (16) indicate that the boundary fields $(\tilde{u} \quad \tilde{v})$ and $(\tilde{U} \quad \tilde{V})$ are defined everywhere in $\bar{A}_N$ and conformity and diffusivity are both satisfied with the system of 24 nodal values shown on Figure 3.

Dual quantity $< w >$ is a sort of mean vertical deflection of the shell.

This element, denominated 'HYTCOQ' constitutes a self-dual metis planar shell element because the strain field and the stress field for the membrane and the bending effects are respectively dual quantities of each other in the sense discussed in the section Duality in the finite element analysis of shells. The details of the stiffness

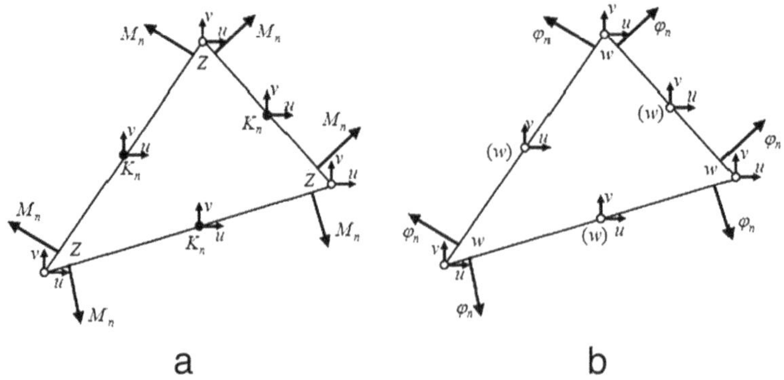

Figure 3 Mixed and self-dual planar shell element. (a) Metis mixed planar shell element. This element is self-dual because its bending and stretching effect are represented by dual models of Figure 1a,c. **(b)** Self-dual metis mixed planar shell element (HYTCOQ). The nodal forces $[\tilde{M}_n \quad \tilde{K}_n \quad \tilde{Z}]$ are replaced by the nodal displacement generalized one $[\varphi_n \quad <w> \quad w]$.

matrix formation for the membrane and bending effects are respectively given in references [16,17].

Here, we merely observe that, for the bending effect, we have formulated the element in such a way that nodal generalized displacements replace nodal forces as unknowns; in this way, no special modifications are required to run this element on existing codes written for displacement elements.

On the other hand, we notice that the system of nodal displacements of this element (Figure 3b) is well suited for easy connection of adjacent elements. In particular, the normal slope is locally defined on the edge of the element; this avoids the drawback frequently encountered with flat shell elements when the slopes are defined at the corners.

One may summarize here the nature of HYTCOQ:

(a) The membrane part possesses displacement metis stretching element with quadratic displacement field defined on the vertexes. The equilibrium stress field (which is derived from a polynomial Airy's function) is defined only inside the element. It appears that when the degree of the Airy's function such that at least $M = 4$, stress field is quadratic the normal rule for kinematic stability is respected. In these conditions, the displacement hybrid or metis formulation does not imply spurious modes, this element leads to good behavior in convergence and precision according to the numerical tests realized in LTAS. Recently (2013), a new examination is performed and it appears that this element leads to very good performance in terms of convergence, precision, and numerical stability [18].

(b) The bending part possesses stress metis element with linear moment field defined on the vertexes. The vertical defection (which is derived from a polynomial function) is defined only inside the element. This bending stress metis element was examined intensively, and the very good results are described in the paper [17].

As both stretching and bending effects are represented by very good elements and there exists no interaction effect due to the flat geometry, we must expect to a good performance of the present self-dual planar shell element.

Results and discussion

Numerical results

Preliminary remarks

This section intends to show the performances of this new mongrel-mixed element by means of a few examples. Simply or doubly curved shells are chose as, namely, cylindrical roof and cylinder or hyperbolic roof. Each example is illustrated by several diagrams. On each of these:

- A small drawing represents the structure, its boundary conditions, its loading, all pertinent data and the finest discretization of mesh.
- The elements being compared are represented by a symbol; their meaning is defined on every figure because it can vary from one figure to the next; the results of a new element called 'HYTCOQ' will be always illustrated in the figures.
- Appropriate references are also given [19].
- The stresses shown are always those obtained with the finest grid; it was deemed useful to represent these stresses even in case where no analytical solution or other numerical results are available.

Cylindrical shell roof supported by two vertical diaphragms and loaded by its dead weight

It is useful to mention that the vertical diaphragms restrain the displacement along X and Z directions but let free Y displacement. The rotation in the direction of X axis is not prevented. The double symmetry of the structure allows considering only a quarter of the structure.

Figure 4 shows the convergence of the strain energy. The analytical solution is taken from Scordelis and Lo [20]. The HYTCOQ element exhibits a relatively fast convergence, and the exact solution is reached with less than 300 degrees of freedom. For comparison motivation, we have chosen the 'GSS3' curved triangular element elaborated by Idelsohn [21]. This latter has really a better behavior than HYTCOQ possibly because the curvature is taken into account.

We can finally notice the following important fact: the convergence of the strain energy seems to be monotonous and upper bounds are obtained for this example; we will see that this monotony is preserved for other examples even if lower bounds are obtained. This remarkable situation has been theoretically discussed by Nguyen Dang Hung [7,8].

Figure 5 illustrates the convergence of the displacement at the point B. The analytical solution has been calculated by Scordelis and Lo [20] and is equal to 6.308 ft.

In this example, only the GSS3 has a better behavior than the HYTCOQ.

MTS2 element behaves exactly like HYTCOQ but the others are rather worse although they are curved and therefore well suited for this example.

Note that the analytical solution is about 3% higher than the 'exact' one towards which elements MTS2 and HYTCOQ converge.

Figure 6 presents bending moments along AB. The finite element stresses are evaluated by calculating a mean value over each element compared with the analytical solution, the results of HYTCOQ with 515 degrees of freedom look excellent: nearly all the points are on the analytical curves.

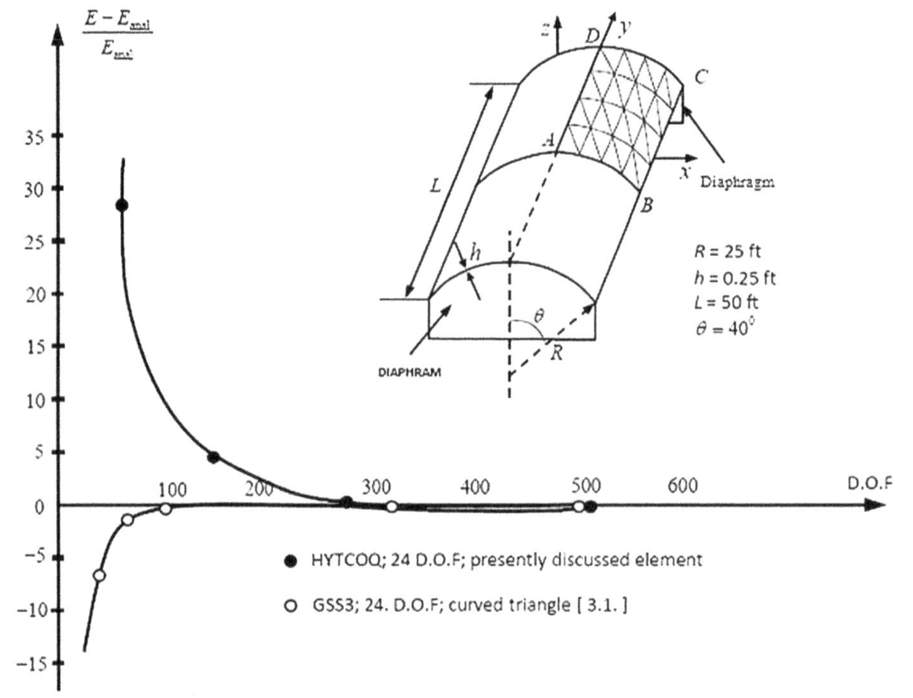

Figure 4 The convergence of the strain energy.

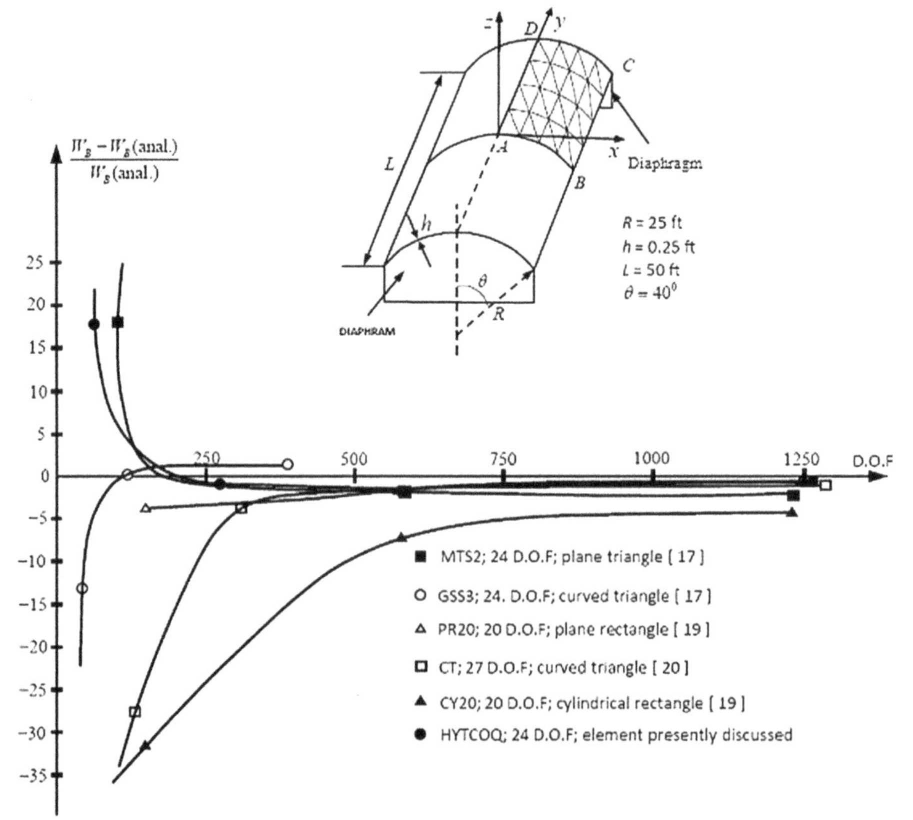

Figure 5 The convergence of the displacement at the point B [21–23].

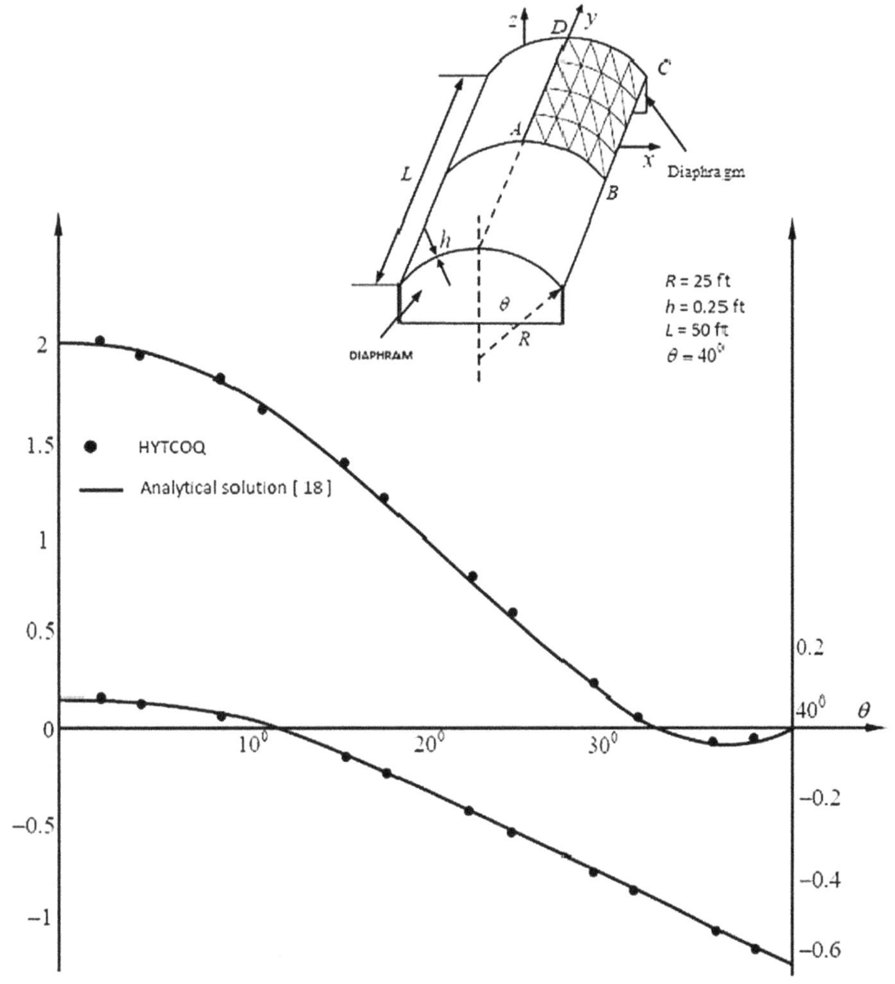

Figure 6 Bending moments along AB [20].

Cylindrical shell

Because of the symmetry, an eighth of the structure is discretized using HYTCOQ.

Figure 7 presents the convergence of the displacement under the load. We can see that the present element has a very good behavior in comparison with cylindrical elements which are theoretically better suited for this problem.

On this diagram, we can also observe that the behavior of the 'CS' element depends on the type of discretization for there are two different curves for this element; it appears better to choose a given discretization along the curvature than along the axis of the cylinder.

The 'exact' solution towards which all the numerical results do converge seems to be 5% higher than the analytical solution given by Timoshenko [26]; but this latter includes only bending effects.

Figure 8 illustrates the bending and the membrane stresses along at $y = L/2$.

No stress diagrams were found in the literature for this example, but all the stresses tend towards an infinite value under the load except for the *Mxy* moment which is equal to zero because of symmetry.

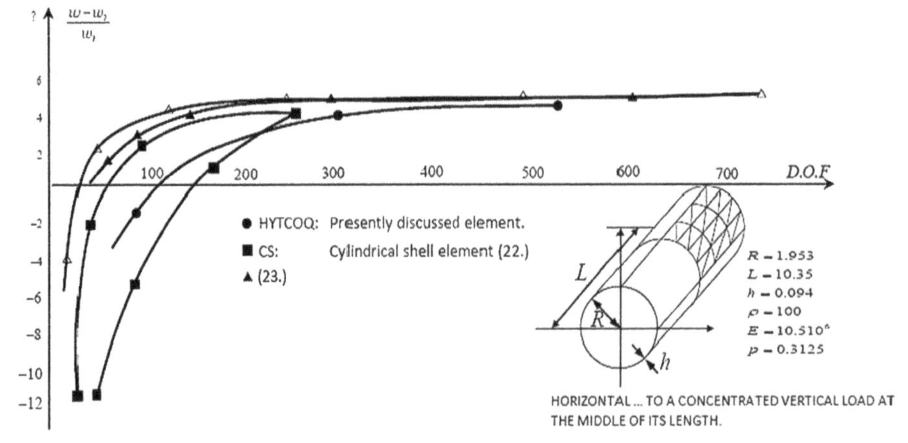

Figure 7 Convergence of the displacement under the load [24,25].

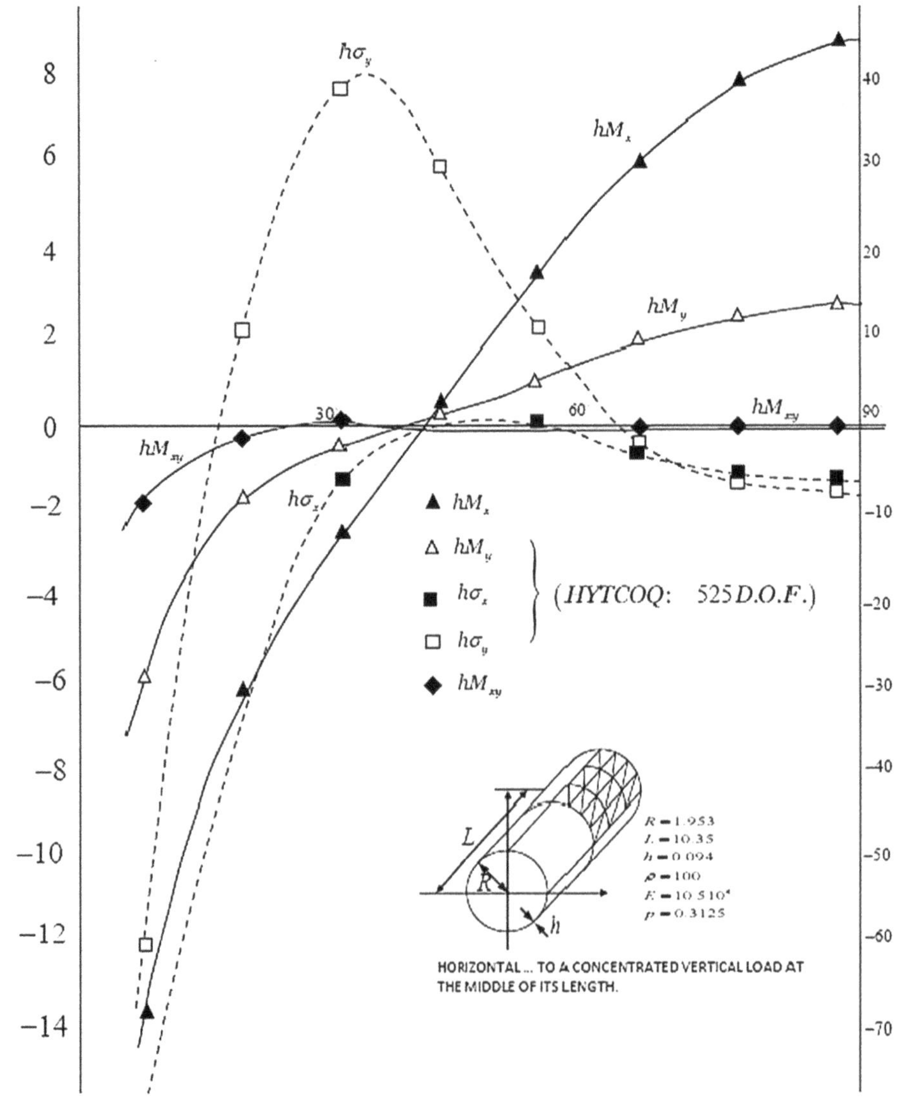

Figure 8 Bending and membrane stress along θ at $y = l/2$.

Clamped square hyperbolic parabolic subjected to a uniform normal pressure

The double symmetry of the structure and the triangular shape of the element allow to study only one quarter of the structure.

Figure 9 presents the convergence of the displacement at the point A. The analytical solution given by Brebbia [27] is equal to $W=$ (where D is represented here the elastic bending rigidity).

The convergence of the HYTCOQ element is not monotonous. This quality is required for only the convergence of the strain energy which indeed does happen (we have not shown it because no reference value was available).

The other elements 'CR20' and 'CR20SE' converge either to another value or more slowly than 'HYTCOQ'.

Figure 10 finally shows the vertical displacement along AD. We compare the result with the result of 'CR20' element. The two solutions are very similar except near the center of the shell, where HYTCOQ gives a better value than CR20 because the exact value obtained from the previous example is $W = -0.02452$ cm. Unfortunately, no analytical solution seems to be available to decide which result is best.

This example is interesting because it deals with a doubly curved structure and we can see that the behavior of HYTCOQ element is still very good.

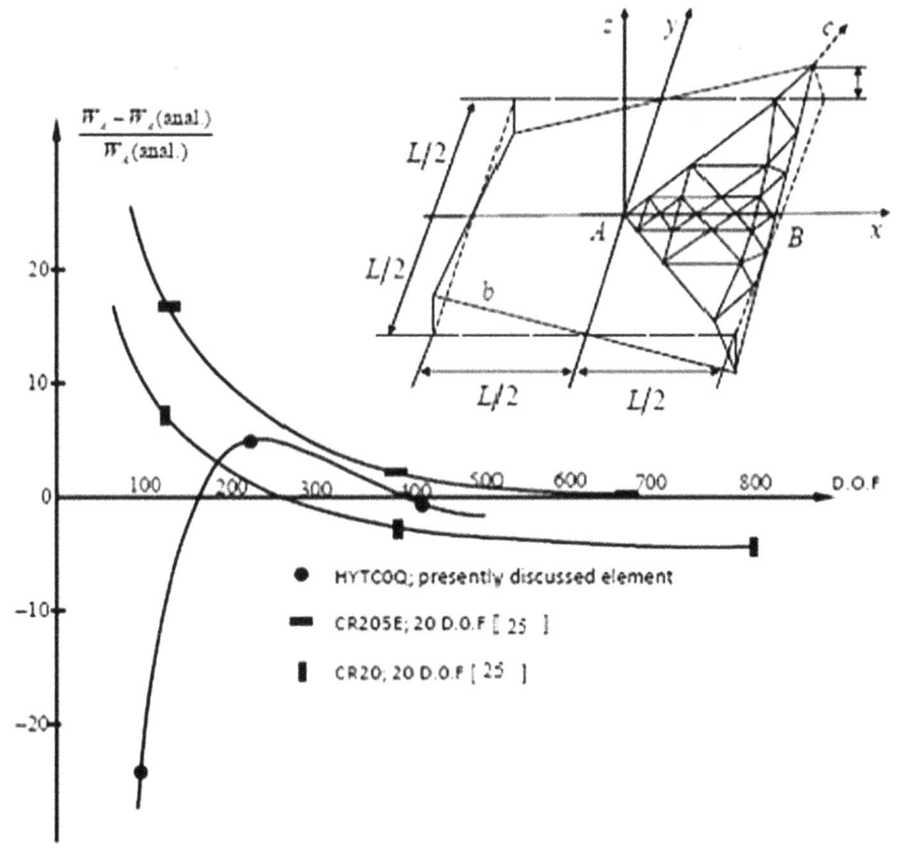

Figure 9 Convergence of the displacement at the point A.

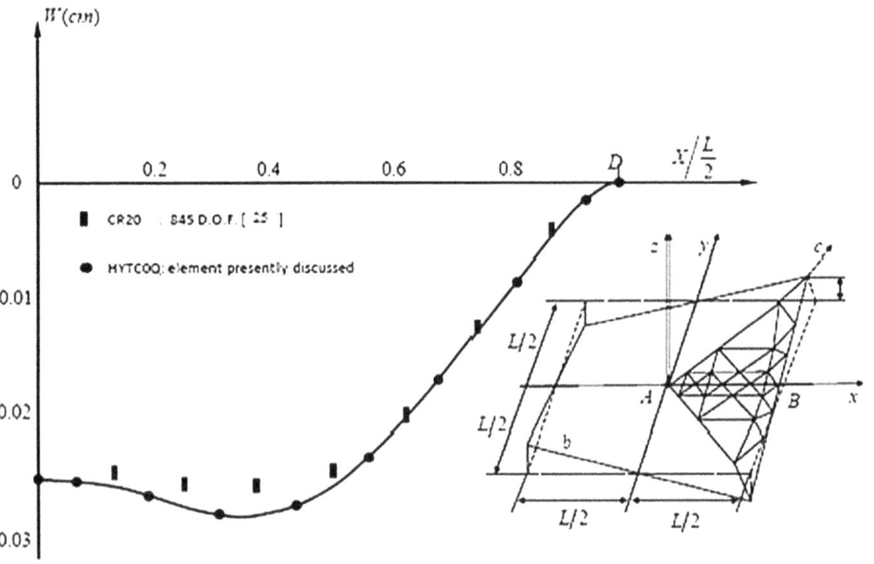

Figure 10 Vertical displacement along AD.

Conclusions

Implementation of the dual properties in shells is a very powerful tool to generate the appropriate finite elements. In this paper, we focus our attention on a special case: derivation of a self-dual metis planar shell element. The versatility and the fast convergence of this type of finite element are confirmed by numerical experiments. It should be interesting to perform a new self-dual pure planar element composed with the quadratic displacement triangle for stretching aspect and the equilibrium model for plate bending proposed very early by Fraeijs de Veubeke and Sander in 1968. On the other hand, we hope that similar duality in shell analysis should be extended to smooth element method [28].

Competing interests

The author declares that he has no competing interests.

References

1. Southwell RV (1950) On the analogues relating flexure and extension of flat plates. Quart Mech Appl Math 3:157
2. Fraeijs De Veubeke B, Zienkiewicz OC (1967) Strain-energy bounds in finite element by slab analogy. J Strain Analysis 2(4):265–271
3. Elias Ziad M (1968) Duality in finite element method. J Engrs Mech Div Am Soc Civ Engrs 94(EM4):931–946
4. Hung ND (1971) Duality in the analysis of shells by the finite element method. Int J Solids and Struct 7:281–299
5. Lure AI (1958) The general theory of thin elastic shells. Prikl Mat Mekh XIV:5
6. Goldenveizer AL (1961) Theory of thin shells. Pergamon Press.
7. Nguyen Dang H (1980) On the monotony and the convergence of a special class of hybrid finite elements: the mongrel elements. In: Nemat N (ed) Proceeding of the IUTAM symposium on variational method in the mechanics. Northwestern University, Pergamon Press, pp 208–213
8. Nguyen Dang H (1979) On a special class of hybrid finite elements: the "metis" (in French). In: Proceedings of the 1st International Congress of GAMNI, (E. ABSI and R. GLOWINSKI), Dunod technique, pp 53–63
9. Nguyen Dang H, Detroux P, Falla PH, Fonder G (1979) Proceedings of World Congress on Shell and Spatial Structures, Theme 4. Madrid, pp 4.1–4.19
10. Novozhilov VW (1955) The theory of thin shells translated by JOVE. In: Noordhoff P (ed) Radok JR. The theory of thin shells translated by JOVE. Groningen
11. Sander G (1970) Application of dual analysis principle. In: Proceedings IUTA symposium high speed computing of elastic structures. Liège
12. Fraeijs De Veubeke B, Sander G (1968) An equilibrium model for plate bending. Int J Solids and Structures 4:447–468
13. Pian THH (1964) Derivation of element stiffness matrices by assumed stress distribution. AIAA Jnl 2:1333–1336

14. Pian THH, Tong P (1969) Basis of finite element methods for solid continua. Int Jnl Num Meth Engr 1:3–28
15. Jones RE (1964) A generalization of the direct stiffness method of structural analysis. AIAA J vol 2, Nr 5:821–826
16. Nguyen Dang H (1976) Direct limit analysis via rigid-plastic finite element. Comp Meth In Mech Engr 8(1):81–116
17. Nguyen Dang H, Desir P (1977) La performance numérique d'un élément fini hybride de déplacement pour l'étude des plaques en flexion » Coll. Publ. Of Faculty of Applied Sciences, vol 33. University of Liège, pp 65–123
18. Dang TD, Hung N-D (2013) A hybrid element model for structural mechanics problems. European Journal of Mechanics - A/Solids 42:469–479
19. Cantin G (1970) Rigid body motions in curved finite elements. AIAA 8(07):1252–1255
20. Scordelis A, Lo KS (1964) Computer analysis of cylindrical shells. J Am Concr Inst 61(5):539–562
21. Idelson S (1974) "Analyse statique et dynamique des coques par la méthodes des éléments finis" Thèse de doctorat ULG
22. Megard G (1969) Planar and curved shell elements. Finite Element Methods in Stress Analysis, Tapir, Trondheim
23. Bunnes G, Dhatt G, Giroux Y, Robichaud L (1968) Curved triangular elements for analysis of shells. In: Proc. 2nd Air Force Conf. on Matrix Methods in Structural Mechanics. Wright-Paterson Air Force base, AFFDL, Ohio, pp 68–150
24. Altman W, Iguti F (1976) A thin cylindrical shell element based on a mixed formulation. Computers & Structures 6(2):149–155
25. Ashwell DG, Sabir AB (1971) A new cylindrical shell finite element based on simple independent strain functions. Department of Civil Engineering, Report, University of Wales, Cardiff
26. Timoshenko SP, Winowsky-Krieger S (1959) Theory of plates and shells. Mc Graw-Hill, New York
27. Brebbia C (1967) Hyperbolic paraboloidal shells, Ph D Thesis. University of Southampton, Department of Civil Engineering
28. Nguyen-Thanh N, Rabczuk T, Nguyen-Xuan H, Bordas S (2008) A smoothed finite element method for shell analysis. Comput Methods Appl Mech Eng 198:165–366

11

Model order reduction for Bayesian approach to inverse problems

Ngoc-Hien Nguyen[1*], Boo Cheong Khoo[2] and Karen Willcox[3]

*Correspondence:
mpennh@nus.edu.sg
[1] Singapore-MIT Alliance, National University of Singapore, Singapore 117576, Singapore
Full list of author information is available at the end of the article

Abstract

This work presents an approach to solve inverse problems in the application of water quality management in reservoir systems. One such application is contaminant cleanup, which is challenging because tasks such as inferring the contaminant location and its distribution require large computational efforts and data storage requirements. In addition, real systems contain uncertain parameters such as wind velocity; these uncertainties must be accounted for in the inference problem. The approach developed here uses the combination of a reduced-order model and a Bayesian inference formulation to rapidly determine contaminant locations given sparse measurements of contaminant concentration. The system is modelled by the coupled Navier-Stokes equations and convection-diffusion transport equations. The Galerkin finite element method provides an approximate numerical solution-the 'full model', which cannot be solved in real-time. The proper orthogonal decomposition and Galerkin projection technique are applied to obtain a reduced-order model that approximates the full model. The Bayesian formulation of the inverse problem is solved using a Markov chain Monte Carlo method for a variety of source locations in the domain. Numerical results show that applying the reduced-order model to the source inversion problem yields a speed-up in computational time by a factor of approximately 32 with acceptable accuracy in comparison with the full model. Application of the inference strategy shows the potential effectiveness of this computational modeling approach for managing water quality.

Keywords: Bayesian; Convection-diffusion equation; Navier-Stokes equations; Markov chain Monte Carlo; Inverse problem; Proper orthogonal decomposition; Reduced-order model

Background

Hydrodynamic processes such as contaminant transport in lakes and reservoirs have a direct impact on water quality. The contaminants will appear, spread out, and decrease in concentration, etc. because of some processes such as convection, diffusion, time rate release of contaminants, and distance of travel. To simulate such processes, a coupled system of partial differential equations (PDEs) including the Navier-Stokes equations (NSEs) and contaminant transport equations needs to be solved. A better understanding of these processes is important in managing water resources effectively.

The direct or forward problems compute the distribution of contaminant directly from given input information such as contaminant location, contaminant properties, fluid flow properties, boundary conditions, initial conditions, etc. On the contrary, the inverse problems infer the unknown physical parameters, boundary conditions, initial conditions, or geometry given a set of measured data. These known data can be obtained experimental or computational. In realistic applications, data are not perfect because of error due to sensor noise. In addition, the model may contain some uncertain parameters such as wind velocity. Thus, inverse problems are generally stochastic problems.

A Bayesian inference approach to inverse problems is one way to deal with the stochastic problem. This approach takes into account both the information of the model parameters with uncertainty and the inaccuracy of data in terms of a probability distribution [1,2]. The Bayesian approach provides a general framework for the formulation of wide variety of problems such as climate modeling [3], contaminant transport modeling [4-6], and heat transfer [7]. Under the Bayesian framework, simulated solutions need to be evaluated repeatedly over different samples of the input parameters. There are available sampling strategies associated with Bayesian computation such as Markov chain Monte Carlo (MCMC) methods [8-11]. However, if we use traditional PDE discretization methods, such as finite element or finite volume methods, the resulting numerical models describing the system will be very large and expensive to solve.

This paper presents an efficient computational approach to solve the statistical inverse problem. The approach uses the combination of a reduced-order model and a Bayesian inference formulation. The Galerkin finite element method [12] provides an approximate numerical solution - the 'full model' or 'forward model'. The MCMC method is applied to solve the Bayesian inverse problems. In particular, we are interested in inferring an arbitrary source location in a time-dependent convection-diffusion transport equation, given a velocity field and a set of measured data of the concentration field at sparse spatial and temporal locations. We obtain the velocity field by solving the Navier-Stokes equations.

Solution of large-scale inverse problems can be accelerated by applying model order reduction [13-15]. The idea is to project the large-scale governing equations onto the subspace spanned by a reduced-space basis, yielding a low-order dynamical system. Proper orthogonal decomposition (POD) is the most popular method to find the reduced basis for a given set of data. The snapshot POD method, which was proposed by Sirovich [16], provide an efficient way for determining the POD basis vectors. Snapshots are solutions of a numerical simulation at selected times or choices of the parameters. The choice of snapshots should ensure that the resulting POD basis captures the most important characteristics of the system.

Since the convection term in contaminant transport equations is a velocity-dependent term, we cannot apply the standard POD reduction framework. The evaluation of the velocity-dependent convection term in the reduced system still depends on the full finite element dimension and has the same complexity as the full-order system. Thus, a system with velocity-dependent convection term needs an additional treatment to obtain an efficient reduced-order model.

This paper is outlined as follows. In the section 'Mathematical model and numerical methods', we introduce the mathematical model, the finite element approximate technique, and the Bayesian inference formulation and its solution using an MCMC method. In section 'Model order reduction', we describe the model order reduction technique and the treatment of the velocity-dependent convection term. In the section 'Numerical example', we use the numerical example to demonstrate the solution of the statistical inverse problem and the reduced-order model performance. We provide some concluding remarks in the final section.

Methods

In this section, the mathematical model, finite element approximation technique, Bayesian inference formulation, and MCMC method are briefly introduced.

Transport model

Consider the fluid flow through a physical domain $\mathcal{D} \subset \mathbb{R}^d, d = 1, 2, 3$ with boundary Γ. The contaminant concentration $c :\equiv c(\mathbf{x}, t; \theta)$ satisfies the dimensionless parabolic PDEs, boundary conditions, and initial conditions as follows:

$$\frac{\partial c}{\partial t} + \mathbf{u} \cdot \nabla c - \frac{1}{Pe}\Delta c = f \quad \text{in } \mathcal{D}\times[t_0, t_f], \tag{1}$$

$$c = g \quad \text{on } \Gamma_D\times[t_0, t_f], \tag{2}$$

$$\frac{\partial c}{\partial \mathbf{n}} = 0 \quad \text{on } \Gamma_N\times[t_0, t_f], \tag{3}$$

$$c(\mathbf{x}, t_0) = c_0(\mathbf{x}) \quad \text{in } \mathcal{D}, \tag{4}$$

where $\mathbf{x} \in \mathcal{D}$ denotes the spatial coordinates, $t \in [t_0, t_f]$ denotes time, and c_0 is the given initial condition. The inlet boundary Γ_D is subjected to a Dirichlet condition, while the remainder of the boundary $\Gamma_N = \Gamma \setminus \Gamma_D$ satisfies Neumann conditions. The external source $f(\mathbf{x}, t; \theta)$ in Equation 1 is used here as a input parameter, where $\theta \in \mathcal{D}$ is the source location. In this study, we suppose that the contaminant source drives the transport process, given a velocity field $\mathbf{u} \in \mathbb{R}^d$. Thus, the Péclet number $\text{Pe} = \frac{\|\mathbf{u}\|\text{L}}{\kappa}$, where κ is the diffusivity and L is the characteristic length. The velocity field is a function of $\mathbf{x}$ and t, $\mathbf{u}(\mathbf{x}, t)$, which can be obtained by solving the Navier-Stokes equations, as follows:

$$\frac{\partial \mathbf{u}}{\partial t} + \left(\mathbf{u} \cdot \nabla\right)\mathbf{u} - \frac{1}{\text{Re}}\nabla^2\mathbf{u} + \nabla p = \mathbf{f}_c \quad \text{in } \mathcal{D}\times\ [t_0, t_f], \tag{5}$$

$$\nabla \cdot \mathbf{u} = 0 \quad \text{in } \mathcal{D}\times\ [t_0, t_f], \tag{6}$$

$$\mathbf{u} = \mathbf{u}_D \text{ on } \Gamma\times\ [t_0, t_f], \tag{7}$$

$$\mathbf{u}(\mathbf{x}, t_0) = \mathbf{u}_0(\mathbf{x}) \quad \text{in } \mathcal{D}, \tag{8}$$

where Re is the Reynolds number, p is the pressure field, and $\mathbf{f}_c$ is the body force. So, for any given f and $\mathbf{u}$, one can solve for the solution $c(\mathbf{x}, t; \theta)$.

Finite element approximations

The finite element method [12] associated with the stabilized second-order fractional-step method is applied to solve the incompressible Navier-Stokes equations (5 to 8). The detailed discussion and derivation of this method is beyond the scope of this paper. For more details, please refer to [17,18].

We also use the finite element method for spatial discretization of the contaminant transport equations in Equations 1 to 4. This leads to the semi-discrete equations

$$\mathbf{M}\dot{\mathbf{c}} + \left(\mathbf{C}(\mathbf{u}) + \mathbf{K}\right)\mathbf{c} = \mathbf{F}(t; \theta), \tag{9}$$

$$\mathbf{c}(t_0) = \mathbf{c}_0, \tag{10}$$

with the output of contaminant solution at sensor locations in the domain

$$\mathbf{y} = \mathbf{B}\mathbf{c}. \tag{11}$$

Here, $\mathbf{c}(t) \in \mathbb{R}^N$ is the discretized approximation of $c(\mathbf{x}, t)$ and contains N state unknowns where N is the number of grid points in the spatial discretization. $\dot{\mathbf{c}}$ is the derivative of $\mathbf{c}$ with respect to time. The vector $\mathbf{y} \in \mathbb{R}^{N_o}$ contains the N_o outputs of the system related to the state through the matrix $\mathbf{B} \in \mathbb{R}^{N_o \times N}, N_o \ll N$. The matrices $\mathbf{M}, \mathbf{K}, \mathbf{C}(\mathbf{u}) \in \mathbb{R}^{N \times N}$ and the vector $\mathbf{F}(t;\theta) \in \mathbb{R}^N$ are defined in the finite element space as follows:

$$\mathbf{M}_{i,j} = \int_{\mathcal{D}} \phi_i(\mathbf{x})\phi_j(\mathbf{x})\, d\mathbf{x}, \tag{12}$$

$$\mathbf{K}_{i,j} = \int_{\mathcal{D}} \frac{1}{Pe} \nabla\phi_i(\mathbf{x}) \cdot \nabla\phi_j(\mathbf{x})\, d\mathbf{x}, \tag{13}$$

$$\left(\mathbf{C}(\mathbf{u})\right)_{i,j} = \int_{\mathcal{D}} \mathbf{u} \cdot \nabla\phi_i(\mathbf{x})\phi_j(\mathbf{x})\, d\mathbf{x}, \tag{14}$$

$$\left(\mathbf{F}(t;\theta)\right)_j = \int_{\mathcal{D}} f(t;\theta)\phi_j(\mathbf{x})\, d\mathbf{x}. \tag{15}$$

Here ϕ_i with $i = 1, \cdots, N$ is the finite element basis and $\theta \in \mathbb{R}^d$ is the coordinate vector of the source location.

Bayesian inference to inverse problems

The Bayesian formulation of an inference problem is derived from Bayes' theorem [1]:

$$p(\theta|\mathbf{y}) = \frac{p(\mathbf{y}|\theta)p(\theta)}{p(\mathbf{y})}, \tag{16}$$

where $\mathbf{y} \in \mathbb{R}^{N_o}$ is the observed data and $\theta \in \mathbb{R}^d \subseteq \mathcal{D}$ is the vector of input parameters. $p(\theta)$ denotes the prior distribution of the parameters, $p(\mathbf{y}|\theta)$ is the likelihood function, and $p(\theta|\mathbf{y})$ is the posterior distribution of parameters given the observed data. $p(\mathbf{y})$ is the prior predictive distribution of $\mathbf{y}$ and may be set to an unknown constant that is not needed in the MCMC solution method. In this case, we write Bayes's formula as

$$p(\theta|\mathbf{y}) \propto p(\mathbf{y}|\theta)p(\theta). \tag{17}$$

A simple model for the likelihood function can be obtained from the following relationship,

$$\mathbf{y} = G(\theta) + \eta, \tag{18}$$

where η is the noise which we assume to be white Gaussian noise $\eta \sim N(0, \sigma^2 I)$. The input-output relative in Equations 1 to 4 is denoted as the forward model $G(\theta)$. Subsequently, the likelihood can be written as

$$p(\mathbf{y}|\theta) = \frac{1}{\sigma\sqrt{2\pi}} \exp\left(-\frac{1}{2\sigma^2}\|\mathbf{y} - G(\theta)\|^2\right). \tag{19}$$

There are many approaches to define the prior information, such as Gaussian Markov random fields or uniform distribution models, etc. In this work, we assume that our only prior information on the source location is given by the bounds on the domain. Thus, using the principle of maximum entropy [19], we take our prior to be a uniform distribution. Therefore, Equation 17 becomes

$$p(\theta|\mathbf{y}) \propto \prod_{i=1}^{K} \exp\left[-\frac{1}{2\sigma^2}\left(\mathbf{y}_i - G(\theta)_i\right)^T\left(\mathbf{y}_i - G(\theta)_i\right)\right]. \tag{20}$$

Here, K is the number of time steps over which we collect the output data.

Markov chain Monte Carlo for posterior sampling

MCMC simulation provides a sampling strategy from a proposal distribution to the target distribution using the Markov chain mechanism. Hastings introduced the Metropolis-Hastings (MH) algorithm [10], which is a generalized version of the Metropolis algorithm [8,9], in which we can apply both symmetric and asymmetric proposal distributions. In this work, the MH algorithm is used to solve the Bayesian inverse problem. The MH algorithm is summarized as follows:

1. Initialize the chain θ^0 and set $n = 0$
2. Repeat
   - $n = n + 1$
   - Generate a proposal point $\theta^* \sim q(\theta^*|\theta)$
   - Generate U from a uniform $\mathcal{U}(0, 1)$ distribution
   - Update the state to θ^{n+1} as
     $\theta^{n+1} = \begin{cases} \theta^*, \text{ if } \beta < \text{U} \\ \theta^n, \text{ otherwise} \end{cases}$
3. Until $n = N_{\text{mcmc}} \rightarrow$ stop.

Here, β is the acceptance-rejection ratio, given by

$$\beta = \min\left(1, \frac{\pi\left(\theta^*\right) q\left(\theta^{n-1}|\theta^*\right)}{\pi\left(\theta^{n-1}\right) q\left(\theta^*\right)|\theta^{n-1}}\right). \tag{21}$$

N_{mcmc} is the total number of samples, $\pi(\theta)$ is the target distribution, $q(\theta^*|\theta)$ is a proposal distribution, and U is a random number.

The discretized model in the form of ordinary differential equations (ODEs) (Equations 9 to 11) may have very large dimensions and be expensive to solve. The MCMC method requires evaluating repeatedly the solution of the forward model (many thousands or even millions of times). Hence, these simulations can be a computationally expensive undertaking. In such situations, the reduced-order model is needed to approximate the large-scale model, which allows efficient simulations.

Model order reduction

This section presents the model order reduction framework. This includes the reduction via projection, the proper orthogonal decomposition method, the additional treatment for the velocity-dependent convection term, and the error estimation.

Reduction via projection

A reduced-order system approximating the ODEs (9 to 11) can be obtained by approximating the full state vector $\mathbf{c}$ as a linear combination of m basis vectors as follows:

$$\mathbf{c} \approx V\mathbf{c}_r, \tag{22}$$

where $\mathbf{c}_r \in \mathbb{R}^m$ is the reduced order state and $V = [v_1\ v_2\ \cdots v_m] \in \mathbb{R}^{N\times m}$ is an orthonormal basis, i.e., $V^T V = I$. The low-order model can be derived by projecting the governing system (9 to 11) onto the reduced space formed by the column span of basis V. This yields

$$\mathbf{M}_r\dot{\mathbf{c}}_r + \big(\mathbf{C}_r(\mathbf{u}) + \mathbf{K}_r\big)\mathbf{c}_r = \mathbf{F}_r(t;\theta), \tag{23}$$

$$\mathbf{c}_r(t_0) = \mathbf{c}_{0r}, \tag{24}$$

$$\mathbf{y}_r = \mathbf{B}_r\mathbf{c}_r, \tag{25}$$

where

$$\mathbf{M}_r = V^T\mathbf{M}V, \tag{26}$$

$$\mathbf{K}_r = V^T\mathbf{K}V, \tag{27}$$

$$\mathbf{C}_r(\mathbf{u}) = V^T\mathbf{C}(\mathbf{u})V, \tag{28}$$

$$\mathbf{F}_r(t;\theta) = V^T\mathbf{F}(t;\theta), \tag{29}$$

$$\mathbf{B}_r = \mathbf{B}V, \tag{30}$$

$$\mathbf{c}_{0r} = V^T\mathbf{c}_0. \tag{31}$$

The model reduction task is to find a suitable basis V so that $m \ll N$ and the reduced-order model yields accurate results. This study will consider POD as the method to compute the basis.

Proper orthogonal decomposition

POD provides a method to compute the reduced-order basis V and construct the low-order system. Here, we briefly describe the general POD method (more details may be found in [16]).

Supposed that we have the snapshot matrix $X \in \mathbb{R}^{N\times Q}$, where Q is the number of snapshot solutions, which are built from the instantaneous solution $\mathbf{c}^s(t_k)$ of the forward model, corresponding to $s = 1, \cdots, S$ random input source locations, picked up at $k = 1, \cdots, T$ different time steps (so that $Q = ST$). The POD basis vectors are the m left singular vectors of X corresponding to the largest singular values ($m \leq Q$). Let $\sigma_i, i = 1, 2, \cdots, Q$ be the singular values of X in decreasing order. We choose the number of POD basis vectors to retain in the reduced-order model as $m \leq Q$ so that

$$\sum_{i=1}^{m}\sigma_i^2 / \sum_{j=1}^{Q}\sigma_j^2 \geq \epsilon_E, \tag{32}$$

where $\epsilon_E(\%)$ is the required amount of energy, typically taken to be 99% or higher.

After obtaining the POD basis vectors for the contaminant, we have defined our reduced-order system. However, as mentioned earlier, the dimension of the system of Equations 23 to 25 is reduced only in state (concentration). The reduced convection matrix ($\mathbf{C}_r(\mathbf{u})$) in Equation 28 still depends on the full dimension of the velocity field as in Equation 14. This means that we have to re-compute the full convection matrix ($\mathbf{C}(\mathbf{u})$) at each time-step before projecting it onto the reduced-space basis to obtain the reduced convection matrix ($\mathbf{C}_r(\mathbf{u})$). Hence, we need an additional treatment to avoid this computational cost.

Linear expansion techniques for velocity-dependent term

We proceed by representing the velocity field as a linear combination of POD velocity basis vectors. The velocity-dependent convection matrix can then be expanded based on this velocity expansion. In particular, let $\mathbf{u}(\mathbf{x}, t)$ be a given velocity field and $\{\mathbf{u}(\mathbf{x}, t_k)\}_{k=1}^{T}$ be a set of 'snapshots' of velocities which are obtained from Equations 5 to 8 and taken over T time steps. The velocity field is decomposed as

$$\mathbf{u}(\mathbf{x}, t) = \mathbf{u}_m(\mathbf{x}) + \mathbf{u}'(\mathbf{x}, t), \tag{33}$$

where $\mathbf{u}_m(\mathbf{x}) = \frac{1}{T}\sum_{k=1}^{T} \mathbf{u}(\mathbf{x}, t^k)$ is the mean velocity field and $\mathbf{u}'(\mathbf{x}, t)$ is the fluctuating velocity field. The fluctuating velocity field is then represented by

$$\mathbf{u}'(\mathbf{x}, t) = \sum_{k=1}^{T} \alpha_k(t)\Psi_k(\mathbf{x}), \tag{34}$$

where $\Psi_k(\mathbf{x})$ is the kth POD velocity basis and $\alpha_k(t)$ is the corresponding time dependent amplitude. We now consider the expansion of the velocity field as

$$\mathbf{u}(\mathbf{x}, t) = \mathbf{u}_m(\mathbf{x}) + \sum_{k=1}^{N_u} \alpha_k(t)\Psi_k(\mathbf{x}), \tag{35}$$

where $N_u \ll T$ is the number of POD basis vectors use to represent the velocity.

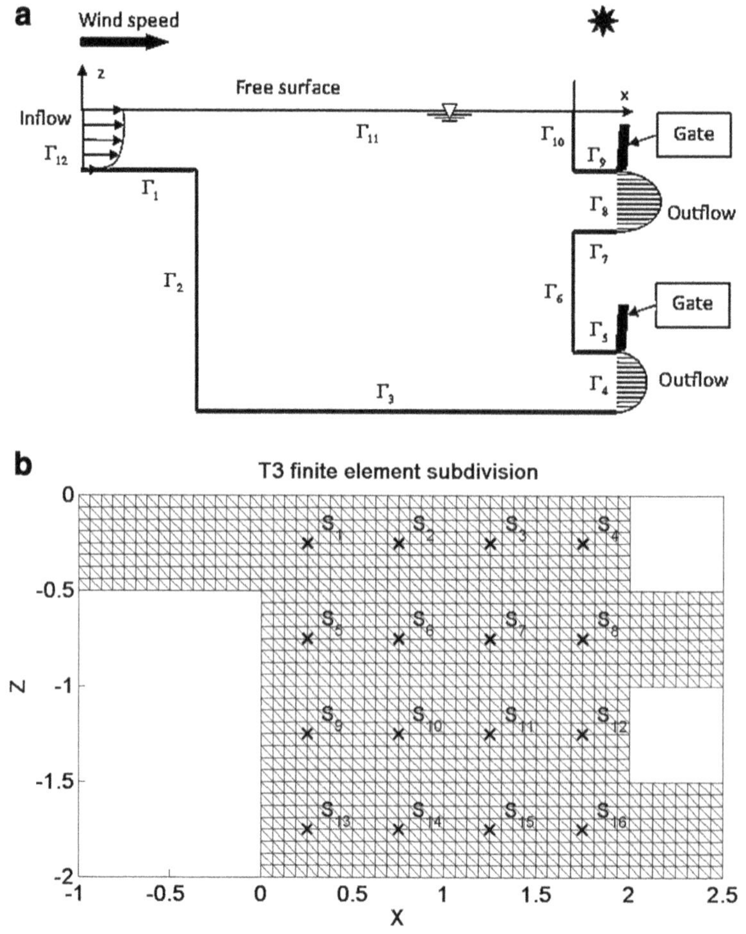

Figure 1 The domain of interest. (a) Physical domain. **(b)** Computational domain.

Galerkin projection of the time-dependent velocity term in Equation 1 has the form as

$$\begin{aligned}(\mathbf{u}\cdot\nabla c, V_i) &= \left(\left[\mathbf{u}_m + \sum_{k=1}^{N_u}\alpha_k\Psi_k\right]\cdot\nabla c, V_i\right)\\ &= [\mathbf{u}_m\cdot\nabla c, V_i] + \left(\sum_{k=1}^{N_u}\alpha_k\Psi_k\cdot\nabla c, V_i\right).\end{aligned} \tag{36}$$

The discrete form of Equation 36 then becomes

$$\begin{aligned}\mathbf{C}_r(\mathbf{u}) &= \left[V_i, \mathbf{u}_m\cdot\nabla V_j\right] + \sum_{k=1}^{N_u}\alpha_k\left[V_i, \Psi_k\cdot\nabla V_j\right]\\ &= \mathbf{C}_{rm}(\mathbf{u}_m) + \sum_{k=1}^{N_u}\alpha_k\mathbf{C}_{rk}(\Psi_k).\end{aligned} \tag{37}$$

Here, $\mathbf{C}_{rm}(\mathbf{u}_m(\mathbf{x}))$ and $\mathbf{C}_{rk}(\Psi_k(\mathbf{x})), k = 1, \cdots, N_u$ are the reduced-order forms of the full-order convection matrices $\mathbf{C}(\mathbf{u}_m(\mathbf{x}))$ and $\mathbf{C}(\Psi_k(\mathbf{x}))$, respectively. They are computed only once in the offline step. Thus, the first case of the reduced-order model (with Equation 28) is only reduced in state (concentration), but the second case (with Equation 37) is now reduced in both state (concentration) and parameter (velocity).

Error estimation

In order to estimate the efficiency of the reduced model relative to the full model, we use the relative errors of state solutions and relative errors of outputs. These errors are defined as follows:

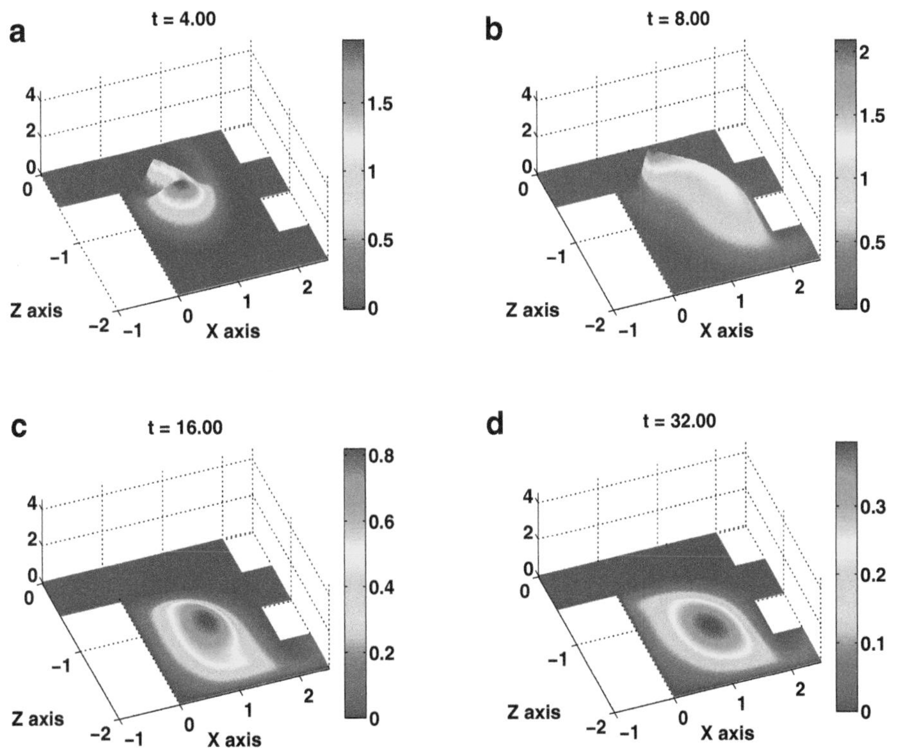

Figure 2 Contaminant field of forward model at specific times. Figures are taken at **(a)** t = 4.0s, **(b)** t = 8.0s, **(c)** t = 16.0s and **(d)** t = 32.0s.

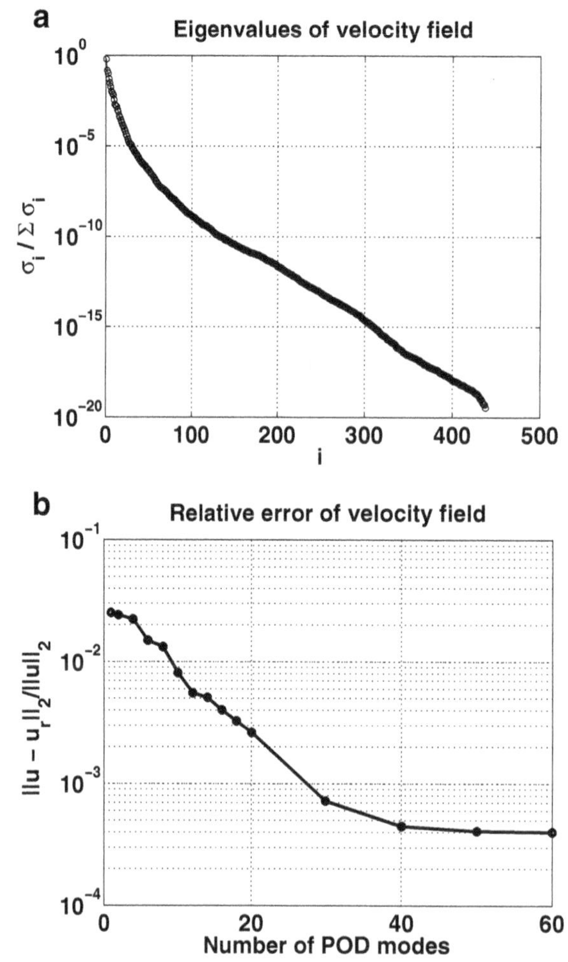

Figure 3 Properties of POD velocity basis vectors: (a) eigenvalues and (b) relative error analysis.

$$\varepsilon_F\left(t^k, \theta\right) = \frac{\|\mathbf{c}\left(t^k;\theta\right) - V\mathbf{c}_r\left(t^k;\theta\right)\|_{L_2(\mathcal{D})}}{\|\mathbf{c}\left(t^k;\theta\right)\|_{L_2(\mathcal{D})}}, \tag{38}$$

$$\varepsilon_S\left(t^k, \theta\right) = \frac{\|\mathbf{y}\left(t^k;\theta\right) - \mathbf{y}_r\left(t^k;\theta\right)\|_{L_2(\mathcal{D})}}{\|\mathbf{y}\left(t^k;\theta\right)\|_{L_2(\mathcal{D})}}. \tag{39}$$

Here, $\mathbf{c}\left(t^k;\theta\right), \mathbf{c}_r\left(t^k;\theta\right), 1 \le k \le T$ are the full and reduced solutions, while $\mathbf{y}\left(t^k;\theta\right)$ and $\mathbf{y}_r(t^k;\theta), 1 \le k \le T$ are the full and reduced outputs of interest, respectively.

Results and discussion

We consider a numerical example based on a 2D mathematical model. The velocity field in the reservoir is obtained by solving a 2D laterally averaged Navier-Stokes model. The Bayesian formulation of the inverse problem is then solved to determine an uncertain contaminant source location. We compare the effectiveness of solving the inverse problem using both the full model and reduced model techniques.

Model setup

The physical domain is illustrated in Figure 1a, which represents a simplified model of a 2D laterally averaged reservoir system. The reservoir system includes a main reservoir section and the river connections. We assume that the contaminant is present within the main reservoir section and that the contaminant transport processes are mainly affected by the inflow and wind velocity. We assume that other factors (such as heat exchange, etc.) have little influence on the processes. The spatial domain is discretized with a finite element mesh, as shown in Figure 1b. The total number of grid points is $N = 1,377$ and the total number of elements is $N_E = 2,560$. The simulation is run from initial time $t_0 = 0$ to final time $t_f = 40$, with time-step size $\Delta t = 0.08$. Thus, the number of time steps is $T = 500$.

A time-dependent velocity field is obtained from the 2D laterally averaged system, which is given in Equations 5 to 8, where the body force $\mathbf{f}_c = [f_{cx}; f_{cz}]^T = [0; g]^T$ with g the gravitational acceleration.

The boundary conditions are set up as follows (refer to Figure 1a for the boundary definitions):

$$(u, w) = (1, 0) \quad \text{on } \Gamma_{12}, \tag{40}$$

$$(u, w) = (-16 * (2.0 + z) * (1.5 + z), 0) \quad \text{on } \Gamma_4, \tag{41}$$

$$(u, w) = (-16 * (1.0 + z) * (0.5 + z), 0) \quad \text{on } \Gamma_8, \tag{42}$$

$$(u, w) = (0.03V_a, 0) \quad \text{on } \Gamma_{11}, \tag{43}$$

$$p = 0 \quad \text{on } \Gamma_{11}. \tag{44}$$

The velocity on remaining boundaries are set to zero. Here, V_a is the wind speed at 10 m above the water surface. In this example, we assumed that $V_a = 2$ m/s for the entire simulation time. The Reynolds number is set to Re $= 5.0e^5$, and a mixing length turbulence model is used [20]. The full model system is given in Equations 9 to 10. The Crank-Nicolson method [21] is used to discretize the system in time.

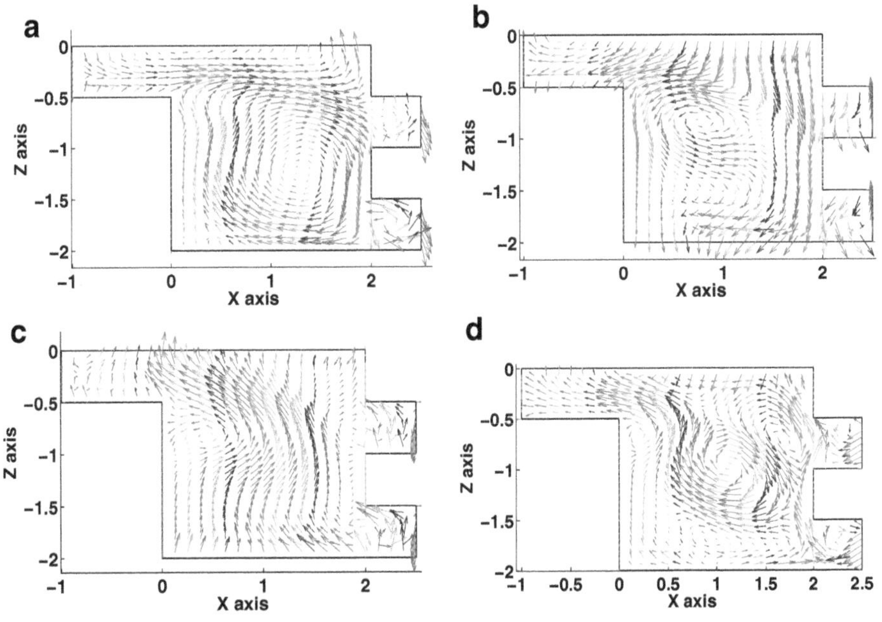

Figure 4 The first four POD basis vectors of the velocity field. (a) First POD velocity basis vector. **(b)** Second POD velocity basis vector. **(c)** Third POD velocity basis vector. **(d)** Fourth POD velocity basis vector.

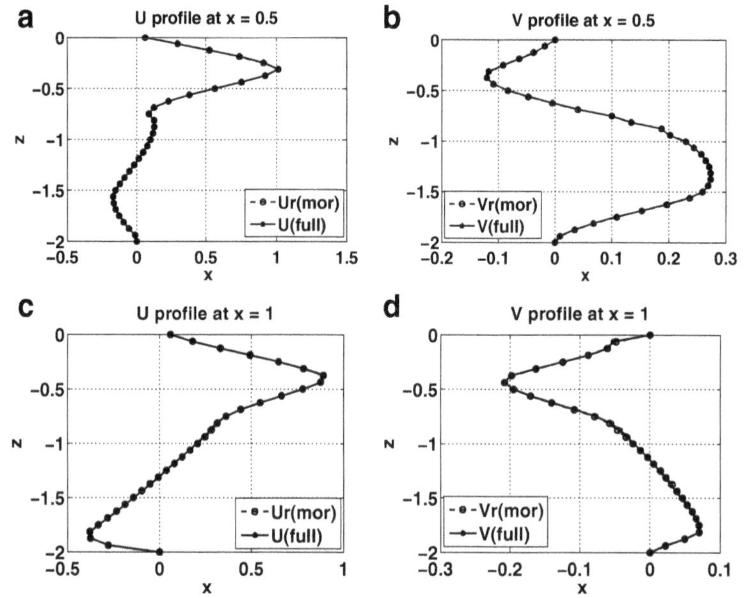

Figure 5 Velocity profile taken at $t = t_f$ at specific locations. Figures are captured **(a)** U profile at $x = 0.5$, **(b)** V profile at $x = 0.5$, **(c)** U profile at $x = 1$ and **(d)** V profile at $x = 1$. Here U(full) and V(full) are the original velocity while Ur(mor) and Vr(mor) are the approximate velocity using a POD expansion with $N_u = 12$ modes.

The setup for the contaminant transport part of the problem is as follows. We use a contaminant source that is defined as the superposition of Gaussian sources, each one active on the time interval $t_{0k} \in [t_0, t_{\text{off}}]$ and centered at $\theta_k \in \mathcal{D}$, with strength h_k and width σ_{sk}:

$$f(\mathbf{x}, t; \theta) = \sum_{k=1}^{n_s} \frac{h_k}{2\pi\sigma_{sk}^2} \exp\left(-\frac{|\theta_k - \mathbf{x}|^2}{2\sigma_{sk}^2}\right) \delta(t - t_{0k}). \tag{45}$$

Here, to simplify the problem, we choose the number of sources to be $n_s = 1$, located at $\theta_1 = (x_c, z_c)$, with strength $h_1 = 0.2$ and width $\sigma_{s1} = 0.05$. The active time of the source is $t_{01} \in [0, t_{\text{off}}]$ with $t_{\text{off}} = 10$. The inflow boundary and other solid boundaries satisfy a homogeneous Dirichlet condition on the contaminant concentration; the outflow boundaries and free surface boundary satisfy a homogeneous Neumann condition. The diffusivity coefficient is assumed to be constant, $\kappa = 0.005$. Thus, the Péclet number $\text{Pe} = \frac{\|\mathbf{u}\|\text{L}}{\kappa} = 100$, where the length of the inflow section is used as the characteristic

Table 1 The properties of various reduced-order models

N_s	m	$\varepsilon_{\text{ROM}-1}$	$\varepsilon_{\text{ROM}-2}$	$\frac{t_{\text{full}}}{t_{\text{ROM}-1}}$	$\frac{t_{\text{full}}}{t_{\text{ROM}-2}}$
10	153	3.25e-1	4.32e-1	0.801	111
20	220	9.81e-2	9.74e-2	0.799	56
30	257	8.03e-3	6.75e-3	0.795	32
40	284	7.53e-3	7.08e-3	0.785	26
50	308	3.39e-3	2.12e-2	0.776	22
60	328	5.83e-3	6.08e-3	0.767	19
70	342	1.41e-2	1.21e-2	0.764	18
80	355	9.09e-3	8.21e-3	0.763	15

length $L = 0.5$. The contaminant concentration is assumed to be zero at initial time $t_0 = 0$.

With this setup, we have specified our forward problem with the input parameter $\theta \in \mathbb{R}^2$ in the range $\Theta := [0, 2] \times [-2, 0]$. Figure 2 shows the contaminant solution $c(\mathbf{x}, t; \theta)$ of the forward model with $\theta_1 = (0.5, -0.5)$ at specific times. The contaminant field grows while the source is active. After the shutoff time of the source, the contaminant moves away, spreads out, and decreases in concentration due to convection and diffusion, until it flows out of the domain.

The outputs of interest are the values of contaminant solution $c(\mathbf{x}, t; \theta)$ at selected sensor locations in the computational domain. These sensors are located on a 4×4 uniform grid covering the reservoir domain as shown in Figure 1b.

Model order reduction

To perform the model order reduction, we need to obtain the POD expansion of velocity field.

Figure 3a shows all eigenvalues of the velocity field. As the number of eigenvalues increases, the significant of eigenvalues decreases, respectively. Figure 3b shows the relative errors of representing the velocity field with various numbers of POD velocity modes.

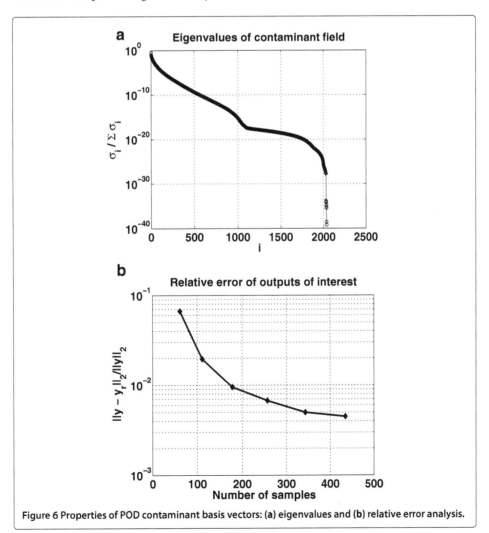

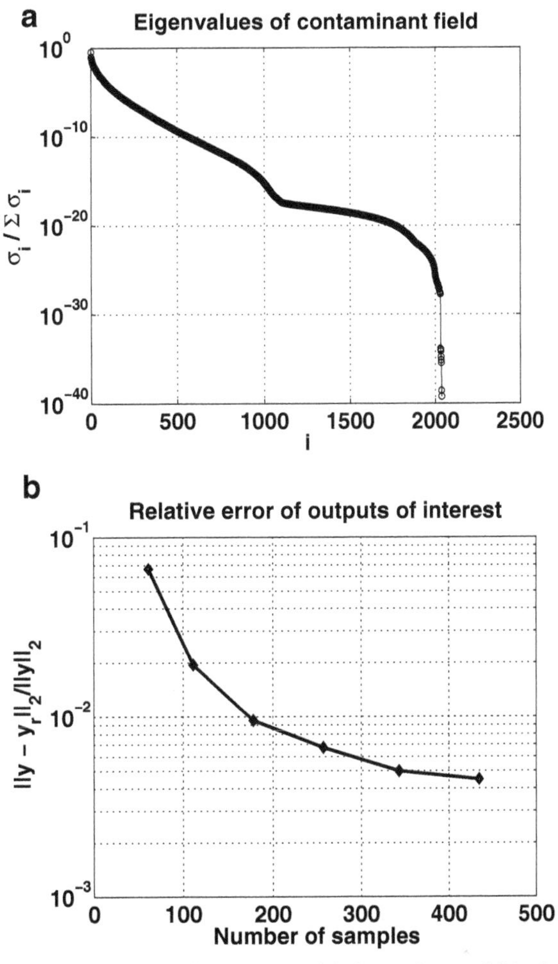

Figure 6 Properties of POD contaminant basis vectors: (a) eigenvalues and (b) relative error analysis.

The goal of this step is to find a suitable N_u that can provide a fast computation of the velocity-dependent convection term and to ensure that the relative errors are acceptable. In this example, we choose the number of terms in the velocity expansion to be $N_u = 12$ yields the relative error around 5×10^{-3}.

Figure 4 illustrates the first four POD basis vectors of the velocity field. Clearly, they represent the most important characteristics of the velocity field.

A comparison between the original velocity and the approximate velocity representation at final simulating time is given in Figure 5. We observe that the approximate velocity profiles at $x = 0.5$ (Figures 5a,b) and $x = 1.0$ (Figures 5c,d) are able to represent well the characteristics of the original velocity profiles.

To generate the snapshots needed for the POD basis to represent the contaminant concentration, we choose S location samples in the computational domain. In this example, we generate random input locations $\theta \in \mathcal{D} \subset \mathbb{R}^2$ for source term $f(\mathbf{x}, t; \theta)$.

Table 1 shows the relative errors and computational time ratio of the reduced-order models (ROM) for different sample sizes of snapshot matrices. Here, we use the notation ROM-1 to denote the reduced model mentioned in the section 'Proper orthogonal decomposition' and ROM-2 for the one mentioned in the section 'Linear expansion techniques for velocity-dependent term'. The POD basis is chosen based on the energy as in Equation 32, with $\epsilon_E = 99.999\%$. We observe that while the relative errors in the outputs are similar for both cases, the ratio of computational time differs significantly. The case ROM-2 shows speedups from 15 to 111 times, while the case ROM-1 is in fact more expensive to solve than the full forward model ($t_{full} \approx 285$ seconds)[1]. This is because the first case consumes a lot of time in re-computing the velocity-dependent convection

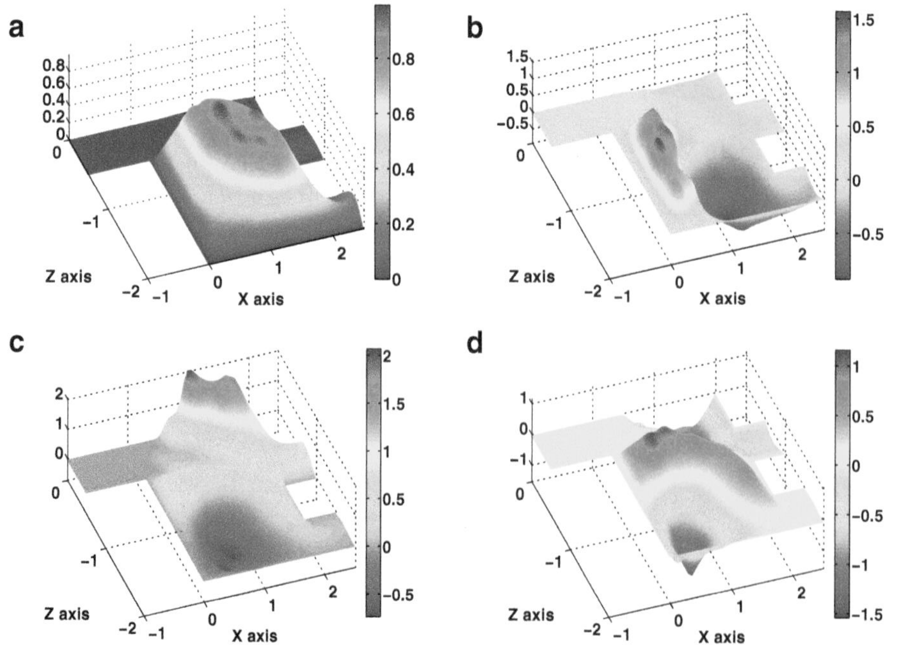

Figure 7 The first 4 POD basis vectors of the contaminant field. **(a)** First POD contaminant basis vector. **(b)** Second POD contaminant basis vector. **(c)** Third POD contaminant basis vector. **(d)** Fourth POD contaminant basis vector.

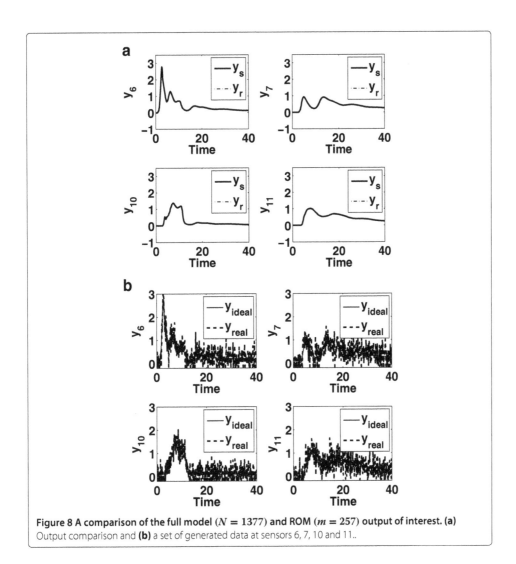

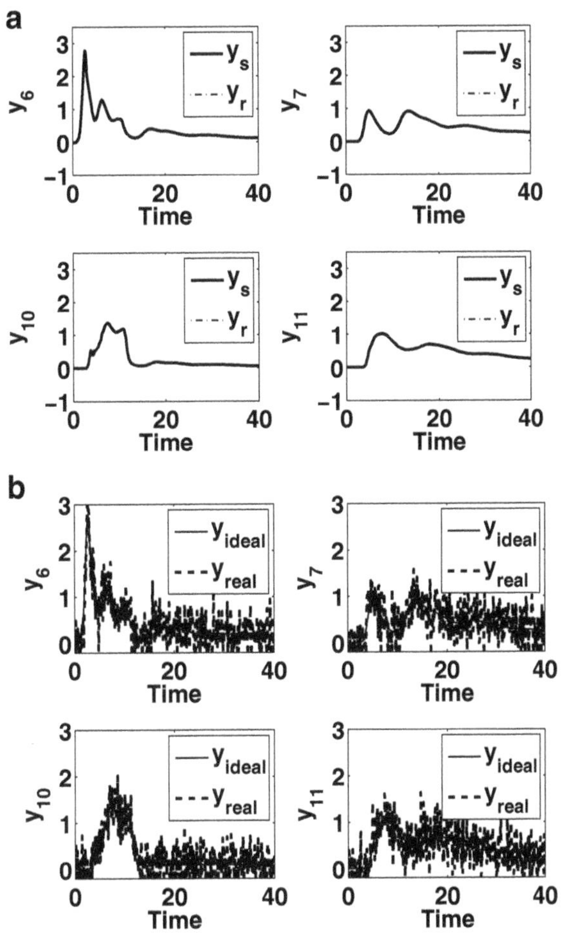

Figure 8 A comparison of the full model ($N = 1377$) and ROM ($m = 257$) output of interest. (a) Output comparison and **(b)** a set of generated data at sensors 6, 7, 10 and 11..

matrix and then projecting it onto the reduced space at each time step. We choose as our reduced-order model the case ROM-2 with sample size $S = 30$.

Figure 6a presents the eigenvalues of contaminant snapshot matrix for the sample test case $S = 30$. We observe that POD eigenvalues of the contaminant field are decayed very fast, and they are significantly important only at the first few hundred values. The first four POD contaminant basis vectors are shown in Figure 7.

Figure 6b shows relative errors of ROMs for different numbers of POD basis vectors. With the energy taken to 99.99999%, the ROM resulted in 434 POD basis vectors with relative error around 4×10^{-3}. In the trade-off between accuracy results and computational

Table 2 Estimated inverse solutions for different numbers of POD basis

$\epsilon_E(\%)$	m	θ_1	θ_2	ε_θ	$t_{mcmc}(s)$
99.0	61	0.788	-0.595	5.31e-1	1.75e+3
90.9	111	0.484	-0.491	6.95e-2	2.74e+3
99.99	178	0.451	-0.471	1.05e-2	7.55e+3
99.999	257	0.443	-0.467	2.42e-3	8.71e+4
99.9999	343	0.446	-0.466	0	5.11e+5

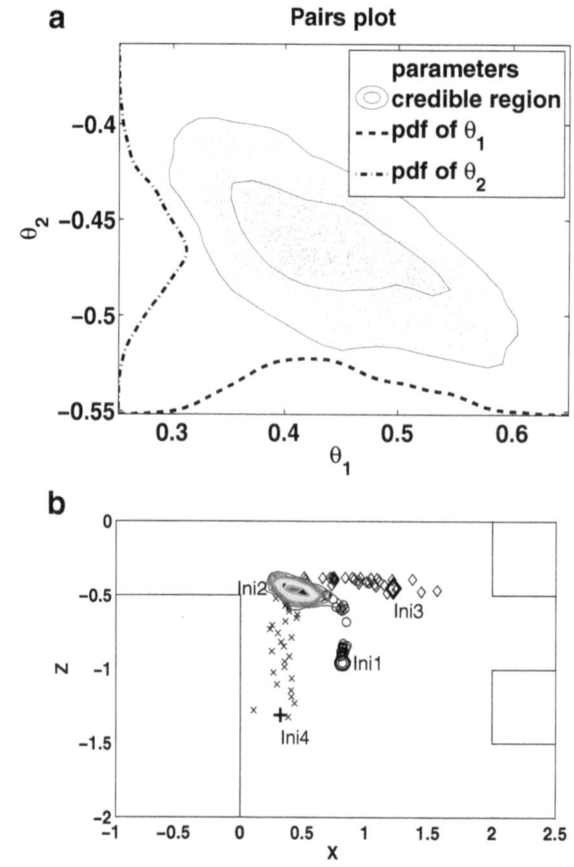

Figure 9 Credible regions and historical trajectory plots of the MCMC convergence. (a) A parameter plot showing estimated source location with credible regions. **(b)** A contour plot of the posterior pdf.

efforts (please refer to Table 1), we can choose our ROM with 99.999% of energy captured which resulting in the size of $m = 257$ POD basis vectors and an acceptably small error.

Figure 8a shows the outputs of the full model ($\mathbf{y}$) and ROM-2 ($\mathbf{y}_r$) with size $m = 257$ at selected sensor locations. The selected sensors (sensor 6, 7, 10, and 11) capture more information of the contaminant than the others for the case studied. We observe that ROM-2 is able to capture well the behavior of the full model at the sensor locations. This reduced-order model will be utilized as the forward solver in solving the inverse problem.

Inverse problems

MCMC is now used to solve the inverse problem for a variety of source locations using the ROM-2 solver above. By accounting for both measured noise and uncertain information in model parameters, Bayesian inference to inverse problem leads to a well-posed problem resulting in a posterior distribution of the unknown [1,2]. Once obtaining the posterior

Table 3 Estimated inverse solutions for different MCMC starting points

Initial	$\theta_{1-\text{ini}}$	$\theta_{2-\text{ini}}$	θ_{1-M}	θ_{2-M}	$t_{\text{mcmc}}(s)$
Ini1	0.821	-0.955	0.451	-0.467	8.71e+4
Ini2	0.322	-0.451	0.458	-0.463	4.53e+4
Ini3	1.222	-0.451	0.452	-0.464	9.80e+4
Ini4	0.323	-1.313	0.456	-0.465	1.05e+5

distribution sample, all statistical questions related to the unknown could be answered with sample averages.

To represent the behavior of uncertain variables such as wind velocity, we generate noisy data at sensor locations. The 'real' data (y_{real}) is generated synthetically by adding noise to the ideal data (y_{ideal}) as in Equation 18. The noise is assumed to be Gaussian $\eta \sim N(0, \sigma^2 I)$. Figure 8b shows the noisy data at sensor locations with $\sigma = 0.3$.

We use the snapshots with $S = 30$ samples above to generate several reduced-order models with different energies. To estimate the relative error of the inverse problem solutions (ε_θ), we choose the solution corresponding to the largest order as a 'truth' solution. We do the MCMC simulation with the starting point $\theta_{\text{ini}} = (0.821; -0.955)^T$. The total number of MCMC samples is set to $N_{\text{mcmc}} = 5000$. The initial burn-in period is set to $N_{\text{burnin}} = 500$. After this stage, data is saved to compute summary statistics of source locations.

Table 2 shows the results of the inverse source problems with different numbers of POD basis. For the case with $m = 257$, the computational time is around 24 h to obtain the solution. If we use the full forward solver, with the speedup factor as given in Table 1, the computational time is estimated around 773 h or approximately 32 days.

Figure 9a shows the credible regions of the source locations θ. In this figure, both a pairwise scatter plot and 1D marginal distributions are displayed. The dash line (in θ_1 axis) and dash-dot line (in θ_2 axis) show the probability density function of each parameter while the solid blue regions show the 95% and 99% credible regions in which the parameters appeared the most (the blue dots).

To assess the convergence of the MCMC approach, we generate four different initial points for the MH sampler. Figure 9b shows the contour plot of the posterior probability density function (the contour plot corresponds to the result of Init1) and the historical trajectories of MCMC samplers for each starting point. We observe that for all four initial points, the MCMC simulations converge to the same final solution. However, depending on the position of the initial points, the computational time varies, as given in Table 3.

Conclusion

This study has applied successfully the combination of a model order reduction technique based on the POD and a Bayesian inference approach to solve an inverse problem that seeks to identify an uncertain contaminant location. Applying an additional POD expansion to approximate the velocity results in a reduced-order model in both state (concentration) and parameter (velocity). The resulting reduced-order model is efficient for solution of the forward problem. Solution of the Bayesian formulation of the inverse problem using the reduced-order solver is much more rapid than using the full model, yielding the probability density of the source location in reasonable computational times. The computational time of using a reduced-order model with $m = 257$ degrees of freedom is about a factor of 32 times lower than using the full model with size $N = 1,377$. This reduction is important in real-time water quality management applications because it reduces time cost and storage requirements.

Endnote

[1]The simulations were performed on a personal computer (PC) with processor Intel(R) Core(TM)2 Duo CPU E8200 @2.66GHz 2.66GHz, RAM 3.25GB, 32-bit Operating System.

Author details
[1]Singapore-MIT Alliance, National University of Singapore, Singapore 117576, Singapore. [2]Department of Mechanical Engineering, National University of Singapore, Singapore 117576, Singapore. [3]Massachusetts Institute of Technology, Cambridge, MA 02139-4307, USA.

References

1. Tarantola A (2004) Inverse problem theory and methods for model parameter estimation. SIAM, Philadelphia
2. Sivia DS, Skilling J (2006) Data analysis: a Bayesian tutorial, Second edition. Oxford University Press Inc., New York
3. Jackson C, Sen MK, Stoffa PL (2004) An efficient stochastic Bayesian approach to optimal parameter and uncertainty estimation for climate model predictions. J Climate 17: 2828–2841
4. Snodgrass MF, Kitanidis PK (1997) A geostatistical approach to contaminant source identification. Water Resour Res 34(4): 537–546
5. Woodbury AD, Ulrych TJ (2000) A full-Bayesian approach to the groundwater inverse problem for steady state flow. Water Resour Res 36(1): 159–171
6. Marzouk YM, Najm HN, Rahn LA (2007) Stochastic spectral methods for efficient Bayesian solution of inverse problems. J Comput Phys 224(2): 560–586
7. Wang J, Zabaras N (2005) Hierarchical Bayesian models for inverse problems in heat conduction. Inverse Probl 21: 183–206
8. Metropolis N, Ulam S (1949) The Monte Carlo method. J Am Stat Assoc 44: 335–341
9. Metropolis N, Rosenbluth AW, Rosenbluth MN, Teller AH, Teller E (1953) Equations of state calculations by fast computing machines. J Chem Phys 21: 1087–1092
10. Hastings WK (1970) Monte Carlo sampling methods using Markov chains and their applications. Biometrika 57: 97–109
11. Gelman A, Carlin J, Stern H, Rubin D (2003) Bayesian data analysis. Second Edition, Chapman & Hall/CRC Texts in Statistical Science
12. Zienkiewicz OC, Morgan K (1983) Finite elements and approximation. Wiley, New York
13. Antoulas AC (2005) Approximation of large-scale dynamical systems. SIAM Advances in Design and Control, Philadelphia
14. Lieberman C, Willcox K, Ghattas O (2010) Parameter and state model reduction for large-scale statistical inverse problems. SIAM J Sci Comput 32(5): 2523–2542
15. Lieberman C, Willcox K (2012) Goal-oriented inference: approach, linear theory, and application to advection-diffusion. SIAM J Sci Comput 34(4): 1880–1904
16. Sirovich L (1987) Turbulence and the dynamics of coherent structures. Part 1: coherent structures. Q Appl Math 45(3): 561–571
17. Codina R, Blasco J (2000) Stabilized finite element method for the transient Navier-Stokes equations based on a pressure gradient projection. Comput Methods Appl Mech Engrg 182: 277–300
18. Ma X, Zabaras N (2008) A stabilized stochastic finite element second-order projection method for modeling natural convection in random porous media. J Comput Phys 227: 8448–8471
19. Jaynes ET (1957) Information theory and statistical mechanics. Phys Rev 104(4): 620–630
20. Wilcox CD (1993) Turbulence Modeling for CFD, DCW Industries, La Cañada, California
21. Crank J, Nicolson P (1996) A practical method for numerical evaluation of solutions of partial differential equations of the heat-conduction type. Adv Comput Math 6(1): 207–226

Permissions

All chapters in this book were first published in APJCE, by Springer; hereby published with permission under the Creative Commons Attribution License or equivalent. Every chapter published in this book has been scrutinized by our experts. Their significance has been extensively debated. The topics covered herein carry significant findings which will fuel the growth of the discipline. They may even be implemented as practical applications or may be referred to as a beginning point for another development.

The contributors of this book come from diverse backgrounds, making this book a truly international effort. This book will bring forth new frontiers with its revolutionizing research information and detailed analysis of the nascent developments around the world.

We would like to thank all the contributing authors for lending their expertise to make the book truly unique. They have played a crucial role in the development of this book. Without their invaluable contributions this book wouldn't have been possible. They have made vital efforts to compile up to date information on the varied aspects of this subject to make this book a valuable addition to the collection of many professionals and students.

This book was conceptualized with the vision of imparting up-to-date information and advanced data in this field. To ensure the same, a matchless editorial board was set up. Every individual on the board went through rigorous rounds of assessment to prove their worth. After which they invested a large part of their time researching and compiling the most relevant data for our readers.

The editorial board has been involved in producing this book since its inception. They have spent rigorous hours researching and exploring the diverse topics which have resulted in the successful publishing of this book. They have passed on their knowledge of decades through this book. To expedite this challenging task, the publisher supported the team at every step. A small team of assistant editors was also appointed to further simplify the editing procedure and attain best results for the readers.

Apart from the editorial board, the designing team has also invested a significant amount of their time in understanding the subject and creating the most relevant covers. They scrutinized every image to scout for the most suitable representation of the subject and create an appropriate cover for the book.

The publishing team has been an ardent support to the editorial, designing and production team. Their endless efforts to recruit the best for this project, has resulted in the accomplishment of this book. They are a veteran in the field of academics and their pool of knowledge is as vast as their experience in printing. Their expertise and guidance has proved useful at every step. Their uncompromising quality standards have made this book an exceptional effort. Their encouragement from time to time has been an inspiration for everyone.

The publisher and the editorial board hope that this book will prove to be a valuable piece of knowledge for researchers, students, practitioners and scholars across the globe.

List of Contributors

Quoc Hung Nguyen
Department of Mechanical Engineering, Industrial University of Ho Chi Minh City, Hochiminh-12 NVBao, Vietnam

Ngoc Diep Nguyen
Department of Mechanical Engineering, Industrial University of Ho Chi Minh City, Hochiminh-12 NVBao, Vietnam

Seung Bok Choi
Department of Mechanical Engineering, Inha University, Incheon 402-751, Korea

Sergei Alexandrov
Laboratory for Strength and Fracture of Materials and Structures, A.Ishlinskii Institute for Problems in Mechanics of Russian Academy of Sciences, Moscow 119526, Russia

Chinh Pham
VAST, Institute of Mechanics, 264 Doi Can, Hanoi, Vietnam

Quy Dong To
Université Paris-Est, Laboratoire Modélisation et Simulation Multi Echelle, MSME UMR 8208 CNRS, 5 Boulevard Descartes, 77454 Marne-la-Vallée, France

Guy Bonnet
Université Paris-Est, Laboratoire Modélisation et Simulation Multi Echelle, MSME UMR 8208 CNRS, 5 Boulevard Descartes, 77454 Marne-la-Vallée, France

Tuyet B Trinh
Lehrstuhl für Mechanik- Materialtheorie, Ruhr-Universität Bochum, Universitätsstr. 150, D-44801 Bochum, Germany

Klaus Hackl
Lehrstuhl für Mechanik- Materialtheorie, Ruhr-Universität Bochum, Universitätsstr. 150, D-44801 Bochum, Germany

Phú Tình Phạm
Faculty of Civil Engineering, Hanoi Architectural University, Nguyen Trai Street, Thanh Xuân District, Hanoi, Vietnam

Manfred Staat
Faculty of Medical Engineering and Technomathematics, Aachen University of Applied Science, Jülich Campus, Heinrich-Mußmann-Str. 1Jülich 52428, Germany

Stefano Secchi
Institute of system science ISIB – CNR, corso Stati Uniti 4, Padua 35127, Italy

Bernhard A Schrefler
Department of Civil, Environmental and Architectural Engineering, University of Padua, 9 via Marzolo, Padua 35123, Italy

Tung Van Phan
R&D Institute, Duy Tan University, 25/K7 Quang Trung, Da Nang 55000, Vietnam Department of Civil and Environmental Engineering, Faculty of Engineering, National University of Singapore, 1 Engineering Drive 2, Singapore 117576, Singapore

Hung Nguyen-Xuan
Department of Computational Engineering, Vietnamese-German University, Binh Duong New City, Vietnam

Chien Hoang Thai
Division of Computational Mechanics, Ton Duc Thang University, HCMC, Vietnam

Jeremy Bleyer
Université Paris-Est, Laboratoire Navier, Ecole des Ponts ParisTech-IFSTTAR-CNRS (UMR 8205), 6-8 av Blaise Pascal, Cité Descartes, 77455 Champs-sur-Marne, France

Phu Vinh Nguyen
Institute of Mechanics and Advanced Materials, School of Engineering, Cardiff University, Queen's Buildings, The Parade, Cardiff CF24 3AA, UK

Nguyen-Thoi Trung
Division of Computational Mathematics and Engineering (CME), Institute for Computational Science (INCOS), Ton Duc Thang University, Hochiminh City, Viet Nam
Department of Mechanics, Faculty of Mathematics and Computer Science, VNUHCM University of Science, Hochiminh City, Viet Nam

Phung-Van Phuc
Division of Computational Mathematics and Engineering (CME), Institute for Computational Science (INCOS), Ton Duc Thang University, Hochiminh City, Viet Nam

Le-Van Canh
Department of Civil Engineering, VNUHCM International University, Hochiminh City, Viet Nam

Nguyen Dang Hung
Vietnamese-German University, Binh Duong New City, Vietnam
University of Liège, Liège B4000, Belgium

Ngoc-Hien Nguyen
Singapore-MIT Alliance, National University of Singapore, Singapore 117576, Singapore

Boo Cheong Khoo
Department of Mechanical Engineering, National University of Singapore, Singapore 117576, Singapore

Karen Willcox
Massachusetts Institute of Technology, Cambridge, MA 02139-4307, USA

Printed in the USA
CPSIA information can be obtained
at www.ICGtesting.com
JSHW051441221024
72173JS00006B/1538

9 781682 850466